Barron's Review Course Series

Let's Review:

Global His
and Geogra

Sixth Edition

Mark Willner
Brooklyn College, City University of New York
Brooklyn, New York
Former Assistant Principal and Chairman, Social Studies Department
Midwood High School at Brooklyn College
Brooklyn, New York

George A. Hero
Brooklyn College
Brooklyn, New York

Mary Martin
Greene Central School
Greene, New York
ARC Otsego, Individual Program Coordinator
Oneonta, New York

David Moore
Webster Central School
Webster, New York

Jerry Weiner
Kean University
Union, New Jersey

BARRON'S

All inquiries should be addressed to:
Barron's Educational Series, Inc.
250 Wireless Boulevard
Hauppauge, New York 11788
www.barronseduc.com

Library of Congress Control Number: 2017961313

ISBN: 978-1-4380-1131-8

PRINTED IN CANADA

9 8 7 6 5 4 3 2 1

About the Authors

MARK WILLNER was the assistant principal and chairman of the social studies department at Midwood High School in Brooklyn, New York, from 1973 to 2005. He was selected as the Outstanding Social Studies Supervisor in the United States for the year 2000. Similar outstanding supervisory honors were bestowed on him in New York State (1991) and in New York City (1984, 1988). In 1997, New York State chose him as its Distinguished Social Studies Educator. In 1995, New York State also selected him to receive the Louis E. Yavner Teaching Award for Outstanding Contributions to Teaching About the Holocaust and Other Violations of Human Rights. In 2004, he was the winner of the Spirit of Anne Frank Outstanding Educator Award, presented by the Anne Frank Center, U.S.A. His most recent honor was in 2006, when he was given the Consul General's Commendation by the Japanese Consulate in New York City.

Mr. Willner obtained a bachelor's degree in history from Queens College and a master's degree in social science education from Yeshiva University. As a recipient of Fulbright, N.E.H., and other grants, he has studied and traveled extensively in Asia and Europe. He has supervised in-service courses, in conjunction with consulates, museums, and universities in New York City, on Africa, China, India, Israel, Japan, Korea, the Middle East, and the Holocaust.

He is past president of the Social Studies Supervisors Association of New York City (SSSA) and has sat on the executive boards of the New York State SSSA and the New York City Association of Teachers of Social Studies (ATSS/UFT). He has served as one of the 12 members on the executive board of the National Social Studies Supervisors Association (NSSSA).

Mr. Willner is the lead author of three Barron's publications: *Global Studies* (Vol. II), *Global History*, and *Let's Review: Global History and Geography*. He has also contributed to Barron's *Regents Exams and Answers: Global History and Geography*, *Regents Exams and Answers: U.S. History and Government*, and *CLEP* (*How to Prepare for the College Level Exam Program*). He is currently a member of the adjunct faculty at Brooklyn College, and has served as an educational coordinator with the Gilder Lehrman Institute of American History and a consultant with New Visions for the Public Schools.

GEORGE A. HERO was a member of the Social Studies Department of Midwood High School at Brooklyn College from 1984 to 2015. He taught Global History, Advanced Placement European History, and Social Science Research, as well as electives in Graeco-Roman, Byzantine, Russian, and Film History. He was the founder and director of the Social Science Research Program at Midwood from 1987 to 2015 and taught History at Brooklyn

College and Long Island University (Brooklyn Campus). He is the coauthor of *Global Studies* (Vol. II) and *Global History* (two volumes), both published by Barron's. In 2004, he won the Bunzel Award for the Outstanding High School Teacher of Social Studies in New York City. He currently teaches history at Brooklyn College.

MARY MARTIN has taught social studies and was Social Studies Department Chairperson at Greene Central School in Greene, New York. She was a contributing author to Barron's *Regents Exams and Answers: Global History and Geography*, for which she wrote the Introduction and Glossary sections. She contributed to the development of several Global Studies, Global History and Geography, and U.S. History and Government Regents and competency exams. She is presently an Individual Program Coordinator for the ARC Otsego in Oneonta, New York.

DAVID MOORE retired from teaching in June 1999 after a 32-year career in the New York State public schools, most of it focusing on Afro-Asian/Global Studies and Humanities. A graduate of Oberlin College (B.A.) and Kent State University (M.Ed.), Mr. Moore taught at the Webster Central School from 1970 after 3 years in the Herricks District. His overseas teaching experience included exchange years in England at the Jack Hunt School in Peterborough (1980–1981) and the Westfield School in Watford (1988–1989) as well as a year at the American Embassy School in New Delhi, India (1973–1974). In addition, he has participated in travel-study programs in India (1971), Indonesia (1978), Jamaica (1984), and Ireland (1997). Mr. Moore served as editor of *Global Studies Resource Guide* for the New York State Council for the Social Studies. He has also worked as a college supervisor of student teachers for SUNY Geneseo.

JERRY WEINER, Ph.D., is a professor at the College of Education at Kean University in New Jersey, where he is the Coordinator of European Programs and Studies and Coordinator of Secondary Education Programs. He also works as a visiting professor at the Ecole Superieure de Commerce in France and the Universidad de Deusto in Spain. Dr. Weiner is a retired New York City high school administrator and supervisor who specialized in social studies education. He was awarded a Fulbright fellowship for study in Brazil. He was also a New York City Supervisor of the Year and was a winner of the John Bunzel Award for supervisors.

T bl of Cont nt

Preface

This book is designed to be used as a review text for the New York State course in Regents Global History and Geography and specifically the "Transition Exam" in Global History and Geography that will be offered beginning in June 2018. The material follows the syllabus of the course, from 1750 to the present, as taught throughout New York State on the secondary level. Although the material has been prepared to meet the needs and standards of New York State students, it can also be helpful to students in any Global History or World History course anywhere in the United States.

• Special Features of This Book

The information in this book parallels the New York State syllabus in Global History and Geography. It serves as an excellent guide for students in two ways: (1) as they take their Global History and Geography course, and (2) as they prepare for the Regents Examination in Global History and Geography. The book begins with an introductory unit that provides important information about the social sciences. Following the introductory unit are four units that cover specific time eras in a chronological pattern. Each unit highlights the significant people and events in the era.

This book also contains references to various global concepts, themes, and issues that appear in the New York State syllabus, and which are used in making up the Regents Exam questions.

1. The ones focused on history are as follows: belief systems, change, choice, citizenship, conflict, culture, diversity, empathy, environment, human rights, identity, imperialism, interdependence, justice, movement of people and goods, nationalism, political systems, power, scarcity, technology, and urbanization.

2. Those focused on geography are as follows: the world in spatial terms, places and regions, physical systems, human systems, environment and society, and the uses of geography.

3. The major world issues are: population, war and peace, terrorism, energy—resources and allocations, human rights, hunger and poverty, world trade and finance, environmental concerns, political and economic refugees, economic growth and development, and determination of political and economic systems.

References to these items are noted in the margins of the book, by icons and call-outs.

Complementing the text in each unit are maps, tables, charts, and illustrations. Also included are review questions that are similar to those that appear on the Regents Exam. These are characterized as multiple-choice questions, thematic essays, and document-based questions (DBQs).

• Taking the Regents Examination

1. Preparation for the Regents Exam begins the first day of class. Good study habits, effective note-taking, completion of all assignments, and a positive attitude throughout the year will make succeeding on any exam an easy task.

2. You will have three hours to complete the exam. The exam will consist of three types of questions.

   A. Multiple-Choice Questions—There will be 30 multiple-choice questions, accounting for 55 percent of the 100 points on the exam. Each question will have four choices, only one of which will be correct. Use the process of elimination if necessary to determine the best answer.

   B. Thematic Essay Question—The exam will have one thematic essay question. It will be worth 15 percent. It will be based on one of the themes, concepts, or issues previously described.

   C. Document-Based Question—There will be one DBQ, worth 30 percent. In answering this question, you will be asked to look at several documents on a single topic. The documents may be written items (for example, speeches, letters, diaries, news articles) or non-written items (for example, maps, cartoons, photographs, paintings, tables, graphs). After each document, there will be a question called a scaffolding question. The answer to these questions will be worth 15 percent and will be labeled as Part A of the DBQ. The remaining 15 percent of the DBQ, Part B, will be an analytical essay. The essay will require an answer built on evidence from the documents as well as from knowledge of global history and geography. Samples of all of these types of questions are present in this book. The questions may be about a single person, place, or time, or may call for connections to be made. Questions that call for making connections across time and place will require you to make comparisons and contrasts.

3. Directions for answering each of the question types will be indicated on the exam itself. The directions will probably use such key skill terms as *define*, *show*, *discuss*, *describe*, *evaluate*, and *explain*.

4. Save all of your notes from your Global History course. Although you will be taking the Regents after the Global History 4 class, you will still have to know material from the Global History 3 class you have taken.

• Conclusion

As you use this book to help with daily lessons and homework assignments, as well as for your Regents Exam preparation, you are certain to find it to be very helpful. Good luck in your studies!

Mark Willner

Introduction to Global History and Geography

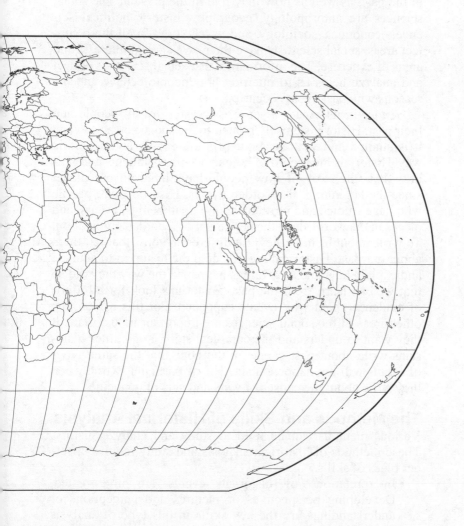

Part A: The Social Sciences

Social science is the term used for all or any of the branches of study that deal with humans in their social, economic, and political relations. These studies are referred to as the social sciences. Modern social sciences use the scientific method, an organized and systematic way of research that dates from the 18th century. Social sciences use quantitative methods and statistical techniques to analyze humans and their behavior toward each other.

The social sciences are sometimes called the people sciences. Social sciences help us to understand how people lived and acted in the past, as well as how they live in the present. The social sciences are anthropology, geography, history, political science, economics, sociology, and psychology. In all these subject areas, social scientists have their own special interests and areas of expertise. The information that social scientists collect and analyze helps us to interpret how people behave and the reasons why past events occurred.

History in its broadest sense is the story of all people and their past. History is closely related to the social sciences when it is studied and written about in a systematic and scientific way. History is the record of human accomplishments and failures. It is the story of how people have lived on our planet since the beginning of recorded events. Historians are people who have studied and written about human beings, events, and places in the world since the beginning of recorded civilization. To write about history, they use different records that tell them about our past. Historical records help the historian to analyze and explain how and why things happened the way they did so that we can learn from the past. Historians look for all kinds of evidence about why events happened. For this reason, the other areas of the social sciences are important to historians if they want to understand the complete story. Sometimes historians write about past events in the hope that the same types of events will not happen again. This is particularly true when they write about the causes of wars and acts of genocide.

The Methods and Skills of Historical Analysis

Various methods can be used to study and analyze history. These methods of historical analysis and study require different types of skills.

- Interpretations of historical events are investigated. Developing perspectives or pictures and perceptions or understandings are the key skills in this type of analysis and study of history.

2

- Hypotheses about interpretations of historical events are investigated. The skill of constructing hypotheses that work is essential in this method of study and analysis.
- Examination of primary historical evidence leads to explanation and analysis. Finding differences and classifying types of evidence are crucial in this method.
- Concepts or ideas and themes are studied over a period of time. Skills in developing a conceptual or thematic framework are important in this method.
- Comparisons and contrasts are made concerning similar types of historical events. Skills in making proper comparisons and contrasts are essential in this method of analysis and study.

Economics is the study of how human beings use resources to produce various goods and how these goods are distributed for consumption among people in society. Throughout human history, people have lived and worked under different economic systems. These economic systems include barter, capitalism, fascism, socialism, and communism. Economists use complex mathematical techniques and statistical data in economic forecasting and analysis and management of resources.

Sociology is the scientific study of human behavior. As the study of humans in their collective or group aspect, sociology is concerned with all group activities—economic, social, political, and religious. Sociologists seek to determine the laws governing human behavior in social contexts. With this objective in mind, they investigate a selected group of social facts or relations.

Psychology is the science or study of living things and their interactions with the environment. Psychologists study processes of how people sense other people, things, and their own feelings. They concentrate on the development of learning, motivations, personality, and the interactions of the individual and the group. Psychology is concerned with human behavior and its physiological and psychological bases.

Anthropology is the study, classification, and analysis of humans and their society—descriptively, historically, and physically. Its unique contribution to studying the links between human social relations has been the special concept of culture. Its emphasis is on data from nonliterate peoples and explorations of archeological remains. Anthropologists study the characteristics, customs, and cultures of people.

Political science is the study of government, political processes, institutions, and political behavior. Political scientists study and comment on fields such as political theory, national and local government, comparative government, and international relations. Political scientists are often called on to make predictions about politics, such as elections and people's reactions to different events.

Geography—The Physical World

Human beings and societies in all regions of the earth share a common global environment. This environment is a closed system consisting of a variety of physical features—landforms, bodies of water, vegetation and animal species, and climatic regions. These physical features are the result of several natural processes including the rotation and revolution of the earth, geological activity, the water cycle, and biological interactions.

The environment provides humans with a variety of renewable and nonrenewable resources, which can be used to meet the needs of both individuals and societies. Though these needs are basic to all humans, the different ways in which they are met are determined by the differences in environments that exist from one part of the earth to another.

The land surface of the earth is generally divided into seven large landmasses called continents—North America, South America, Asia, Africa, Europe, Australia, and Antarctica. Large bodies of water, called oceans—Atlantic, Pacific, Indian, and Arctic—and smaller ones called seas cover about 70 percent of the earth's surface. These bodies of water separate some continents from one another.

In recent centuries, humans have improved their abilities to use more of the earth's limited resources, and technology has created closer contacts among peoples of different cultures. This global interdependence has made it increasingly important to understand the similarities and differences among cultures. It is hoped that such understanding will aid in solving shared problems and resolving disputes between peoples of different cultures.

Maps and Their Uses

We can illustrate much information about the world with maps, but we must be aware of their limitations and distortions. Projecting the features of a sphere (the globe) on a flat surface (a map) can distort sizes and distances, especially when we attempt to show the entire world.

Attempting to illustrate the shapes of landmasses correctly can distort the sizes of the landmasses. On the other hand, trying to show size can distort shape, as in the Gall-Peters projection. Thus, maps can convey inaccurate impressions of the importance and influence of certain areas of the world.

Placement or location can give false impressions of the relationships among regions or the relative importance of an area. For example, in the Mercator projection, with the Atlantic Ocean in the middle, North America and Europe are located top center. This seems to illustrate both the importance and the closeness of their relationship. Compare the Mercator projection and the Japan Airlines map. The Japan Airlines map centers on the Pacific Ocean and therefore islands in the Pacific become important. If you look at the Macarthur corrective map, which was created by Australians, you will see a different story and emphasis in which land areas in the South Pacific are prominent.

Reading maps requires an understanding of their language. The scale provides a tool for determining distances. A map's legend or key provides information about the meaning of lines, symbols, colors, and other markings found on the map itself.

Modern technology has changed how we think about the size of the world. Actual (or absolute) distance has become less important than relative distance—how quickly communication and transportation can move ideas and people from one part of the world to another. Cultural regions once separated by thousands of miles or formidable physical barriers now interact with one another.

Maps can present information in many ways. A topographical map attempts to show physical features, a political map focuses on the way humans divide up the world (the boundaries of nations), and an economic map illustrates the ways in which people use the environment and resources. Comparing specific maps, such as those showing rainfall patterns and population distribution, can be useful in understanding ways of life and the relationships between humans and the world in which they live.

FOUR PARTS OF THE NATURAL ENVIRONMENT

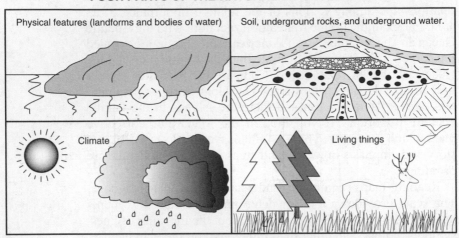

Physical features (landforms and bodies of water)

Soil, underground rocks, and underground water.

Climate

Living things

CONTINENTS AND OCEANS

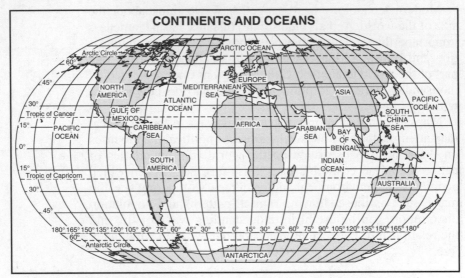

MERCATOR PROJECTION

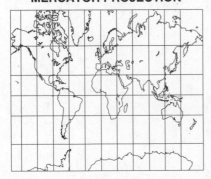

GALL-PETERS PROJECTION

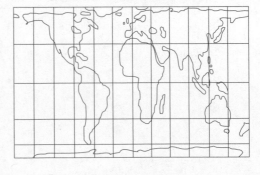

6

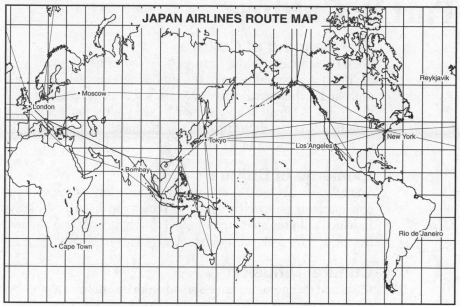

JAPAN AIRLINES ROUTE MAP

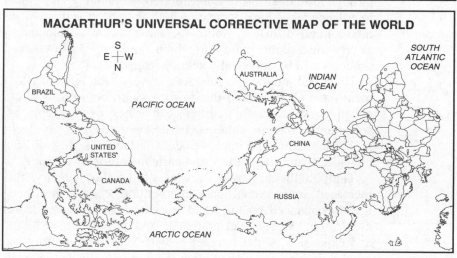

MACARTHUR'S UNIVERSAL CORRECTIVE MAP OF THE WORLD

Part B: Culture

The Meaning of Culture

Social scientists use the term *culture* to define the total way of life of a group of people. It includes actions and behaviors, tools and techniques, ideas and beliefs. Culture is preserved by the group, is taught to and learned by the young, and provides a pattern of interrelationships for the group, as well as a way for them to use their natural environment.

Elements of Culture

Social scientists look at cultures from a variety of viewpoints, concentrating on specific factors as they try to discover the ways in which cultures are similar to and different from one another. See page 9 for a closer look at the elements of culture.

Cultural Diffusion

Ideas and technologies have spread from one culture to another throughout human history, but modern technology and global interdependence have increased both the speed and extent of this cultural diffusion. Some see these recent developments as creating a global culture in which similar styles, tastes, and products will be universally acknowledged.

Trade, aid, migration, conquest, slavery, war, and entertainment have all promoted this process, with both positive and negative results. Useful traditions can be destroyed or replaced; social and economic patterns can be disrupted. But new technology can also bring improvements in standards of living, and new ideas can bring variety and enrichment to any culture.

Through the first two decades of the 21st century, this increased international and intercultural contact has been greatly enhanced by the rapid escalation of electronic communication. Widespread computer and cellular phone usage and expansion of the Internet provide opportunities for both good and ill. Knowledge of other cultures is more readily available to more people with the potential for greater tolerance and understanding. At the same time, these devices enable the spreading of grievances, hatred, prejudices, and intolerance while enabling those who would put these feelings into action. The relative ease of communication can facilitate planning of violence and terrorist acts as well as aid those who would organize and protest peacefully.

Increased contact between cultures can also bring about exploitation and help to create or at least emphasize differences in prosperity and standards of living from one culture region to another. The "developed" regions—Europe (East and West), Anglo-America, Japan, and Australia/Oceana—have been greatly influenced by the Industrial Revolution. The people of these regions have a more abundant supply of material goods and personal services.

In the "developing" (once called "less developed" or "Third World") regions, the populace generally has fewer comforts and

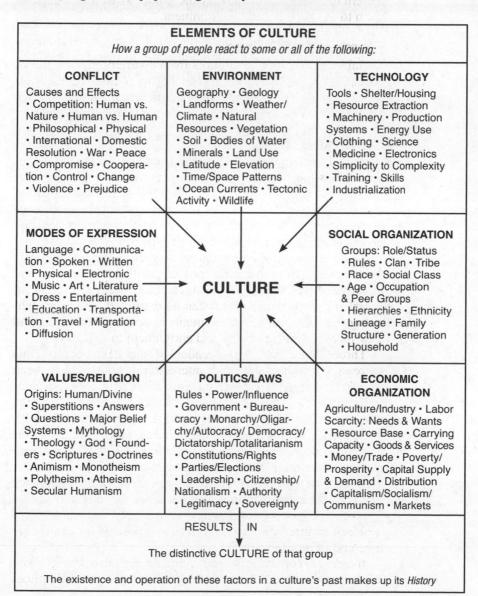

ELEMENTS OF CULTURE
How a group of people react to some or all of the following:

CONFLICT

Causes and Effects
• Competition: Human vs. Nature • Human vs. Human • Philosophical • Physical • International • Domestic Resolution • War • Peace • Compromise • Cooperation • Control • Change • Violence • Prejudice

ENVIRONMENT

Geography • Geology • Landforms • Weather/ Climate • Natural Resources • Vegetation • Soil • Bodies of Water • Minerals • Land Use • Latitude • Elevation • Time/Space Patterns • Ocean Currents • Tectonic Activity • Wildlife

TECHNOLOGY

Tools • Shelter/Housing • Resource Extraction • Machinery • Production Systems • Energy Use • Clothing • Science • Medicine • Electronics • Simplicity to Complexity • Training • Skills • Industrialization

MODES OF EXPRESSION

Language • Communication • Spoken • Written • Physical • Electronic • Music • Art • Literature • Dress • Entertainment • Education • Transportation • Travel • Migration • Diffusion

CULTURE

SOCIAL ORGANIZATION

Groups: Role/Status • Rules • Clan • Tribe • Race • Social Class • Age • Occupation & Peer Groups • Hierarchies • Ethnicity • Lineage • Family Structure • Generation • Household

VALUES/RELIGION

Origins: Human/Divine • Superstitions • Answers • Questions • Major Belief Systems • Mythology • Theology • God • Founders • Scriptures • Doctrines • Animism • Monotheism • Polytheism • Atheism • Secular Humanism

POLITICS/LAWS

Rules • Power/Influence • Government • Bureaucracy • Monarchy/Oligarchy/Autocracy/ Democracy/ Dictatorship/Totalitarianism • Constitutions/Rights • Parties/Elections • Leadership • Citizenship/ Nationalism • Authority • Legitimacy • Sovereignty

ECONOMIC ORGANIZATION

Agriculture/Industry • Labor Scarcity: Needs & Wants • Resource Base • Carrying Capacity • Goods & Services • Money/Trade • Poverty/ Prosperity • Capital Supply & Demand • Distribution • Capitalism/Socialism/ Communism • Markets

RESULTS | IN

The distinctive CULTURE of that group

The existence and operation of these factors in a culture's past makes up its *History* conveniences, and significant numbers of people may survive at a subsistence level. A major goal for most countries in these areas is *economic development*—an increase in the capacity to produce goods and services in order to make life safer and healthier.

In the last decades of the 20th century and the early years of the 21st century, significant numbers of people in some "developing" nations, particularly China, India, and several countries in Southeast Asia have benefited from increased standards of living. The growth of a vigorous middle class in these countries has been based on enhanced educational opportunities and access to more complex technology and communication. In many cases it has also accentuated economic discrepancies within these nations.

Part C: World Regions

We can view the world as being divided into different regions based on cultural, economic, political, and physical features. This means that large sections of the globe can be classified as regions depending on what type of culture, economic and political systems, or physical characteristics they have. The identification of factors shared by most people in a regional area provides a tool for studying similarities and differences among regions. It can also be a basis for understanding relationships within a given region, as well as contacts between regions.

Classification of World Regions by Common Characteristics

Each region possesses a set of common characteristics that sets it apart from other regions. The world regions defined below share a number of classification factors. These regions have their own special combinations of characteristics. Some characteristics may not be typical of all nations in a specific region because these countries have their own special features.

Western Europe. Judaic-Christian religious ethic, Greco-Roman traditions, industrial economies, temperate-type climate, Latin and Germanic languages, members of the European Union.

Central and Eastern Europe. Primarily Slavic languages, Orthodox Christian religious ethic, formerly communist/socialist economies, developing capitalist economies, recently obtained membership in or candidates for admittance to the European Union.

Latin America. Primarily Roman Catholic religion, Latin-based languages (Spanish/Portuguese), heritage of European colonialism, Native American cultural influences.

Sub-Saharan Africa. Tropical or semitropical climate, multiple religious traditions (animism, Christianity, Islam), strong tribal identities and ethnic-group social organizations, agricultural.

Middle East. Islamic religious ethic, crossroads location with connecting waterways, Arabic language and culture, arid climate, abundance of oil, birthplace of three major religious systems (Judaism, Christianity, and Islam), authoritarian governments.

South Asia and Southeast Asia. Monsoon climatic conditions, Hindu, Buddhist, and Islamic religious traditions, floodplain agriculture, colonial experiences, transition to more industrial economies from agricultural economies.

East Asia. Confucian/Taoist/Buddhist traditions and ethic, hierarchical social systems, character-based alphabet, developing industrialized economies based on trade priorities.

West Asia. Former republics of the Soviet Union, Islamic religious ethic, authoritarian secular governments, mineral resources (particularly oil).

Within individual regions there are often great differences among the individual countries and peoples. For example, in the Middle East the nation of Israel has a Judaic tradition and a democratic government. Turkey and Iran are Islamic but do not have Arabic cultures. In Latin America, the climate varies from tropical in the Amazon basin to temperate further south in the Argentine pampas. Sub-Saharan Africa has hundreds of distinct ethnic groups with a wide variety of cultural characteristics.

Muslims make up the majority in some South Asian and Southeast Asian countries, thereby giving nations such as Pakistan, Bangladesh, and Indonesia a cultural tradition strongly influenced by Islamic traditions. This is not true of other nations in this region. In Eastern Europe, Poland has a Christian yet non-Orthodox religious tradition, and Bosnia and Albania have primarily Islamic cultures.

In addition there are transition or diffusion zones between regions that are hard to define by distinct cultural characteristics. In these zones or areas, cultures meet, mix, and produce unique combinations. The area of the former Soviet Union known as the Trans-Caucasus is such a subregion, having traditions from both the Orthodox and Islamic cultures. The Caribbean subregion of Latin America combines Latin, African, and Anglo-European traditions.

There has been a recent development of more integrated global economic systems that transcend regions. For example, the European Union and the North American Free Trade Association (NAFTA), which operate as integrated economic systems, are creating bridges and interconnections between different world regions. This is particularly true in Central and Eastern Europe where many nations are joining or seeking to join the European Union. Even Turkey, a nation that is mostly Middle Eastern and Islamic, is a candidate for membership in the European Union. Heavy immigration to the more industrialized nations is also leading to changes in the cultural characteristics that traditionally defined these nations. This is particularly true in Western Europe and the United States. The

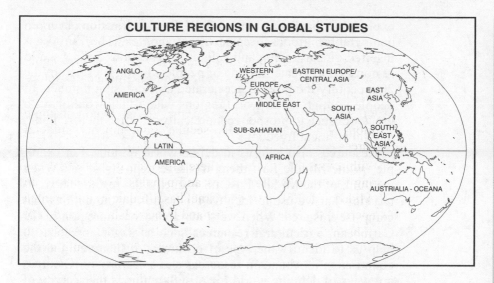

CULTURE REGIONS IN GLOBAL STUDIES

end of communism and the trend away from military-led governments have led to fundamental changes in the political systems that characterized some world regions.

The Impact of Resources, Demography, and History

The history, demography, and resources of any region influence the characteristics of that defined world region. The nations of India, China, Peru, and Egypt have long historical traditions that influence their national characteristics and the cultural traits of other nations within their regions. For example, in China the long Confucian ethic tradition has survived the nation's experience with a recent communist political system. In India, attempts at modernization conflict with a social system strongly influenced by the Hindu cultural tradition. Other nations in East Asia, South Asia, and Southeast Asia are also influenced by this strong Confucian or Hindu cultural tradition. Ecuador and Bolivia are influenced by the heritage of the Peruvian Inca civilization.

Demography also continues to play a strong role in determining the characteristics of any world region. We are all the same in that we are human beings who, according to one scientific theory based on genetics, descended from a common ancestor. Yet over the course of human evolution people have developed differences that have distinguished them and others like them from other peoples. For example, there are cultural differences based on demographic identification that separate Asians, Africans, and Caucasians. After the great voyages of exploration that began in the 1400s, the identification of certain demographic groups became more complex. The European-inspired global trading and colonial connections among world regions led to greater mixing of peoples. In the later part of the 20th century the process accelerated as increasing numbers of people immigrated to world regions where they would have a greater chance to prosper economically, practice their religion, or gain political freedom.

Resources also help us to define world regions. For example, in the Middle East there are large deposits of oil. When we think of the Middle East, oil is one of the resource characteristics that we use to identify this region or the nations that comprise this area. When we study about the subregion of the Caribbean, agricultural resources such as sugar and tobacco help us to identify the type of economy of this area and the countries in it. Abundant resources and a scarcity of resources are ways of defining world regions. Sometimes the scarcity of resources influences the development of a world region. This is true when we look at the history of Western Europe where during the Age of Exploration nations went to other world regions to gain access to resources. The rise of European industry is tied to this development of trade and colonialism, which heavily influenced all the regions that the Europeans penetrated. In East Asia, the economic and political history of Japan continues to be greatly influenced by the lack of natural resources in this island nation. It seems safe to say that the issue of resources (for example, oil, water, and timber) will continue to influence the development of different world regions and the nations within them in the years to come.

We now begin our world journey from 1750 to the present.

ERA I

An Age of Revolutions (1750–1918)

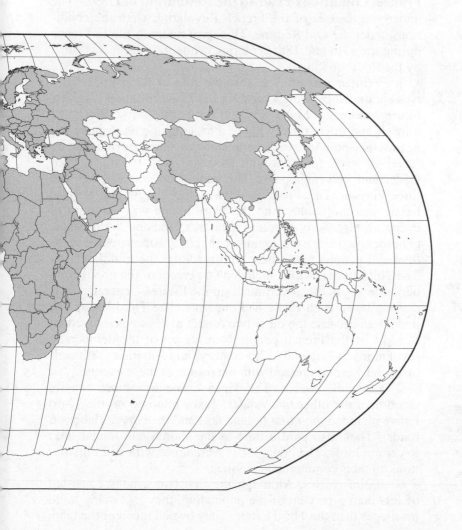

Part A: The French Revolution, the Enlightenment, and the Napoleonic Era

The French Revolution

France: Conditions Prior to the Revolution of 1789. The underlying causes of the French Revolution were the conditions under the Old Régime. This term refers to life in France during the 17th and 18th centuries, while the nation was ruled by the Bourbon kings.

GLOBAL CONCEPTS

Human Rights

CONCEPTS GLOBAL

1. *Political causes.* The absolute rule of King Louis XIV was continued by King Louis XVI (1774–1792) and his wife, Marie Antoinette. Louis XVI did not permit any criticism of himself and imprisoned without a trial anyone who spoke out against his policies. Imprisonment was often carried out by *lettres de cachet*, letters with the royal seal. He was a poor leader and very unpopular. The population was divided into three classes. The First Estate was the clergy; the Second Estate was the nobles; and the Third Estate was made up of everyone else—city workers, peasants, and the bourgeoisie. (The bourgeoisie were mainly bankers, businesspeople, professional people, and others who made up the middle class.) The Third Estate, which included 90 percent of the population, had little say in the government. In the Estates-General, a law-making body, each estate had one vote. The Third Estate felt powerless because the other two estates always voted together.

GLOBAL CONCEPTS

Citizenship

CONCEPTS GLOBAL

Most of the French people were aware of the democratic revolutions in England (17th century) and America (18th century) and were impressed with the results of these events.

GEOGRAPHY

Human Systems

2. *Economic causes.* The Third Estate was more heavily taxed than the other two estates. Taxes imposed on the Third Estate included the *taille* (a land tax) and the *corvée* (labor on roads). They also paid a tithe to the church and feudal dues to certain lords. The bourgeoisie were upset with strict restrictions on their commercial activities.

3. *Social causes.* Although the first two estates consisted of less than 5 percent of the population, they had many more privileges than the Third Estate. They owned much of the land,

were exempt from most taxes, and generally lived much better than members of the Third Estate.

4. *Influence of the Enlightenment.* The Enlightenment, also called the Age of Reason, was an intellectual movement in the 17th and 18th centuries. It was sparked by the scientific progress of the previous age (the Scientific Revolution). Educated Europeans had learned that natural laws governed the physical universe. They reasoned that similar laws must govern human society as well. If people were able to discover these laws, they might be used to construct a better government and more just societies. The thinkers, philosophers, and writers who examined the political and social problems of the time were known as Philosophes. They believed that everything, even government and religion, should be open to reason and criticism. They were convinced that through the use of reason, logic, and experience, people could improve their society—its laws, economy, and so on. The Philosophes claimed that humans had certain natural rights. Traditional royal and Church authority, particularly in France, were in conflict with these rights and had to undergo change. The most important French writers of the Enlightenment are listed in the chart below.

GLOBAL
CONCEPTS

Change

CONCEPTS
GLOBAL

FRENCH WRITERS OF THE ENLIGHTENMENT

Name	Major Work and Ideas
Montesquieu (1689–1755)	*The Spirit of the Laws.* There should be a separation of powers in government as well as a system of checks and balances. These features would prevent tyranny and absolutism.
Voltaire (1694–1778)	*Letters Concerning the English.* Written in support of the concepts of England's limited monarchy and its ideas on freedom of speech and religion.
Rousseau (1712–1778)	*The Social Contract.* Inequality among people can be ended by citizens coming together and agreeing to a general will. The general will is what the majority desires and should be carried out by the government.
Diderot (1713–1784)	*The Encyclopedia.* Absolutism and the injustices of the Old Regime were wrong.

There were also other important Enlightenment writers. Adam Smith of England (*The Wealth of Nations*) said that people should be free to conduct business without government interference. This was the laissez-faire philosophy of economics. The American Thomas Paine (*Common Sense*) claimed that it was right and natural for the American colonists to revolt against England, a tyrannical government that was thousands of miles across the Atlantic Ocean. John Locke was also a major Enlightenment writer.

The Enlightenment's concern with natural rights and the use of reason, logic, and experience was seen in the field of science as well as in politics and economics. During the 16th and 17th centuries, the way the people of Europe viewed themselves and the universe underwent a dramatic transformation in what was called the Scientific Revolution. The discoveries of a succession of astronomers, physicists, and mathematicians undermined many ideas that had been accepted for centuries. A new system of ideas and theories was created, based on the direct observation of nature and a belief in the power of reason. The scientific method, based on carefully planned experiments, observation of results, and the formulation of general laws, was the basis of the Scientific Revolution. Scientists such as Isaac Newton (1642–1727) of England used the scientific method to investigate nature. Newton, the leading figure in the Scientific Revolution, put forth important theories about gravity and the movement of planets. His famous book was the *Principia Mathematica*.

The French Revolution of 1789: Outbreak and Major Developments. In 1789 King Louis XVI called the Estates-General into session because he needed money to solve France's financial problems. This was the first time this body had been summoned since 1614 (175 years before). When the Estates-General met, the Third Estate refused to accept the traditional method of voting—each estate met separately and had one vote—because it would be outvoted by the other two estates. It demanded that all three estates meet together and that each deputy have a vote. When the king refused, the Third Estate, on June 17, 1789, declared itself to be the National Assembly and in the Tennis Court Oath pledged to write a constitution for the nation. This declaration was the beginning of the French Revolution. On July 14, 1789, the revolution spread as a mob stormed and destroyed the Bastille—a prison that was a symbol of the Old Regime. The next day the king recognized the National Assembly. The National Assembly, which was made up of moderates, took power and began to carry out reforms. They passed the Declaration of the Rights of Man on August 27, 1789. This document was similar to the American Declaration of Independence and the English Bill of Rights. It stated the following democratic ideals:

1. The class structure and privileges connected with the three estates were ended, abolishing the remains of feudalism.

GLOBAL CONCEPTS

Change

CONCEPTS GLOBAL

GLOBAL CONCEPTS

Justice

CONCEPTS GLOBAL

2. All people were equal before the law and had certain basic freedoms, including freedom of religion, speech, and the press.

3. The spirit of Liberty, Equality, and Fraternity was to guide the nation. In 1790 the National Assembly abolished the special taxes and privileges of the Catholic Church in the Civil Constitution of the Clergy. It also granted freedom of worship, confiscated all Church land, and placed the Church under the government's control.

The French Constitution was written in 1791, and it created a limited, or constitutional, monarchy and established separate executive, legislative, and judicial branches of government.

However, King Louis's unsuccessful attempt to flee the country and war with Austria and Prussia enabled radicals, such as Robespierre, Danton, and Marat, to take over the Revolution. In 1792 delegates were elected by universal manhood suffrage to the National Convention, which took the place of the National Assembly and contained more radical members, such as the Jacobins. The first act of the National Convention was to declare France a republic. Louis XVI was brought to trial and executed in 1792.

The National Convention was soon taken over by extremist groups, who formed the Committee of Public Safety, which put the executive, legislative, and judicial powers of government in the hands of a small group of revolutionaries. The committee was given power to conduct the war with France's enemies and to enforce the ideals of the Revolution by all means possible. The leading figures were Danton and Robespierre, who began a Reign of Terror (1793–1794) in which they executed at the guillotine all enemies of the revolution, who were to them the nobles or anybody who spoke out against them.

GLOBAL
CONCEPTS

Human Rights

CONCEPTS
GLOBAL

Eventually, more moderate groups, anti-Jacobins, took over the National Convention. Danton and Robespierre were themselves sentenced to die by the guillotine in 1795. The Convention wrote a new constitution in 1795 that made France a republic. It established a five-member Directory government that ruled France until 1799, when it was replaced by the military dictatorship of Napoleon Bonaparte. (See The Rise and Fall of Napoleon, on the next page.) This return of government to moderate control is called the Thermidorian Reaction.

Importance of the French Revolution. The French Revolution had many important and long-lasting results. It brought about a basic change in the relationship between the government and the governed. Along with the revolutions in England and the United States, the French Revolution advanced democracy by recognizing the value and worth of the individual. Political power passed from an absolutist monarch who ruled by Divine Right and the nobles to the masses of people. A greater sense of nationalism and patriotism developed. Also, the remaining feudal features of French society were removed. The growing power of the bourgeoisie helped France to become a strong capitalist nation.

The Rise and Fall of Napoleon (1799–1815)

Napoleon Bonaparte was an ambitious, brilliant military officer who won many victories in wars against France's enemies. In 1799 in a coup d'etat (a sudden takeover of a government), he came to power in France in a new government called the Consulate. The Directory had lost support because of worsening economic problems and its inability to defeat Russia and Austria in the war. The Consulate was headed by three consuls, with Napoleon as First Consul. The new government, France's fourth in ten years, was called a republic, but it was a military dictatorship under the control of Napoleon. He took the title of Emperor Napoleon I in 1804. The French people accepted his ruthless methods because they believed he would bring peace and stability to the nation.

At first, Napoleon was brilliantly successful in his war against France's European enemies. Under Napoleon's leadership, French forces won victories and took large amounts of land in Europe. By 1808 Napoleon dominated Europe, and he reorganized many parts of Europe, making members of his family rulers in Italy, Spain, and other places.

The Napoleonic Empire soon became too large to control, however, and in time Napoleon suffered severe military setbacks. His attempt to conquer Russia in 1812 failed due to the harsh winter conditions and the scorched-earth fighting tactics of the Russians. At the Battle of Waterloo in 1815, fought near Brussels in Belgium, Napoleon's forces were defeated by the combined forces of European nations led by the Duke of Wellington of Britain.

Results of the Napoleonic Era. Napoleon made many significant contributions to governing France. Both within France and in the areas he conquered, Napoleon sought to carry out the ideals of the French Revolution as he interpreted them. Indeed, he called himself a son of the Revolution and carried out the following reforms:

1. The Code Napoleon brought all the laws, regulations, and reforms of the revolution into a single system of law. Based on

GLOBAL CONCEPTS
Political Systems

CONCEPTS GLOBAL

GEOGRAPHY

Use of Geography

WORLD ISSUES

War
and
Peace

the belief that all people are equal before the law, the Napoleonic Code became the fundamental law of France and the parts of Europe governed by France.

2. The Concordat of 1801 provided for a peaceful relationship between the French government and the Catholic Church.

3. An efficient, centralized government was created in France, with specific power over the education and banking systems. Government officials were selected based on merit through an examination system, and a public school system was established.

4. Many European monarchs lost their thrones to Napoleon's armies. In the last decade of the 18th century and continuing into the 19th century, ideas that developed during the Enlightenment and the French Revolution resulted in a growing sense of nationalism in different parts of the world. Peoples in these areas, such as Spain and Italy, learned of the ideals of the French Revolution. At first, some of these people welcomed Napoleon because they believed he had liberated them from foreign and unjust rule. Eventually, they turned against Napoleon's dictatorial rule and fought against him. However, as a result of Napoleon's conquests, the ideas of the French Revolution were spread throughout Europe. The ideals of social justice, liberty, and democracy became rallying cries for reformers. Combined with the rise of the spirit of nationalism, which was stirred by the struggle against Napoleon's armies, the dreams of liberty and equality made many national groups determined to gain self-government in the years after 1815.

GEOGRAPHY

Environment and Society

Part B: Nationalism and Unification in Europe

The Metternich Age and the Growth of Nationalism (1815–1871)

After Napoleon's defeat, five major European powers—England, Russia, Prussia, France, and Austria—met at the Congress of Vienna in 1814 and 1815 to draw up peace plans and settle a number of important territorial questions by redrawing the map of Europe. Under the leadership of Austria's Count Metternich, the Congress of Vienna sought to restore political life in Europe, including former rulers and boundaries, to what it had been prior to Napoleon and to maintain peace and stability. Such a policy of restoring past ways and turning the clock back is called reactionary. Metternich wanted to wipe out the ideas spread by the Napoleonic era and return to the old days of absolutism and special privilege. The decisions reached at the Congress of Vienna were based on three principles—legitimacy, the balance of power, and compensation. Legitimacy meant restoring the ruling families that reigned before the French Revolution to their thrones. Balance of power meant that no one nation should be strong enough to threaten the security of the others. To do this, shifts of territory were necessary. This involved compensation, or providing one state with territory to pay for territory taken away from that state.

Metternich opposed the French Revolution's ideas of freedom and equality. He sought to maintain what had been the status quo prior to the French Revolution. During the Metternich age (1815–1848), there were challenges to the status quo. However, most attempts by European peoples against these reactionary policies in order to achieve national unity were put down by force. These attempts, which led to revolutions in 1830 and in 1848, were inspired by a nationalistic spirit, whereby a group of people, such as the Italians, Poles, or Germans, sought to create their own nation and establish self-government. Although most of these revolutions failed, two successful attempts were made in Belgium and Greece in 1830. The Quadruple Alliance, representing the four powers that had defeated Napoleon, did not want these revolutionary movements to succeed. From this alliance emerged the Concert of Europe. This was a form of international government, arranged by concert, or agreement, among its members. It wanted to keep the balance of power that the

Congress of Vienna had set up. Although the Congress could not suppress nationalism permanently, it was able to postpone its success for a half century. The unification of Italy and of Germany in the later 1800s were the first breaks in the territorial settlements of 1815.

The spirit of nationalism influenced the political history of Europe from 1815 to 1914. Nationalism is the belief that a group of people who share a common culture, language, and historical tradition should have their own nation in a specific area of land. Once the people accomplish their nationalistic goals and form a nation-state, they can then make their own laws and are said to be sovereign and to have autonomy. Nationalism was the guiding force that led to the unification of both Italy and Germany in the late 19th century. The Italians, Poles, Hungarians, Turks, and others who were ruled by the large dynastic states that dominated Europe—the Austrian Empire, the Russian Empire, and the Ottoman Empire—all struggled to win freedom and form their own nation-states.

Unification of Italy. In 1815 there was no nation called Italy; Italy was really a geographic expression. The Italian Peninsula was divided among large and small states, such as the Lombardy province and the kingdom of Sardinia-Piedmont. Austria, which controlled the states in the northern part of the Italian Peninsula, was against any kind of unity. But by 1861 all the Italian states had become unified into a nation. Those most responsible for bringing unification about were:

1. *Cavour*. Considered the brain of unification, he was a successful diplomat who got France to help him fight the Austrians. He also expanded the power of Sardinia-Piedmont by adding to it other Italian states.

2. *Mazzini*. The soul of unification, he wrote and spoke eloquently about his desires for Italian unity. He was the founder of the Young Italy movement. This movement wanted a free independent nation. It was created in the mid-1800s in a time period known as the Italian *risorgimento* (reawakening, resurgence).

3. *Garibaldi*. The sword of unification, he conquered southern Italy and joined it to the state that Cavour had unified under the control of Sardinia-Piedmont in the north.

4. *King Victor Emmanuel*. Formerly the King of Sardinia-Piedmont, he became the ruler of a united Italy in March 1861.

Unification of Germany. In 1815 there was no nation called Germany. Instead, there were more than thirty independent

GLOBAL CONCEPTS
Change

CONCEPTS GLOBAL

GEOGRAPHY

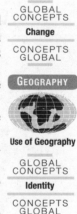

Use of Geography

GLOBAL CONCEPTS
Identity

CONCEPTS GLOBAL

GEOGRAPHY

Use of Geography

German states that had their own traditions, laws, and economic regulations. The largest of these states, Prussia, located in northern Germany, led the movement for unification. The chief obstacle to Prussia's leadership was Austria. It sought to dominate German affairs and did not want to see the German states unified. But by 1871, under the leadership of Prussia's chief minister, Otto von Bismarck, Austria's power was weakened and the German states achieved unification.

Otto von Bismarck

Following a policy of blood and iron, Bismarck used military means to achieve his goal of German unity under Prussia's leadership. Under this policy, Prussia won victories in the Danish War (1864), the Austro-Prussian War (or Seven Weeks' War, 1866), and the Franco-Prussian War (1870–1871). As a result of these wars, Prussia was able to gain land, such as Schleswig-Holstein from Denmark and Alsace-Lorraine from France, unite other German states with Prussia, and reduce the influence of Austria in German affairs. King William I of Prussia was declared the ruler of a united Germany in 1871 and was called emperor, or kaiser. This declaration was made by Bismarck at the Versailles Palace in France. This action, along with France's defeat in the war, caused much anger and resentment in that country. These feelings lasted into the early years of the 20th century.

Conclusion. Nationalism can be positive (a force for good) or negative (a force for evil). The desire by Italians and Germans to form their own nations brought together people with common ties and histories. The wishes of a group of people to achieve sovereignty and self-determination are common themes throughout history and exist even in our own day. However, nationalistic desires can become so intense that hatred and unnecessary bloodshed can result. The reign of terror in France was one example; Bismarck's humiliation of France after the Franco-Prussian war was another. Intense nationalism can also be dangerous when it turns into chauvinism and excessive ethnocentrism. This occurs when a group of people claim to be superior to another group of people. Such claims have often led to prejudice and wars.

GLOBAL
CONCEPTS

Identity

CONCEPTS
GLOBAL

Part C: The Industrial Revolution

WORLD ISSUES

Economic
Growth and
Development

A major upheaval in the way people live, work, and think began about 200 years ago and in many ways is still going on today. This change is called the Industrial Revolution, and it accomplished on a massive scale the replacement of human power and animal power with the power of machines. The Industrial Revolution began in England in the 1750s and involved vast changes in the production of goods. These changes were as follows:

1. From handmade goods to machine-made goods.

2. From production at home to production in factories (from the domestic system to the factory system).

3. From producing small amounts to producing large amounts (mass production).

GLOBAL
CONCEPTS

Technology

CONCEPTS
GLOBAL

4. The increased use of science and new forms of energy (steam power, for example) to speed up production and meet human needs. The use of science in these ways is referred to as technology.

Causes and Preconditions in 18th-Century England. The Industrial Revolution began in England because of a combination of fortunate conditions that existed at the time.

1. *Natural resources*. Britain was fortunate to have large amounts of coal and iron ore.

2. *Geography*. England had many good harbors, and coastal and river trade was well developed. England also had relatively good roads and numerous canals for the cheap transport of raw materials and finished goods.

3. *Investment capital*. Entrepreneurs and other private individuals had money that they, as capitalists, were willing to invest and risk in business ventures.

4. *Labor supply*. There were large numbers of skilled workers in the population.

5. *Increased demand*. There was a great demand for British products, both in the domestic market (within the nation) and in foreign markets.

6. *Transportation and colonial empire*. Britain had a good navy and had built up a shipping industry. Its expanding colonial empire furnished raw materials and markets for goods.

7. *Agricultural changes*. An agricultural revolution that occurred in the 1700s brought changes in farming that made the Industrial Revolution possible. These changes resulted in the production of more food and required fewer farmers to produce it. Many people left the farms and went to the cities to find work in factories.

8. *Role of government*. Britain had a stable government that had established a good banking system, promoted scientific experimentation, and passed laws to protect business.

9. *Inventions*. The changes in production came first in the cotton textile industry. Several inventors devised inventions that sped up and improved the manufacture of textiles.

EUROPEAN INVENTORS OF THE INDUSTRIAL REVOLUTION

Inventor	Invention and Its Importance
John Kay	Flying shuttle—speeded up the weaving process
James Hargreaves	Spinning jenny—could spin many threads at one time
Richard Arkwright	Water frame—used water power to increase spinning; first machine to replace human hand power with another power source
Edmund Cartwright	Power loom—used water power to make weaving faster
James Watt	Steam engine—use of steam as a source of power
George Stephenson	Steam locomotive—improved ground transportation

The locomotive was developed during the Industrial Revolution.

Responses to the Industrial Revolution. The Industrial Revolution fundamentally changed the way people lived. Families moved to industrial cities by the millions to work in the new factories. The first years of adjustment to the new industrial society were a period of severe difficulty for workers. Men, women, and children worked long hours under deplorable conditions in factories. People were crowded into towns and cities that had made little provision for housing or for sanitation. With more people working in factories and living in cities, occupational, health, and housing problems developed. Moreover, even though they were becoming more populated than rural areas, cities had not gained political power. These problems associated with industrialization developed in Britain as well as in other areas of Europe where industrialization took place. In response to workers' protests and reformers' appeals, various reform measures were adopted. These reforms indicated that Europeans had begun to understand the changes in the working and living conditions of those who labored under the factory system. Reform measures in Britain were as follows:

1. *Social and economic reforms.* Harmful working conditions such as child labor, low wages, faulty ventilation, and dangerous equipment were brought to public attention by the Sadler Report on factories and the Ashley Report on mines. In time, members of Parliament became concerned about children as young as five or six working long hours in factories and mines and about the dangerous, unhealthful conditions for all workers in factories. Laws such as the Factory Act (1833) and the Mines Act (1842) were passed to improve conditions for workers. The need for workers to unite to protect and advance their interests led to the formation of labor unions.

2. *Political reforms.* The move to reduce property rights as the basis for suffrage (the right to vote) and to give cities more representation in Parliament led to the passage of the Reform Bill of 1832. This bill also did away with most "rotten boroughs" (areas that no longer had many people but had kept the same amount of representation in Parliament). The middle class, workers, and women were to benefit from the Reform Bill of 1832 and similar legislation passed in the 19th and early 20th centuries. By 1928, for example, Britain provided for universal suffrage. This meant that both women and men had the right to vote. The expansion of suffrage in Britain and other European countries was partially due to changes brought about by the Industrial Revolution.

The Development of Socialism. Political scientists and philosophers struggled with the problems presented by industrialization, seeking to discover how the political system should respond.

One of these solutions was socialism, which was a criticism of capitalism and called for a basic change in the economic system in order to correct these problems. Socialists maintained that it was necessary to transfer ownership of the means of production (factories, mines, railroads, land) from private individuals to the state. According to socialist theory, the government, as elected by the people, should own all the means of production and should also make all the key economic decisions. These decisions included: What should be produced? Who should produce it? What should the price be? and How should the product be distributed? This kind of planned, or command, economy is in contrast to a free-enterprise or market economy. In a market economy, according to capitalist principles, the key economic decisions are basically made by private individuals acting on their own.

GEOGRAPHY

Environment and Society

One group of socialists wanted to create an ideal society, or a utopia. Utopian socialists believed that a socialist society would emerge peacefully and that even capitalists would be willing to help create it. Among the utopian socialists of the 19th century were a wealthy British manufacturer, Robert Owen, and a French philosopher, Charles Fourier.

In contrast to utopian socialists were those people who believed in a radically different type of socialism called sci-

Karl Marx

entific socialism or communism. That was a type of socialism based on what they believed were scientific ideas about the way society operates. The leading scientific socialist thinkers were Karl Marx and Friedrich Engels of Germany. Their ideas were contained in two books: *The Communist Manifesto* (1848) and *Das Kapital* (1867). Their major ideas came to be known as Marxism and included:

1. *Economic interpretation of history.* All history is determined by economic conditions. Whichever group or class controls the means of production will control the government.

2. *Class struggle.* In all societies throughout history, there have been struggles for power between two economic groups—the haves and the have nots. In industrial societies the struggle has taken place between the capitalists, or bourgeoisie, and the workers, or proletariat.

3. *Surplus value theory.* Surplus value was the difference between the price of a good and the wage paid to a worker. According to Marx, this difference was kept by the capitalists as their profit. For Marx, this was wrong, especially as he felt that workers were paid far too little in wages. Such abuse, or exploitation of workers, was unjust.

4. *Inevitability of socialism.* Eventually all these conditions would lead to depressions and poverty and would result in a violent overthrow by the workers of the government, primarily because the capitalists would not peacefully give up their economic and political power. This communist revolution would result in a dictatorship of the proletariat, a government that would be more just and would rule on behalf of the working class. The government would operate under the theory of socialism. Eventually, a classless society would emerge, and there would be no need for a government; the government would wither away.

The Impact of Communism. The history of communism since Marx put forth his ideas shows a wide difference between what Marx said and what has actually happened.

1. His prediction that communist revolutions would occur mostly in Western European industrialized societies was wrong. The first two communist revolutions took place in agricultural societies—Russia (1917) and China (1949).

2. Communism never won control in industrialized societies in Western Europe or in North America. Marx failed to see the growth of unions and their ability to work toward their goals in a free, democratic system. He also did not realize that the living conditions of the workers would improve in the 19th century and that workers would become part of the middle class.

3. As the 1990s began, it was clear that communist societies had failed to achieve their goals. Economic and political problems in Eastern Europe and the Soviet Union led to the collapse of communism in those areas (1989–1991). In addition, throughout this century, there have been constant attempts by people in these communist nations to leave, seeking a better life elsewhere, specifically in non-communist countries.

Part D: Imperialism

Imperialism can be defined as the control by one nation over a weaker area or nation. This control has usually been both political and economic. Since the areas under control are called colonies, the practice of imperialism can be referred to as colonialism. There were two distinct periods of imperialism—the "old imperialism" (1500–1800) and the "new imperialism" (beginning in the 1880s). The old imperialism had the following characteristics: concerned with establishing trade routes and obtaining resources; carried on at first by private individuals and companies; took place mainly in the western hemisphere, the Americas. (See the section on Latin America.) The new imperialism had these general characteristics: concerned with establishing trade and markets, obtaining resources, and making large financial investments; carried on by governments as official policy; took place mainly in the eastern hemisphere, Africa, and Asia. There were many reasons for the new imperialism.

WORLD ISSUES

World Trade and Finance

GEOGRAPHY

Use of Geography

1. *Economic*. The increased supply of manufactured goods produced by the Industrial Revolution encouraged European nations to find new markets for these goods. Investors with surplus capital looked overseas to make investments that would bring them profits. The need for raw materials to produce more goods was another important consideration.

GLOBAL CONCEPTS

Interdependence

CONCEPTS GLOBAL

2. *Political*. Nations hoped to gain prestige and glory by expanding their power. These nationalistic desires sparked nations to achieve a balance of power with other nations that were also seeking to build colonial empires.

3. *Social*. European nations felt that they were superior to other global areas. They felt that they had both an obligation and a right to spread their culture and way of life into these areas. These feelings of ethnocentrism can be seen in Rudyard Kipling's poem *The White Man's Burden,* which concerns the obligation of carrying Western civilization to those considered less fortunate. These feelings were also the result of 19th-century notions of white racial superiority and the theory of social Darwinism. This was the belief that social progress depended on competition among human beings, resulting in the survival of the fittest.

GEOGRAPHY

Human Systems

Forms of Imperialist Control. Imperialism took many different forms in the 19th century.

1. *Sphere of influence.* A nation gained sole economic power in a region and had exclusive economic rights to trade, to invest, and to develop mines, railroads, or factories. It could not be interfered with by other nations. This form of imperialism was used in China, where each foreign nation—for example, Germany—had economic control in a specific area.

GEOGRAPHY

Use of Geography

2. *Concession.* In this form, a foreign nation obtained special privileges. An underdeveloped area gave permission to a technologically advanced nation to do something of economic value in the area. (For example, the Arabs let the British drill for oil and build a railroad in the Middle East.)

3. *Protectorate.* A colonial nation allowed the native ruler of an area to remain in office as a figurehead, while in reality the colonial power made all the major decisions (France in Tunisia). The former Eastern European satellite nations controlled by the former Soviet Union after World War II can be thought of as protectorates.

4. *Colony.* An imperialist nation takes total control over an area and makes it part of its empire. (France in Indochina, the Netherlands in Indonesia, Britain in India.)

Colonial Policies. The major imperialist nations followed different policies in ruling their empires. These policies influenced the patterns of independence that took place after 1945.

GLOBAL
CONCEPTS

Choice

CONCEPTS
GLOBAL

1. *England.* Its policy of indirect rule permitted local rulers to retain some power in an area. Nevertheless, because the British felt that their democratic values were superior and should be spread, they sought to educate selected Africans and Asians in English schools. It was hoped that these natives would plant British political and social ideals in their native lands. People who received such an education, such as Gandhi and Nehru in India, eventually led their people to independence in nonviolent ways, based on democratic ideas. Britain was never involved in harsh colonial wars for independence as were some of the other European nations.

2. *France.* Its policy of direct rule viewed colonies as if they were actually parts of France. Decisions for the colonies were made directly in Paris. Since the French language and culture were assumed to be preferable, all people were to learn them in colonized areas. These attitudes were the basis for France's claim to carry out a civilizing mission and to accomplish assimilation of native peoples. Since France viewed areas such as Algeria and Indochina as much a part of French territory as Paris, the French were unwilling to give in to demands for independence that grew

GEOGRAPHY

Use of Geography

after the end of World War II. Consequently, France fought bitter, unsuccessful colonial wars in these areas.

3. *Portugal.* Its policy of paternalism viewed colonies as though they were children, and Portugal did little to prepare its colonies for independence. As with France, it looked on its colonies as parts of Portugal. Consequently, it too was unwilling to grant independence to its colonies in Angola and Mozambique without military struggle.

4. *Belgium.* It followed policies of paternalism and exploitation in the Congo. Belgium did little to pave the way for independence and left the area amid much bloodshed in 1960. Consequently, this former colony had severe political problems in creating a stable government when it became independent.

Independence and Decolonization. During the period after World War II, independence came to almost all areas that had come under European imperialist control. This period of decolonization saw the emergence of over fifty new nations. The end of imperialism after 1945 was a result of many factors: nationalist movements in the colonies grew powerful, gaining support from native people as well as from some people in the imperialist nations; the Western European nations were weary after fighting World War II; the creation of the United Nations was linked to global concern for human rights and recognition of the need for people to achieve self-determination.

GLOBAL CONCEPTS

Change

CONCEPTS GLOBAL

GEOGRAPHY

Use of Geography

Although decolonization was achieved in both peaceful and violent ways, many former colonies retain ties today to their former foreign rulers. Many of Britain's colonies, after independence, voluntarily chose membership in the British Commonwealth of Nations. The organization meets to discuss matters of mutual interest and provides certain economic privileges for members. Although it no longer exists, the French Community was an organization similar to the British Commonwealth. It included France and several of its former colonies. France's interest in its former colonies can be seen in its giving economic aid and in providing military support when requested. For example, in recent years, French forces were sent to the African nations of Chad and Gabon to put down armed opposition to the governments there.

WORLD ISSUES

Human Rights

Evaluation of Imperialism. European imperialism had both positive and negative consequences, as summarized in the following table.

EUROPEAN IMPERIALISM

Consequence	Positive	Negative
Political	Brought stability and unification; training for independence; promoted the nation-state idea	Colonial wars; discrimination; drew boundaries without consulting native peoples
Economic	Introduced modernization; improved means of transportation and communication; created industries; taught new skills; improved the standard of living; provided employment	Took wealth away from colony; treated workers badly; did not provide for advancement or mangement by colonized people; destroyed traditional industries and patterns of trade
Social	Introduced Christianity and other aspects of Western culture; built schools and hospitals; modern medicine	Looked down on native cultures; promoted racism and cultural inferiority; introduced Western vices and diseases

SECTION 1: SOUTH ASIA

The British Raj (Rule) (1760–1947)

The British involvement in India, an example of imperialism, grew from economic contact to direct political control. Britain was able to outmaneuver its European rivals, most notably the French, build alliances with native Indian rulers in some areas of the subcontinent, and inflict military defeat on other rulers.

WORLD ISSUES

Determination of Political and Economic Systems

The British East India Company. Granted a charter from Queen Elizabeth I in 1600, the British East India Company received permission from the ruling Mughal Dynasty to trade in India as early as 1613. From this time until 1858, the company exercised powers usually associated with a government. It had, for example, its own private army. One of its employees, Robert Clive, led military forces to victories over both French and native Indian armies. As a result of the most important of these victories, at Plassey in 1757, the British became the dominant economic and unofficial political power in the subcontinent.

The Sepoy Mutiny and Direct Rule by Britain. The Sepoy Mutiny of 1857 was fought against the British for both religious and political reasons. It began when Indian soldiers serving in the British colonial army (sepoys) suspected that the grease used on bullet cartridges came from cows and pigs. If so, to bite into these cartridges would have violated Hindu and Muslim beliefs. These suspicions led to a rebellion that gradually spread beyond the military and became an anti-Western movement. Some Indian historians view the Sepoy Mutiny as a war of independence, similar to movements in Europe and the Americas. Eventually it was severely crushed. Nevertheless, the East India Company was abolished and replaced as a governing body by the British Crown. In 1876 Queen Victoria was proclaimed Empress of India. What was now called the Crown Colony of India actually included present-day Pakistan, India, and Bangladesh.

GLOBAL CONCEPTS

Human Rights

CONCEPTS GLOBAL

Rule by Britain brought some benefits to the colonized people of the subcontinent, such as improved transportation and communication, health services, education, and political unity. However, colonial rule was more beneficial for the British, allowing them to exploit Indian resources and provide employment for many British people. British government administrators and business people formed a dominant ruling and decision-making class. In addition, Indians felt that their cultural values, beliefs, and practices were threatened because they clashed with those of the British. British ethnocentrism stirred bad feelings.

Growth of an Indian Nationalist Movement. The movement for Indian independence grew from distrust of British economic, cultural, and political practices. In addition, Indians felt it was wrong for the British to preach democratic ideals while denying Indians democratic rights, such as self-determination. The Sepoy Mutiny could be viewed as the first major step in an Indian nationalist movement. Other important developments included:

1. In 1885 the Indian National Congress was founded, initially to promote a gradual relaxation of British economic and political control. It eventually became known as the Congress Party. In the 20th century, leading political figures associated with the Congress Party were Mohandas Gandhi, Jawaharlal Nehru, and Indira Gandhi.

2. In 1906 the Muslim League was created by those Muslims who feared that the Congress Party was becoming too strongly dominated by Hindus. One of its founders was Mohammed Ali Jinnah.

3. From 1914 to 1918 British participation in World War I adversely affected Britain in the colony of India. Indian soldiers fought in Europe and gained military distinction. However, they soon began to question for whose interests they were really fighting. Also, they came to realize that the terrible tragedies associated with the war cast doubt on the British claim of the superiority of European culture and civilization.

4. In 1919 the Amritsar Massacre occurred when British troops fired on unarmed Indians attending a political rally. The death of hundreds of people in this town in the northern province of Punjab infuriated Indians.

5. In 1921 the Montagu-Chelmsford Reforms provided for a limited amount of self-government. This included a two-chamber legislature with limited powers that would have more members elected by Indians than appointed by the British.

6. In 1935 the Government of India Act extended the policy of limited self-government by letting Indian provinces have more control over their own affairs. It was intended to set the groundwork for India to become a self-governing dominion within the British Empire, like Canada.

7. Gandhi's nonviolent movement. Known as Mahatma ("the great soul"), Mohandas K. Gandhi organized boycotts and

other nonviolent activities, such as a march to the sea to protest a salt tax, in an attempt to shame the British and achieve swaraj (self-rule). Gandhi also went on frequent hunger strikes. His nonviolent actions stemmed from the Hindu idea of "ahimsa." His ideas and tactics were described as examples of passive resistance and civil disobedience. They inspired other campaigns for political equality and civil rights, including those led by the Reverend Martin Luther King, Jr. in the United States and Nelson Mandela and others in South Africa.

World War II, Partition, and Independence. With the end of World War II in 1945, Britain moved to seek a peaceful transition for Indian independence. Britain was exhausted after the war and did not want to spend the money or use the personnel needed to maintain the colony. It also wanted to adhere to the principles of the United Nations charter concerning self-determination for all people. However, even though the British had hoped to leave behind them one united country, there was much tension between Hindus and Muslims. The Congress Party, led by Jawaharlal Nehru, and the Muslim League, led by Mohammed Ali Jinnah, were unable to resolve all their differences. These differences led to much bloodshed and threatened to bring on a civil war if no agreement was reached on a partition plan. Eventually, on August 15, 1947, independence came with the creation of two independent nations, India, with a Hindu majority, and Pakistan, which is predominantly Muslim, formed by a partition, or division, of the subcontinent.

WORLD ISSUES

War
and
Peace

GLOBAL
CONCEPTS

Change

CONCEPTS
GLOBAL

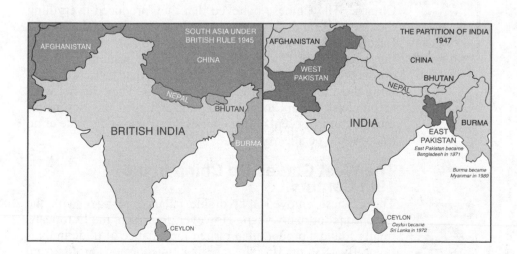

SECTION 2: CHINA

China's Relationships with the West

Westerners became interested in opening relations with China for a number of reasons. Western missionaries wished to convert the Chinese to Christianity. Western traders were interested in obtaining Chinese silks, tea, ceramics, spices, and other luxury goods and in selling Western goods to the Chinese. In the 19th century, during the period of European imperialism, the Europeans sought to conquer Chinese territory and exploit its resources.

Chinese interest in Christianity and foreign trade was limited, however. The government, in an effort to limit foreign influence, restricted the activities of the missionaries. European trade with China was restricted to the port of Guangzhou (Canton) in 1757, and severe restrictions were placed on that trade. Foreign relations with the Chinese could only be conducted through the tributary system. The Chinese considered themselves superior to all other nations, and all non-Chinese were considered "barbarians."

The Tribute System and Trade

The Chinese applied the idea of the tribute system to trade with the Europeans. As long as trade didn't interfere with the Chinese way of life and economy, and as long as the Westerners "knew their place," the Chinese would allow trade, but they believed they controlled that trade. The Europeans sought trade, not the Chinese. The Chinese believed that they produced everything they needed, and they saw trade as a favor extended to the Europeans. They were willing to sell to the Europeans because they could understand that Europeans would want fine Chinese products. However, they did not believe that there was anything they might want from the Europeans. They did not wish to purchase European products, and believed the Europeans must therefore accept all the Chinese restrictions on trade or no trade would be allowed.

GEOGRAPHY

Use of Geography

The West Carves Up China in the 19th Century

GEOGRAPHY

Human Systems

The Chinese enjoyed a favorable balance of trade with the Europeans for many years. However, in opium, the Europeans finally found a product that turned the balance of trade in their favor. By 1839 the British were making enormous profits from the opium trade, and the Chinese government took steps to end the trade. British opium was confiscated and destroyed, and the British were informed they could no longer trade with China. In 1840 the British sent warships to China and the Opium War began. In 1842 the Chinese were defeated because of the superior technology of the West.

The treaty ending the war, the Treaty of Nanjing (Nanking) (1842), was the first of the unequal treaties forced upon China. The Chinese were forced to open five ports to trade; Hong Kong was ceded to the British; China was to pay a $21 million indemnity to Britain; foreign merchants were to be allowed to reside in the treaty ports; and the Chinese were not allowed to set tariffs (taxes on imports) in the treaty ports. Other nations, including the United States, Germany, Russia, and France,

---

Causes of the Opium War

Background Causes

Chinese:

1. British imported opium from India into China; addiction became a problem in China, upsetting society.
2. As demand for opium increased, silver was drained from China to pay for it, upsetting the economy and resulting in an unfavorable balance of trade.
3. Chinese law made opium trade illegal; British continued the trade.

British:

1. British resented being treated as inferiors under the tribute system.
2. Chinese put such a high tariff on British products most Chinese couldn't buy them.
3. British resented being restricted to Canton.
4. Chinese refused to import British textiles, one of Britain's most important industries.
5. Chinese law was applied to British citizens in China, and Chinese law was harsh.
6. British wanted free trade but did not want to trade through guilds or trade associations called cohongs, which was required in China.

Immediate Cause

Chinese officials burned British opium.

---

quickly followed suit, and China was forced to agree to more demands. Western diplomats were allowed to live in Beijing (Peking), Christian missionaries were able to establish churches, foreign powers were granted concessions in Chinese ports, and foreigners gained the right of extraterritoriality.

Furthermore, China was carved into spheres of influence, areas of China where only one imperialist Western power was allowed to dominate, with exclusive rights to trade. In 1894 China and Japan went to war over their interests in Korea, a Chinese tributary state. The Japanese, who had instituted rapid industrialization and militarization in the 1860s to prevent Western nations from carving up Japan, defeated China. China was forced to cede Taiwan and the Pescadores Islands to Japan, and Chinese influence in Korea was ended. Within a few years, Japan annexed Korea. China was being whittled away, but the Chinese, because of their lack of technological progress, were powerless to stop it. To prevent its exclusion from the China trade, in 1899 the United States encouraged Western nations to adopt the Open Door Policy: all nations would have equal trading rights in China and would recognize the territorial integrity of China.

WORLD ISSUES

Economic
Growth and
Development

Treaty of Nanjing (Nanking): The First Unequal Treaty

Britain Gained:

1. Payment for the opium
2. Control of Hong Kong
3. Freedom to trade in five cities
4. Abolition of the tariff on British goods or the right to set the tariff low
5. Extraterritoriality
6. Most-favored nation clause

China Lost:

1. The right to control the British in China
2. Control over parts of Chinese territory and the Chinese people in it
3. The right to control their own infant industries with the tariff
4. Control of trade
5. Prestige—they were defeated by the "barbarians" and couldn't compete with them

Chinese Response to Foreign Imperialism

Although the scholar-bureaucrats of China were resistant to change, some attempts at reform were made. The tributary system was replaced by a government office to deal with foreign representatives as diplomatic equals. Those in the government who favored reform wished to adopt Western technology without making any major changes in China's government or society. These reformers believed that the Chinese had been defeated only because of the superior armaments of the West. Western experts were employed to create and train a modern army and navy. A small effort was also made at industrialization. Coal mines were opened, arsenals and dockyards were built, and railroads and telegraph lines were constructed.

The real power in China between 1861 and 1908 was the Empress Dowager Cixi (Tzu-hsi), who ruled as regent for her son and then her nephew. In 1898 Guang-Xu (Kuang Hsu) took control of the government from his aunt and issued daily edicts calling for reforms. This period was called the Hundred Days Reform. Guang-Xu's edicts called for changes in government, education, foreign policy, agriculture, technology, and the military. These reforms threatened the interests of Confucian scholars, government officials, Cixi, and also foreign interests in China. Cixi regained control of the government within three months and ended the reform movement. In 1900 anti-foreigner Chinese called "Boxers," with the secret support of the Empress Dowager, attacked the foreign delegations in Beijing, hoping to expel the foreigners (Westerners) from China. The Boxers were defeated by combined foreign forces after 55 days.

Overthrow of the Emperor (1911–1912)

Revolts against the Manchu Qing (Ch'ing) Dynasty began in the late 1700s. However, most of the rebellions were limited and easy to suppress. One of the strongest uprisings against the Manchu was the Taiping Rebellion, which spread across southern and central China from 1850 to 1864.

GLOBAL
CONCEPTS

Change

CONCEPTS
GLOBAL

A successful rebellion—the Chinese Revolution—against the Manchus began on October 10, 1911. The revolutionaries declared a republic and elected Sun Yat-sen as the provisional president. His program for China was known as the Three Principles of the People, and the party to carry it out was the Kuomintang, the National People's Party, or the Nationalist Party.

Three Principles of the People

1. Nationalism meant both restoring the pride of the Chinese people and Chinese rule and removing the foreigners, their concessions, and their spheres of influence.

2. Democracy meant popular sovereignty, but it was to be approached in three stages: first, a military government to remove the Manchu Dynasty and defeat the Westerners; second, rule of the Kuomintang; and third, constitutional government, with popularly elected executive, judicial, and legislative branches called yuans.

3. Livelihood meant a program of land reform, the redistribution of land to the peasants, and the elimination of the system of tenant farming. The government was to control transportation, communication, and heavy industry.

The Manchus turned to Yuan Shih-kai (a former general in the Manchu army) to defeat the Chinese Revolution of 1911. Instead, Yuan reached an agreement with the revolutionaries and used his power to force the abdication of the Manchu emperor. In return, Sun Yat-sen resigned as president of the republic and was replaced by Yuan. Yuan became a military dictator and eliminated the democratic reforms instituted by Sun and the Kuomintang. Sun and his followers tried to overthrow him, but Sun was forced into exile. Yuan died in 1916, and Sun returned to China. However, warlords who had been building up their own power in the provinces began to struggle against each other to gain control of the country. China fell into a decade of total chaos, with warlords fighting each other.

SECTION 3: JAPAN

Americans Arrive in Japan

On July 14, 1853, Commodore Matthew Perry, in command of four U.S. ships, sailed into Tokyo Bay. The Japanese had never seen steamships before and were astonished at the fire power of the warships. Perry carried with him a letter from U.S. President Millard Fillmore, demanding that Japan open its ports to American trade and ships, and that the government guarantee fair treatment of American sailors (shipwrecked sailors were badly treated).

The Japanese were opposed to the American demands, but the government of the shogun realized that the Japanese could not defend themselves against American technology. In 1854 the shogun's government signed a treaty opening two Japanese ports to American ships to take on supplies, and an American consulate was opened. Within four years, the United States had been granted full trade rights in several other ports, extraterritoriality, and limitations on the Japanese right to impose tariffs on American goods. Soon the European powers were demanding the same rights. The Japanese believed that Japan would be cut up into spheres of influence, as China had been, unless they took steps to prevent it.

Meiji Restoration (1868–1912)

Many Japanese blamed the shogunate for failing to defend Japan against foreign interference and believed that the Tokugawa could not resist the foreigners. In 1868 samurai forces overthrew the shogunate and restored the emperor's rule. This so-called Meiji Restoration brought to the throne Emperor Matshuhito, who was only fifteen years old.

Changes by 1912

The Japanese who led the overthrow of the shogun and the restoration of the emperor believed that the only way to remove the threat of the Western powers was a rapid program of modernization to enable Japan to compete with the West. Japan already had a high literacy rate, a high degree of urbanization, a large pool of skilled labor, and channels for mass training of citizens. What stood in the way of full-scale modernization was the feudal system, which the leaders of the restoration set about to destroy.

The daimyo (feudal lords) were persuaded to give up their estates, and Japan was divided into prefectures under the direct control of the government in Tokyo (the new name for Edo). Class divisions and restrictions were abolished, and equality of all people was declared. The samurai lost all their special privileges, and universal military service was adopted. An education system was established.

The leaders of the restoration created a highly centralized bureaucratic government, which was an oligarchy (a small group controlling the government and allowing little opposition). In 1889 the Japanese were presented with a written constitution, a "gift from the emperor." The new constitution established a two-house legislature, called the Diet. This was a severely limited democracy, and the small elite group who took control of the government in 1868 remained in control. The Western powers recognized Japan's efforts to provide at least a limited democracy.

A program of rapid modernization was begun. The government constructed railroads, highways, and telegraph lines and also built industries—textile mills, armaments factories, shipbuilding facilities—and opened mines. Later these industries were sold to private enterprise, thereby sponsoring the development of the zaibatsu (Japanese industrial monopolies that controlled all aspects of an industry). Japanese students were sent to Western nations to study, and Western advisers were employed. Western experts were hired to assist the Japanese in developing a modern army and navy. By the close of the 19th century, the foundations of a truly modern state had been laid.

Japanese Expansion Prior to World War II

Japanese aggression against weaker neighbors resulted from its need to acquire raw materials for its industrialization. Such aggression was modeled after imperialist actions of the Western powers in the late 19th and early 20th centuries. By the late 19th century, Japan's rulers were concerned that Korea, "a dagger pointed at the heart of Japan," would fall into the hands of an imperialist Western power because the Manchu Dynasty in China could not defend it. This led to the Sino-Japanese War (Sino means Chinese) of 1894 to 1895, which was won by Japan. The Treaty of Shimonoseki granted Japan control of Taiwan, the Pescadores, and China's Liaotung Peninsula, plus an indemnity of several hundred million dollars and trade concessions in China. Korea was declared to be independent of China, and Japan began to seek control of the region.

Japan's chief rival in Korea was Russia, and the Japanese launched an attack in 1904 against the Russian fleet based at Port Arthur, beginning the Russo-Japanese War. The Russians were driven out of Korea and southern Manchuria, and Japan captured Port Arthur. In 1905 U.S. President Theodore Roosevelt negotiated peace between the two belligerents. The Treaty of Portsmouth gave Russia's lease on Port Arthur and its concessions in southern Manchuria to Japan. By 1910 Korea had been annexed by Japan.

SECTION 4: AFRICA

European Imperialism in Africa

In the late 19th century, the Europeans began to explore the interior of Africa and to expand their control. This imperialist expansion was made possible by their technological superiority. As the Europeans expanded in Africa, they dominated the African people as well as their territory. They used the excuse of "the white man's burden," a legacy of the slave trade, to justify this expansion, claiming that it was their duty to bring civilization, progress, and Christianity to the less developed regions of the world. In reality, their major goal was to accumulate profit and power. This period of European imperialism was influenced by industrial capitalism and the increasing demands for raw materials for European factories and for markets for European manufactured goods. The Europeans needed African resources—mineral, land, forest products. They also desired greater power and prestige. The more territory they controlled, the more powerful and important they became, and European nations became rivals for African territory.

GLOBAL CONCEPTS

Power

CONCEPTS GLOBAL

The Africans resisted the intrusion of Europeans and felt they were defending themselves against invasion. The Zulu fought the British and Boers in South Africa. The Sudanese fought the British. The Mandingo fought the French in West Africa. The Germans were forced to fight in East Africa. The Africans fought conventionally and also used guerrilla tactics, but their weapons were no match for those of the Europeans. Some of the African peoples used passive resistance. The Bushmen and Hottentots in South Africa simply disappeared into the bush.

GEOGRAPHY

In 1875, European holdings in Africa were fairly small, but by 1914 all of Africa except Ethiopia and Liberia were under European control. The scramble for Africa began after King Leopold of Belgium announced he was taking control of the vast Congo Free State in Central Africa in 1879. In 1885, at the Berlin Conference, the European nations reached agreement on how Africa should be divided into colonial territories.

Use of Geography

Some Africans served as mercenaries in the European armies or worked with the colonial governments. The British used a colonial policy known as indirect rule. They left tribal leaders in charge, but the Africans were actually puppet rulers who followed directions from the British colonial administrators.

GLOBAL CONCEPTS

Political Systems

CONCEPTS GLOBAL

The French practiced a policy of assimilation. Their hope was to make the Africans "French" by changing their culture

GLOBAL CONCEPTS

Change

CONCEPTS GLOBAL

GEOGRAPHY

Human Systems

and traditions. The French ruled more directly than the British and removed the traditional rulers.

The Belgians used a policy of paternalism, treating the indigenous peoples as children who needed to be cared and provided for.

The Portuguese at first believed the Africans needed to be taught discipline and obedience. In the 20th century, however, this attitude changed, and they adopted a policy of assimilation intended to eventually make the Africans citizens of Portugal.

German rule in Africa was different in different colonies. In some they used forced labor. In others they tried the indirect rule approach.

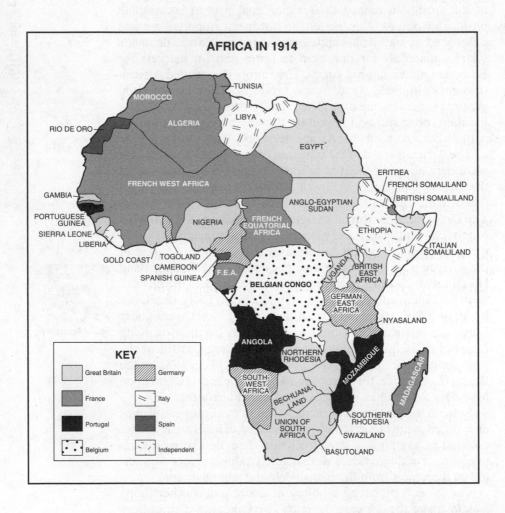

AFRICA IN 1914

KEY

- Great Britain
- France
- Portugal
- Belgium
- Germany
- Italy
- Spain
- Independent

Effects of European Rule on Africa

1. *Establishment of boundaries.* When the Europeans divided Africa, they drew up boundaries that had nothing to do with physical features or ethnic boundaries. As a result, ethnic groups found their territories divided among more than one colony; some were within boundaries with traditional enemies. Because the colonies were granted independence based on the European-drawn boundaries, the problems created by dividing ethnic territories or expecting enemies to coexist remain in modern Africa.

2. *Changes in agriculture.* To provide raw materials for their industries, the Europeans encouraged the development of plantations and the cultivation of cash crops such as cocoa, cotton, coffee, peanuts, and palm oil. Many Africans concentrated on the cultivation of these cash crops, and they had to import food crops to feed themselves. In areas of heavy European settlement, such as South Africa and the Kenya highlands, the best farmland was reserved for Europeans.

3. *Transition from barter to money economy.* Taxes such as the head tax or the hut tax had to be paid in cash. To pay the tax, many Africans were forced to work for Europeans. They had to move to the city, sometimes with their families, sometimes leaving the family in the countryside to work the land, thereby destabilizing the family system. In addition, the money economy created greater disparities in wealth. Some Africans accumulated capital, while others did not. As a result, social tension was created between the haves and the have nots.

4. *Changes in the landholding system.* Europeans introduced the idea of individual ownership of land. This weakened tribal ties and also meant that for some, there was no land, thus destroying the Africans' traditional way of making a living.

5. *Exploitation of resources.* The Europeans needed raw materials for their factories, so they developed the resources of Africa by opening mines and plantations. The benefits of this development went to the Europeans, not the Africans.

6. *Improved transportation and communications.* In order to exploit the resources of Africa, the Europeans had to build railroads and communications systems. These improvements benefited the Africans by assisting in the development of national unity and opening remote regions of the interior to economic development. However, they also accelerated the migration of African labor to areas where work could be found, further weakening tribal and family ties.

7. *New legal and judicial systems.* The European nations introduced their own ideas of law and justice in the colonies.

GLOBAL CONCEPTS

Identity

CONCEPTS GLOBAL

GEOGRAPHY

Human Systems

WORLD ISSUES

Determination of Political and Economic Systems

GEOGRAPHY

Environment and Society

GEOGRAPHY

Human Systems

Era I **AN AGE OF REVOLUTIONS (1750–1918)**

WORLD ISSUES

Determination
of Political
and Economic
Systems

Secular law and religious law were separated, while traditional law was changed or abolished, again weakening group ties and eroding traditional authority systems.

8. *Education.* Although education was not freely available to all Africans, some education was provided. Through European education, Africans learned of democracy and natural human rights and again began to reject traditional authority systems. Traditional African culture was downgraded and European culture upheld as the example of how things should be. Educated Africans became the core of the nationalist movements in Africa and led the struggle for political independence from colonial domination.

WORLD ISSUES

Population

9. *Preventive medicine and improved nutrition.* Because of Western medicines and medical practices, the infant mortality rate and overall death rate dropped dramatically. As a result, Africa has the most rapidly increasing population growth rate (about 3 percent) of any of the continents.

Part E: Global Changes and Revolutions (1750–1914)

SECTION 1: RUSSIA

Expansion and Modernization Under the Tsars (1725–1905)

Under the tsars and tsaritsas who succeeded Peter I, Russia continued to expand its empire and its involvement with Western Europe. During the reign of Ekaterina or Catherine II (1762–1796), usually referred to as "the Great," Russia regained the parts of Ukraine and Belarussia lost under the last Rurik tsars, as well as Lithuania. In the southeast, the last of the Tartar tribes were defeated, thus gaining the entire Crimea and much of the northern coast of the Black Sea at the expense of the Ottoman Empire. This began a traditional policy that was pursued by the Soviet government as well as the later tsars—to gain Constantinople (modern-day Istanbul) and the straits that connect the Black Sea with the Aegean and the Mediterranean (the Dardanelles) in order to have access to major trade routes. In addition, much of Siberia was explored and settled by Russians.

GLOBAL CONCEPTS

Empathy

CONCEPTS GLOBAL

Tsar Alexander I (1801–1825) was credited as the monarch who defeated Napoleon. This victory was due to the "Scorched Earth" policy (retreating and burning anything that could not be taken rather than leaving it for the enemy) that the Russians adopted in response to Napoleon's invasion. A lack of supplies and the severely cold winter devastated the French Army. Thousands died during the chaotic retreat. At the Congress of Vienna, Russia acquired most of Poland. Alexander also gained Finland from Sweden in 1809.

WORLD ISSUES

| War |
| and |
| Peace |

GEOGRAPHY

Use of Geography

Under the strong autocratic rule of Nikolai or Nicholas I (1825–1855), Russia was unsuccessful in further expansion. Greatly shaken by the Decembrist Revolt of 1825 (in which officers favoring democratic reforms tried to overthrow Nicholas), the tsar fought any movement for change. Fearing that reform would undermine his authority, Nicholas followed repressive policies at home and abroad (he earned the title "Policeman of Europe"). Yet, Russia's defeat in the Crimean War (1854–1856) revealed the need for both reform and modernization.

RUSSIAN EXPANSION IN EUROPE

KEY

- Original area
- Alexis
- Peter
- Catherine
- 19th Century
- - - Polish boundary before partitions

Archangel

FINLAND (1809)

(1721)

St. Petersburg

RUSSIAN EMPIRE

SWEDEN

ESTONIA (1721)

Novgorod

BALTIC SEA (1795)

(1772)

Moscow

(1816-1855)

PRUSSIA (1815)

(1793)

POLAND

GALICIA (To Austria)

AUSTRIA

(1812)

(1792)

(1783)

(1783)

(1783)

CASPIAN SEA

CRIMEA

(1801-1864)

ADRIATIC SEA

OTTOMAN EMPIRE

BLACK SEA

(1878)

AEGEAN SEA

GREECE

Alexander II (1855–1881), the son of Nicholas I, made many of the necessary changes that his father would not. Known as the "Tsar Liberator," Alexander ended the institution of serfdom (peasants were bound to the land they farmed and were therefore controlled by the landowner), which held back the expansion of Russian agriculture and promoted many abuses and social evils. Industrialization was also started in order to make Russia competitive with other European nations. Finally, Alexander

Tsar Nicholas I

Tsar Alexander II

instituted reforms in government, education, and the military that ended many abuses and cruelties and modernized the Russian system. Despite the many changes made by Alexander II, new problems were created by the reforms themselves.

1. The liberation of the serfs created many small farmers who could not pay off their debts. This resulted in mass foreclosures and enormous migrations of unskilled workers to the cities.

2. The abundance of unskilled labor gave factory owners the opportunity to exploit the workers, or proletariat.

3. Widespread exploitation of workers resulted in poverty, slums, and unsafe working conditions in Russian cities and industrial centers.

4. The exploited workers became strong supporters of revolutionary ideas and parties, particularly the Socialists, Communists, and Anarchists. The assassination of Alexander II in 1881 resulted in the end of reform and a renewal of repression.

Alexander III (1881–1894) reacted to his father's murder by enforcing strict control over his subjects. Reinstituting a policy of Russification (forcing Russian language, culture, and religion on all peoples in the Russian Empire), Alexander created resentment and revolutionary feelings.

SECTION 2: OTTOMAN EMPIRE (1453–1918)

During the 1800s, the Ottoman Empire began to decline. Reasons for its decline included corruption and inefficiency on the part of the rulers as well as their inability to hold together so many different peoples. Many of the subject people wished to break free from Ottoman control. Several short wars with other nations weakened Ottoman rule and caused a loss of territory. Finally, the Ottomans failed to modernize and keep up with the growth in industry, technology, learning, science, weapons, and trade that was occurring in Western Europe. As a result, the declining empire became known as "the Sick Man of Europe."

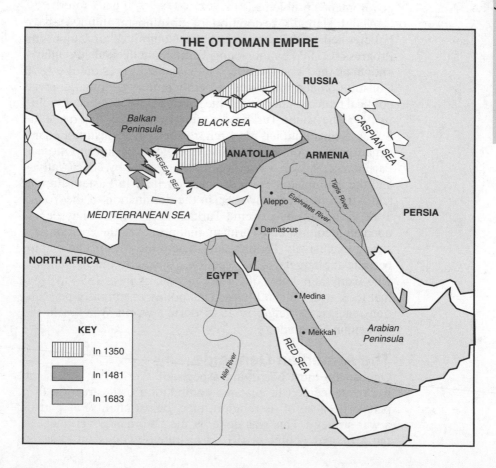

THE OTTOMAN EMPIRE

RUSSIA

Balkan Peninsula

BLACK SEA

CASPIAN SEA

ANATOLIA

ARMENIA

AEGEAN SEA

Tigris River

MEDITERRANEAN SEA

• Aleppo

Euphrates River

PERSIA

• Damascus

NORTH AFRICA

EGYPT

• Medina

• Mekkah

Arabian Peninsula

Nile River

RED SEA

KEY

In 1350

In 1481

In 1683

THE GROWTH OF TURKISH NATIONALISM (1876–1912)

By the mid-1870s the weaknesses in the Ottoman system had made it clear that reform was needed if the Turkish empire were to continue to exist. Under the influence of young Turkish intellectuals who had been educated in Western Europe, the Ottoman government allowed the creation of a constitution in 1876. Supported by the leaders of the non-Turkish minority groups as well, the reformers proposed the transformation of the empire into a constitutional monarchy with a freely elected assembly in which all groups would be proportionately represented. Sultan Abdul Hamid II (r. 1876–1909) responded by revoking the constitution and beginning a period of political repression in 1878. He ordered the massacre of over 200,000 Armenians, claiming this large Christian minority was responsible for revolutionary activity. This began a tradition in the Ottoman Empire of "scapegoating" or blaming others for a government's problems.

Abdul Hamid's restoration of absolutism and repressive policies led to the creation of the Committee of Union and Progress (C.U.P.) by the young Turkish intellectuals. Popularly known as the "Young Turks," they wanted to restore the 1876 Constitution and implement a democratic system that allowed political representation for all the nations in the Ottoman Empire. In 1908, the Young Turks led a military takeover that made the Sultan a constitutional monarch, restored the Constitution, and began preparations for the first free elections for an Ottoman Parliament. Strong opposition to the reforms by conservatives and the continued loss of Ottoman territory in Eastern Europe and Africa resulted, however, in the domination of the Young Turk leadership by extreme Turkish nationalists. They developed an ideology, Pan-Turkism, that proposed the creation of a strong exclusively Turkish state. The minorities of the empire became the targets of persecution, especially the Armenians, who were the victims of further massacres from 1894 to 1896 that took over 300,000 lives. This policy of minority persecution reached its height in 1915 during World War I with the Armenian Genocide.

The Armenian Genocide

One of the most horrifying aspects of World War I was the use of genocide (the planned annihilation or destruction of a people because of its religion, race, or nationality) as part of a war strategy. This was done by the Ottoman government to the Armenian people in 1915. Frustrated by constant losses in the war, the Ottoman leadership made the Armenians "scape-goats" and claimed they were responsible for the Empire's poor military performance. The leaders of the government, a group of army officers known as the Young Turks, adopted this policy as a means of shifting the population's anger and dissatisfaction with the war effort away from themselves. Accusing Armenians of working with the Allies against the Ottoman Empire, the government began a systematic extermination of them on April 24, 1915. Armenian men were rounded up and massacred while the women and children were taken on death marches into the desert. Armenia's political and religious leaders were publicly executed. Armenian churches and institutions were destroyed and their confiscated homes given to Turkish people. Some Armenians were able to escape into Russia or Syria, but the majority were slaughtered. Out of a population of only three million, almost two million were massacred. The surviving Armenians established a republic in the Soviet Union after the war. The Young Turk leaders, who had fled Ottoman Turkey after the defeat of the Central Powers, were found guilty of war crimes by an Ottoman military court, but were never punished. After the modern nation of Turkey was established in 1922, the new government under Mustafa Kemal (later known as "Atatürk") denied the Armenian Genocide ever occurred. This policy of official denial has been continued by successive Turkish governments until the present day.

THE GREEK WAR OF INDEPENDENCE (1821–1832)

The first people in the Ottoman Empire to rebel against Turkish rule were the Greeks. In 1821, they rose up inspired by a new sense of nationhood led by young Greeks who had been educated in Western Europe and exposed to the concepts of nationalism and democracy. Using the slogan "Freedom or Death" to rally the population, they were supported by the clergy of the Greek Orthodox Church and foreigners who were **philhellenes** or "friends of Greece," such as the English poet Lord Byron. Unsuccessful at first, they soon gained support by the British, French, and Russians who were hoping to gain influence in the region. Both Austria and Prussia opposed their support as they feared it would encourage the other Eastern Europeans to demand independence as well. This produced a conflict of interests that permanently ended the agreements made by the Great Powers at the Congress of Vienna to oppose revolution. The Greek cause also had support from famous writers, artists, and composers throughout Western Europe. By 1832, parts of

Greece had been freed from Ottoman control and formed the modern Greek state.

Independence and Pan-Slavism (1821–1914)

The Greek struggle for independence in 1821 touched off a movement throughout Eastern Europe to end Turkish domination in that region. As revolutions broke out in each country, the rivalry between Russia and Austria intensified. The other major European powers became involved, trying to maintain the balance of power. In 1683 the Habsburgs defeated the Turks and captured Hungary. In 1815 Russia and Austria divided Poland at the Congress of Vienna after the Napoleonic Wars. By 1900, Austria had also gained Bohemia (modern-day Czech Republic) and Croatia. Both Russia and Austria had great interest, therefore, in the shape of the new independent Eastern European states.

GLOBAL CONCEPTS

Change

CONCEPTS GLOBAL

Use of Geography

Throughout the 19th century, Russia financed and supported wars for independence in Greece, Serbia, Montenegro, Bulgaria, and Romania. Developing the concept of Pan-Slavism (political, religious, and cultural unity of all Slavs and/or Orthodox Christians), Russian tsars came into conflict with the British, Germans, and French, as well as the Austrians and Turks. Territorial gains made by the Eastern European nations from the Ottomans in the Second Russo-Turkish War (1877–1878) and the Balkan Wars (1912–1913) were limited by the rest of the Great Powers, who feared Russia's growing influence in the region. The modern nation of Albania was created in 1913, as a compromise between Russia and the other Western powers concerning Serbian expansion. By 1914 tensions had grown so great in Eastern Europe, especially in the Balkans, that it was called the "Tinderbox of Europe." The incident that set off World War I, the assassination of the Austrian Archduke Franz Ferdinand by a Serbian nationalist, was one further example of how explosive tensions in Eastern Europe had become.

SECTION 3: LATIN AMERICA

Establishment of Political Independence in Latin America

The 1700s was a period of great political, social, and economic change for the European powers. Britain's thirteen colonies in North America won their independence as a result of the American Revolution. In the late 1700s the French Revolution shook the stability of Europe. The writings of the Enlightenment, expressed in the works of Locke, Rousseau, Voltaire, Montesquieu, and others, led to the spread of revolutionary ideas in Europe and the Americas. In the 1700s Spain sought to reform its American empire. New viceroyalties were created, and an intendancy system was introduced to increase revenues and improve the colonial administration. A Spanish officer appointed by the crown, an *intendente*, had complete control in matters of justice, war, fiscal problems and general public administration over a given area. Despite these reforms, the foreign policy of Spain's Bourbon monarchy, which allied the nation with France, led to a series of military engagements that greatly weakened the Spanish empire. Spain's economic situation and military power continued to decline into the 1790s.

The Napoleonic era that followed the French Revolution caused dislocations that eventually led to a period of Latin American revolutions from 1808 to 1826. Despite the distance and isolation of Spain's colonies from Europe, the political ideas of the Enlightenment and the American and French revolutions affected the people in the Spanish colonies. The English, Dutch, French, and Americans increasingly traded with Spain's American empire. Moreover, some of the Creole elite in the Spanish colonies, such as the Venezuelan Francisco Miranda, promoted the independence of Spanish America.

Napoleon's armies invaded Spain and Portugal in 1806 to 1807. The capture and exile of the Spanish royal family to France and the placement of Joseph Bonaparte on the Spanish throne broke the bond that tied Spanish America to Spain. The ideas that influenced the French Revolution and the revolts against Napoleon in many parts of Spanish Latin America had an enormous influence that led to important political changes throughout the region. A movement that began as a rejection of French control ended as a series for wars of independence against Spain.

The liberators, Simón Bolívar and José San Martín, and their supporters raised armies to drive the Spanish out of South America. In Mexico the leadership of Fathers Hidalgo and Morelos and other revolutionaries led to the eventual success of

Agustín de Iturbide, who established Mexican independence in 1821. Creole nationalism was too strong to overcome, and with the help of the mestizo population, the Spanish were driven out.

Case Study in Independence: Haiti

The movement toward Haitian independence was sparked by the French Revolution. Throughout the 1790s, the former slaves, first led by Toussaint L'Ouverture, increasingly sought to drive out the white slave owners. Despite a major attempt by Napoleon to restore French authority in 1802, independence was inevitable. In 1804 Jean-Jacques Dessalines, an ex-slave, was able to drive out the French, and Haiti became the second nation in the western hemisphere to win complete independence.

Case Study in Independence: Mexico

In 1810 Miguel Hidalgo, a priest, joined with other Creole plotters, most notably Ignacio de Allende, and issued the famous Grito de Dolores. This symbol raised the cry of rebellion against the Spanish government in New Spain. The first phase of the struggle for independence ended with the royalists' defeating the insurgents and executing many of the leaders of the rebellion. Despite this setback, one of Hidalgo's lieutenants, Jose Morelos, called together a congress, which wrote a constitution and declared independence. Morelos was captured and executed in 1815. However, independence was finally secured in 1821 when Agustín de Iturbide, a Creole military officer who had helped defeat the earlier rebellions, negotiated with Vincente Guerrero, by then the principal insurgent leader, to form the Plan of Iguala, which called for independence under a monarchy. Iturbide forced the Spanish out and briefly ruled Mexico as emperor.

LATIN AMERICAN INDEPENDENCE MOVEMENTS TO 1828

Country	Year of Independence	Independence Movement Leaders
Haiti	1803–1804	Toussaint L'Ouverture
Mexico	1821	Father Miguel Hidalgo
		José Morelos
		Agustín de Iturbide
Colombia	1819	Simón Bolívar
Venezuela	1821	Francisco de Miranda
		Simón Bolívar
Ecuador	1822	José de Sucre
		Simón Bolívar
Argentina	1816	José de San Martín
Chile	1818	José de San Martín
		Bernardo O'Higgins
Peru	1824	José de Sucre
		Simón Bolívar

Country	Year of Independence	Independence Movement Leaders
Bolivia	1825	Simón Bolívar
Uruguay	1814, 1828	José Artigas
Brazil	1822	José Bonifacio Emperor Dom Pedro
Paraguay	1811	Fulgencio Yegros
Central American Republics	1812–1825	José Delgado José del Valle

Case Studies: Argentina, Chile, and the Role of José de San Martín

In 1810 a revolutionary regime in Buenos Aires declared independence. José de San Martín, the real architect of independence, had liberated the future Argentina by 1816. He crossed the Andes Mountains with an army in 1817 and helped Bernardo O'Higgins drive the Spanish army out of Chile the following year. San Martín was also involved in the liberation of Peru, but he left the final military struggle in that country after an historic meeting with Simón Bolívar, the Liberator.

Case Study: The Andean Region and the Role of Simón Bolívar, "the Liberator"

Simón Bolívar, by birth a member of the Creole landowning elite, supported the growing independence movement. Between 1810 and 1821, the Liberator was involved in wars to free the future nations of Venezuela, Colombia, Ecuador, Bolivia, and Peru. He was made the first constitutional president of Gran Colombia in 1821. With the help of Francisco Santander and Antonio José de Sucre, Bolívar defeated the Spanish royalist forces by 1826, and they withdrew from Peru.

Case Study: Brazil

Napoleon's invasion of Portugal resulted in the royal family leaving for Brazil. Joao VI became king of Portugal, Brazil, and the Algarve in 1816. Joao helped the British commercial interests by opening the Brazilian ports to trade with friendly nations. This measure also resulted in promoting Brazil's economic autonomy. However, in 1821 political events in Portugal caused Joao to return there. He left behind his son, Pedro I, as regent of Brazil. In 1822, Pedro issued his famous "I am staying" statement after the Portuguese parliament ordered him to return to Portugal. Later that year, independence was declared. In contrast to Spanish America, Brazilian independence was achieved peacefully. Pedro I was declared emperor of Brazil in 1822.

Case Study: The Caribbean

The one area where Spain retained its colonies was in the Caribbean. Cuba and Puerto Rico remained possessions of Spain until the Spanish-American War in 1898. The sugar-plantation owners dominated the economies of these two Greater Antilles islands, and slavery was the main source of labor, particularly in Cuba. The cooperation of Spanish and Creole landowners, merchants, and government officials prevented an independence movement from developing on these islands.

In the British, French, and Dutch Caribbean colonies, with the exception of Haiti, independence has been attained more recently, if at all. Many of the British-held islands did not achieve independence until the post-World War II period. Some islands have remained attached to Great Britain. The French-speaking islands were made overseas departments, which gave them the privilege of representation in the nation's politics and the right of French citizenship. However, the real political power remained in France.

Early Attempts at Unification Fail

The initial attempts at unification of the newly independent states did not last, mainly because nationalistic feelings in the Latin American countries led to political fragmentation. The political union of present-day Colombia, Venezuela, Ecuador, and Panama in Gran Colombia was established in 1819 through the efforts of Simón Bolívar, Francisco Santander, and others. At the Congress of Cucuta in 1821, a constitution was adopted. Bolívar and Santander were elected the first president and vice president for all of Colombia. Santander remained to direct the government after Bolívar went off to liberate Peru. The central government promoted a program of liberal reform. However, attempts by the landed elite to safeguard their local authority and autonomy in Venezuela and Ecuador led in 1826 to an open revolt that broke out in Venezuela. The return of Bolívar temporarily brought unity and peace. However, a brief war soon began between Peru and Gran Colombia in 1828, and this caused the local landed elite to renew their struggle for a political entity that would be more easily influenced and run in their interests. In 1830 first Venezuela and then Ecuador formally seceded. The remaining part of Gran Colombia became the Republic of New Granada.

The Federation of Central America was created when the five provinces—Guatemala, El Salvador, Honduras, Nicaragua, and Costa Rica—declared independence in 1821 and joined the Mexican Empire under Iturbide. They drafted a constitution and adopted a republican form of government. The new government immediately had political difficulties, and in 1823 the five provinces left the federation and became independent states. By the 1840s the federation had ceased to exist.

Sources of Stability and Power: The Landed Elite, the Military, and the Roman Catholic Church

The failure of unification in South America and in Central America was a result of the concentration of power in the hands of the Creole landed elite in the independent nations of Latin America. The large landowners gained enormous power in their local areas and were unwilling to surrender it to a strong central government. The Creole aristocracy, who owned large estates called latifundio, replaced the Spanish officials and peninsulars. They were unwilling to share political power, and the large landowners became a conservative force that sought to maintain stability and their traditional local powers. Instead of unity, Latin America fell victim to frequent disputes concerning ownership of land within each nation and along border areas. These problems have continued to our present day.

The role of the military also proved to be a continuing problem in Latin America. In the early years, military leaders were called on to maintain law and order and act as a stabilizing influence. The military shared a common goal with the landed elite, which was to preserve the status quo. In some countries, the military was the only organized force that could prevent chaos after the wars of national independence.

The rebellions that frequently broke out in the Spanish-speaking republics in the 1800s led the armed forces of many nations to control their countries for long periods. The rise of the military dictator, the caudillo, became a tradition in many countries. José Antonio Paez of Venezuela and Andres Santa Cruz of Bolivia are early examples of caudillos in their nations. Venezuela suffered fifty revolutions and Bolivia sixty revolutions by 1900.

Military figures continued to gain and hold onto power in the 20th century. The military continues to see itself as the preserver of stability and tradition. Today, a military coup d'état is justified to prevent the possibility of a communist takeover and social disintegration. This was the case in Chile when General Augusto Pinochet seized power in 1973.

After the wars of independence, the Roman Catholic Church remained a key institution throughout Latin America. Until recently, the Church often supported the landed elite and military in their efforts to preserve tradition and social order and showed little concern for social problems. However, in recent years the role of the Church in some Latin American nations has changed, as the clergy has taken a more active role in causes concerning human rights. Some members of the clergy have supported the ideas of the liberation theology, a church of the people and even rebellions against the government in power. The struggle within the Church between conservatives, who believe that the clergy should continue its traditional historic role, and radicals, who want the clergy to play a more social and political role, continues. In addition, the Roman Catholic Church is also under pressure due to inroads made by Protestant denominations, particularly the evangelical movements that stress the importance of reconciliation and personal experience with God.

Political Evolution Since Independence

In Latin America, a concept of citizenship was slow to develop after independence. There also were difficulties in attempting to institute a republican form of government. Political participation was open primarily to the wealthy members of society. The landed elite consolidated their hold on the executive and legislative branches of government. In theory, some democratic traditions were established in many Latin American countries in the 19th century. For example, constitutions were written, elected legislative bodies were provided for, and judicial systems were created. However, in practice, the *caudillo* acted as a dictator and often ignored the democratic features of government.

Mexico

In the late 1820s a military caudillo, Antonio Santa Anna, rose to power. He dominated Mexican politics to the mid-1850s and supported a conservative and centralist concept of government. Unfortunately, Santa Anna resorted to dictatorial rule and corrupt policies that had disastrous consequences. Mexico, under Santa Anna's leadership, fell victim to U.S. expansionism. The successful rebellion led by Americans in Texas in the 1830s and the Mexican War in the 1840s led to a loss of over 40 percent of Mexico's territory.

After Santa Anna's exile in 1855, Benito Juárez tried to rule Mexico under more democratic ideals. In the mid-1870s, Porfirio Diaz, a soldier and protégé of Juárez, was elected president and held political power until the Mexican Revolution of 1911. During Díaz's rule, Mexico was transformed into a politically stable and economically progressive nation, but at the expense of political freedom and democratic government. Foreign investment was encouraged in railroads, oil, and mining. Díaz's political power was based on the use of a repressive police force, the *rurales*, to control his opponents. The peasants continued to live under terrible conditions, and the urban labor movement was suppressed. Díaz was supported by the elite hacienda owners, the Roman Catholic Church, and the military.

REVIEW QUESTIONS

Multiple Choice. Select the letter of the answer that correctly completes the statement.

1. The ideas of the European Enlightenment encouraged revolution in
   A. Europe and Asia
   B. Europe and its colonies
   C. Europe and the Middle East
   D. Europe and Africa

2. The revolutions of the 19th century were similar in that they were all
   A. inspired by the French Revolution of 1789
   B. the result of the development of nationalism
   C. inspired by European ideas or events
   D. the result of industrialization

3. Which of the following groups consists of revolutionary leaders only?
   A. Toussaint L'Ouverture, Maximillian Robespierre, Klemens
      von Metternich
   B. Simón Bolívar, Sun Yat-sen, Friedrich Engels
   C. Guiseppe Mazzini, Napoleon Bonaparte, Otto von Bismarck
   D. Fr. Miguel Hidalgo, Karl Marx, Emperor Matshuhito

4. Which of the following was not nationalist in origin?
   A. Greek War of Independence (1821)
   B. Meiji Restoration (1868)
   C. Boxer Rebellion (1900)
   D. Industrial Revolution (early 1800s)

5. Which of the following revolutions did not replace a monarchy with
   a democracy?
   A. France (1789)
   B. Colombia (1821)
   C. Japan (1868)
   D. China (1911)

6. The only African nations to avoid European imperialism in the
   19th century were
   A. Congo Free State and Sierra Leone
   B. Union of South Africa and Angola
   C. Ethiopia and Liberia
   D. Orange Free State and Transvaal

7. Which of the following did not occur during the 19th century?
   A. Industrial Revolution in Western Europe
   B. Division of China into "protectorates"
   C. European imperialism of Latin America
   D. Rise of nationalism in Eastern Europe

8. Which of the following leaders encouraged 19th-century imperialism?
   A. King Louis XVIII of France
   B. King Leopold of Belgium
   C. Dr. Sun Yat-sen
   D. Mohandas K. Gandhi

9. The region least affected by 19th-century imperialism was
   A. Asia
   B. Africa
   C. Middle East
   D. Latin America

10. Which was the only non-European nation to practice imperialism in the 19th century?
   A. India
   B. Ethiopia
   C. Japan
   D. Brazil

THEMATIC ESSAYS

Essay #1 Theme: Revolution

Throughout the period of 1750–1914 revolutions erupted throughout the world. Some were the result of political, economic, or social dissatisfaction within a nation, whereas others were in response to foreign domination.

Task:
1. Define the term "revolution."
2. Select one nation that you have studied and give one specific historical example showing why revolution developed in that nation.
3. Assess whether or not the revolution was successful and whether it was either positive or negative for that nation.

Essay #2 Theme: Imperialism

The Industrial Revolution in Western Europe during the 19th century led to shortages of much needed natural resources and raw materials. This resulted in these nations imperializing nonindustrialized regions of the world.

Task:
1. Define the term "imperialism."
2. Select one nation you have studied that either practiced imperialism or was imperialized and give one specific example showing how imperialism affected that nation.
3. Assess whether imperialism was either positive or negative for that nation.

DOCUMENT-BASED ESSAY QUESTIONS

Essay #1
This task is based on the accompanying documents (Documents 1–4). Some of these documents have been edited for the purposes of this task. The essay is designed to test your ability to work with historical documents. As you analyze the documents, take into account both the source of each document and the author's point of view.

Historical Context: The 19th and early 20th centuries saw the growth of nationalism. The documents relate the nationalistic beliefs of four leaders of different nations during this period.

Task:
  Analyze the statements of each leader in order to understand how nationalism influenced the historical events of that nation.

Part A: The documents below relate the nationalistic ideas of four leaders during the 19th and early 20th centuries. Examine each document carefully and then answer the question that follows it.

Part B: Write a well-organized essay that includes an introduction with a thesis statement, several paragraphs explaining the thesis, and a conclusion. Use evidence from the documents to support your position. Do not simply repeat the contents of the documents. You should also include specific related outside information based on your study of history.

DOCUMENT 1

"Soldiers of France! . . . All of you are consumed with a desire to extend the glory of the French people; all of you long to humiliate those arrogant kings who dare to contemplate placing us in chains; all of you desire to dictate a glorious peace, one which will repay the Patrie (Nation) for the immense sacrifices it has made."
                    —Napoleon Bonaparte (1796), *The Corsican:*
                        A Diary of Napoleon Bonaparte's Life

According to the reading, how does Napoleon Bonaparte appeal to nationalism in order to encourage support for his military conquests?

_____

_____

_____

DOCUMENT 2

"Young Italy is a brotherhood of Italians who believe . . . that Italy is destined to become one nation. . . . They join this association in the firm intent of consecrating both thought and action to the great aim of reconstituting Italy as one independent sovereign nation of free men and equals. . . . The means by which Young Italy proposes to reach its aim are education and insurrection, to be adopted simultaneously, and made to harmonize with each other."

—Giuseppe Mazzini (1831),
Young Italy

According to the text, how did nationalism influence the vision Italian leaders had of their country after independence?

_____

_____

_____

DOCUMENT 3

"We are not Europeans; we are not Indians; we are a mixed species of aborigines and Spaniards. Americans by birth and Europeans by law, we find ourselves engaged in a dual conflict: we are disputing with the natives for titles of ownership, and at the same time we are struggling to maintain ourselves in the country that gave us birth against the opposition of foreigners . . . for we, having been placed in state lower than slavery, have been robbed not only of our freedom, but also of our rights."

—Simón Bolívar (1819), Address to
the Congress of Angostura

According to the text, in what ways was national identity even more difficult for the peoples of Latin America than those of Europe?

_____

_____

_____

DOCUMENT 4

"People all over the world refer to Japan as the Land of the Gods and call us descendants of the gods. Indeed, it is exactly as they say: our country, as a special mark of favor from the heavenly gods, was begotten by them, and thus there is an immense difference between Japan and all other countries . . . . Ours is a splendid and blessed country . . . and we, down to the humblest man and woman, are the descendants of the gods."

—Hirata Atsutane (19th-century writer)

According to the reading, how did traditional national beliefs prepare Japan to be an imperialist power?

_____

_____

_____

Essay #2
This task is based on the accompanying documents (Documents 1–4). Some of these documents have been edited for the purposes of this task. The essay is designed to test your ability to work with historical documents. As you analyze the documents, take into account both the source of each document and the author's point of view.

Historical Context: The industrialization of Western Europe in the 19th century created a need for raw materials and natural resources. This led many Western European nations to imperialize non-European nations that possessed these resources. The documents relate different opinions on 19th- century imperialism by both Europeans and non-Europeans.

Task: Analyze the opinions on 19th-century imperialism in order to evaluate its effects on both the Europeans and the peoples they imperialized.

Part A: These documents relate the opinions of both Europeans and imperialized peoples on 19th-century imperialism. Examine each document carefully and then answer the question that follows it.

Part B: Write a well-organized essay that includes an introduction with a thesis statement, several paragraphs explaining the thesis, and a conclusion. Use evidence from the documents to support your position. Do not simply repeat the contents of the documents. You should also include specific related outside information based on your study of history.

DOCUMENT 1

"We now feel that British rule over these territories . . . has brought security, peace and comparative prosperity to countries that never knew these blessings before. In carrying out this work of civilization, we are fulfilling what I believe to be our national mission. . . . You cannot destroy the practices of barbarism, of slavery, of superstition, which for centuries have desolated the interior of Africa, without the use of force; . . . we may be rest assured that for every life lost, a hundred will be gained, and the cause of civilization and prosperity of the people will in the long run be eminently advanced."
—Joseph Chamberlain (1897),
Foreign and Colonial Speeches

According to the text, how does Chamberlain justify British colonialism in Africa?

_____

_____

_____

DOCUMENT 2

"History shows one way, and one way only, in which a high state of civilization has been produced, namely the struggle of race with race, and the survival of the physically and mentally fitter race. . . . The great function of science is to show us . . . how the nation is a vast organism subject . . . to the great forces of evolution. . . . Is it not a fact that our strength depends . . . upon our colonies, and that are colonies have been won by the ejection of inferior races? . . . . This struggle of . . . nation with nation, may have its mournful side; but we see as a result of it the gradual progress of mankind to higher intellectual and physical efficiency."

—Karl Pearson (1900), "National Life
from the Standpoint of Science"

According to the reading, how does Pearson use Darwin's theories to justify European imperialism?

_____

_____

_____

DOCUMENT 3

"Decades of imperialism have been prolific in wars; most of these wars have been directly motivated by aggression of white races upon 'lower races' and have resulted in the forcible seizure of territory. . . . Imperialism is only in the interests of competing groups of businessmen . . . that these groups . . . use public resources to push their private businesses, and spend the blood and money of the people in a vast and disastrous military game. . . . Nowhere under such conditions is the theory of white government as a trust for civilization made valid. . . . This failure to justify by results the forcible rule over alien peoples . . . is inherent in the nature of such domination."

—John Atkinson Hobson (1902), *Imperialism*

According to the text, why does Hobson reject the nationalistic and scientific arguments for European imperialism?

_____

_____

_____

DOCUMENT 4

"It was not that Masoudi was any the less convinced about the desirability of many of the things the White Man had to offer. Their clothes were far superior, even if . . . they were the real reason why his villagers had to plant that ridiculous cotton which everyone knew ruined the soil. The oil lanterns and bicycle were also good things, and so was the hospital in Matadi. . . . But what Masoudi could never understand was why the White Man expected him and the others to change their beliefs, to abandon the ways of the ancestors. . . . Did the Black Man expect the White Man to change his beliefs, to abandon his traditions?"

—Colin M. Turnbull, *The Lonely African*

According to the reading, why did the imperialized peoples become resentful of European domination?

_____

_____

_____

ERA II

A Half-Century of Crisis and Achievement (1900–1945)

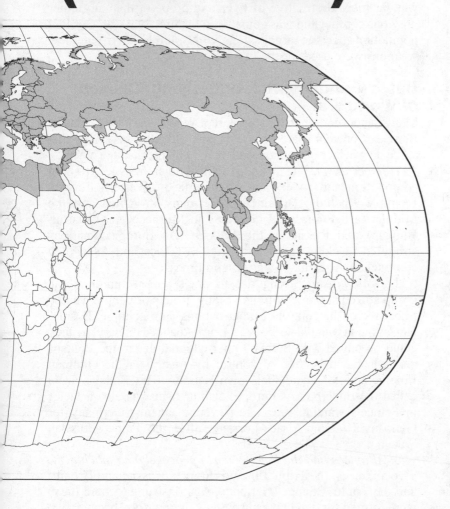

Part A: World War I

The Congress of Vienna laid the foundation for a century of peace in Europe, broken only by a few brief and local wars (Franco-Prussian, Russo-Turkish, and Crimean). Beginning about 1870, a series of forces combined to move Europe toward war. These forces included a growing spirit of nationalism, increasingly dangerous colonial conflicts, a complex system of entangling alliances, and a rising tide of militarism.

Between 1914 and 1918 war swept across Europe. This war was far more destructive of lives and property than any other previous conflict and was considered the first total war. Civilian populations became targets along with soldiers. Terrifying new weapons were used for the first time.

Basic (Fundamental, Underlying) Causes of World War I

Many factors contributed to the start of World War I. All the major European powers shared some blame, although historians disagree on whether one nation was more to blame than the others.

1. *Imperialism.* The desire to control other areas led to sharp competition and rivalry among nations of Western Europe. Examples include: Britain and Germany in Africa and the Middle East; France and Germany in Morocco; and Austria-Hungary and Russia in the Balkans. As European nations struggled to claim more territories in Africa and Asia, they approached the brink of war several times.

2. *Nationalism.* Strong ties to one's nation and/or ethnic group stirred strong emotions. Many groups of people wanted to be free of the control of other nations. For example, Bosnia-Herzegovina wanted to be free from Austria-Hungary so they could be united with Serbia. Other nationalities in the Balkans also wished to be free of control by Austria or the Ottoman Empire and to create their own nations. The Balkans were called the tinderbox of Europe. Nationalism was also a factor in France's wanting *revanche* (revenge) against Germany for Germany's taking Alsace-Lorraine after the Franco-Prussian War.

3. *Alliances and the lack of world peacekeeping machinery.* Two alliances, the Triple Entente (France, Russia, and Britain) and the Triple Alliance (Germany, Austria-Hungary, and Italy) were formed for defensive purposes, but they soon became two

EUROPE IN 1914

KEY

Allied powers

Central powers

Neutral countries

armed camps. At this time no organization existed, such as the United Nations, to foster world peace or to help settle disputes among the major powers.

4. *Militarism.* As the alliance system divided Europe into two opposing camps, each nation began to increase its military strength. The growth of armies and navies, as well as the development of weaponry, added to the mood of belligerence (warlike attitude) and a tendency to settle disputes by fighting. Manufacturers of arms increased production, as governments sought to build up their military strength. Economic rivalry between Germany and Britain poisoned relations between the two nations. Germany's growing navy was seen by Britain as a threat to its security and its colonies.

EUROPE IN 1919

ICELAND

NORWAY

SWEDEN

FINLAND

UNITED KINGDOM

ESTONIA

SOVIET UNION

LATVIA

LITHUANIA

IRISH FREE STATE (1922)

NETHERLAND

E. PRUSSIA

GERMANY

POLAND

BELGIUM LUXEMBOURG

CZECHOSLOVAKIA

FRANCE

AUSTRIA

HUNGARY

RUMANIA

SWITZERLAND

YUGOSLAVIA

BULGARIA

ITALY

PORTUGAL

SPAIN

TURKEY

GREECE

ALBANIA

KEY

New countries

Countries with border changes

Immediate Cause of the War

The spark that set off World War I was the assassination of the Austrian Archduke Francis Ferdinand in June 1914 in the town of Sarajevo. The assassin was a Serbian nationalist, Gavrilo Princip, who wanted to free Bosnia-Herzegovina from the Austro-Hungarian Empire and unite them with Serbia.

Developments in the War

Austria, backed up by Germany and glad to receive Germany's blank check, threatened Serbia. This angered Russia, causing it to get its armed forces ready for war. Because of the alliance system, country after country was drawn into the conflict and all the major powers were soon fighting each other. A local, regional crisis thus became the spark of a major war. The war, known as the Great War at first, turned into the most violent European conflict since the Napoleonic Wars, almost 100 years before. With neither side able to win, the armies faced one another from trenches. The war was a stalemate until 1917, when the United States entered the war on the side of the Triple Entente nations, or the Allies (Britain, France, and Russia). This helped to bring victory against the Central Powers (Germany, Austria-Hungary, Italy, and Turkey—a late entrant into the war). The war ended in November 1918, having lasted over four years.

Results of World War I

The war changed the course of the world's history, causing economic chaos and radical social changes in many countries. Some of the most powerful nations in Europe lost their influence and began to decline. Many monarchs lost their thrones. A communist government came to power in Russia, and the seeds of a second great conflict (World War II) were sown when World War I ended and the peace treaty was drawn up.

GLOBAL CONCEPTS

Change

CONCEPTS GLOBAL

1. *Economic.* The war was very costly to the participants. The losers became debtor nations. Many economic problems arising from the war were partly responsible for the worldwide depression that began in 1929.

2. *Social.* Millions were killed and wounded from the fighting. More than 8 million soldiers died, and almost as many civilians were killed. Several deadly weapons were used for the first time in warfare—gas, tanks, airplanes, submarines, and the machine gun. Most Europeans failed to understand the destructive power of these weapons and how horrible modern warfare had become.

MAJOR TERRITORIAL CHANGES AFTER WORLD WAR I

Changes	Taken From
1. Poland recreated, with a corridor to the sea	Germany and German-conquered area of Russia
2. Romania enlarged	Austria-Hungary
3. Yugoslavia and Czechoslovakia created as new nations	Austria-Hungary
4. Austria and Hungary became separate nations	Austria-Hungary
5. Finland, Estonia, Latvia, and Lithuania created	Russia
6. Alsace-Lorraine to France	Germany
7. Syria, Lebanon, and Palestine became mandates	Turkey

WORLD ISSUES

War
and
Peace

3. *Political.* The League of Nations was formed in an effort to secure world peace. The political problems and hatreds that emerged in some nations provided a basis for the rise of dictatorships later in Germany and in Italy.

The Versailles Treaty (1919)

The Versailles Treaty officially ended World War I. It was drawn up at the Paris Peace Conference by David Lloyd George (Britain), Georges Clemenceau (France), Vittorio Orlando (Italy), and Woodrow Wilson (United States). It forced Germany to accept "war guilt" and stripped Germany and Austria-Hungary of much territory. Germany was also forced to pay huge amounts of money to the victors as reparations. It was prohibited from uniting with Austria and required to limit its armed forces (demilitarization). This *diktat* (dictated peace), as it was called by Germany, caused much resentment in that country and was later used by Hitler as propaganda in his rise to power in the 1930s. The treaty also created the League of Nations. The League was one of the Fourteen Points that America's Wilson had asked for in an attempt to prevent future wars. The U.S. Senate refused to ratify (approve) the Versailles Treaty. Therefore, the United States did not become a member of the League. For this reason, as well as the fact that it had no enforcement powers, the League was seen as a weak organization.

Part B: The Rise of the Modern Totalitarian State

Totalitarianism is a political philosophy that emerged in the 20th century. Totalitarianism describes governments in which one political party monopolizes all power and exercises complete authority over the people and their activities. It involves total control of all aspects of an individual's life by the government, with both civil and political rights being curtailed. Although various forms of totalitarianism exist in parts of the world today, its earliest examples were in three European nations during the 20-year period following World War I. These nations were the Soviet Union (under communism), Italy (under fascism), and Germany (under Nazism). Totalitarian societies look down on individual human rights and civil liberties. The values of democracy are not found in such societies. Totalitarian states emphasize: (1) glorification of the whole community (that is, the state); (2) authoritarian rule by a dictator or by selected members of the one political party allowed to exist; (3) control of the individual citizen's life; (4) belief in the idea that the individual should benefit the state and exists solely to serve the state's interests. In Western Europe, these features of totalitarianism were most characteristic of Germany under the control of Adolf Hitler and the Nazi Party, from 1933 to 1945. This government, known as the Third Reich, arose after the period of the Weimar Republic.

WORLD ISSUES

Determination of Political and Economic Systems

SECTION 1: GERMANY

Germany Under the Weimar Republic (1919–1933)

The Weimar Republic was the name of the German government that came to power after World War I. It was a democratic government, with a constitution that was drawn up in the city of Weimar. However, this experiment with democracy in Germany faced many problems, including economic chaos and street violence. It was not successful for a number of reasons.

GEOGRAPHY

Spatial Terms

WORLD ISSUES

Hunger
and
Poverty

1. In the early 1920s the Weimar government printed paper money with little to back it, resulting in severe inflation. This devastated the German economy and resulted in severe unemployment and street violence.

2. When Germany was unable to meet its reparations payments in 1923, France sent troops to occupy the Ruhr Valley, Germany's chief industrial area.

3. There was terrible unemployment in Germany in the early 1920s and again in the 1930s.

4. The German economy was restored after 1923 and conditions improved. However, in 1929 a worldwide depression that threatened the stability of democratic governments everywhere brought much suffering to Germany. Unemployment rose to 6 million in 1932, and Germans lost faith in their political leaders. This further fueled the bad feelings that had been caused by the Versailles Treaty.

5. The government was unstable because no single party was able to achieve a majority in the Reichstag, the more powerful of the two legislative houses created by the Weimar constitution. As a result, German political leaders seemed helpless to deal with the severe economic problems.

These problems led many Germans to conclude that democracy was ill-suited to their nation and that autocracy was preferable, especially since it had brought Germany political unification, economic growth, and respect as an international power. A strong democratic tradition did not exist in German history.

The Role of Adolf Hitler

Hitler was born in Austria and served in the German army during World War I. He joined the Nazi Party (National Socialist German Workers Party). He spoke out against the Weimar government and was arrested for his role in the Munich Putsch of 1923, an unsuccessful attempt to overthrow the government. While imprisoned, he wrote the book *Mein Kampf* (My Struggle) that contained his ideas for a stronger and more powerful German nation. It also revealed his racist beliefs concerning the alleged superiority of Aryans as a "master race" and the need to eliminate all groups he considered inferior, such as Jews, Slavs, Gypsies, homosexual people, and blacks. Hitler was a stirring and charismatic speaker when addressing large crowds, thereby attracting many people to the Nazi Party.

Rise of the Nazis to Power

In addition to the problems of the Weimar government and the powerful role played by Hitler, a number of other factors led to the rise of the Nazis in Germany:

1. *Economic problems.* The Nazis offered simple explanations for both the causes of Germany's economic problems and its cures. These problems, as described above, affected millions of Germans. The reparations demanded by the Versailles Treaty were condemned as unjust and blamed for causing the economic crisis.

2. *Patriotic appeals.* The Nazi program stirred German nationalism. It called for:

- a large increase in the armed forces;
- the expansion of the German fatherland to include territory in Europe where people of German descent lived (Austria, parts of Poland, and Czechoslovakia);
- control over educational and cultural institutions to teach Nazi principles of racism and physical fitness for the glory of the state;
- ignoring the Versailles Treaty and refusing to accept the war-guilt clause;
- regaining land that Germany had held in Europe and its overseas colonies prior to World War I;
- the use of violence as a legitimate means to achieve domestic and international goals;
- the importance of looking back to and glorifying the mythical German race (the so-called *Volk*) as the source of all strength and power.

The Nazis also claimed that Nordic Germans were destined to rule the world and to eliminate undesirable peoples. They blamed the Weimar government for accepting the Versailles Treaty and said it had been forced to do so by Jews, communists, and others. Finally, the Nazis claimed that German forces had not been defeated in World War I but had been stabbed in the back.

3. *Anti-Semitism.* Prejudice toward Jews had existed in Germany for hundreds of years, resulting in exile, loss of life and property, and hatred. However, Hitler's prejudice against

GEOGRAPHY

Places and Regions

WORLD ISSUES

Terrorism

Jews was fanatical; he used Jews as scapegoats and blamed them for his own personal failures and also for Germany's problems. These false notions became persuasive parts of Nazi propaganda, especially when they were blended with Hitler's master race theories. Hitler claimed that the Aryans (Germans) were a master race who were naturally entitled to control and rule peoples of less "pure" blood, such as Slavs and Jews. (The Holocaust, in which 6 million Jews were systematically murdered after Hitler came to power, was the tragic consequence of these misguided notions.)

WORLD ISSUES

Human Rights

4. *Fear of communism and of Soviet Russia.* The Nazis played upon these fears with much success and portrayed themselves as the only ones capable of protecting Germany from foreign beliefs and potential aggressors. In this way, they were able to win the support of large segments of the German population, such as bankers and industrialists.

5. *Use of private, illegal armed groups.* Many of Hitler's followers were organized into private armies. One such group was the Storm Troopers (S.A.), or Brown Shirts, who used scare tactics and violence to terrorize Jews and opponents of the Nazis.

6. *Lack of meaningful opposition.* Few strong voices inside Germany spoke out against the Nazis. Many Germans came to gradually support Hitler, while others were apathetic. Others feared speaking against him, and many who did were intimidated. Internationally, there was little awareness of or concern about the Nazi movement.

GLOBAL CONCEPTS

Power

CONCEPTS GLOBAL

The Nazis Come to Power. The formal takeover of Germany by the Nazis took place in January 1933 when the president of the Weimar Republic, Paul von Hindenburg, appointed Hitler as chancellor. By this time, the Nazis had become the largest political party in Germany, and they formed the single largest block in the Reichstag, the German parliament. Yet they had never won a clear majority in any national election. (In 1932, for example, they won slightly less than 40 percent of the seats in the Reichstag.) Although Hitler promised to preserve the Weimar constitution, he soon carried out policies that destroyed the democracy that had existed under the Weimar Republic. The result was a totalitarian dictatorship, known as the Third Reich, that eventually brought about World War II and brought devastation to Germany and to most of Europe.

GLOBAL CONCEPTS

Political Systems

CONCEPTS GLOBAL

Hitler's distorted ideas, along with his antidemocratic beliefs and tactics, unfortunately found a receptive audience in post–World War I Germany. He was called *der Führer*, or leader.

SECTION 2: ITALY

Italy Under a Fascist Government (1922–1943)

Italy experienced totalitarian rule under a fascist government headed by Benito Mussolini. The word "fascist" comes from the word "fasces," an axe-like weapon that was a symbol of the ancient Roman Empire. Mussolini wanted Italians to feel a strong sense of nationalism and to remember the glory of the Roman Empire. Mussolini and his Black Shirt followers came to power for some of the same reasons that led to the rise of the Nazis in Germany.

GLOBAL
CONCEPTS

Identity

CONCEPTS
GLOBAL

1. *Economic.* The costs of World War I had been staggering. After the war, there was high unemployment, strikes, and severe inflation.

2. *Political.* The weak and divided government of King Victor Emmanuel III was unable to provide leadership or to inspire confidence in its ability to solve the postwar crisis. Also, there was no strong democratic tradition in Italy. Moreover, the fear of communism and a communist-led revolution was seized upon by Mussolini, who promised to defend Italy and thereby won followers.

3. *Social.* Italy was suffering from low morale, and was saddened by the many deaths in World War I. Mussolini promised the Italian people security, order, and economic progress in exchange for their liberties and freedom.

Mussolini in Power. As a result of his famous March on Rome in 1922 supposedly to save Italy from a communist revolution, Mussolini came to power. Neither the king nor the army opposed him. He soon established a police state, destroying civil liberties and demanding that people recognize him as Il Duce, the leader. Mussolini reorganized the economy of Italy, establishing fascist-controlled associations in all industries, and Italy was run as a corporate state.

GLOBAL
CONCEPTS

Power

CONCEPTS
GLOBAL

SECTION 3: RUSSIA

The Russian Revolution (1905–1917)

During the reign of Nicholas II (1894–1917), Russia made its greatest strides toward reform, modernization, and, ironically, revolution. From 1894 to 1905, Nicholas followed his father's (Alexander III) policies in opposing reform. Despite great gains made in the industrialization program under the direction of Finance Minister Sergei Witte, the conditions in urban slums and factories were still terrible. After the embarrassing defeat in the Russo-Japanese War (1904–1905) and the massacre of peaceful demonstraters in St. Petersburg in January of 1905, known as *Bloody Sunday*, uprisings broke out in every major Russian city and industrial center. Known as the 1905 Revolution, this series of revolts frightened the government into making reforms, most notably the creation of the *Duma*, or parliament. While Russia technically became a constitutional democracy, the Duma was little more than an advisory body that could be dissolved by the tsar at will.

World Issues

War
and
Peace

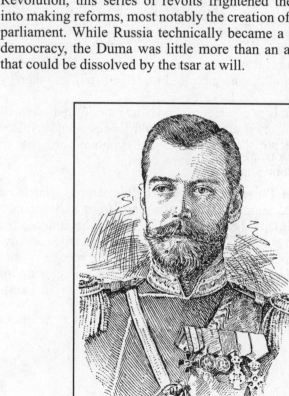

Tsar Nicholas II

In 1906 the monarchy instituted its own reforms in order to restore public confidence. Under the guidance of Prime Minister Piotr Stolypin, a program of industrial expansion, foreign investment, and land reform was instituted.

In 1914 Russia entered World War I (1914–1918), a conflict that it was neither militarily nor economically ready to fight. For three years the Russians suffered defeats by the technologically superior German forces. (See "World War I," page 76.) Enormous casualties and government inefficiency led to widespread dissatisfaction with the conduct of the war. Scandal within the royal family also hurt the prestige of the monarchy. Tsaritsa Aleksandra had fallen under the influence of a fraudulent "holy man," Grigorii Efimovich Rasputin, who was able to control the Tsarevitch (Prince) Alexei's hemophilia (probably through hypnosis).

While the tsar was away at the front running the war, Rasputin exercised a destructive domination over the German-born tsaritsa, who was already suspected by many of being a spy. His influence produced corruption and even greater inefficiency. By February 1917, food shortages and an outbreak of strikes and riots led to the collapse of the tsar's authority in St. Petersburg and other cities. Nicholas II was forced to abdicate, and a provisional (temporary) democratic government was formed by the Duma, headed first by Prince Georgii L'vov and later by Aleksandr Kerenskii.

The Provisional Government attempted to make Russia a democracy by instituting political reforms. By October of 1917, however, it was overthrown by the Bolshevik (Communist) Party. There were a number of reasons for this:

GLOBAL
CONCEPTS
Change
CONCEPTS
GLOBAL

1. Kerenskii's decision to continue fighting the war was very unpopular.

2. Russia did not have a democratic tradition. Most of the Provisional Government's goals were not understood and appeared to be irrelevant to the majority of the population.

3. The war continued to create shortages and strain the economy. Conditions in the cities did not improve, and unrest began again.

4. The Bolsheviks capitalized on the unpopularity of the war. They undermined support for the Provisional Government through antiwar propaganda.

5. The monarchy had held the Russian Empire together. With the traditional symbol of unity (the tsar) gone, the Provisional Government could provide no equivalent institution.

6. Kerenskii was experimenting with democracy in a nation with no democratic heritage during a war, a time when most democracies temporarily suspend civil liberties.

7. The war wasted the best troops the Provisional Government had. The regiments that remained to protect the Provisional Government were poorly trained and unreliable.

8. The Bolshevik leader Lenin promised "bread, peace, and land" as well as a "workers' state," promises that were better understood than the democratic principles put forth by the Provisional Government.

9. The Bolsheviks influenced the soviets, or local committees, that represented workers, soldiers, and farmers. Closely linked throughout Russia, they became influential, especially in the cities.

Lenin (1917–1924). Born Vladimir lllich Ulianov, Lenin founded the Bolshevik, or "Majority," Party at a 1903 Socialist Party Conference in London. While the Bolsheviks were never a majority, they were "professional revolutionaries" who ruthlessly pursued power, using any means necessary in order to succeed. The other Russian Socialists, the Mensheviks, or "Minority," favored gradual, peaceful change, without the violence and terror advocated by the Bolsheviks.

When the Bolsheviks seized power in 1917, Lenin immediately made peace with Germany and took Russia out of the war. Giving away sizable parts of Russia in a peace agreement (Treaty of Brest-Litovsk) and having no widespread support, the Bolsheviks soon faced strong opposition throughout Russia. A civil war followed (1918–1921) in which the Bolsheviks, or Reds, fought the combined forces of anti-Bolshevik groups, or Whites. The dependence of the White Army on foreign nations for military supplies as well as the disunity among its leadership eventually led to a Bolshevik victory.

Once the Bolsheviks were firmly in power, Lenin realized that Russia was not ready to adopt communism. In the new political order, the Bolshevik Party would run the state until such time as society could be transformed into a pure communist state. The central government planned and controlled all aspects of political, social, and economic life through a series of party organs.

WORLD ISSUES

Determination
of Political
and Economic
Systems

Facing great opposition, especially from the peasants, Lenin tried to ease the population into communism by instituting the N.E.P. (New Economic Program) in 1921. This policy combined features of both capitalism and socialism by allowing private enterprise on a small scale while the state retained control of large industries. Under the N.E.P. (1921–1928), the Soviet economy experienced only limited growth.

When Lenin died in 1924, a struggle for power developed between Leon Trotskii, Lenin's chosen successor, and Joseph Dzhugashvili, known as Stalin ("Man of Steel"), who was Communist Party Secretary. By 1925 Stalin had gained control and removed Trotskii from all official positions. In 1929 Trotskii was deported as Stalin began to remove all possible opposition and rivals (Trotskii was assassinated by Stalin's agents in Mexico in 1937).

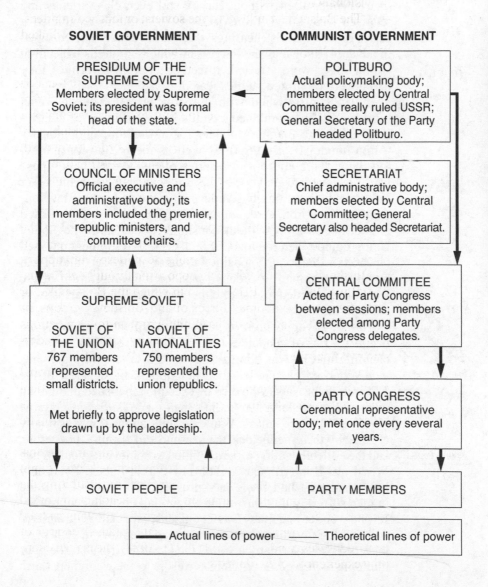

SOVIET GOVERNMENT

PRESIDIUM OF THE SUPREME SOVIET
Members elected by Supreme Soviet; its president was formal head of the state.

COUNCIL OF MINISTERS
Official executive and administrative body; its members included the premier, republic ministers, and committee chairs.

SUPREME SOVIET

SOVIET OF THE UNION
767 members represented small districts.

SOVIET OF NATIONALITIES
750 members represented the union republics.

Met briefly to approve legislation drawn up by the leadership.

SOVIET PEOPLE

COMMUNIST GOVERNMENT

POLITBURO
Actual policymaking body; members elected by Central Committee really ruled USSR; General Secretary of the Party headed Politburo.

SECRETARIAT
Chief administrative body; members elected by Central Committee; General Secretary also headed Secretariat.

CENTRAL COMMITTEE
Acted for Party Congress between sessions; members elected among Party Congress delegates.

PARTY CONGRESS
Ceremonial representative body; met once every several years.

PARTY MEMBERS

━━━ Actual lines of power ──── Theoretical lines of power

GLOBAL CONCEPTS

Political Systems

CONCEPTS GLOBAL

GLOBAL CONCEPTS

Human Rights

CONCEPTS GLOBAL

GLOBAL CONCEPTS

Justice

CONCEPTS GLOBAL

WORLD ISSUES

Economic
Growth and
Development

GEOGRAPHY

Human Systems

WORLD ISSUES

Hunger
and
Poverty

Stalin (1925–1953). Stalin's rule proved to be one of the most brutal and ruthless dictatorships in modern history. From his consolidation of complete power in 1929 until his death in 1953, he was responsible for millions of deaths, starting with the elimination of all possible rivals. Stalin created his own secret police, which spied on, arrested, tortured, and executed party members, government officials, artists, writers, clergy, workers, and peasants he suspected of not supporting his policies. In time, his fears became paranoia (fear and suspicion of everyone, often without cause), and even close friends and relatives were killed. From 1935 to 1936 Stalin conducted a series of show trials (hearings where the verdicts were decided in advance) known as the Purges, in which hundreds of leading Communists were arrested, forced to confess to crimes they had never committed, and executed.

In 1928, dissatisfied with the slow growth rate of Soviet industry, Stalin abandoned Lenin's N.E.P. in favor of centralized economic planning. Goals for agriculture and industry (often unrealistically high), as well as the means for achieving them, were laid out in a series of Five-Year Plans. These were designed to make the U.S.S.R. catch up with the other industrialized nations by emphasizing the industrial development of steel, iron, coal, and oil. The population was expected to sacrifice and do without consumer goods until the Soviet Union could reach the level of industrial development attained by capitalist nations. Opposition to these plans was quickly and brutally put down. In order to pay for the importation of the technology needed to institute the Five-Year Plans, farms were collectivized.

To end the opposition of peasants to collectivization, Stalin began a series of genocides (mass killings) from 1932 to 1937, claiming that he was eliminating the *kulaks* (wealthy peasants who supposedly exploited their neighbors). In fact, few of the 14.5 million peasants who died by execution, perished in Siberian labor camps, or starved in Stalin's man-made famine in Ukraine (1932–1933) were kulaks. While outright opposition was finally crushed by these genocides, the peasants did not fully cooperate, and the collectivization program failed to achieve its goal. When World War II interrupted the Third Five-Year Plan in 1941, only heavy industry had made any progress. The loss of life and human suffering that this modest gain had cost was enormous. It is no wonder that many Soviet citizens, especially Ukrainians, first saw the invading German armies as liberators in 1941.

When Nazi Germany invaded the U.S.S.R. in 1941, the population was forced once again to resort to the Scorched-Earth policy used so effectively against Napoleon. By 1944 over-extension of supply lines, the harsh climate, and stiff military resistance by the Red Army, despite heavy losses, had worn down the German forces. By 1945 the Soviet Army had pushed the Nazis out of the U.S.S.R. and Eastern Europe into Germany and occupied the eastern portion of that nation. Despite an agreement made with the Allies earlier that year (the Yalta Conference) that the U.S.S.R. would only occupy Eastern

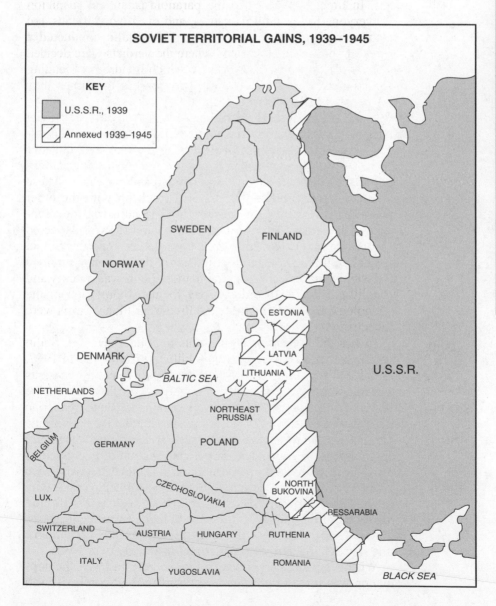

SOVIET TERRITORIAL GAINS, 1939–1945

KEY

U.S.S.R., 1939

Annexed 1939–1945

NORWAY

SWEDEN

FINLAND

DENMARK

BALTIC SEA

ESTONIA

LATVIA

LITHUANIA

NETHERLANDS

NORTHEAST PRUSSIA

U.S.S.R.

BELGIUM

GERMANY

POLAND

LUX.

CZECHOSLOVAKIA

NORTH BUKOVINA

BESSARABIA

SWITZERLAND

AUSTRIA

HUNGARY

RUTHENIA

ITALY

YUGOSLAVIA

ROMANIA

BLACK SEA

Europe temporarily, Soviet forces remained. Instead of holding free elections for self-determination in each Eastern European nation, Stalin placed puppet communist governments throughout Eastern Europe. These countries became satellites, controlled by the Soviet government. By Stalin's death in 1953, Eastern and Western Europe were divided by ideological differences and mutual fear. This last legacy of Stalin became known as the Iron Curtain.

Part C: World War II

Although the war started in Europe, it soon became a global conflict that dwarfed all previous wars in geographical extent and in human and material losses suffered. Fighting took place on three continents—Europe, Africa, and Asia—and on the seas, lands, and oceans around the globe. More nations (over fifty) were belligerents (fighters in the war) than in any war in history. The chief antagonists on the Allied side were Great Britain, France, the United States, the Soviet Union, and China. On the opposing side were Germany, Italy, and Japan, the so-called Axis powers.

WORLD ISSUES

War
and
Peace

Causes

Many of the causes of World War II were similar to those that brought on World War I. After World War I, many nations hoped to prevent another war by establishing what could be called a house of peace. The foundations of this house included: the Versailles Treaty, the League of Nations, disarmament conferences (held in Washington, D.C., and in London), and the Kellogg-Briand Pact, which attempted to outlaw war. Unfortunately, the house of peace crumbled for a number of reasons, most of them due to the actions of the Axis powers (Germany, Italy, and Japan). The basic causes of the war were:

1. *Militarism.* Large amounts of money were spent on weapons. Military strength was seen as a source of national pride. The leaders of the Axis nations were always seen in military dress.

2. *Nationalism and racism.* The Axis nations saw themselves as superior to others and with the right therefore to extend their culture and their borders (the German "master race" theory, the Italian wish to revive the ancient Roman Empire, the Japanese pride based on Shinto teachings and the necessity to establish a new order in Asia).

3. *Imperialism.* The Axis nations sought to take over other lands for political, racist, and economic reasons. Japan moved into China (1931, 1937); Italy conquered Ethiopia (1938); and Germany annexed Austria (the *Anschluss*, or union) and Czechoslovakia (1938, 1939).

GEOGRAPHY

Spatial Terms

4. *Failure of collective security.* The democratic nations of Europe and the United States did little to curb the aggressive policies of Germany, Italy, and Japan. The League of Nations condemned some of these aggressive moves but was unable to take any other action.

5. *Appeasement*. To give in to a potential aggressor, hoping that the aggressor will be content and not commit any further harmful acts, is called appeasement. It later came to mean the policy of accepting territorial aggression against small nations in the hope of avoiding a general war. This policy was followed by the British prime minister, Neville Chamberlain, at the Munich Conference in 1938. Here, he agreed to accept German annexation of the Sudetenland portion of Czechoslovakia in return for Hitler's guarantee of independence for the rest of Czechoslovakia. The policy proved to be a failure when Hitler later sent the German army to occupy all of Czechoslovakia in violation of the Munich Agreement.

The Start of the War

GLOBAL
CONCEPTS

Power

CONCEPTS
GLOBAL

The German attack on Poland in September 1939 was the actual start of the war. Britain and France finally realized that they would have to use military force to stop Hitler's aggression and threat to conquer all of Europe. Just prior to its attack on Poland, Germany signed a nonaggression pact with the Soviet Union. Under this agreement, Russia would take over eastern Poland and the Baltic states of Estonia, Latvia, and Lithuania and would not contest Hitler's attempt to take over western Poland. Also, Russia and Germany promised not to fight each other.

Developments in the War

Using blitzkreig warfare ("lightning war"), Germany over-ran most of Europe, except for England, by 1941. In June of that year, Germany broke its promise not to attack Russia and invaded that nation. The Russians suffered great losses and were driven back to the outskirts of Moscow, Leningrad, and the Volga River, where they held and gradually began to turn the tide. Also, in 1941 the United States entered the war after its navy was attacked by Japan at Pearl Harbor, Hawaii. The nations now fighting the Axis powers were known as the Allies (United States, Britain, France, Soviet Union). With the invasion of Normandy in western France on June 6, 1944 ("D-Day"), Allied forces began to retake German-held lands and pushed the Germans eastward. Russian forces entered the German-held Eastern European nations and pushed the Germans westward. On May 8, 1945 ("V-E Day"), Germany surrendered. In Asia, by 1941 Japan had conquered large areas of East and Southeast Asia. These Pacific areas were slowly retaken by U.S. forces between 1942 and 1945. In August 1945 the United States dropped two atomic bombs on the Japanese cities of Hiroshima and Nagasaki. On September 2, 1945 ("V-J Day"), Japan surrendered.

TERRITORIAL CHANGES IN EUROPE 1945–1948

NORWAY

Leningrad ■

ESTONIA

0   300 miles

0   300 km

SWEDEN

LATVIA

DENMARK

LITHUANIA

*NORTH
SEA*

BALTIC SEA

ODER–NEISSE
LINE

E. PRUSSIA

Stettin ■

U.S.S.R.

(TO POLAND)

U.S.

Berlin ■

NETH.

BR. ZONE

Warsaw ■

BELG.

SOV. ZONE

GERMANY

POLAND

(TO U.S.S.R.)

LUX.

Nuremberg

■ Prague

FRANCE

CZECHOSLOVAKIA

(TO CZECH.)

U.S. ZONE

SOV. ZONE

FR. ZONE

AUSTRIA

Vienna ■

FR. ZONE

U.S. ZONE

SWITZ.

BR. ZONE

Budapest ■

ROMANIA

HUNGARY

Trieste ■

(TO FRANCE)

(TO YUGOSLAVIA 1954)

Bucharest ■

Belgrade ■

ADRIATIC SEA

YUGOSLAVIA

ITALY

(TO BULGARIA)

CORSICA

BULGARIA

■ Rome

ALBANIA

SARDINIA

GREECE

DODECANESE ISLANDS
(TO GREECE)

MEDITERRANEAN SEA

KEY

Territorial changes after World War II

Soviet occupation zones

Occupation zones of Western powers

International boundaries after World War II

The Holocaust

WORLD ISSUES

Terrorism

This word refers to the intentional persecution and systematic murder of European Jews by the Germans from 1933 to 1945. Six million Jews were exterminated, mostly in concentration and death camps such as Auschwitz, Dachau, and Treblinka. The planned extermination of a group of people because of their religion, race, or ethnicity is called genocide. The genocidal tactics of the Nazis were a horrible extension of Hitler's anti-Semitic attitudes. The Nazi plan to kill all Jews was known as "the final solution." The world stood by and did nothing while these tactics such as gas chambers, ovens, medical experiments, and firing squads were being used. There were scattered instances of Jewish armed resistance, such as in the Warsaw Ghetto Uprising in 1943 and the destruction of a crematorium in Auschwitz in 1944. After the war, at the Nuremberg War Crimes Trials, several Nazis were found guilty of genocide and of crimes against humanity.

GLOBAL CONCEPTS

Justice

CONCEPTS GLOBAL

In addition to Jews, other groups of people labeled "inferior" by the Nazis were also sent to the concentration camps. These included homosexuals, Jehovah's Witnesses, Gypsies, Slavs, and mentally retarded people.

WORLD ISSUES

Human

Rights

Results of World War II

The world of 1945 bore little resemblance to the world of the 1930s. Europe was shattered and lay in ruins, its people facing an uncertain future.

GLOBAL CONCEPTS

Change

CONCEPTS GLOBAL

1. *Political.* The United States and the Soviet Union became the two leading superpowers and eventually clashed on many issues in what became known as the Cold War. Germany was divided into four zones of occupation—American, British, French, and Soviet. Poland's boundaries with the Soviet Union were changed, moving further westward. The Soviets established a sphere of influence, as an imperialist power, in many Eastern European nations. Some Soviet activities were in violation of the Yalta agreements of 1945. Britain and France lost some of their status as world powers; nationalistic movements in their colonies were to lead to a loss of their empires. The Allies helped to create the United Nations.

GEOGRAPHY

Use of Geography

2. *Economic.* The war proved to be the most costly ever fought. The loss of life and property in World War II far surpassed that of any previous conflict. The economies of many European nations were destroyed. Communism spread into the nations of Eastern Europe.

3. *Social.* More people, soldiers and civilians, were killed than in any other war. Much of this was due to new highly destructive weapons, as well as to the racist policies of the Axis powers. At war's end, millions of people had become refugees and displaced persons.

4. *Scientific.* The Atomic Age had begun with the dropping of atomic bombs on Hiroshima and Nagasaki.

Multiple Choice. Select the letter of the answer that correctly completes the statement.

1. Stalin, Hitler, and Mussolini were similar in that they
   A. belonged to the same political party
   B. permitted many political parties to exist
   C. permitted only one political party to exist
   D. favored both the Democratic and Republican political parties

2. What was true of both the Paris Peace Conference (1919) and the Yalta Conference (1945)?
   A. Russia was represented by Stalin.
   B. Treaties were signed.
   C. England had a delegate.
   D. World wars had just ended.

3. Winston Churchill was most concerned about his nation's
   A. struggle against Germany
   B. agricultural production
   C. economic competition with the United States
   D. construction of a tunnel under the English Channel

4. The technology developed in World War I resulted in
   A. a smaller number of refugees during the war
   B. smaller nations becoming part of larger empires after the war
   C. increased military casualties in battles fought during the war
   D. a reduction in transportation improvements after the war

5. Which was one part of "the final solution"?
   A. attack in Pearl Harbor
   B. blitzkrieg over Poland
   C. killings at Auschwitz
   D. bombings of Hiroshima and Nagasaki

6. "Weimar Republic to institute changes in Germany."
   "Provisional government stirs Russian hopes."

   These headlines reflected attempts to establish a
   A. monarchy
   B. dictatorship
   C. democracy
   D. colony

7. "Italy conquers Ethiopia"
   "Japan seizes Manchuria"

   Both headlines best reflect the concept of
   A. imperialism
   B. nationalism
   C. totalitarianism
   D. isolationism

8. The failure of collective security in the 1930s was interpreted as a sign of
   A. racism
   B. appeasement
   C. alliance building
   D. militarism

9. The Russian Duma and the German Reichstag exercised power that was
   A. authoritarian
   B. legislative
   C. executive
   D. judicial

10. Which pair favored collectivization and an end to private property?
    A. Lenin and Stalin
    B. Hitler and Mussolini
    C. Churchill and Roosevelt
    D. von Hindenburg and Nicholas II

THEMATIC ESSAYS

Essay #1 Theme: Conflict
At various times in global history, nations have acted in ways that caused armed conflict with other nations.

Task:
1. Choose two nations from your study of global history and geography.
2. For *each* nation:
   - Describe one action it took that caused armed conflict with another nation.
   - Explain why it took this action.
   - Evaluate whether it would take this action today.

You may use any example from your study of global history and geography. Some suggestions you might wish to consider include: Germany in the 20th century, Italy in the 20th century, Japan in the 20th century.

Hint: You are not limited to these suggestions.

Essay #2 Theme: Change
Throughout history, changes of government in a nation have frequently occurred. These changes have at times been led by a single group or political party.

Task:
1. Select two nations from your study of global history and geography.
2. For *each* nation:
   - Name the group or political party, and its leader, that caused a change in government.
   - Describe how the group or political party was able to bring about the change.
   - Analyze one reason why the group or political party was successful in bringing about the change.

You may use any example from your study of global history and geography. Some suggestions you may wish to consider include: Russia in the 20th century, Germany in the 20th century, Italy in the 20th century.

Hint: You are not limited to these suggestions, but you cannot use the United States in your answer.

DOCUMENT-BASED ESSAY QUESTIONS

Essay #1
This task is based upon the accompanying documents (1–6). Some of these documents have been edited for the purposes of this task. This task is designed to test your ability to work with historical documents. As you analyze the documents, take into account both the source of each document and the author's point of view.

Directions: Read the documents in Part A and answer the questions after each document. Then read the directions for Part B and write your essay.

Historical Context: Throughout history, societies have held different viewpoints on governmental decision-making, power, and the role of the citizen. These viewpoints can range from absolute control to democracy.

Task:
Using information from the documents and your knowledge of global history and geography, write an essay in which you
• Compare and contrast the different viewpoints societies have held about the process of governmental decision-making and about the role of citizens in the political decision-making process.
• Discuss the advantages and disadvantages of a political system that is under absolute power or is a democracy.

Part A
Short Answer

Directions: Analyze the documents and answer the questions that follow each document in the space provided.

DOCUMENT 1
"We are a democracy because the power to make the laws is given to the many rather than the few. But while the law gives equal justice to everyone, it has not failed to reward excellence. While every citizen has an equal opportunity to serve the public, we reward our most distinguished [best] citizens by asking them to make our political decisions. Nor do we discriminate against the poor. A man serves his country no matter how low his position on the social scale.

An Athenian citizen does not put his private affairs before the affairs of the state; even our merchants and businessmen know something about politics. We alone believe that a man who takes no interest in public affairs is more than harmless—he is useless."

—"Pericles' Funeral Oration"
Athens, 5th century B.C.

According to Pericles, what is the responsibility of a citizen in a democracy?

_____

_____

_____

DOCUMENT 2

"The one means that wins the easiest victory over reason: terror and force."

"A majority can never replace one man . . . Just as a hundred fools do not make one wise man, an heroic decision is not likely to come from a hundred cowards."

"In the size of the lie there is always contained a certain factor of credibility, since the great masses of the people . . . will more easily fall victims to a great lie than to a small one."

—Adolf Hitler, *Mein Kampf*
Germany, 1924

Is Hitler willing to let ordinary citizens have a role in political decision-making? Explain.

_____

_____

_____

DOCUMENT 3

"The State of Israel will be open for Jewish immigration and for the ingathering of the exiles; it will foster the development of the country for the benefit of all inhabitants; it will be based on freedom, justice, and peace as envisaged by the Prophets of Israel; it will ensure complete equality of social and political rights to all its inhabitants irrespective of religion, race, or sex; it will guarantee freedom of religion, conscience, language, education, and culture; it will safeguard the Holy Places of all religions; and it will be faithful to the principles of the Charter of the United Nations."

—Declaration of the Establishment
of the State of Israel, 1948

Why can Israel be called a democracy?

_____

_____

_____

DOCUMENT 4

"After socialism, Fascism combats the whole complex system of democratic ideology [theory], and repudiates [denies] it, whether in its theoretical premises [basis] or in its practical application. Fascism denies that the majority, by the simple fact that it is a majority, can direct human society; it denies that numbers alone can govern by means of a periodical consultation [elections], and it affirms the . . . beneficial, and fruitful [useful] inequality of mankind, which can never be permanently leveled through . . . universal suffrage."

—Benito Mussolini, 1932

What was the basis of Mussolini's arguments against democracy?

_____

_____

_____

DOCUMENT 5

". . . Whereas . . . King James II, . . . did attempt to undermine . . . the laws and liberties of this kingdom . . . Therefore, the Parliament declares:
1. That the King's supposed power of suspending laws without the consent of Parliament is illegal.
4. That the levying of taxes for the use of the King without the consent of Parliament is illegal.
8. That the King should not interfere with the election of members of Parliament.
13. And that to redress grievances and amend, strengthen, and preserve the laws, Parliament ought to be held [meet] frequently."

—English Bill of Rights

How did the English Bill of Rights change government decision-making?

_____

_____

_____

DOCUMENT 6

"But what happens when the sun sets?"

Based on this illustration, who controlled the government of France from the mid-1600s to the early 1700s?

_____

_____

_____

Part B
Essay

Directions:
• Write a well-organized essay that includes an introduction, several paragraphs, and a conclusion.
• Use evidence from the documents to support your response.
• Do not simply repeat the contents of the documents.
• Include specific related outside information.

Historical Context:
Throughout history, societies have held different viewpoints on governmental decision-making and the role of citizens in this decision-making process. The decision-making process can range from absolute control to democracy.

Task:

Using information from the documents and your knowledge of global history and geography, write an essay in which you

- Compare and contrast the different viewpoints societies have held about the process of governmental decision-making and about the role of citizens in the political decision-making process.
- Discuss the advantages and disadvantages of a political system that is under the absolute control of a single individual or a few individuals, or a political system that is a democracy.

Be sure to include specific historical details. You must also include additional information from your knowledge of global history and geography.

Essay #2
This task is based upon the accompanying documents (1–5). Some of these documents have been edited for the purposes of this task. This task is designed to test your ability to work with historical documents. As you analyze the documents, take into account both the source of each document and the author's point of view.

Directions: Read the documents in Part A and answer the questions after each document. Then read the directions for Part B and write your essay.

Historical Context: Throughout history, nations have gone to war for various reasons. The reasons can be categorized as political, economic, or social (cultural).

Task:
Using information from the documents and your knowledge of global history and geography, write an essay in which you
• Compare and contrast the different reasons why nations have gone to war.
• Evaluate why nations go to war.

Part A
Short Answer

Directions: Analyze the documents and answer the questions that follow each document in the space provided.

DOCUMENT 1

"The history of recent years, and in particular the painful events of the 28th June last, have shown the existence of a subversive movement with the object of detaching a part of the territories of Austria-Hungary from the Monarchy. The movement which had its birth under the eye of the Serbian government has gone so far as to make itself manifest on both sides of the Serbian frontier in the shape of acts of terrorism and a series of outrages and murders."

—Austrian ultimatum to Serbia
July 23, 1914

Why is Austria-Hungary so angry with Serbia?

_____

_____

_____

DOCUMENT 2

"Our general purpose is to redeem Europe from the perpetually recurring fear of German aggression and to enable the peoples of Europe to preserve their independence and their liberties. No threats will deter us or our French allies from this purpose."

—Neville Chamberlain,
British Prime Minister, 1939

Why is Chamberlain willing to go to war against Germany?

_____

_____

_____

DOCUMENT 3

"I am not now thinking of the loss of property involved . . . but only of the wanton and wholesale destruction of the lives of non-combatants, men, women and children engaged in pursuits which have always, even in the darkest periods of history, been deemed innocent and legitimate. Property can be paid for; the lives of innocent people cannot be. The present German submarine warfare against commerce is a warfare against mankind. There is one choice we cannot make . . . we will not choose the path of submission and suffer the most sacred rights of our nation and our people to be ignored or violated. The wrongs against which we now array ourselves are no common wrongs: they cut to the very roots of human life."

—Woodrow Wilson, Address to
Congress Recommending War,
April, 1917

Why is Woodrow Wilson asking for a declaration of war from Congress?

_____

_____

_____

DOCUMENT 4

"The greatest single underlying cause of the War was the system of secret alliances . . . It gradually divided Europe into two hostile groups of Powers who were increasingly suspicious of one another and who steadily built up greater and greater armies and navies."

Sidney Fay, "The Origins of
The World War," 1928

What does Sidney Fay think was the main reason for the outbreak of war in Europe?

_____

_____

_____

DOCUMENT 5

"A government should not mobilize an army out of anger, military leaders should not provoke a war out of wrath. Act when it is beneficial, desist when it is not. Anger can revert to joy, wrath can revert to delight, but a nation destroyed cannot be restored to existence, and the dead cannot be restored to life."

—Sun Tzu, *The Art of War*, 300 B.C.E.

Does Sun Tzu think it is good to begin a war because of anger? Explain.

_____

_____

_____

Part B
Essay

Directions:
• Write a well-organized essay that includes an introduction, several paragraphs, and a conclusion.
• Use evidence from the documents to support your response.
• Do not simply repeat the contents of the documents.
• Include specific related outside information.

Historical Context:
Throughout history, nations have gone to war for various reasons. The reasons can be characterized as political, economic, or social (cultural).

Task:
Using information from the documents and your knowledge of global history and geography, write an essay in which you
• Compare and contrast the different viewpoints about why nations go to war.
• Make a ranking list of the three major reasons why nations go to war. Explain the reasons for your choices and explain whether each reason for war is political, economic, or social.

Be sure to include specific historical details. You must also include additional information from your knowledge of global history and geography.

ERA III

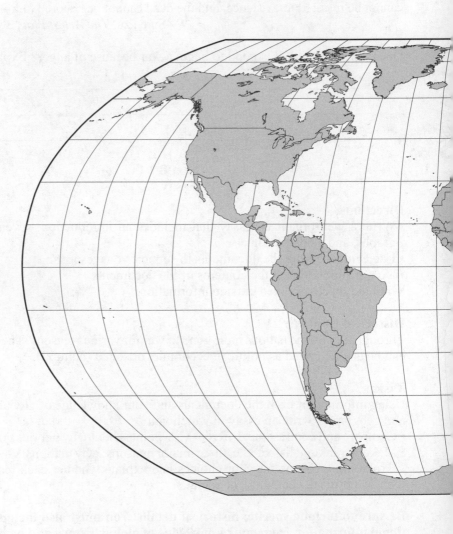

The World
Since 1945

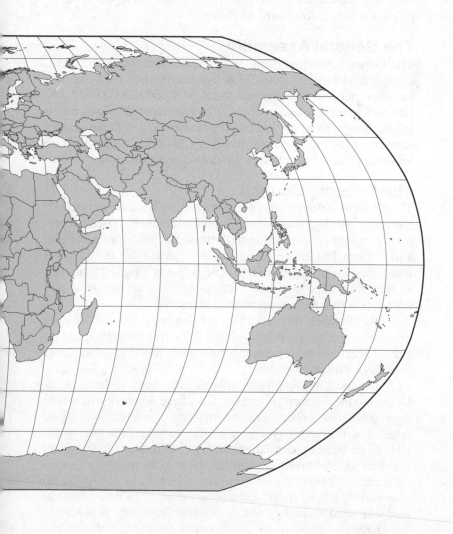

Part A: The United Nations

The United Nations was created in 1945. Its founders included the United States and the other World War II Allies. They hoped to make the UN a more effective international peacekeeping organization than the League of Nations had been. The UN Charter listed the organization's goals: to maintain peace and prevent war; to fight against hunger, disease, and ignorance; to improve social and economic conditions; and to build friendship and cooperation among nations. To accomplish these goals, the UN is structured as follows:

The General Assembly

The General Assembly has 193 member nations, as of 2017. Each nation has one vote. This figure contrasts with the fifty member nations that signed the UN Charter in 1945. The General Assembly meets to consider international problems. It has the power to admit and expel members and to make recommendations to members and to other UN bodies. A decision on important questions requires a two-thirds majority.

The Security Council

The Security Council has fifteen members. Five are permanent members, while ten are nonpermanent members. The five permanent members are the United States, Britain, France, Russia, and China. The other members are elected by the General Assembly for a two-year term. The Security Council functions as the UN's executive body; it can investigate problems and take action to maintain international peace.

1. Resolutions for action in the Security Council require nine votes, including the votes of all the five permanent members. Therefore, each permanent member has veto power over Security Council proposals.

2. The most important UN official is the head of the Security Council—the Secretary-General. The office involves overseeing the organization's operations and includes media relations. In the latter area, the Secretary-General often serves as the face of the UN. Even before the establishment of the UN, U.S. President Franklin D. Roosevelt envisioned the role as that of a "world moderator." The office is generally filled by a career politician and diplomat, from a country considered to be a small- to medium-sized neutral power, and whose nomination is sent to the General Assembly by the Security Council. The position

rotates among the various world regions for no more than two five-year terms of office. Elected in 2016, António Manuel de Oliveira Guterres, previously the Prime Minister of Portugal and the United Nations High Commissioner for Refugees, is the ninth person to hold this office. His three immediate predecessors came from South Korea, Ghana, and Egypt.

Specialized Agencies

The United Nations oversees a number of specialized agencies that administer specific social and economic programs. Among these organizations is UNESCO (United Nations Educational, Scientific and Cultural Organization) whose "mission is to contribute to the building of peace, the eradication of poverty, sustainable development and intercultural dialogue through education, the sciences, culture, communication and information." The World Health Organization (WHO) is "responsible for providing leadership on global health matters and providing technical support to countries (by) monitoring and assessing health trends." "Raise levels of nutrition, improve agricultural productivity, better the lives of rural populations and contribute to the growth of the world economy"—this is the mandate of the Food and Agricultural Organization (FAO) of the UN. Altogether about two dozen other groups promote progress in such areas as the status of women, banking, labor, trade, weather, tourism, and atomic energy.

GEOGRAPHY

Places and Regions

Activities and Challenges

The UN has generally been more successful in dealing with social and economic issues than with political ones. Examples can be seen in its virtual elimination of smallpox and in the reduction of other diseases through the effort of WHO. On the other hand, there has been frustration with the lack of success in dealing with the AIDS epidemic, especially in African nations. FAO programs have succeeded in handling some famine situations around the world, but North Korea's adamant, self-imposed political isolation has prevented the UN from helping with that country's ongoing food crisis. UNESCO and WHO have promoted a worldwide focus on women's equality and health issues, improving conditions in a number of regions. Under UN sponsorship, the Kyoto Protocol set standards for environmental protection in spite of the lack of support from some critical highly industrialized nations including the United States.

Since 1946 the UN International Court of Justice has delivered dozens of judgments on disputes concerning land frontiers and maritime boundaries, territorial sovereignty, the nonuse of force, noninterference in the internal affairs of states, diplomatic relations, hostage taking, the right of asylum, nationality, guardianship, rights of passage, and economic rights.

In the political arena, the United Nations has had limited success, although it did provide a forum for ongoing diplomacy in diffusing potentially dangerous situations during the Cold War period. Peacekeeping forces have served in numerous contentious areas: Cyprus during Greek-Turkish disputes in the 1970s, several areas in the Middle East including Lebanon, the Indian-Pakistani quarrel over Kashmir (1947 and 1966), newly independent East Timor after the attempted Indonesian takeover of that former Portuguese colony in 1999, and Bosnia and Kosovo following the breakup of the former Yugoslavia during the 1990s. However, the UN was faulted for failing to prevent ethnic cleansing, especially the mass killings at Srebenica.

Peacekeeping efforts benefit from substantial investment in both finances and personnel. These efforts generally have admirable goals, but can be thwarted by the nations where conflicts occur. UN membership is balanced with national sovereignty. Although the host governments of some nations have rejected or limited UN attempts to protect civilian populations, several "stabilization missions" have recently achieved partial success, especially in Africa. Some of the UN's more successful supportive efforts have been:

- Combating famine, warfare, and human rights abuses in Darfur with the African Union (2007)
- Consolidating peace in the Democratic Republic of the Congo (before and after 2010)
- Protecting civilians and monitoring human rights in South Sudan (2011)
- Deploying its largest peacekeeping force in Mali (2013)
- Protecting civilians and supporting the transition processes in the Central African Republic (2014)

Unfortunately, efforts to moderate the escalating civil war in Syria lasted less than three weeks in 2012, illustrating the United Nations' limited ability to resolve serious conflicts. In spite of difficulties, as of 2017, there were 16 active peacekeeping missions across four continents involving 125,000 field personnel, including military, police, and civilians from over 120 nations.

In the area of nuclear nonproliferation, the UN has achieved some modest results but has also failed to deal effectively with the ambitions of Iran and North Korea and the perceived instability of a nuclear-armed Pakistan. In 2015, a UN conference on the Non-Proliferation Treaty ended without the adoption of a strengthened review process designed to ensure accountability regarding nations' activities in the use of nuclear materials. This lack of consensus was considered by many to be a setback in the campaign to control the development and spread of nuclear weapons. At the same time, its resolutions regarding international terrorism did enlist near-unanimous support of the membership in the wake of the September 11, 2001, destruction of the World Trade Center in New York and subsequent terrorist attacks elsewhere.

In the Middle East, the United Nations has been consistently criticized for its lack of success in dealing with Arab-Israeli relationships, in spite of the passage of numerous resolutions. When the UN's recognition established the legitimacy of Israel at its birth in 1948, it also created the basis for a "two-state" solution to the Arab-Jewish question as it existed at the time. Arabs continue their adherence to the quest for a Palestinian state while Israeli conservatives oppose such an outcome in both action and word. In 2015, future Israeli prime minister Benjamin Netanyahu announced that "there would be no Palestinian state under his watch." A 2016 UN Resolution called on Israel to "cease all settlement activities in the occupied Palestinian territory." In the ongoing attempt to increase recognition of Arab claims, a campaign led by Palestinian National Authority President Mahmoud Abbas has pressed the UN to once again consider Palestine's application for membership. In spite of nominal support from some influential European nations, the issue seemed to have little chance of success in the short run, given opposition by influential Security Council members.

Since its birth, perhaps the UN's greatest accomplishments have been creation of the Universal Declaration of Human Rights, the relatively rapid phasing out of colonialism with surprisingly little bloodshed, and the enlistment and retention of a virtually universal membership.

South Sudan became the UN's 193rd member after a UN-administered referendum helped it become independent. Looking to the future and its potential to improve conditions in war-torn, ethnically fractious, poverty-stricken, and famine-riddled nations like Sudan, the UN in 2000 adopted a set of Millennium Development Goals. These goals have targeted poverty and hunger, universal education, gender equality, maternal and child health, AIDS/HIV, environmental sustainability, and global partnerships as focal areas for emphasis. A "global action plan" resolution passed in 2011 reiterated the organization's commitment, engaged world leaders and nations, gained support of private groups, and gained pledges of $40 billion in the campaign to achieve measurable results.

Part B: Western Europe and the Cold War

The Cold War and the Era of the Superpowers

WORLD ISSUES

Determination
of Political
and Economic
Systems

GLOBAL
CONCEPTS

Change

CONCEPTS
GLOBAL

WORLD ISSUES

Determination
of Political
and Economic
Systems

The period after World War II (the postwar period) was marked by the dominance of two superpowers—the United States and the former Soviet Union. Each nation had different philosophies about politics, economics, and human rights. Each thought it was superior to the other. The two nations engaged in a cold war, which was not a shooting war but a war of words and propaganda; it also involved competition in science, weapons, and seeking friends among the new emerging nations in Africa and Asia. Western European nations sided with the United States in what was called the free world. The Soviet Union occupied the Eastern European nations and, with them, formed the communist bloc. As the 1990s began, however, the Cold War came to an end, seen in the peaceful overthrow of communist governments in Eastern European nations such as Poland and Czechoslovakia. But the most striking event marking the end of the Cold War and the decline of communism occurred on December 8, 1991, when the leaders of Russia and other Soviet republics announced that the Soviet Union no longer existed. Taking its place would be several independent nations, for example, Russia, Ukraine, and Belarus, that would be members of the Commonwealth of Independent States. The Cold War era, from 1945 to 1991, was distinguished by certain key events in Western Europe.

Today, the era of superpower absolute supremacy has ended despite the fact that the U.S. and Russia are still, in terms of military capabilities, the most powerful nations. Other nations, such as China and India, have greatly improved their military capabilities. In addition, the rise of international terrorism, particularly Islamic Jihadism, has changed the nature of warfare and reduced the advantages of the nuclear-armed, once totally dominant superpowers. Nations such as North Korea and Iran already have or are attempting to obtain intercontinental nuclear capabilities. Also, in the Middle East and Asia, military conflicts have proven that overall military superiority does not guarantee victory or prevent atrocities from happening. In Syria, Iraq, Afghanistan, and elsewhere in Africa and Asia, military conflicts continue, and solutions to end these conflicts are difficult to find. In addition, in the 21st century, the strongest military nations, the United States, Russia, and China, are increasingly using their military power and other resources to combat national and international terrorism as opposed to fighting each other.

NATO

NATO, the North Atlantic Treaty Organization, was formed in 1949. It was a defensive alliance consisting of the United States, Canada, and ten Western European nations. The twelve founding members expanded to sixteen member states during the Cold War. After the fall of communism in Eastern Europe, ten former Eastern Bloc nations joined NATO from 1999 to 2004. By 2005, NATO had twenty-six member nations. Its formation was part of the U.S. policy of containment, through which the United States and its European allies hoped to prevent the spread of communism by the threat of military power. Two important parts of the containment policy in 1947 were the Marshall Plan (to provide economic aid) and the Truman Doctrine (to provide military aid to prevent a communist takeover in Greece and Turkey). To counter NATO, the Soviet Union and its allies formed the seven-member Warsaw Pact in 1955.

GEOGRAPHY

Use of Geography

However, in March 1991 the former Soviet Union and five Eastern European nations agreed to dissolve the Warsaw Pact. This dramatic event, along with others that marked the end of the Cold War, caused NATO members to reconsider the role of the organization. They discussed the possibility of changing NATO from an alliance focused on collective defense against a specific threat to an alliance based on extending democracy and providing stability throughout Europe. Key episodes during 1994 illustrated how such changes could develop.

GLOBAL
CONCEPTS

Choice

CONCEPTS
GLOBAL

1. In April, the NATO alliance carried out its first bombing raid. NATO bombed Serbian positions in Bosnia-Herzegovina to protect UN officials under fire and to protect thousands of people in the town of Gorazde from being attacked.

2. In January, U.S. President Bill Clinton and other NATO leaders proposed a Partnership for Peace program, which was intended to bring about closer ties between NATO and its former Warsaw Pact enemies. It would allow these former communist nations to join military exercises, peacekeeping operations, and other activities without actually granting them NATO membership or security guarantees. As of June 1994, eighteen Eastern European nations and former Soviet republics had signed the partnership agreement. In 1999, Poland, the Czech Republic, and Hungary joined NATO. In April of 1999, NATO intervened in Kosovo after Yugoslav forces began ethnic cleansing of the Albanian majority as a response to violence by the KLA (Kosovo Liberation

Army), which demanded the independence of the province from Yugoslavia. Through a massive air campaign against targets in both Kosovo and Serbia, NATO eventually forced the Yugoslav troops to leave the province. As the basis of the peacekeeping force in Kosovo after the withdrawal of Yugoslav troops and Serbian paramilitaries, NATO encountered problems both with the population and the Russian troops who were serving them. Despite efforts by NATO to create a democratic, multiethnic state in Kosovo, a divided state, as in Bosnia, seemed likely.

In recent years, NATO has expanded in terms of the number of member nations. One of NATO's primary goals in the 21st century is to block Russian expansionism and lessen the possibility of Russia's influence in nations that border a resurgent Russia. Ukraine has been a key concern for NATO since the eastern portion of that nation has sought to break away. The need to prepare for a possible war with Russia has also been a priority.

The election of Donald Trump as U.S. president has shaken the foundations of NATO because President Trump has complained that NATO nations do not pay their fair share of the expenses needed to maintain NATO's readiness. In the coming years, NATO will be tested as a viable multi-nation military force in terms of the organization's military preparedness and the member nations' willingness to pay their fair share for the upkeep and overall expenses. NATO will also be tested for its ability to contribute to resolving difficult issues, such as illegal immigration and terrorist activities.

GEOGRAPHY

Human Systems

GLOBAL
CONCEPTS

Change

CONCEPTS
GLOBAL

WORLD ISSUES

Determination
of Political
and Economic
Systems

Germany

In the years immediately after World War II, the question of what to do about Germany caused much tension between the superpowers. At the end of the war, most of Germany was divided into four occupation zones—American, British, French, and Soviet. The city of Berlin was also divided into four such zones. Some territories in East Germany were put under Polish control. Since the four Allies were unable to agree on a plan for German reunification, the Western nations permitted their zones to come together in 1949 as the Federal Republic of Germany (West Germany), with its capital at Bonn. The Soviet zone became the German Democratic Republic (East Germany), with its capital in East Berlin. West Berlin, although surrounded by East Germany, became part of West Germany. The Soviets tried to cut off access to West Berlin in 1948 and 1949 by imposing the Berlin Blockade. However, the Western Allies sent in food and supplies by plane (the Berlin Airlift). The Soviet Union subsequently backed down and ended the blockade.

1. *The Berlin Wall.* The Soviets again made Berlin a tension spot in 1961 when they built a wall (the Berlin Wall) separating the Western section from the Eastern section. These areas had been used as escape routes for people who wanted to flee from communist rule. The wall was another example of the Soviet policy of restricting the flow of ideas, goods, and people between the free world and the communist world. This restrictive policy became known, in the words of former British Prime Minister Winston Churchill, as the Iron Curtain.

The many historic changes in the European communist world that occurred in 1989 and 1990 can be thought of as cracks in the Iron Curtain. One crack was the destruction of the Berlin Wall by the communist authorities, making Berlin a more open city. From November 1989 onward, when the wall was opened, it lost its significance as a political, economic, and social barrier.

2. *German reunification.* With the end of the Berlin Wall and the friendlier relationship (détente) between the superpowers, the chances of reunifying Germany became a very distinct possibility. In 1990 free elections were held in East Germany. West German political parties, such as the Christian Democrats and Social Democrats, ran candidates and won the support of some voters. In July 1990 an economic merger occurred when

GEOGRAPHY

Human Systems

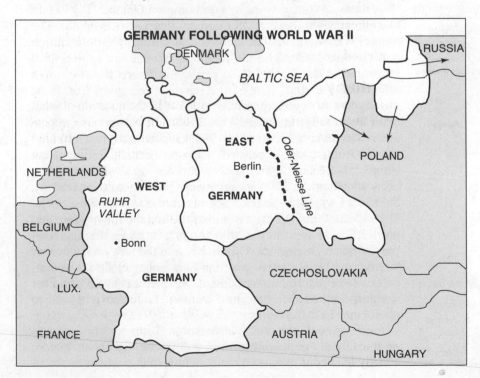

GERMANY FOLLOWING WORLD WAR II

DENMARK

RUSSIA

BALTIC SEA

EAST

Berlin

Oder-Neisse Line

POLAND

NETHERLANDS

WEST

GERMANY

RUHR VALLEY

BELGIUM

• Bonn

GERMANY

LUX.

CZECHOSLOVAKIA

FRANCE

AUSTRIA

HUNGARY

the West German mark became the unit of currency in East Germany. This meant that even though Germans were still living in two separate nations, they would use the same money. East Germans were allowed to move into West Germany; West German companies were allowed to set up capitalist-style businesses in East Germany. With these developments, it became likely that German reunification would occur by 1991. Indeed, discussions about a reunited Germany were held throughout 1990. The major discussants were the four victorious World War II Allies, as well as representatives from the two Germanies. These discussions were thus known as the four-plus-two negotiations. Poland wanted to be included in the talks, because it had suffered more from German occupation in World War II than any other European nation. It wanted assurance that a reunited Germany would respect Polish sovereignty and would not seek to retake any land given to Poland after the war. Specifically, Poland wanted to be sure that the Oder-Neisse boundary line between East Germany and Poland would remain intact. A promise to maintain this boundary was made by West German Chancellor Helmut Kohl in the spring of 1990, on the assumption that he would become the first head of a reunited German nation.

A reunited Germany came into being on October 3, 1990. In December 1990 the first all-German elections were held. The winner was the Christian Democratic Union (CDU) coalition party and its leader, Helmut Kohl. To finance the huge cost of reunification and to fight the economic depression that now affected the eastern part of the new nation, taxes had to be raised. The new government also decided to move the capital from Bonn to Berlin by the year 2000. The move was made in 1999. Two events occurred in 1994, to mark the new Germany: (1) In August, all American, British, French, and Russian troops left Berlin; (2) In October, the second all-German elections were held. In 1999, a third election was held with Gerhard Schroeder winning. Gerhard Schroeder, the leader of the Social Democratic Party (SPD), remained the chancellor of Germany until 2005. In November 2005, Angela Merkel, the leader of the Christian Democratic Union, became the new chancellor of Germany after her party won the September elections and all parties later reached an agreement. Ms. Merkel's rise to power is significant, as she is the first woman chancellor and is from the former East Germany.

Under Angela Merkel's leadership, Germany continues to be the leading economic power within the European Union. However, recent events, which include the rising number of immigrants (both legal and illegal) entering into a reunited and wealthy Germany, have led to problems of integrating people of other cultures into a German- and European-based culture. The differences between the more prosperous Germany and some southern Mediterranean nations have led to problems as well. Greece, Portugal, Spain, and Italy have seen their economies decline in the post 2007–2008 era. Germany's willingness to help these economically challenged economies has been questioned because of its concern for a stable euro currency.

Furthermore, the election of President Donald Trump has caused concern because of his call for more of a protectionist trading policy, which would affect Germany's export-dominated economy. President Trump is also asking Germany to pay more of a share in financing and exercise more active military participation in NATO.

Other Important Issues at the Turn of the 21st Century

The consequences of German reunification, as well as the influx of refugees from Asia and Africa, are just a few of the political issues that will concern European nations in the 21st century. Some of the others are:

GLOBAL
CONCEPTS
Human Rights
CONCEPTS
GLOBAL

Ireland

The Irish question has been a source of controversy between Ireland and England for centuries. By 1600, Protestant England had gained control over Catholic Ireland. From that time until the 20th century, British imperialist treatment of the Irish was cruel and harsh. During the 17th century, when Oliver Cromwell ruled England, many Irish were killed by British forces; in addition, Protestants from England and Scotland took over large areas of land in Northern Ireland. Until the 1800s, Irish Catholics could not hold political office and were taxed to support the Anglican (Protestant) Church.

GLOBAL
CONCEPTS
Change
CONCEPTS
GLOBAL

In 1905 the Sinn Fein Party was formed as a nationalist group to press Britain for Irish independence. Its leader was Eamon de Valera. Although the Easter Rebellion in 1916 against the British was unsuccessful, the Sinn Fein continued its campaign for independence. In 1922, the southern four-fifths of the island of Ireland became a free nation known as the Republic of Ireland. The remaining one-fifth, Northern Ireland, also known as Ulster, decided to remain as part of the United Kingdom (Great Britain). Catholics in Northern Ireland wanted the area to be united with the Irish Republic to the south, as

WORLD ISSUES

Terrorism

did the new Republic of Ireland itself. These requests were turned down by Britain, particularly because the majority of Ulster citizens were Protestants and wanted to stay under the British Crown. Extremist groups, both Catholic and Protestant, began to fight an undeclared civil war in Northern Ireland. The IRA (Irish Republican Army) and its political party, Sinn Fein, spoke for many Ulster Catholics and demanded a united Ireland. Militant Protestants, headed by the Reverend Ian Paisley, are against unification. British troops have been sent to Ulster since 1976 to help maintain peace and stop the killings and terrorist actions of both sides. These efforts have not been very successful. A 1985 agreement between Ireland and Britain, the Hillsborough Agreement, attempted to end what has been called the Troubles. It provided for greater cooperation against extremist groups, stopping discrimination toward the Catholic minority in the north, and giving the Republic of Ireland some involvement in the governing of Northern Ireland. The agreement has had mixed results and has been criticized by both Catholics and Protestants.

In December 1993, Prime Ministers John Major of Britain and Albert Reynolds of Ireland signed a declaration of principles in London to encourage talks for a peace plan. The agreement's highlights were: (1) all groups that promise to renounce violence, such as the I.R.A. and Protestant guerrilla organizations, would be invited to join negotiations on the future of Northern Ireland; (2) Northern Ireland would remain a province of Britain for as long as most of its people want it to; (3) the Irish government agreed to amend its constitutional claim to the territory of Northern Ireland. Although little progress toward peace was made in the early months of 1994, there was a reduction in the bloodshed that had claimed over 3,100 lives in the preceding 25 years.

From 1995 to 1998, efforts to end the violence progressed slowly. Due to the efforts of the American Senator George Mitchell, a peace plan was reached on April 10, 1998 (Good Friday). The accord, known as the Good Friday Agreement, set up a timetable in which the British would withdraw and a government made up of representatives of both the Protestant Unionists and the Catholic Nationalists, including Sinn Fein, would share power and the decision-making process.

Ratification of the Good Friday Agreement by the political parties of Northern Ireland progressed slowly as the extremists on both sides found objections. In the summer of 1999, the whole process temporarily stopped over the issue of the IRA disarming before the new power-sharing executive was set up.

By the autumn of 1999, due to the efforts of Unionist leader David Trimble and Nationalist leader Gerry Adams, the Good Friday Agreement seemed back on track. Despite good intentions, implementation of the Good Friday Agreement proved difficult from 1999 to 2005. However, in 2005, hopes for peace in Northern Ireland increased when the Irish Republican Army (IRA) officially gave up its armed struggle and agreed to hand in its weapons.

Today, the IRA has essentially disarmed, and they are no longer a threat to peace and prosperity in Ireland. Ireland went through a severe economic crisis as a result of the world recession in 2007–2008, which severely damaged its technology-based economy and banking system. However, for the most part, Ireland's economy has improved in recent years and, once again, Ireland's liberal and open economic policies are bringing prosperity to this nation.

The European Union

GEOGRAPHY

Human Systems

The political unification of European nations is an idea that has been under consideration since the end of World War II. There already exists a European Parliament, a European Court of Justice, and a European Commission. These organizations have limited powers but stand for some attempt at international cooperation. The twelve nation European Union (EU) (formerly known as the European Community) has made great strides toward economic cooperation. At its June 1990 meeting in Dublin, the EU agreed to consider proposals for a political union. These have been discussed further in conferences at Rome and elsewhere. French presidents and German chancellors have spoken of a single European currency as well as possible political unification.

One factor that helped to set the stage for consideration of political and economic cooperation was the Helsinki Pact of 1975. This was a treaty signed by the United States, Canada, and 33 European nations, at what was called the Conference on Security and Cooperation in Europe. The signing nations agreed to accept the post–World War II boundaries in Europe. They also agreed to recognize the importance of promoting human rights throughout Europe and to investigate any governmental actions that violated such rights. A Helsinki Watch Committee was established to conduct such investigations.

In 1992, the members of the European Union signed the Maastricht Treaty, which began the process of creating a unified Europe. This included an end to tariffs and passports between members. This process was taken further in 1999, when members of the European Union began to replace their national currencies with the euro. The EU also began to consider the applications of the Eastern European nations formerly in the Soviet bloc to join. By 2005, the European Union had twenty-five members. In 2007, two additional countries, Romania and Bulgaria, were allowed to join, bringing the EU membership to twenty-seven nations. The new members were primarily nations from Eastern Europe. Other nations, including Turkey, were candidates for membership. The issue of Turkish membership in the EU is complicated by the fact that Turkey is a mostly Islamic nation.

In 2016, the majority of voters in Great Britain chose to leave the European Union. This vote to leave, called "Brexit," calls into question the durability of the European Union. The terms of the "Brexit" departure will be difficult to negotiate. In addition, other nations are increasingly questioning their continuing membership in the European Union. The situation in Greece is particularly troublesome as that nation seeks to improve its weak and basically bankrupt economy. In Greece, as well as in other EU nations, both rich and poor, populist forces are questioning the value and the benefits of being an EU member. In the coming years, the EU will have to find solutions for its member nations' living standard inequalities, immigration policies, excessively high rates of unemployment, and various trade issues. The EU will also have to be capable of improving its military preparedness if it will be able to survive as a viable political and economic union.

Part C: Eastern Europe, the Cold War, and the Transition to Democracy

The Cold War (1953–1990)

As a result of the division of Europe, a cold war (political, economic, and diplomatic conflict without open military conflict) developed. In 1949 the countries of Western Europe and the United

THE DIVISION OF EUROPE

KEY

◼ NATO Countries
Other NATO members include: Canada, Iceland, and the United States

▨ Warsaw Pact Countries

☐ Neutral Countries

0   200   400

ATLANTIC OCEAN

FINLAND

NORWAY

SWEDEN

DENMARK

BALTIC SEA

U.S.S.R.

IRELAND

UNITED KINGDOM

NETH.

POLAND

EAST GERMANY

BELGIUM

LUX.

WEST GERMANY

CZECHOSLOVAKIA

FRANCE

AUSTRIA

HUNGARY

ROMANIA

SWITZ.

ITALY

YUGOSLAVIA

BLACK SEA

BULGARIA

PORTUGAL

SPAIN

MEDITERRANEAN SEA

ALBANIA

GREECE

TURKEY

States formed a military alliance, NATO (North Atlantic Treaty Organization), in response to Stalin's takeover of Eastern Europe and his unsuccessful attempts to install communist governments in Greece, Turkey, and Iran. This policy, called containment (to limit the spread of communism to areas where it already existed), was answered by the U.S.S.R. with the creation of the Warsaw Pact, an alliance of the Soviet Union and the Eastern Bloc or communist satellite countries. The military buildup that resulted from the Cold War put an even greater strain on the Soviet economy, which was still suffering from the devastation of World War II. The U.S.S.R.'s new superpower status was expensive to maintain, and Soviet consumers bore the burden.

GEOGRAPHY

Use of Geography

With the death of Stalin, there was a period of readjustment from the fear and suffering the Soviet dictator's rule had brought. The "Great Thaw" from Stalinism (1953–1958) allowed some freedom of political and cultural expression (mostly denouncing Stalin). However, this was short-lived. When Nikita Khrushchëv (r. 1958–1964) took power as First Secretary and Premier, these freedoms ended. Khrushchëv attempted to increase industrial and agricultural production through a series of plans, particularly productivity incentives and an expansion of agricultural development into thinly populated areas (Virgin Lands Program). Khrushchëv's policies failed due to the inefficiency of the bureaucratic Soviet system, the lack of incentives to produce in the factories, and the severe forces of nature in Russia. Many conservatives from the Stalinist period resented Khrushchëv. They used his setback in the Cuban Missile Crisis and the failures of his economic reforms to oust him from power in 1964.

WORLD ISSUES

Economic
Growth and
Development

Khrushchëv was succeeded by Leonid Brezhnev (r. 1964–1982), who, unlike Stalin or Khrushchëv, did not have complete power and was answerable to top Communist Party officials. Despite the great need for change that had prompted Khrushchëv's programs, Brezhnev feared that reform would undermine the authority of the Communist Party. The policy of concentrating on heavy industry was therefore continued, except for one unsuccessful experiment to expand consumer goods production in the Ninth Five-Year Plan (1971–1975). By 1972 the antagonism between the Soviet Union and Communist China and the fear produced by improved relations between China and the United States forced Brezhnev to adopt a policy of détente (understanding) with the United States and Western Europe. This first thaw in the Cold War also resulted in the first of two SALT (Strategic Arms Limitation Talks) agreements, in which both NATO and the Warsaw Pact nations agreed to restrict the development of antiballistic missile systems. These

GLOBAL CONCEPTS

Choice

CONCEPTS GLOBAL

were followed by START (Strategic Arms Reduction Talks) in the Gorbachëv era. Despite détente, Brezhnev continued to suppress dissent and oppose any domestic reform.

Gorbachëv (r. 1985–1991)

After the brief period of rule by Yurii Andropov (r. 1982–1984) and Konstantin Chernenko (r. 1984–1985), Mikhail Gorbachëv became General Secretary of the Communist Party. He quickly consolidated his power by removing the older, more conservative members of the U.S.S.R.'s ruling Politboro (chief political committee of the Communist Party) and replacing them with younger reformers like himself. The stagnation of the Soviet economy had reached a crisis, and Gorbachëv proposed sweeping economic reforms known as perestroika, or "restructuring." Gorbachëv also adopted a policy of glasnost (openness), which was aimed at destroying the secrecy and suspicion of Soviet life. Public criticism and suggestions about national problems were encouraged as well as the expression of opposing ideas, which had previously been censored. Literature, films, music, and art that had been banned were now reinstated as cultural life was given new freedoms. As the Russian Orthodox Church celebrated its millennium (1,000-year anniversary), in 1988 Gorbachëv lifted many of the restrictions on Orthodox Christianity and the practice of religion in general.

From 1988 to 1989, Gorbachëv reorganized the entire Soviet political system. Communist Party control over the government was reduced; a popularly elected assembly (the Congress of People's Deputies) was established, which was a structure for a multiparty system; and a presidency with control over domestic and foreign affairs was created. In March 1989 the U.S.S.R. held its first elections, in which many non-Communist Party candidates were elected, yet the majority of representatives were Communists who ran unopposed. When the Congress first met in June, it elected a smaller body (the Supreme Soviet) to deal with daily legislation. It also elected Mikhail Gorbachëv as the U.S.S.R.'s first (and only) president.

Gorbachëv also greatly improved relations between the U.S.S.R. and the West. In 1987 the U.S.S.R. and the United States agreed to the I.N.F. (Intermediate-Range Nuclear Forces) Treaty, in which both sides would destroy two classes of nuclear weapons. He also implemented the Gorbachëv Doctrine, a policy of noninterference in Eastern Europe. By the autumn of 1988, he began to reduce the number of Soviet troops in some of the satellite nations, which helped to bring about the collapse of the communist regimes in those countries a year later.

GLOBAL CONCEPTS
Change
CONCEPTS GLOBAL

GEOGRAPHY

Human Systems

GLOBAL CONCEPTS
Political Systems
CONCEPTS GLOBAL

The Decline and Collapse of the Soviet Regime (1989–1991)

By 1989 Gorbachëv began to retreat from his reforms. The election to the Congress of People's Deputies of dissidents, such as the prominent scientist Andrei Sakharov, and officials who were openly critical of the regime, such as the President of the Russian Republic Boris Yeltsin, was seen by Gorbachëv as a threat to the survival of the Soviet system. Yeltsin had risen to power by promoting Russian nationalism and downplaying the Soviet Union. This gave the population a new pride in their nation and directed their anger at the Soviet government. Gorbachëv, who never understood this, continued to support dominance by the Communist Party. In so doing, he became as unpopular as the system he defended. By 1991 he had backed down from his reforms and appointed conservative Communists to important government positions.

GLOBAL CONCEPTS

Change

CONCEPTS GLOBAL

With Gorbachëv's new policies, many of the U.S.S.R.'s republics, beginning with the Baltic nations, demanded independence. Gorbachëv was totally overwhelmed by the rise in nationalism and agreed to sign a union treaty with the leaders of most of the republics that would have given these nations greater autonomy. This frightened the conservative Communists into attempting a military coup d'état (an unexpected seizure of power) in August 1991. Gorbachëv, who was on vacation in the Crimea, was put under house arrest. The coup lacked any public support or the support of the bulk of the military, and it collapsed after three days. Yeltsin, who had defied the takeover, became a national hero. Gorbachëv returned, and the leaders of the coup were arrested or committed suicide. This series of events became known as the Russian Revolution of 1991.

GEOGRAPHY

Use of Geography

The coup had made Gorbachëv seem weak and incompetent. Rumors circulated that he had actually planned and ordered the coup as a way of undoing his reforms before the Communist Party leadership had completely lost power. The failed overthrow discredited both the Communist Party and the KGB (secret police). Disregarding the unsigned agreement, Yeltsin declared Russia to be an independent state. One by one, the other republics also claimed independence. Unable to stop the swift breakup of the Soviet Union, Gorbachëv resigned on December 25, 1991, from the presidency of an empire that no longer existed. Communism in both Russia and the U.S.S.R. had ended.

WORLD ISSUES

Determination
of Political
and Economic
Systems

The Commonwealth of Independent States (1991–   )

When the U.S.S.R. disbanded, each republic held its own elections and established its own independent government. Russia, as the largest and most populous of these states, took a leadership position in creating a new federation of autonomous nations, the Commonwealth of Independent States (C.I.S.). The United Nations recognized each new nation, giving them their own representatives in the world body.

Some republics did not make a smooth transition. Civil war flared up in Georgia between the newly elected government and rebels. Fighting between the Christians of Armenia and the Muslims of Azerbaijan, which had started in the last years of the Soviet Union, also continued. From 1992 to 1993, Russia and Ukraine negotiated a compromise over the Black Sea fleet in the Crimea (an area in southern Ukraine that had been a very important naval base for the Russians). The two nations finally agreed that it would belong to Ukraine, but the Russian fleet would be allowed to use it.

GLOBAL
CONCEPTS
Political Systems
CONCEPTS
GLOBAL

GEOGRAPHY

Use of Geography

Russia and the Transition to Democracy (1991–   )

In the fall of 1993, President Yeltsin dismissed the Congress of People's Deptuies. Composed mainly of Communists from the Gorbachëv period, the former Soviet parliament had blocked all efforts to turn the Russian economy into a capitalist free market. Yeltsin demanded that new elections be held since most of the parliament's deputies had never been elected, but had run unopposed as Communist Party candidates in 1989. Realizing it would probably not be returned to office, the Congress refused to stop meeting and the members barricaded themselves in the parliament building. Yeltsin brought in troops to storm it and arrest rebellious deputies. These decisive actions added to Yeltsin's popularity. He also took steps toward creating a new constitution that would give greater powers to the presidency. The enormous suffering that the economic transformation brought created new problems that threatened the development of democracy in Russia.

The national elections of 1994 confirmed popular support for both Yeltsin and a new constitution. Within the year, however, the Russian Army's inability to put down rebellion in Chechnya (a republic within Russia), a rise in government corruption and organized crime, and the hardships created by economic reforms, overwhelmed the Yeltsin presidency. Despite

GEOGRAPHY

Human Systems

these problems, Yeltsin campaigned successfully on a platform of commitment to reform and a moderate choice over both right-wing nationalists and old-style Communists in the 1996 elections. Soon after both his health and popularity faded as the struggling president continuously shifted ministers.

By late 1997, the economy declined steadily and with it the standard of living for most Russians. Popular anger forced Yeltsin to remove reformers from his cabinet. The economic relapse continued into 1998, made worse by a decline in the Russian president's health and a rise in organized crime.

Resentment and anger toward the Russian president was compounded by government scandals involving the laundering of money by Russian banks. On January 31, Yeltsin resigned, making Vladimir Putin acting president until the national elections scheduled for March of 2000.

In the March 2000 election, Putin was elected president with a strong popular mandate. His platform of ending corruption in government and opposing the "oligarchs" (government "insiders" who took illegal advantage of their positions to gain control of newly privatized industries, becoming extremely wealthy and influential) gave him enormous public support. His KGB background gave Putin the image of a strong, decisive leader who would both strengthen internal security against terrorism and restore Russia's declining military power.

Despite Putin's authoritarian style in implementing his reforms, he remained popular. Over the next six years he increased the strength of the national government. He greatly weakened the power of local governments, creating seven new supraregional governors appointed by the president. Putin also obtained legislation allowing the president to remove any regional leader accused by federal authorities of wrongdoing. He gained greater influence over the Duma by creating federal requirements for political parties.

Putin placed restrictions on the Russian media's ability to criticize the government. While seen by many, especially outside Russia, as censorship of free speech, control of much of the media gave the president surprising popular support. Exposure of the corruption of the oligarchs and their responsibility for the 1998 economic collapse gave Putin the political mandate to make needed economic reforms. In 2001, he designed a new land code allowing the purchase and sale of land in Russian cities for the first time since the Bolshevik Revolution of 1917. It generated a new housing market attracting both domestic and foreign investment. The expansion of privatization and free enterprise resulted in the development of stock exchanges to provide investment capital throughout Russia in the 1990s. The lack of regulation, however, as well as the problems the government experienced in tax collecting, resulted in the creation of a small, aggressive class of wealthy entrepreneurs, often tied to organized crime, with government connections. Most ordinary Russians with low-paying jobs and the elderly, dependent on small pensions, became extremely resentful of the rise of this group. Social ills, such as crime, prostitution, and alcoholism, combined with high unemployment and government corruption, led to disillusion with the new system and the flight of many young people to the West in search of economic opportunities. On coming to power, Putin took steps to correct these problems by reducing taxes, implementing reforms to curb corruption within the government bureaucracy, cracking down on organized crime, and waging a war on the oligarchs in which the government seized control of their industries.

Putin's use of authoritarian means resulted in strong criticism from both within and abroad; by 2002 it appeared that the Russian economy had stabilized. The government's budget showed a surplus, and Russia had paid off all of its foreign debts in full for the first time since 1991. Putin's strong action restored public confidence in the economy, which revived foreign investment. The government seizure of control of the oil and gas industries from the oligarchs, which benefited from the high prices on the international market, contributed greatly to the economic recovery. Finally, the successful humbling of the oligarchs created greater confidence in the government and opened up new opportunities for small, independent entrepreneurs.

In 2004, Putin won reelection and his party, United Russia, took 50 percent of the seats in the State Duma (Parliament). From 2004 to 2007, Putin instituted changes to limit other parties from running candidates. These included creating difficult requirements for candidacy and ending local parliamentary districts, replacing them with a system of nationwide closed party lists. In 2007, United Russia won a huge majority in the Duma, giving Putin the ability to pass legislation. In 2008, Putin could not run for reelection due to a constitutional limitation of two consecutive terms. He supported fellow United Russia candidate Dimitry Medvedev, who won the election easily. Putin became prime minister. Many believed that he was still really running the government. During the Medvedev presidency, there was increasing criticism of government corruption and the growth of a wealthy elite connected to United Russia, which was shrinking the newly created Russian middle class.

In 2011, Medvedev chose not to run for reelection, supporting Putin, who could legally seek the presidency again in 2012. This meant Putin could remain in power for an additional 12 years (United Russia used its parliamentary majority to extend the presidential term from 3 years to 4). In the parliamentary elections of 2011, United Russia lost a large number of seats, barely retaining its majority. The losses were surprising considering the reports of election fraud and vote rigging by the government from international observers. This was seen as a growing disillusion with both Putin, whose popularity had started to fall, and United Russia. Following the December 2011 elections mass protests began, with citizens demanding an investigation of election fraud and new elections. Despite Putin's election as President in March of 2012, popular discontent with United Russia continued.

In July of 2012, a law that required all nongovernmental organizations that were receiving funds from outside Russia to register as foreign agents came under heavy criticism as a means of further repressing political opposition. In July of 2013, opposition activist and anti-corruption blogger Alexei Navalny was sentenced to five years in prison in a controversial trial that appeared to be politically motivated. The assassination of opposition activist Boris Nemtsov in February of 2015 raised suspicions that it had been ordered by the government. This led to protests and criticism from within and outside Russia, where people further questioned Putin as a democratic leader.

The July 2014 seizure and annexation of the Crimea region in southern Ukraine and evidence of military support of Russian separatists in Eastern Ukraine in the months following led to sanctions by the U.S. and the EU, as well as Russia's suspension from the G-8 group of industrialized nations. Beginning in 2015, Russian involvement in the Syrian Civil War created further tensions with the U.S. and the EU. While claiming to be fighting ISIS, the Putin government was accused of aiding Syrian President Bashar al-Assad, who was committing atrocities against the civilian population, in order to gain influence in the Middle East.

Despite a downturn in the economy due to falling gas prices, mounting evidence of government involvement in the violent removal of political opposition, increasing repressive legislation to maintain political control, and worsening relations between Russia and both the U.S. and the EU due to Russian involvement in Ukraine and Syria, United Russia and other pro-Putin parties increased their majority in the September 2016 parliamentary elections. The legitimacy of the election was questioned by opposition groups and outside observers because key opposition leaders, such as Alexei Navalny, were prevented from running, and legal obstacles removed many independent parties from the ballot. This led to more protests throughout 2016 and into 2017.

While Putin appears to retain a strong popular base of support, economic problems, continued corruption in government, increasing criticism of his use of political power, and worsening international relations all pose many challenges. As internal opposition increases and as the nation grows more isolated internationally, the Russian government may find it difficult to solve the economic and social problems that continue to confront the nation.

The NATO military invasion on the side of the ethnic Albanians of Kosovo and the bombing of Serbia in the spring of 1999 created strains in relations between Russia and the West and the United States. Russia supported Serbia and was highly critical of the NATO actions in the Yugoslav province. Its role in ending the conflict and the involvement of Russian troops in the peacekeeping force resulted in further tensions and mutual suspicions.

Terrorist attacks in Russian cities during the summer of 1999 were blamed on Chechen separatists. This resulted in a full scale Russian military invasion of Chechnya in autumn. By the winter, Russian troops had captured much Chechen territory and forced thousands of refugees to flee. The international community, including the United States, was critical of Russia's harsh reaction to the terrorist attacks. Yeltsin responded that it was an internal matter and it was hypocritical of the West to criticize Russia's actions after NATO's military interference in Kosovo and bombing of Serbia.

On coming to power in 2001, Putin escalated Russian military action in Chechnya. Although the campaign was successful in crushing rebel resistance and recapturing the Chechen capital city of Grozny, as well as most of the lowlands, it devastated both the country itself and the economy. By 2002, the cost of the war and the continuation of Chechen terrorism within Russia forced Putin to rethink his strategy. A new policy of supporting pro-Russian Chechen president Ramzan Kadyrov to end the fighting and create a compromise that would allow Chechnya autonomy while remaining part of Russia was adopted. Kadyrov's continued support for Russian President Vladimir Putin became a source of international criticism when a member of the Chechen Security Services murdered Russian liberal opposition leader Boris Nemtsov in February of 2015. Open threats against other opponents of President Putin and continued violent political repression in Chechnya have further harmed the reputation of the Kadyrov government. Awarded a medal by the Russian president the day after Nemtsov's murder, Kadyrov is viewed by many as "Putin's hit man." Kadyrov continues to receive funding from Russia, and he rules Chechnya as a personal kingdom, using extortion, torture, and killing to keep the population under control.

Former Soviet Republics

Ukraine

In Ukraine, Russia's largest neighbor, a political division between the western and eastern regions became clear soon after independence in 1991. The western Ukrainians were highly nationalistic and anti-Russian, favoring stronger ties with Western Europe and joining both NATO and the European Union. Eastern Ukrainians, many of whom were primarily Russian speaking, wanted closer ties with Russia and opposed joining any Western organization. The Ukrainian Duma (Parliament) became a battleground between these opposing political views, often resulting in angry debates and physical violence.

From November to December 2004, a series of mass protests took place in response to charges of massive corruption, voter intimidation, and electoral fraud in the 2004 Ukrainian presidential elections. In late December, Ukraine's Supreme Court ordered a revote. Under the close supervision of Ukrainian and international observers, the runoff election resulted in a victory for Viktor Yushchenko, who became president in January 2010. These events became known as the "Orange Revolution." Initially his main rival, Viktor Yanukovych, had won the election. Yanukovych was very pro-Russian and had his main support in Eastern Ukraine. Yushchenko, who was the candidate of a coalition of nationalist groups (Orange parties) with support in Western Ukraine, ran on a program of reform and pro-Western policies. Orange, the color adopted by Yushchenko's election campaign, became the symbol of political change that Ukrainians hoped his election would bring.

Under the Yushchenko presidency, the Ukrainian constitution was changed to shift power from the presidency to the parliament. The Orange Coalition was unable to make successful economic reforms due to divisions between the parties and the enormous corruption within the government. Creating a rival coalition with the pro-Russian Socialist and Communist parties, Yanukovych became prime minister, which created permanent conflict within the government. In 2007, new parliamentary elections were held in which the Orange parties won a narrow majority, but were unable to achieve further reforms or pro-Western policies such as NATO or EU membership.

In the presidential election of 2010, Yanukovych was elected in response to the failure of the Orange parties to push through reform. He consolidated his personal power and began to attack his political opponents. An unpopular law that gave the Russian language regional status was pushed through Ukrainian Parliament in July of 2012. It led to protests in the capital city of Kiev as the government's pro-Russian stance became clear. Despite this, Yanukovych's Party of Regions and its ally, the far-right Freedom Party, won the December parliamentary elections. Opposition leaders and international observers criticized the integrity of the election.

When the Yanukovych government suddenly refused to sign the EU Association Agreement in November of 2013, pressure from Russia was blamed for the refusal. This led to massive protests in cities throughout Ukraine during the winter of 2013–2014. Despite Russian offers to slash gas prices and give generous loans to Ukraine, the protests became larger and increasingly violent. Known as the "Maidan Uprising," named after the square in Kiev where the protests began, the unrest led to President Yanukovych fleeing Russia and the opposition groups forming a temporary coalition government in February of 2014. Russian President Putin refused to recognize the new leaders. In March of 2014, Russian forces invaded and annexed the southern Ukraine region of Crimea (which had a Russian majority population). In April, this was followed by Russia providing military support to Russian separatists who seized parts of Donetsk and Luhansk in eastern Ukraine (which also had majority Russian populations). This prompted sanctions by both the U.S. and the EU, creating tensions that had not existed since the Cold War.

The May 2014 presidential election was won by businessman Petro Poroshenko, who headed a pro-Western coalition government. The EU Association Agreement was finally signed the same month. The October 2014 parliamentary elections produced a majority for the pro-Western parties, which formed a new coalition government under Prime Minister Arseny Yatseniuk. A fragile cease-fire in eastern Ukraine, established in February of 2015, was broken as hostilities resumed in January of 2017. The situation remains unstable as fears of its escalation into a large-scale war have made Ukraine, Russia, the U.S., the EU, and Ukraine's immediate neighbors very cautious in trying to resolve the crisis.

The Poroshenko government faces many challenges and dangers in terms of improving Ukraine's economy and building up its infrastructure, ending government corruption, fighting organized crime, and becoming closer to the EU without a major conflict with Russia. Regaining lost territories in Crimea and eastern Ukraine remains another problem that will not likely be resolved in the near future.

Belarus

In 1994, Aleksandr Lukashenko was elected president of Belarus. By 1996, he had annulled the constitution and began to rule the nation alone. His popularity with extreme nationalists, less educated farmers, the elderly, and those who were sympathetic to the old Soviet regime gave him a base of support. He began arresting, imprisoning, and killing all political opposition and critics, taking complete control over the mass media. He consolidated control over the armed forces and established a dictatorship. Lukashenko claimed he was "saving" the nation from the problems of capitalism and democracy; he transformed Belarus back into a Soviet-style state. Initially purposing union with Russia, he was able to gain its support to keep the Belarusian economy from collapsing. Lukashenko also reached out to the West for economic integration, trying to play the Europeans against the Russians. These tactics managed to keep him in power despite strong criticism from the foreign press and human rights groups. This policy eventually backfired as the Belarusian economy began to fail when the foreign loans finally stopped in 2010. In November 2011, Lukashenko was forced to give Russia complete control of Belarus' gas pipeline network, including the right to raise prices, in return for a $14 billion rescue plan. Alienated from the West due to his recent crackdown on political opposition, Lukashenko appeared to have put his nation under Russian influence. In January 2012, a new law restricted access to foreign websites and required the registration of all users. Angry with the increasingly repressive nature of the Lukashenko regime, popular protests began throughout Belarus.

In October 2015, President Lukashenko won his fifth consecutive term in an election that both opposition parties and international observers maintained was unfair. The September 2016 elections, in which the pro-government candidates gained almost full control of the Belarusian Parliament, were equally criticized as being rigged by the authorities. Despite strong government control, popular protests throughout Belarusian cities continued into 2017.

While President Lukashenko retains a strong base of support, economic decline, which has resulted in unpopular tax policies, has led to protests and a growth in open opposition. Increasing control over the electoral process, growing censorship, and repressive actions against political opponents have all created popular discontent. Lukashenko's dependence on Russia has hurt the image of Belarus as an independent nation. The goal of his policies, which seems to be complete control over the nation, may have unintended negative consequences for both himself and Belarus.

Moldova

The nation of Moldova was part of Romania until after World War II when the U.S.S.R. annexed it and made it a Soviet Republic. Repopulating it with Russian-speaking Eastern Ukrainians and ethnic Russians, who became a majority (54 percent), the ethnic Romanians were forced to accept separation from their nation. When Moldova became independent in 1991, ethnic Romanians, especially in the region of Transnistria, demanded reunification with Romania. This led to uprisings (1991–1992) that were put down with the help of the former Soviet military. In 1992, economic reforms and a market economy were adopted by the government. A parliamentary democracy was established. Appealing to the non-Romanian Russianized population, the communists came to power in 2001. Unable to deal with the global economic crisis of 2007–2010 and discredited by government corruption, their victory in the 2009 elections led to civil unrest, forcing President Vladimir Voronin to resign. A coalition of liberal democratic parties, the Alliance for European Integration, formed a new government. Two seats short of a majority, the coalition was unable to elect a new president. In the November 2012 election, Nicolae Timofti was elected president, ending years of parliamentary deadlock.

In November of 2012, a Russian ultimatum made Moldova withdraw from its energy agreement with the EU. In March of 2013, the coalition government collapsed as the Liberal Democratic Party left due to political scandals and tensions between its members. In May of 2014, acting Prime Minister Iurie Leancă formed a new government. Russia's actions to annex Moldova's breakaway Trans-Dniester region angered the government and resulted in Moldova signing the Association Agreement with the EU in June of 2014. While pro-EU parties retained their majority in Parliament in the November 2014 elections, the pro-Russian Socialists became the largest single party.

In July of 2015, a major banking scandal led to the creation of a new coalition government of pro-EU parties, which fell in October of that same year due to continued protests over the banking scandal. Despite the creation of another coalition of pro-EU parties, popular unrest directed at the Parliament led to Moldova's Constitutional Court ruling in March of 2016, which determined that presidential elections must be decided by a popular vote rather than by parliamentary representatives. In November 2016, pro-Russian candidate Igor Dodon won the presidential election, which appeared to be a shift in government away from the EU. As the poorest nation in Europe, Moldova faces great challenges in ending corruption, overcoming internal divisions between ethnic Romanians and Russians, and balancing policies between Russia and the EU.

Baltic Nations

Unlike the other former Soviet republics, the Baltic nations became democratic states with free market economies after independence in 1991. Lithuania, Latvia, and Estonia quickly established constitutions and parliaments with multiple political parties. Alternating between capitalist and socialist policies, governments struggled to expand their economies. All three joined the European Union in 2004. Resentful of past Russian and Soviet domination, they immediately developed strong economic and political ties to the West. They also had to deal with the problem of large ethnic minorities in each nation. In Lithuania, tensions between the large Polish minority and the Lithuanian government over restitution of prewar Polish property and language rights in Lithuanian schools have developed. In Latvia and Estonia, the large Russian populations have created separate cultural, religious, and social institutions, as well as political parties. Resentful of past Russian control, this has created divisions in Latvian and Estonian society. Despite these problems, the transition from Soviet satellites to free democratic nations has been peaceful and successful.

Caucasian Nations

The nations in the Caucasian Mountain region have experienced turbulent relations with both Russia and each other. The former Soviet republics of Georgia, Armenia, and Azerbaijan have had difficulties transforming into independent nations.

In 2003, American-educated Mikheil Saakashvili became president of Georgia. Promising economic and institutional reforms, he defeated Eduard Shevardnadze, a Soviet-era leader who had been president since Georgian independence in 1991. Tired of corruption in government and the poor economy, the population hoped the election would bring real change. It became known as the "Rose Revolution." Saakashvili and his United National Movement (UNM) party strengthened state institutions, such as security and the military, and made reforms to end corruption in government. He also made economic reforms, which encouraged foreign investment. Saakashvili's pro-Western/American policies, which included proposing to join NATO and the European Union, strained relations with Russia, which wanted Georgia to stay within its sphere of influence.

In 2004, Georgia tried to regain control of South Ossetia and Abkhazia, two regions that had become autonomous (self-governing) after the breakup of the U.S.S.R. in 1991. Both regions have Muslim Turkic populations within Georgian minorities. Fearful of losing influence in the region after Georgian independence, Russia supported both regions' autonomy by providing peacekeeping forces to protect them in 1992. Saakashvili's attempts to restore Georgian control were unsuccessful and led to both regions voting to become independent nations in 2006. This led to tensions between Georgia and Russia, resulting in war by August 2008. Claiming to be protecting the autonomy of South Ossetia and Abkhazia, Russia sent troops to the region and bombed the Georgian capital city of Tbilisi. This forced Saakashvili to end the campaign to restore Georgian control over these areas. The autonomous statuses of both regions were restored and EU peacekeepers replaced the Russians in 2009. Russia was criticized for its actions by Western nations, including the United States, which believed that Russia had used the conflict as a means of regaining control of the Caucasus area. In November of 2014, Russia signed the Strategic Partnership Treaty with Abkhazia. This was followed by the Alliance Aid Integration Treaty with South Ossetia in March of 2015. In August of 2017, Russian forces moved the border with South Ossetia a few miles inside Georgia, threatening the main road that connected the eastern and western parts of the country. A lack of an international reaction to this incident created further tensions between Georgia and Russia as well as fears that this incident would encourage further conflicts.

Despite much criticism from Georgian opposition parties and the failure to regain South Ossetia and Abkhazia, Saakashvili remained popular and was reelected in 2009. In

October of 2010, the UNM lost the parliamentary elections to the Georgian Dream Party (GDP), an alliance created by wealthy businessman Bidzina Ivanishvili. This was largely due to the unpopularity of Saakashvili's repressive use of the judicial system to push through reforms and anti-corruption laws. After the October 2012 election, the GDP took control of the Georgian Parliament, making Ivanishvili the prime minister. In the presidential elections of October 2013, Saakashvili was defeated by Giorgi Margvelashvili. Despite an economic decline, the GDP continued to make even greater gains in the elections of October 2016. Beginning in 2014, an investigation of the Saakashvili government, which the UNM claimed was politically motivated, led to the arrest of many of its leaders on corruption charges and the collapse of the party by 2016. It was replaced by a popular new pro-EU party known as the Movement for Liberty—European Georgia (MLEG) in May of 2017. Conflicts between Prime Minister Ivanishvili and President Margvelashvili and continuing economic problems led to a loss of support for the GDP. The MLEG party's growing popularity seems to reflect a movement away from nationalism and back toward reform and European integration. An economic decline, continued internal corruption, and the threat of conflict in Georgia's breakaway regions all present great challenges for this nation in the future.

Armenia established a stable and democratic government after independence in 1991 largely due to the economic assistance and support from its larger diaspora (Armenians living in other nations). With limited resources, the nation had a difficult time building its economy.

Despite a relatively smooth transition to a free market democracy under Presidents Levon Ter-Petrosyan (1991–1998) and Robert Kocharyan (1998–2008), Armenia's economy was limited by its small population due to high levels of emigration, few resources, and little industry. A controversy surrounding the election of Serzh Sargsyan as president in 2008, in which the opposition parties disputed the results of the election, led to violent protests that required military intervention to restore order. President Sargsyan was reelected in February of 2013 after managing modest economic growth and modernization in his first term, despite great challenges. Balancing policies to bring Armenia closer to Western Europe, while maintaining ties to Russia, on which its military is dependent in case of a renewed conflict with Azerbaijan, has put the Sargsyan government in a very difficult situation. Armenia faces an uncertain future.

Armenia's largest problem has been conflict with its neighbor Azerbaijan, which has brought tensions to the Caucasian region. Beginning in the 1990s, the two nations fought over the region of Nagorno-Karabakh, an area with an Armenian majority within Azerbaijan's borders. With Russian support, Armenian forces gained control over the region along with seven additional Azerbaijan provinces, from which the Azeri populations were chased out. In 1994, Russia, the U.S., and France brokered a cease-fire that, despite occasional shooting incidents, held until April of 2016 when Azerbaijan's forces invaded territory on the border of the region. Both sides accused the other of starting the conflict, and each claimed to have gained or regained the territory. The situation remains tense, and the possibility of renewed hostilities is very likely.

Armenia also has strained relations with its other neighbor Turkey, which closed its border to Armenia in 1993. The poor relations are due to continued Turkish denial of the Armenian Genocide by the Ottoman and Nationalist Turkey from 1915 through 1922 (in which almost two million Armenians were slaughtered), and its support of the Turkic Azeris over Nagorno-Karabakh. The Armenians maintain that the conflict was instigated by Turkey, a longtime ally of Azerbaijan and a traditional rival of Russia, which supported Armenia throughout the conflict.

After its independence in 1991, Azerbaijan's economy grew due to its wealth of gas and oil. Instead of becoming a free market democracy, the nation developed into an oligarchy run by wealthy tycoons, organized crime, and corrupt politicians. Oil money created a political system that is inefficient, corrupt, and resistant to reform.

In 1991, former KGB general Heydar Aliyev, communist leader of Azerbaijan under Soviet rule, became president. Ruthless and repressive, he established a personal dictatorship, crushing all political opposition and eliminating his rivals. Aliyev gained control of the mass media and Parliament, placing the nation under his personal rule. Azerbaijan remained under the control of the Aliyev family as the dictator's son Ilam took over as president in 2003.

Despite much corruption and the brutal repression of political opponents, the government was able to maintain a strong economy. It built up the country's infrastructure, expanded the military, and created projects to gain popular support for the Aliyev regime. When oil prices collapsed in 2016, the economy declined severely, resulting in protests and riots that were brutally put down. Through a crackdown on political opposition and democratic freedoms, President Aliyev kept tight control over power. He has made reforms to limit government corruption and improve the economy in order to keep the support of the middle class. The lack of a bureaucracy capable of reform and the opposition of the wealthy Azeri clans that Aliyev depends on for power make these changes extremely difficult and unlikely.

The buildup of Azerbaijan's military and the use of nationalism to gain support for the government has created a dangerous situation. Aliyev's policies have made the tensions between Azerbaijan and Armenia over Nagorno-Karabakh, which were already high, potentially explosive. Russia's strong support of Armenia raises the danger to an even higher level. The Caucasian region remains highly unstable and problematic.

Central Asian Nations

The Central Asian nations continued to be ruled by one party after independence in 1991. The leaders of the Communist Party became presidents and adopted more nationalist policies, but the Soviet system initially continued. The Central Asian states continue to be ruled by one party and/or one leader.

In Kazakhstan, Communist Party leader Islam Nursultan Nazarbayev, who came to power in 1989, was elected president in 1991 after the nation became independent. Making needed economic reforms to end the Soviet-style system, he began developing the country's oil and hydrocarbon industries. Reaching out to the West while maintaining good relations with Russia and China, Nazarbayev built up the Kazakh economy, creating a middle-class society. This made the leader very popular, despite his repression of political opponents, rigging of elections, control of the mass media, and domination of his Otan Party (former Communists) in the parliament (as a presidential republic, most power is in the hands of the executive). Tolerant of both religious and ethnic minorities, Kazakhstan has avoided the bloody conflicts between ethnic groups in its Central Asian neighbors. Reelected several times, Nazarbayev remains popular. In 2017, Kazakhstan opened up to Chinese investment, creating tensions with its traditional economic partner, Russia, which claims an interest in the nation as a fifth of the population are ethnic Russians. The effect of outside investment remains limited, however, due to systemic corruption and the government's inability to make real reforms.

In Kyrgyzstan, tension between ethnic Kyrgyz and Uzbeks, which began under Soviet rule with the Osh Riots in the 1990s (in which the Kyrgyz majority tried to take Uzbek farms), threatened to create a civil war when the nation became independent in 1991. Communist Party leader Askar Akayev was elected president and immediately imposed strong central control to create stability. He began economic reforms and limited political freedom. Corruption in government and organized crime made most government reforms ineffective. Akayev's successor, Kurmanbek Bakiyev, encountered similar problems. The corruption in government, poor economic conditions for most people, and brutal repression led to civil unrest in the capital in April 2010. President Bakiyev was forced to resign and flee to Kazakhstan. A transitional government led by former foreign minister Roza Otunbayeva took power. In June, fighting between ethnic Kyrgyz and Uzbeks erupted. Many believed it had been instigated by the supporters of exiled president Bakiyev. The government was able to restore order by August.

In October of 2010, the first parliamentary elections under the new constitution failed to produce a majority party. In December of 2010, a coalition government under Roza Otunbayeva and Almazbek Atambayev was formed. Known as the "Tulip Revolution," the new government promised to make reforms to end corruption, fight organized crime, build up the economy and infrastructure, and end the conflict between the nation's ethnic groups. In October of 2011, Atambayev won the presidency in a very questionable election. His administration soon abandoned the reforms, becoming repressive and pro-Russian. Political opponents were systemically removed, and democratic freedoms were ignored. Kyrgyzstan faces an uncertain future as its government has become Atambayev's personal dictatorship.

In Tajikistan a destructive civil war between the nation's clans (1992–1997) after independence in 1991 led to the deaths of over 100,000 people. Unlike the other Central Asian nations, the Soviet-era leaders were not able to keep the nation together. In 1997 a cease-fire was reached, and in 1999 elections were held. President Emomali Rahmon, who first came to power in 1994 in a highly controversial election, was reelected. He was strongly criticized from both within and outside the nation for manipulating the election. The Rahmon government gained control over the military, mass media, and Parliament repressing all political opposition. Rahmon's People's Democratic Party of Tajikistan (PDPT) continues to dominate Parliament as he continues to follow repressive policies. These have led to the rise of Islamic militants in the nation's eastern provinces, which the government continues to fight. Tajikistan has retained good relations with Russia, China, and the United States, assisting NATO in fighting the Taliban in Afghanistan.

The Rahmon government, however, has failed to build up the economy, end corruption, or improve the quality of life for its citizens. It faces a very uncertain future.

In Turkmenistan, Communist Party leader Saparmuray Niyazov, who took power in 1985, was elected "President for Life" after independence in 1991. Promoting policies of traditional Muslim and ethnic Turkmen culture, he established a dictatorship, brutally removing all political opposition. Isolationist and repressive, Niyazov developed a cult of personality (similar to Stalin), making himself "Turkmenbasy" or "Leader of the Turkmens." With his sudden death in 2006, there was a hope for change. In 2007, Gurbanguly Berdymukhammedov was elected president. He began to make political reforms, establishing a constitution and a Parliament. While allowing the creation of multiple political parties, Berdymukhammedov gained control over the mass media, blocked political freedoms, and repressed political opposition, dominating the Parliament with his Democratic Party of Turkmenistan (DPT), which was formerly the Communist Party. While he increased contact with his neighbors and the West as well as developing the nation's largest resource of natural gas, the economy has not grown. Most of the nation's wealth remains in the hands of the DPT and corrupt government officials. Most of the population remains uneducated and poor as the government continues to follow repressive policies.

In Uzbekistan, Communist Party leader Islam Karimov was elected President after independence in 1991. He created a Presidential republic, in which the executive holds most of the power. While multiple political parties are allowed to exist, Parliament is dominated by the President. Karimov remained in power through manipulating elections, crushing political opposition, controlling the mass media, and exploiting the ethnic conflicts between Uzbeks and other ethnic minorities, in particular the Tajins, both in Uzbekistan and neighboring nations. Most of the nation's wealth remains under the control of the President and his supporters.

Karimov ruled until his death in August of 2016. He was replaced by his prime minister, Shavkat Mirziyoyev, who won the presidency in a sham election. His rule has been more brutal and repressive than Karimov's rule. With no free press, no independent judiciary, and no political opposition, most Uzbeks accept the government's propaganda that the president's autocratic rule, while repressive, is the only alternative to political chaos and fanatic Islamism. Yet his rule has led to a small but growing number of young disaffected men becoming radical Islamists. While Mirziyoyev has announced plans for economic reforms and investment infrastructure, Uzbekistan faces a very uncertain future.

The Soviet Bloc (1945–1989)

Unlike the Byzantine Commonwealth or the Pan-Slavic alliances of the 19th century, the creation of the Communist Eastern, or Soviet, bloc was forced on the nations of Eastern Europe by Stalin. The bloc consisted of Hungary, Czechoslovakia, Bulgaria, Albania, Poland, Romania, and East Germany. From the start, Yugoslavia under Tito refused to take orders from Moscow. The formation of NATO in 1949 and the subsequent creation of the Warsaw Pact in 1955 once again divided Europe into two camps, the East and the West.

Starting with riots after Stalin's death in 1953, the nations of the Eastern bloc began to oppose control by the U.S.S.R. In 1956 a revolution overthrew the puppet communist government in Hungary, but Soviet troops were sent in to restore it. In 1961 Albania's extremist communist government, under the leadership of the Stalinist dictator Enver Hoxha, left the sphere of Soviet domination and allied itself with Communist China. In Berlin, the Berlin Wall was built to stop the embarrassing flow of East Germans and Eastern Europeans from the East to the West. In 1968, after the Czechoslovakian government under Alexander Dubček tried to initiate democratic reforms (the Prague Spring), Soviet troops invaded that nation and installed a government more obedient to Moscow. From 1970 to 1980, food riots and worker unrest in Poland grew, as the trade union *Solidarity* was formed under the leadership of Lech Walesa. In 1981, the puppet Polish government began a series of unsuccessful moves (pressured by Moscow) to crush Solidarity. By 1989, Solidarity was legalized. In addition, domestic and international pressure forced the Polish government to hold free elections, in which the Communists were swept out of power. Solidarity formed a new government, with Solidarity leader Tadeusz Mazowiecki as prime minister. Encouraged by Mikhail Gorbachëv's reforms and his policy not to interfere in Eastern Europe (Gorbachëv Doctrine), other countries began to break away from the Communist Bloc.

The Collapse of Communism and the Transition to Democracy in Eastern Europe (1989–)

In the fall of 1989, Hungary allowed thousands of East Germans to escape through that nation. Faced with enormous protest

GEOGRAPHY

Use of Geography

GLOBAL CONCEPTS

Change

CONCEPTS GLOBAL

GEOGRAPHY

Human Systems

and pressure, both internal and external, the East German government allowed free travel, and citizens began to dismantle the Berlin Wall. Realizing that their authority had gone when Gorbachëv refused to support them, the East German communists resigned their monopoly of power. A noncommunist government was elected, and the reunification of Germany took place the following year.

WORLD ISSUES

Determination
of Political
and Economic
Systems

In the manner of dominoes, Hungary, followed by Czechoslovakia, began reforms and free elections. By 1990 both nations had ousted their communist governments and established democracies, electing former dissident writers Arpad Goncz (Hungary) and Vaclav Havel (Czechoslovakia) to lead the new governments.

Hungary

In 1989, a multiparty system began to develop as negotiations were held between Communist leaders and representatives of the new political parties that had formed to ensure an orderly transition of power. In the October elections, the Communists (who had changed their name to the Hungarian Socialist Party) were badly defeated. In December, the parliament was dissolved. In the 1990 elections, the remaining Communists were swept from power. The new parliament began the transition to a free market democracy under President Goncz.

Throughout the 1990s, Hungary made enormous progress toward transforming itself into a fully capitalist economy, shifting policies between right-, center-, and left-leaning parties. From 2002 to 2006, the Socialist Liberal Coalition under Prime Minister Peter Medgyessy expanded the Hungarian infrastructure and improved the standard of living. In 2004, Hungary joined the European Union. In 2006, the Socialist Liberals were reelected under a new prime minister, Ferenec Gyuresany. The global financial crisis of 2007–2010, however, led to a decline in the economy and a break up of the Socialist Liberal Coalition in 2008.

In the elections of 2010, the center-right Fidesz Party won. Under Prime Minister Viktor Orbán, strong nationalist, more Eurosceptic policies were adopted. From 2010 to 2011, the Fidesz government restricted the role of the Constitutional Court and adopted the "Basic Law," which replaced the 1989 Constitution. This restricted individual rights and gave the government more power. A media council was also created, which would issue fines to material it found offensive. In December of 2011, the Hungarian Parliament approved a controversial election law that halved the number of representatives and redrew electoral districts. The opposition parties and critics claimed it favored the ruling Fidesz Party. An equally controversial bank reform law was also passed. It gave the government greater control over monetary policy.

By January of 2012, protests began in the capital city of Budapest in response to the new constitution. In January of 2013, the Constitutional Court struck down the electoral law amendment. The Orbán government retaliated by passing an amendment to the constitution that curbed the power of the Constitutional Court. Another amendment, passed in September, banned political advertising in the media despite criticism from within and outside of Hungary.

In April of 2014, Fidesz won a sweeping victory in the parliamentary elections. The opposition parties claimed that restrictive campaign rules and biased media coverage gave the governing party an unfair advantage. In September of 2015, the government passed a law that blocked migrants, mainly from the Middle East, from coming into Hungary in defiance of the EU policy to relocate them among member states. A national referendum held in October of 2016 overwhelmingly supported the rejection of the EU migrant policy.

Relations with the EU worsened in 2017 in response to the government's attempt to close the liberal European University in Budapest. In June, Parliament passed a law that required all nongovernmental organizations that receive outside funding to register as foreign entities. This was seen by many as targeting groups that were critical of the government. Under the continued threat of Hungary's membership in the EU being suspended, and amid much domestic opposition, the Orbán government still maintains a strong base of support and has moved closer economically to Russia. This has raised concerns about the future of democracy in Hungary.

Czechoslovakia

Following Czechoslovakia's independence from communist rule in 1990, tensions soon developed between the Czech and Slovak leadership. In 1992 nationalist Slovak Prime Minister Vladimir Mečiar succeeded in getting his country to vote for independence. On January 1, 1993, Czechoslovakia separated into the nations of the Czech Republic and Slovakia.

Czech Republic/Czechia

After the separation, the Czech Republic was able to make the transition to a free market democracy with relatively few problems. Under successive governments ranging from moderately left and right of center, state control of the economy gradually diminished in exchange for employment and social stability. In 2004, the Czech Republic was accepted for membership in the European Union.

Despite its membership in the European Union, the government of the Czech Republic has followed Eurosceptic (distrustful of European integration) policies since 2003 with the election of Vaclav Klaus and the center-right Civic Democratic Party (CDP). A long-time opponent of centrally developed economic policies in the European Union, Klaus has maintained the Czech Republic's independence in financial decisions. He has also developed strong ties with Russia and the West. Reelected in 2008, the CDP and President Klaus remained popular and continued to follow a cautious policy balancing European integration and independence until he left office in 2013.

In January of 2013, former Prime Minister Miloš Zeman of the Social Democratic Party won the Czech Republic's first directly elected presidential election. Social Democrat Jiří Rusnok was appointed prime minister, but his government was forced to resign in August due to a scandal. While the Social Democrats won the October 2013 parliamentary elections, they fell short of a majority and were forced to form a coalition government with the Anti-Corruption Movement (ANO) and the Christian Democrats. In July of 2016, the Czech Republic was officially renamed Czechia.

Slovakia

In contrast, Slovakia became increasingly conservative and nationalistic. Under Mečiar (1993–1998) privatization and the transition to a free market economy was slowed down as he built up his own personal power base. His attempts to censor the free press greatly damaged Slovakia's world image as a developing democracy. Mečiar's nationalistic policies hurt the economy, as they discouraged badly needed foreign investment to build industries and relations with Slovakia's neighbors, because of the harsh treatment of its large Hungarian minority. By 1998, Slovakia's health and education systems were bankrupt, the economy was on the verge of collapse, and privatization had failed as state enterprises were sold to Mečiar's political appointees at bargain prices.

In the elections of September 1998, Mečiar and his nationalist party were voted out. New democratic and pro-Western parties dominated successive governments that took Slovakia in a different direction. The nationalist policies of the Mečiar era were abandoned, and greater efforts were made to develop a free market economy by encouraging foreign investment, increasing privatization, ending government corruption through reforms, and increasing democratic participation by amending the constitution to provide for direct popular election of the president.

In 2004, Slovakia joined the European Union. Succeeding left- and right-wing coalitions tried to end the problem of corruption in government, which greatly hurt Slovakia's efforts to create an efficient free market economy. In 2010, a center-right coalition led by Iveta Radicova was elected. An Oxford-educated sociology professor, the new prime minister adopted strong policies to end corruption. By October of 2011, the coalition government collapsed, forcing early elections in the spring.

In March of 2012, the leftist party, Smer, led by Robert Fico, won a landslide victory in the parliamentary elections. Beginning in 2014, the Fico government defied the EU by refusing to support sanctions against Russia or cooperate with the policy allowing migrants, mostly from the Middle East, into Slovakia. While Smer emerged as the largest party in the March 2016 parliamentary elections, it lost its majority and was forced to form a coalition government. As the elections were dominated by the migrant issue, the nationalist Slovak National Party and the far-right Our Slovakia Party became prominent in Slovak politics. In June of 2016, the government came under criticism over alleged corruption. Facing declining approval ratings and competition from the right-leaning nationalist parties, the Fico coalition faces great challenges.

Poland

In Poland, the 1990 elections revealed the great divisions in the post-communist leadership. Despite his lack of education and political experience, Solidarity leader Lech Walesa was elected president as a compromise among the various factions. After the election of October 1991, Walesa formed a series of coalition governments with a variety of political parties from both the left and right. They were unable to make a real transition to a free market economy as the rapid pace of reforms had created great economic hardship for many Poles, especially the elderly and farmers. In November 1995, Walesa was replaced by Aleksander Kwaśniewski, a moderate who believed the economic transition had to be slowed down and monitored. Successive Polish governments alternating between right- and left-wing parties managed the nation's transition into a free market economy. By 2004, Poland had been accepted for European Union membership.

147

In the elections of 2005, two conservative parties that came from the Solidarity movement emerged as dominant—the victorious Law and Justice (PiS) and the second-place Civic Platform (PO). Led by the twin brothers, Lech and Jarosław Kaczyński, PiS formed a coalition government that promoted foreign investment and a free market economy. However, by 2007, despite the economic progress, some Poles began to dislike the government's social conservatism and Eurosceptic (distrustful of Europe) foreign policy. As a result in that year's parliamentary elections the more socially moderate PO won a majority of seats, replacing Jarosław Kaczyński with Donald Tusk as prime minister. This created conflicts within the government.

On April 10, 2010, a Russian-built plane carrying President Kaczyński and ninety-five other top Polish officials crashed in Smolensk, Russia, killing everyone on board. The Polish delegation was on its way to commemorate the anniversary of the infamous Soviet genocide of Polish army officers at Katyń during World War II. The tragedy generated great national unity, especially during the week of official mourning. Bronisław Komorowski of the PO assumed presidential powers upon Kaczyński's death, due to a constitutional clause. Although relations with Russia temporarily improved due to Russian sympathy, the ambiguous circumstances of the plane crash prevented a real thaw in relations between the two nations. An independent Polish investigation blamed both the Polish pilots and the Russian infrastructure, whereas a Russian state investigation refused to review the Polish report and put the full blame on the pilots.

GEOGRAPHY

Human Systems

In October 2011, the PO won the presidential and parliamentary elections. Komorowski formally became president and the PO became the first party ever to win consecutive elections in post-Communist Poland. The government continued to follow policies of close economic integration within the EU, as well as promoting progressive social changes.

In May of 2015, Andrzej Duda of the conservative Law and Justice Party (PiS) won the presidential election. His party also won an overwhelming majority in the Polish Parliament. In December, the Duda government passed a controversial reform that made it harder for the Constitutional Court to make majority rulings. This was followed by a new media law in January of 2016 that allowed the government to appoint the heads of state TV and radio stations. This led to large protests in Polish cities. In May of 2017, huge protests followed an attempt to adopt laws that would give the government extensive power over the judiciary by allowing it to remove and replace judges.

President Duda was forced to veto his party's controversial legislation due to popular anger. While maintaining a strong base of support due to its conservative social policies and its defiance of the unpopular EU migration policy, the Duda government's attempts to expand its authority have divided the nation.

Romania

In Romania, a major uprising in December of 1989 overthrew the communist dictator Nicolai Ceauşescu, executing him and his closest followers. The new Romanian government, the National Salvation Front, led by a former associate of Ceauşescu, Ion Iliescu, came under much criticism as a disguised continuation of the previous dictatorship. Popular discontent to governments run by ex-communists continued until 1996 when a reformist coalition was elected. Disputes within the coalition, corruption within the bureaucracy, and the inability to provide strong leadership resulted in a sharp decline in the economy. The elections of 1998 led to a new, but similar, reformist coalition.

The determination to implement free market reforms led to strikes by miners and other groups adversely affected. As crime and the economy worsened, a disillusioned population brought former leader Ion Iliescu and his right-wing party to power in 2000. While supporting Romania's integration with the Western European democracies and free market reforms in general, he also pledged to end corruption in government and crime. President Iliescu soon encountered the same problems as his predecessors when trying to balance the need for free market reforms with the economic hardships they created.

In 2004, Traian Băsescu was elected president with a coalition known as the "Justice and Truth Alliance." Under the Băsescu government, Romania joined NATO in 2004 and the EU in 2007. The global financial crisis of 2007–2010 greatly weakened the Romanian economy. Băsescu was barely reelected in 2009, and he was forced to form a coalition government. The implementation of harsh austerity measures led to waves of strikes and protests throughout 2010 and 2011. The austerity policies, combined with continued corruption in government, led to the resignation of Prime Minister Emil Boc in February of 2012. In May, the left-wing Social Liberal Union formed a new coalition government under Prime Minister Victor Ponta. While failing to impeach President Băsescu in July of 2012, the Social Liberal Union won the parliamentary elections in December of that same year. In November of 2014, Klaus Iohannis of the Conservative Party was elected president.

The subject of a high-level corruption scandal, Prime Minister Ponta resigned the same month.

Despite a victory in the November 2016 parliamentary elections, the Social Democrats were forced to form a coalition government with the Alliance of Liberals and the Democratic Party under Prime Minister Sorin Grindeanu in January of 2017. Massive protests against continued government corruption and new austerity measures led to the resignation of Grindeanu in June. The coalition government currently under Prime Minister Mihai Tudose continues to face the challenges of making needed economic reforms and fighting internal corruption while facing popular unrest because of the problems in implementing the needed changes.

Bulgaria

Bulgaria's communist government also started to make concessions to reform following Gorbachëv's lead, but seemed to stop short of making real changes. Bulgarian Communist Party leader Todor Zhivkov tried to overcome criticism by launching a campaign to nationalize by ousting the country's Turkish Muslim minority. However, Zhivkov was forced to resign in 1989, and parliamentary elections were held. In 1990, the Bulgarian Parliament ended the Communist Party's domination of the government. Yet, from 1991 to 1997 governments consisting of ex-communists ruled Bulgaria. Public dissatisfaction with corruption in the bureaucracy and economic stagnation led to the election of the nation's first real reformers in 1997. Under the leadership of Prime Minister Ivan Kostov, a reformist coalition began a program of economic reforms to transform Bulgaria into a free market economy. Under Kostov (1997–2001) crime was reduced, foreign investment began, privatization was implemented, economic productivity rose, and the private sector grew for the first time in the post-communist era. Despite these gains, the standard of living for the average Bulgarian had stagnated. The transition to a free market had been particularly difficult for the urban populations, especially the elderly who depended on pensions.

In 2001, the former Bulgarian King Simeon II and his Simeon National Movement Party seemed to offer a "third way" between Kostov's reforms and the socialists who wanted to reverse the reforms. Simeon became prime minister, forming a government that included many returning Bulgarian émigrés who had been educated in the West. This led to a growth in foreign investment and efficiency in government due to experienced ministers trained outside Bulgaria.

Economic, social, and political conditions improved. In 2004, Bulgaria joined the EU. The global financial crisis of 2007–2010 greatly weakened the Bulgarian economy. Succeeding governments were unsuccessful in stemming corruption and organized crime. In the elections of 2009, the Citizens for the European Development of Bulgaria Party took power. Prime Minister Boyko Borisov instituted policies to end corruption and fight organized crime, as well as build up the nation's infrastructure.

In the October 2011 election, Rosen Plevneliev of the center-right Citizens for European Development of Bulgaria party (GERB) won the presidency. GERB also swept the parliamentary elections, forming a government under Prime Minister Boyko Borisov. By February of 2013, growing protests and violence due to the government's unpopular austerity measures forced Borisov to resign. Unable to form a coalition, President Plevneliev appointed a caretaker cabinet to run the government temporarily and organize elections. GERB narrowly won the May 2013 elections, but failed to gain a majority and was forced to form a coalition government with the Socialist Party under Prime Minister Plamen Oresharski.

Anti-government protests erupted over unpopular policies, corruption scandals, and a banking crisis from June 2013 to July 2014, which led to Oresharski's resignation. The October 2014 elections resulted in the Bulgarian Parliament being divided between eight political parties. In November 2014, GERB formed a center-right coalition government under Prime Minister Borisov, which promised reforms. In November of 2016, former general Rumen Radev of the Socialist Party won the presidency, resulting in the resignation of Borisov and the formation of a new coalition. The Radev government faces great challenges as Bulgaria must overcome its economic problems and internal corruption, which continue to prevent its development into a successful free market democracy.

Albania

Albania, the most xenophobic (fearful of foreigners), isolated, and ruthless communist regime, showed the first signs of change in 1990. Hoxha's successor, Ramiz Alia, was forced to begin political and economic reforms as he saw the rest of Eastern Europe abandoning the communist system. He was forced to allow thousands of Albanians to leave the economically devastated country and hold free elections for the first time. In the spring of 1992, the communists were removed from power in Albania following national elections. The new

GEOGRAPHY

Use of Geography

government, under President Sali Berisha, began to make economic and political reforms to transform Albania from one of the poorest nations in the world to a functioning free market economy and democracy. The popular Berisha government's involvement in a disastrous investment scheme that cost thousands of Albanians their life savings in 1996 created a scandal that resulted in riots and rebellion. By 1997, a state of civil war erupted between forces loyal to the government and those that opposed it. Forcing thousands of Albanians to flee, the fighting brought an international peacekeeping force to restore order. UN-monitored elections were held in April of 1998, bringing to power a coalition of Socialist parties under Fatos Nanos. Fighting, however, continued through the year as the new government slowly regained control of southern Albania, which remained loyal to Berisha. Unable to keep the fragile coalition together, Nanos resigned in September.

Pandeli Majko then became prime minister. A member of the new post-Hoxha generation, he enjoyed great popularity, especially among younger people. Denounced by Berisha as a "Nanos puppet," he faced enormous opposition from a coalition of parties determined to prevent reform toward a free market. Committed to ending government corruption and ending crime, the Majko government found itself overwhelmed as thousands of refugees flooded Albania from Kosovo in the spring of 1991. The crisis had an unexpected positive effect economically, as the arrival of UN troops, foreigners, and Western aid created new employment in the construction and humanitarian service industries, especially in the Albanian capital city of Tirana. The infusion of foreign money to help the nation deal with the cost of the refugees stimulated economic productivity and raised the standard of living, especially in cities. This allowed the Majko government to pursue privatization and reforms toward a free market economy.

Despite having led the country through a difficult period of crisis, Majko was forced to resign in October 1999. In the elections of 2000, the Socialists won a majority in the Albanian Parliament, allowing the government to pursue its goals of economic reform, fighting organized crime, ending government corruption, and ending civil fighting within Albania.

The Socialists' reforms had limited success as political divisions and entrenched government corruption frustrated their efforts. Succeeding right- and left-wing governments encountered similar problems. Conflict between Prime Minister Berisha and opposition leader Edi Rama paralyzed the Albanian Parliament and divided the population. The situation grew worse after the Republican Guard fired on protesters in December 2011.

The June 2013 general elections were a huge victory for the Socialist Party, which formed a government under Prime Minister Edi Rama. Under the pro-Western Rama, Albania applied for membership in the EU. In March of 2015, the government announced a plan to privatize the state oil company, Albpetrol. In July of 2015, the Socialists and the opposition Democratic Party agreed to judicial reforms to prepare for EU membership.

The challenges facing the Rama government are enormous as it must fight internal corruption in both the government and in civil society, build a modern infrastructure, make reforms to transform an economy devastated by years of isolation and destructive communist mismanagement, and overcome traditional clan divisions that still plague the northern part of the country. The unprecedented cooperation between two rival parties in making reforms is a sign of hope for Albania's transition into a modern free market democracy.

Yugoslavia

After Tito's death in 1980, the independent communist government of Yugoslavia began to allow civil liberties unheard of in the Eastern Bloc. Yet, despite these, a poor economy caused riots and strikes, forcing several of Tito's successors to resign. The forces of local nationalism also reappeared. This became evident in 1990 when the republics of Slovenia and Croatia declared independence from Yugoslavia. This led to conflict between those republics and the Yugoslavian government, which opposed the breakup of the federated nation. Slovenia was able to repulse the Yugoslav government's troops and force recognition of its independence. The Croatian government, however, became involved in a civil war against the sizable Serbian minority, which was assisted by the Serbian-dominated Yugoslav Army. Acts of brutality were committed on both sides, with ethnic cleansing (the violent removal of people) being practiced to drive Serb and Croatian civilian populations out of one region into another. As a truce was finally reached between Croatians and Serbians in 1991, hostilities broke out between the Serbians and the Muslims of Bosnia-Herzegovina, after that republic declared its independence from the Yugoslav federation. The conflict soon became a three-way ethnic war between Bosnia's Serbs, Croats, and Muslims, with the Yugoslav and Croatian governments arming their Bosnian kinsmen. The war was also encouraged by the nationalist politicians of the

GEOGRAPHY

Use of Geography

Yugoslav republics (Serbian President Slobodan Miloševič, Croatian President Franjo Tudjman, and Bosnian President Alija Izetbegovič). In late 1992, the former Yugoslav Republic of Macedonia declared independence, leaving only the republics of Serbia and Montenegro. The killing in Bosnia continued into 1994, despite the efforts of the United Nations and European Union to resolve the conflict. In 1995, the Dayton Peace Conference divided Bosnia-Herzegovina into a Serb Republic and Bosnian state. Even though the Dayton Accord reduced the conflict, it did not end it, as an international peacekeeping force remained in Bosnia-Herzegovina. In 1997, U.S. air strikes against military positions violating the cease-fire agreement further helped to keep the peace.

Croatia, Slovenia, and Bosnia

In Croatia, Tudjman's death in 1999 led to the defeat of his nationalist HDZ party in the 2000 elections. A center-left coalition under Prime Minister Ivica Racan amended the constitution, making Croatia a parliamentary system rather than a presidential one. The Racan government also brought the nation out of semi-isolation under Tudjman and began to transform the economy into a free market. In 2003, a reformed HDZ took power under Prime Minister Ivo Sanadar. Reelected in 2007, Sanadar abruptly resigned in 2009 due to charges of criminal involvement (he was later arrested on corruption charges). In the 2010 elections, the HDZ lost to the Social Democratic Party of Croatia (SDPC). Under SDPC Prime Minister Ivo Josipović, the economy was further liberalized. The Josipović government also began a policy of improving relations with Serbia in 2010.

A center-left coalition led by the Social Democrats won the December 2011 parliamentary elections, replacing the HDZ as the dominant party. Croatia joined the EU in July of 2013. In January of 2015, moderate conservative Kolinda Grabar-Kitarović was elected as the nation's first female president. No party won a majority in the November 2015 general election, which resulted in the creation of a coalition government under Prime Minister Tihomir Oreskovic, a nonpartisan technocrat. By June of 2016, the government fell due to disputes between the coalition's parties. In September of 2016, the HDZ won the most seats in Parliament, forming a center-right coalition under HDZ leader Andrej Plenković.

After Slovenia became independent in 1992, the Liberal Democracy of Slovenia Party (LDS) dominated Slovenian politics. Under President Milan Kučan and Prime Minister Janez Drnovsek, who led the LDS government from 1992 to 2002, the nation was transformed into a free market democracy. That same year, a right-wing coalition led by Janez Jansa came to power. In 2008, a left-wing coalition under Borut Pahor won the election by a narrow margin. Both coalitions were unsuccessful in gaining strong popular support. In 2004, Slovenia joined NATO and the European Union. In September of 2011, the Pahor government was removed after a no-confidence vote in the Slovenian Nation Assembly (Parliament). In December, the centrist Positive Slovenia Party under Zoran Janković was elected. The Slovenian Parliament, however, refused to accept Janković as prime minister. A new right-wing coalition under Prime Minister Janez Jansa was created in February of 2012.

The Jansa government's unpopular austerity measures and corruption scandals led to massive protests. In December of 2012, former Prime Minister Borut Pahor was elected president. The civic unrest led to the collapse of the Jansa coalition in March of 2013. Liberal opposition leader Alenka Bratušek became prime minister of a new center-left coalition. Faced with economic collapse, the Bratušek government was forced to implement unpopular austerity measures, which resulted in more protests and civic unrest. In May of 2014, Bratušek resigned.

The July 2014 general election was won by the Miro Cerar Party (SMC). Its founder, Miro Cerar, became prime minister, forming a center-left coalition. Facing many challenges, Slovenia's current government continues to implement tough economic reforms.

Since the end of the war, Bosnia has remained ungovernable. Bosnia-Herzegovina is divided into two parts: the Serb-dominated Republina Srpsha (Serbian Republic) and the Bosniak-Croat Federation. The two governments function independently of each other and the threat of renewed civil war is constant. Milorad Đodik, president of the Serbian Republic, continues to demand the dissolution of Bosnia-Herzegovina. The government of the Bosniak-Croat Federation was divided as many Croatian political parties refused to join or recognize the mainly Bosniak government of the Social Democratic Party that won the elections of 2010. The nation is in danger of fresh conflict or breakup and faces great challenges to its survival. In December of 2011, the political leaders of the Bosniaks and the Croatians reached an agreement to form a new SPD-led coalition under Vjekoslav Bevanda, a Croatian prime minister.

GEOGRAPHY

Use of Geography

Accused of corruption in 2012, President Živko Budimir refused to step down, splitting the ruling SPD coalition. In April of 2013, he was arrested. In the elections of May of 2014, the Party of Democratic Action (PDA) emerged as the largest party.

A new coalition under Prime Minister Denis Zvizdić was created in February of 2016. Despite the Zvizdić government's efforts to make economic reforms and fight corruption, the coalition remains fragile because there is a fear of ethnic and religious divisions reemerging to destroy the newly unified central government.

Macedonia voted to leave Yugoslavia in 1992. A nation with an Orthodox Christian Slavic majority, its large Muslim Albanian minority objected to independence, claiming that they would be persecuted because of long-standing ethno-religious conflicts between the two groups. There was also Greek objection to its name (based in part by historically inaccurate claims by some leaders that they were descendants of the ancient Macedonians). This forced the nation to call itself the Former Yugoslav Republic of Macedonia (FYROM) when it became independent in 1993.

Tensions between Slavic Macedonians and Albanians in the 1990s resulted in the creation of a coalition government in 1998 led by Prime Minister Ljubčo Georgievski and President Boris Trajkovski, which included Albanian representatives. An uprising by the Albanians in February of 2001, which included the formation of an Albanian National Liberation Army, demanding equal rights led to the creation of a new coalition government known as National Unity under Georgievski and Trajkovski in May. In August 2001, the government and the rebels signed the Ohrid Peace Agreement in which the Albanian minority was guaranteed full rights in return for the disbanding of the National Liberation Army. In November, the Macedonian Parliament approved a new constitution with Albanian becoming the second official language in 2002. In August of 2004, Parliament approved legislation to give Albanians greater autonomy in areas where they were a majority. By 2005, Macedonia was a candidate for EU membership.

In the July 2006 elections, the victorious VMRO-DPMNE Party formed a coalition government with the center-right Democratic Party of Albania under Prime Minister Nikola Gruevski. The Gruevski coalition government was reelected in June of 2008. A power struggle with the government led to the opposition Social Democratic Party boycotting Parliament in January of 2011. While the VMRO-DPMNE won the parliamentary elections in June of 2011, it failed to get a majority and was forced to create a new coalition. There was a rise of new tensions between Macedonians and Albanians in 2012 because of agitation from outside Islamists in Muslim areas. In March of 2013, with EU intervention, the Social Democrats ended the boycott and joined a new coalition. By April, the government collapsed under internal disputes. The VMRO-DPMNE won the general parliamentary election and the presidency later that month, forming another coalition with the Albanian Democratic Union for Integration Party. The Social Democrats claimed there was electoral fraud. By February of 2015, an open feud between the nation's two main political parties led to a breakdown of government, often with violent protests against each other. The chaotic situation was taken advantage of by Islamists and extreme Albanian nationalists from Kosovo, who incited violence against Macedonians as well as against Slavic nationalists who retaliated. In January of 2016, Prime Minister Gruevski resigned as part of an EU negotiated deal to end the political crisis. A temporary coalition government was formed under Prime Minister Emil Dimitriev until elections could be held.

Political tensions and ethnic violence continued to rise, forcing the postponement of the June 2016 elections. The December 2016 general election failed to produce a winning party, resulting in the creation of yet another weak coalition. When the Parliament attempted to heal the ethnic division by electing an Albanian as speaker in April 2017, it was stormed by angry Slavic Macedonian nationalists. At present, the situation is extremely volatile, with both parties unwilling to work with each other, effectively paralyzing the government. The ethno-religious divisions continue to grow, incited by extremists from both within and outside the country. The enormous gains made by Macedonia in creating a unified and stable nation seem likely to be lost if the present disunity continues.

Kosovo

In 1998, conflict erupted in the Yugoslav province of Kosovo between the Yugoslav police and Albanian separatists demanding union with Albania (known as the Kosovo Liberation Army or KLA). In April of 1999, NATO began a massive air campaign against Serbia. This led to a new campaign of ethnic cleansing by Serbian President Milošević using the Yugoslav military to drive out the Albanian majority from Kosovo. Although NATO claimed that the action was only to stop the ethnic cleansing in Kosovo, the bombing of civilians and foreign embassies in the Serbian capital city of Belgrade as well as Albanian refugee convoys raised questions about the role of NATO after the Cold War. The Yugoslav government and some nations, especially Russia and China, viewed the military action as a violation of national sovereignty. The countries of NATO and other nations saw the military interference as a stand against ethnic cleansing

157

and the violation of human rights. The United Nations, while condemning Milošević's actions, resented NATO's unilateral action as it undermined the UN's authority.

The air campaign and the inclusion of Serbia's traditional ally Russia in the peace negotiations resulted in the withdrawal of the Yugoslav Army by June. This failed to solve the long-term problems and created new ones in Kosovo. The destruction and flood of refugees that resulted from the bombing destabilized the entire Balkan region. Despite his indictment as a war criminal by the International Court and Serbia's exclusion from all Western economic aid until his removal as Serbian President, Milošević remained in power. A weak and divided Serbian political opposition and a population angry at NATO for the bombing of their cities made it possible for the unpopular leader to continue. The NATO/Russian peacekeeping forces came into conflict with both the population of Kosovo and each other. The withdrawal of Yugoslav troops quickly resulted in massacres of Serbs by vengeful ethnic Albanians. Attempts to prevent these by the peacekeepers proved difficult. Serbians fled into Serb-dominated areas in northern Kosovo or Yugoslavia, while the KLA, disregarding NATO demands to disband, took over local administration. The exiled Kosovo Albanian leadership came into conflict with them when they returned.

In December of 2010, flawed elections were held in Kosovo. A government was only formed the following February. The elected prime minister, Hashim Thaci, is reported to be an organized crime leader involved with the sale of heroin and illegal human organs. The continued persecution of Serbians and destruction of their property in Kosovo has raised doubts about the viability of it as an independent state. Despite international efforts, and the normalizing of relations with Serbia in 2013, the creation of a stable democratic multiethnic country seems very unlikely in the near future.

Serbia

The aftermath of the NATO military intervention in Kosovo in 1999 severely weakened Milošević politically. Economic decline in Serbia and growing political opposition led to his defeat in the elections of September 2000. Despite his efforts to contest the election results, public anger against him made it clear that his 13-year rule was over.

Vojislav Kostunica became the new Serbian president. In an attempt to maintain good relations with the West, he sent Milošević to The Hague for trial in the International Court of Justice for his role in the war crimes committed during the

Yugoslav civil war. (Milošević died in 2006 before the court was able to make a decision on his case.) This turned out to be a decision that divided the Serbian population. Kostunica also worked to keep Kosovo as part of Serbia. Finally, he was determined to prevent Montenegro from leaving what was left of Yugoslavia.

Kostunica's preoccupation with maintaining Serbia's borders and the division over Milošević prevented him from dealing with growing domestic problems. Economic assistance from the West in order to prevent further problems in Serbia helped the Kostunica government to spur economic growth.

In the 2004 elections, the center-left Democratic Party (DP) won a majority and its leader Boris Tadić became president. The new government adopted pro-Western policies that included applying for EU membership. This brought much criticism from Serbian nationalists and right-wing parties who felt the Europeans had betrayed Serbia during the wars in Bosnia and Kosovo. In 2006, the Tadić government accepted separation with Montenegro when the nation declared its independence and ratified a new Serbian Constitution, which allowed greater political freedoms. In the 2008 presidential elections, Tadić was narrowly reelected. In the parliamentary election later that year, Tadić's coalition "For a European Serbia" fell short of a majority and needed to work within a leftist coalition to form a new government under Prime Minister Mirko Cvetković. Its hopes of becoming a candidate for EU membership improved after the Serbian government handed over the Serbian general Ratko Mladić to the international war crimes tribunal. This brought further anger and criticism from conservative and national Serbs, especially after the EU granted candidacy to Montenegro and Croatia, but not Serbia, in December 2011. In March of 2012, Serbia officially became a candidate for the EU. With an economy that was struggling and a growing feeling that the price of EU membership might be too high, the pro-European Serbian government was defeated in the elections of May 2012 and populist Tomislav Nikolić of the nationalist Serbian Progressive Party (SPP) gained the presidency. The SPP also made large gains in the Serbian Parliament. In July of 2012, President Tomislav Nikolić formed a coalition government with the Socialist Party, whose leader, Ivica Dačić, became prime minister.

In April of 2013, Serbia and Kosovo normalized relations after the EU-mediated talks guaranteed the rights of the Serbian minority in that country. The SPP won a huge victory in the March 2014 parliamentary election. While Aleksandar Vučić of the SPP became prime minister, the coalition with the

Socialists continued. In the April 2016 election, the SPP won a majority in Parliament, which was seen as a mandate for the party to push through reforms in order to qualify for EU membership. In August of 2016, Prime Minister Vučić formed a new coalition government with the Socialists. In April of 2017, Vučić won the presidential election, giving him greater authority to pursue reforms.

In 2002, Serbia and Montenegro agreed to a partnership that would keep them allied but give each domestic autonomy (self-rule). Serbia also came to an understanding with the other former Yugoslav states.

Montenegro

In 2006, Montenegro declared itself an independent nation. Serbia did not object to the declaration. Since that time relations between the two nations have been good. In November of 2010, Montenegro became a candidate for EU membership. In December of 2012, Milo Đukanović of the Democratic Party of Socialists (DPS) became prime minister for the seventh time, leading a coalition government. In April 2013, Đukanović's ally Filip Vujanović was reelected for a third term as president. Protests against the Đukanović government over accusations of corruption, and in opposition to joining NATO, took place throughout 2015–2016, splitting the governing coalition. Despite losses in the parliamentary elections of October 2016 and the replacement of Đukanović with Duško Marković as prime minister, the DPS-led coalition remained in power. In June of 2017, Montenegro joined NATO. Despite strong opposition to moving closer to the West and the need for economic reform, the Marković government seems determined to continue a course toward Montenegro's greater integration with Western Europe.

The violence and disorder in Eastern Europe following the collapse of communism presents new challenges to the world community. On July 6, 1990, NATO issued an official statement proclaiming the end of the Cold War. Yet, in its place old ethnic and religious hatreds have reappeared. Many question if NATO, in its new role as the "Policeman of Europe," can or should use its military power to control ethnic and religious conflict within individual nations. While the communist regimes were able to suppress these conflicts, they did not resolve them. In addition, the nations of Eastern Europe must deal with the legacy of communist "progress"—economic and environmental damage. In their new-found freedom, these countries face enormous obstacles that will require all their resources to solve.

Multiple Choice. Select the letter of the answer that correctly completes the statement.

1. Starting with Brezhnev, the U.S.S.R. followed a policy of détente, or
   A. understanding with the West
   B. openness with the West
   C. standing firm to the West
   D. suspicion of the West

2. Gorbachëv's policy of glasnost was aimed at creating greater
   A. job opportunities and work incentives
   B. efficiency, especially in industry
   C. openness, with an end to the secrecy and suspicion in Soviet society
   D. patriotism and faith in communism

3. The event that led to the Russian Revolution of 1991 and the collapse of communism in the U.S.S.R. was
   A. the elections of 1991
   B. the signing of the Union Treaty
   C. the unsuccessful coup d'etat by the conservative Communists
   D. Gorbachëv's election as president of the U.S.S.R.

4. Which of the following former Soviet republics engaged in a conflict after the collapse of the Soviet Union?
   A. Russian and Ukraine
   B. Moldova and Belarus
   C. Georgia and Uzbekistan
   D. Armenia and Azerbaijian

5. Russian President Yeltsin dismissed the Congress of People's Deputies in the fall of 1993 because
   A. he wanted dictatorial powers
   B. it continued to block all economic reforms
   C. it had tried to impeach him
   D. it was making too many reforms too quickly

6. Which of the following leaders dominated Russian politics in the early part of the 21st century?
   A. Mikhail Gorbachëv
   B. Boris Yeltsin
   C. Vladimir Putin
   D. Dmitry Medvedev

7. The formation of NATO in 1949 resulted in the creation of an Eastern European communist military alliance under Soviet domination known as
   A. SEATO
   B. EEC
   C. the Eastern bloc
   D. the Warsaw Pact

8. The two Eastern European nations that unsuccessfully attempted to free themselves of Soviet domination in 1956 and 1968 were, respectively,
   A. East Germany and Czechoslovakia
   B. Hungary and Poland
   C. Hungary and Czechoslovakia
   D. Poland and Czechoslovakia

9. The Polish Communist Party was forced out of power in 1989 largely due to
   A. the Polish Liberation Army
   B. the trade union Solidarity
   C. NATO
   D. détente between the U.S.S.R. and the United States

10. Democratic reform and ethnic struggles began in Yugoslavia after the death of
    A. Josip Broz (Tito)
    B. Nicolai Ceausescu
    C. Joseph Stalin
    D. Alexander Dubček

11. "Ethnic cleansing" is defined as
    A. mass killing of a people
    B. persecution of a minority within a country
    C. violent removal of a people
    D. destruction of a people's culture

12. Which leader is *incorrectly* paired with his nation?
    A. Milošević/Serbia
    B. Tudjman/Croatia
    C. Izetbegovič/Slovenia
    D. Nanos/Albania

13. The Dayton Accord of 1995 reduced the conflict in
    A. Albania
    B. Bosnia-Herzegovina
    C. Kosovo
    D. Croatia

14. The NATO air strikes against Serbia are in response to its
    A. violations of the Dayton Accord
    B. ethnic cleansing of Albanians from Kosovo
    C. attacks on Bosnian Croats
    D. ethnic cleansing of Bosnian Muslims

Part D: The Middle East

20th-Century Nationalism

The desire of a group of people to establish their own nation in a specific territory can be described as nationalism. Nationalist movements in the 20th century have resulted in many new nations in the Middle East and elsewhere.

The Establishment of Modern Turkey

The Ottoman Empire was divided after World War I. Spheres of British and French influence were created in the Middle Eastern lands. Western Asia Minor, which included the city of Constantinople, was given to Greece while the eastern part was to be the nation of Turkey (despite vague promises from the victorious Allies, nothing was done to restore the Armenian people to their traditional lands in eastern Asia Minor). Angered by the Allied division and the weakness of the Ottoman government, the Nationalist Party was formed by a group of army officers under the leadership of war hero Mustafa Kemal. The Nationalists set up a rival government in the city of Ankara in 1920, proclaiming it the Turkish Republic and rejecting the authority of the Sultan. Kemal was elected president of the new republic as well as commander-in-chief. Gaining the support of the army, the Nationalists invaded western Asia Minor. Taking advantage of the war-weariness of the Allies (upon whom the Greeks newly established in western Asia Minor depended), Kemal's forces were able to drive the Greek army back into Greece by 1922. Claiming that atrocities had been committed against the Turkish population while under Greek occupation, the Nationalist forces massacred the Greek population (the ancient city of Smyrna was burned to the ground). This began a policy of persecution to drive out non-Turkish populations in order to create an exclusively Turkish state ("ethnic cleansing"). In the 1923 Treaty of Lausanne, Turkey gained control of Constantinople and changed the city's name to Istanbul. The victory of the Nationalists made Kemal a national hero. In the Turkish Constitution of 1923 he was given almost dictatorial powers. This enabled him to make radical changes that transformed Turkish society:

- There was separation of the state from traditional Islamic law and custom.
- Traditional Islamic clothing, in particular the wearing of the veil by women and the fez (tall brimless cap) by men was replaced by Western clothing.
- The Latin alphabet replaced the Arabic.
- Mandatory public education was established.
- Women were given the right to vote (1929) and encouraged to participate in public life.
- Sunday replaced the traditional Islamic Friday as the state "Day of Rest."
- Western technology was introduced to Turkish society.
- The Turkish army was modernized.

Kemal's role as the "Father of Modern Turkey" earned him the title of "Atatürk" or "Head Turk." His close relationship with the army gave the military enormous influence over succeeding governments after his death in 1938. Seeing themselves as the protectors of the established order, the military had exercised a strong and secular control over Turkish politics until the 21st century.

A major change in Turkish politics took place with the election of Recep Tayyip Erdogan as president in 2014. He reduced the influence of the military and began to rule in an authoritarian manner. Restrictions on journalists and news outlets were evident. While claiming not to be an Islamist, he nevertheless promoted policies that appeared to make Turkey less secular. Examples included increased references to Islam in the school curriculum, excluding the topic of evolution in schools, removing many teachings about Atatürk, and overseeing the growth of more religious schools. In July of 2016, an attempted coup against his rule was viciously put down. He subsequently declared a state of emergency and arrested hundreds of people. This purge also saw over 50,000 people being dismissed from their jobs. That number included members of parliament, teachers, and judges.

The year 2017 presented further tensions. In April, Erdogan organized a referendum on expanding his powers. Although almost half of Turkey's voters voted against him, he prevailed. The referendum also led to a problem with Germany, as that nation prevented his followers from campaigning among Germany's large Turkish population. Relations with Germany were also harmed in July when Turkey arrested some German human rights activists and accused them of involvement with terrorist groups. One such group, according to Turkey, is the

PKK or the Kurdistan Workers' Party. (See page 184.) These issues, along with Erdogan's authoritarian rule, could affect the long-stalled talks on Turkey potentially joining the European Union.

Arab Nationalism

The nationalistic desires of different groups of Arabs were evident in both the African and Asian parts of the Middle East.

Use of Geography

1. *Algeria.* Algeria came under French control in the 19th century. Algerian nationalism grew in the 20th century and posed a problem for France after the end of World War II in 1945. France's refusal to leave Algeria led to a long and bloody war between 1954 and 1962. Peace talks in 1962 finally brought an end to the war, and Algeria became an independent nation. Its first leader was Ahmed Ben Bella.

2. *Lebanon and Syria.* After World War I, France held mandates in Lebanon and Syria. However, after World War II, Lebanon and Syria became free nations when the French left peacefully. Independence came to both nations in 1946.

3. *Iraq and Jordan.* Britain was given mandates over both Iraq and Jordan after World War I. Iraq became independent in 1923, but Britain held on to its mandate in what was then called Trans-Jordan until 1946. This was part of the area that was the British mandate in Palestine.

4. *Egypt and Saudi Arabia.* From the late 1800s until 1922, Egypt was a British protectorate. However, in 1922 Egypt became a free constitutional monarchy, although Britain controlled Egypt's foreign affairs. This lasted until 1936, when Egypt gained more self-government. Saudi Arabia, never formally colonized, became a nation in 1927. Its name came from Ibn Saud, the head of a Muslim sect that had established its power in most of the Arabian Peninsula.

GEOGRAPHY

Human Systems

Zionism

This term is used for the nationalistic desire of Jews to reestablish a nation of their own. The Zionist goal was achieved in 1948 with the establishment of Israel, which was located in Palestine, with borders somewhat similar to those of the ancient Israelite kingdoms. The territorial goals of Zionists and Arab nationalists conflicted in Palestine, especially while the area was a British mandate from 1920 to 1948. The conflict continues to the present day, with four major wars having been fought between Israel and the Arabs since 1948. (A brief examination of this conflict follows.)

WORLD ISSUES

Political and
Economic
Refugees

Background of the Arab-Israeli Conflict

The conflict between Israel and the Arab nations is over sovereignty (political control) in the land called Palestine. This small strip of land on the eastern shore of the Mediterranean Sea has been inhabited by Jews and Arabs for thousands of years and has been under the dominance of different rulers at many times in history. The word "Palestine" refers to a geographical area, not to a nation. There has never been a nation or state called Palestine. Therefore a Palestinian is a resident in the area but not a citizen of any nation called Palestine.

1. *Jewish sovereignty* in Palestine existed for about 1,000 years, 1,600 years prior to the emergence of Islam. However, with the Roman conquest in 70 C.E., many Jews were forced to leave what for them was "the holy land." This dispersion of Jews, with many eventually settling in Europe, North Africa, Asia, and later in the Americas, is known as the diaspora. (The word "diaspora" today can mean any place in the world where people live outside of their original homeland.) Jews in the diaspora generally led difficult lives, especially in Europe. They were often persecuted for their religious beliefs (such persecution against Jews is referred to as anti-Semitism) and were frequently forced to live in separate areas of cities, called ghettoes. The ghettoes, as well as village settlements, often suffered from violent attacks, called pogroms. By the late 19th century, the majority of Jews lived in the diaspora; yet there was continuous Jewish habitation in Palestine from the Roman conquest into the 20th century. The movement for the restoration of a Jewish nation in Palestine (Zionism) was sparked in the late 1800s by Theodore Herzl, an Austrian Jew and journalist who wrote a book called *The Jewish State*. In the early 1900s, Zionists increased their efforts to help persecuted Jews immigrate to Palestine. At the same time, Zionists tried to get the ruling Ottoman Turks to grant territory for a Jewish state. Jews supported Britain in World War I against the Turks; Chaim Weizmann, an English Jewish chemist, contributed to the British war effort with his scientific achievements.

2. *Arab sovereignty* in Palestine can be traced to the Umayyad conquest in 637 C.E., which began a long era of Muslim control that lasted until the end of World War I (1918). Different Arab dynasties held power in Palestine from the 7th to the 15th centuries. From 1453 until World War I, sovereignty was held by the Ottoman Turks, who were not Arabs, but were Muslims. However, Arab habitation in Palestine was continuous during the period of Ottoman Turkish rule. The Arabs did not like the Turks and wanted to establish their own nation in the area, as did the Jews. Consequently, the Arabs sided with the British in

WORLD ISSUES

War and Peace

WORLD ISSUES

Political and Economic Refugees

GEOGRAPHY

Use of Geography

WORLD ISSUES

Human Rights

GLOBAL CONCEPTS

Identity

CONCEPTS GLOBAL

Era III **THE WORLD SINCE 1945**

World War I in the struggle against the Turks. With the end of the war, Britain was given temporary control (the British mandate) over Palestine by the League of Nations.

3. During the period when Palestine was under the British mandate (1920–1948), Jews and Arabs continued to press their nationalistic claims. Britain had made territorial promises to both groups and issued an important document in 1917, while defeating the Turks in Palestine, called the Balfour Declaration. Named after Lord Balfour, the English statesman, the document proposed that Great Britain would view ". . . with favor the establishment in Palestine of a national home for the Jewish people . . . it being . . . understood that nothing shall be done which may prejudice the civil and religious rights of . . . non-Jewish communities . . ." In 1922, acting on their own behalf, the British also carved out over half the mandate area, 77 percent, as a separate Arab enclave to be known as Trans-Jordan. This was the first partition of Palestine.

WORLD ISSUES

War
and
Peace

Encouraged by the Balfour Declaration, Jews began to increase their immigration to what little remained of Palestine, where they bought land from some Arabs and cultivated areas left unused by the Turks. Only 23 percent of the original Palestine remained for what might be a Jewish state. Nevertheless, Arab protests against Jews grew into riots and violent confrontations. Britain found it difficult to maintain peace between the two sides and was further weakened by its involvement in World War II (1939–1945). World War II was also the time when persecution against Jews in Europe reached an unprecedented level, with the killing of 6 million Jews by the Germans and their collaborators in the Holocaust. This tragedy convinced many Jews that the only safe place for them would be their own nation in Palestine.

WORLD ISSUES

Terrorism

WORLD ISSUES

Determination
of Political
and Economic
Systems

At the end of World War II, Britain decided to give up its mandate over Palestine and asked the United Nations to resolve the conflict between the Arabs and Jews in Palestine. By a majority vote in 1947 the UN decided to partition the remaining non-Arab 23% of Palestine into two states—a Jewish state and an Arab state. This was the second partition of Palestine. The city of Jerusalem, which was holy to both Jews and Muslims, was to be under UN supervision. Jews accepted this decision and declared their state of Israel in 1948. Arabs both in Palestine and in the new Arab nations outside of Palestine rejected the partition plan. In May 1948, six Arab nations—Egypt, Iraq, Trans-Jordan (later to be called Jordan), Syria, Lebanon, and Saudi Arabia—declared war on Israel. Although the combined Arab forces were larger and better equipped, they were unable

GEOGRAPHY

Use of Geography

to accomplish their goal of destroying Israel. A UN-arranged truce in 1949 ended the fighting.

The Four Arab-Israeli Wars

1. *The War for Independence, 1948–1949.* (This was described above.) Even though the Arabs failed in their goal to drive "the Jews into the sea," they still refused to accept the UN Partition Plan of 1947. In addition, they also refused to recognize the state of Israel even though the United States, the Soviet Union, and most of the world recognized the new state.

Israel is the only democracy in the Middle East, and although it was established as a Jewish state, Israel permits religious freedom to all people within its borders. Nevertheless, during the 1948 to 1949 war, over 700,000 Palestinian Arabs fled from Israel to Arab lands, thus becoming refugees. Some of these people fled because they feared the fighting. Many others were urged to leave by Arab armies, who promised to let the Palestinians return once the expected victory over Israel had been achieved. As another result of the Arab reaction to the Partition Plan, as well as to the fighting, many Jews in Arab nations suffered persecution. Consequently, almost 800,000 of them fled to Israel as refugees.

This first Arab-Israeli war also affected the status of Jerusalem. The Israelis gained control of the western part of the city, while Jordan illegally seized East Jerusalem, which contained the city's important holy sites. Jordan promised to permit equal access to these holy Christian, Jewish, and Muslim sites for members of the three religions. (However, Jordan never

WORLD ISSUES

Political and

Economic

Refugees

WORLD ISSUES

Human

Rights

The holy city of Jerusalem

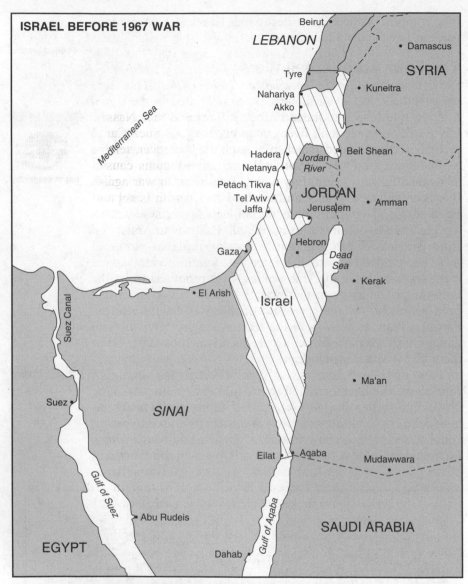

ISRAEL BEFORE 1967 WAR

The patterned area shows the nation of Israel that existed between 1949 and 1967. At its narrowest point, near the city of Netanya, Israel is only 9 miles wide.

permitted Jews to visit their holy sites.) Jordan also seized and occupied the West Bank (the area west of the Jordan River). These actions violated the UN Partition Plan, as this area was supposed to become an independent Palestinian Arab state. The Jordanian occupation received international condemnation and was never recognized by any Arab nation. It lasted for nineteen years, until 1967. The Arab view of the 1948–1949

War is different from the Israeli view. The Arab world labels the war's events as the nakba, or "disaster." This word is used because of the defeat of the Arab armies along with the flood of Arab refugees. (Some Arabs did not flee Israel. Today, they and their descendants make up about 20 percent of the Israeli population.)

2. *The 1956 War.* Under President Gamal Abdel Nasser, Egypt nationalized (took over) from England the Suez Canal in 1956 and prohibited Israel from using it. Moreover, terrorist raids into Israel by Egypt and other Arab nations caused many deaths. As a result, Egypt and Israel went to war again. However, this time France and England joined with Israel and attacked Egyptian forces along the Suez Canal. Israel defeated the Egyptian army in the Sinai Peninsula and occupied the entire region. The UN arranged a cease-fire ending the second Arab-Israeli war. Egypt kept the Suez Canal and demanded that Israel give back the Sinai Peninsula. Israel agreed to give back the Sinai, hoping that in return Egypt would recognize the state of Israel and agree to peace. A United Nations Emergency Force (UNEF) was sent to keep peace on Israel's borders.

GEOGRAPHY

Use of Geography

3. *The Six-Day War, 1967.* Egypt and the other Arab nations continued to refuse to recognize Israel and stepped up their terrorist attacks. Egypt built up its forces in the Sinai Desert, forbade Israel to use the Suez Canal, and closed the Gulf of Aqaba to Israeli shipping. It also ordered the UNEF to leave. These measures, along with Egypt's continued threats to destroy Israel, led the Israelis to strike at Egypt in early June 1967. Although Egypt was well supplied with Soviet equipment and was supported by other Arab nations that attacked Israel, Israel was able to defend itself successfully for the third time in 19 years. Arab armies that attacked Israel from the north, east, and south were thrown back, and Israel took over large amounts of land—the Sinai Peninsula and Gaza (from Egypt), the West Bank of the Jordan River and East Jerusalem (from Jordan, which had illegally taken these areas in the 1948 to 1949 war and was asked by Israel not to attack her in 1967), and the Golan Heights (from Syria). The war lasted for six days. Israel annexed East Jerusalem and the Golan Heights, making them part of Israel. Israel offered to negotiate for the other newly won territories if the Arabs would sign a peace treaty and recognize Israel's right to exist.

WORLD ISSUES

War

and

Peace

After the war, Israel held occupied territory, such as the West Bank, that contained a large Arab population. The area was also known by its ancient names: Judea and Samaria. As thousands of people fled, the number of Arab refugees in Arab

WORLD ISSUES

Politics and

Economic

Refugees

nations such as Lebanon and Syria increased. Many Arab refugees were forced by their Arab host nations to live in camps with poor facilities that served as training grounds for terrorist activity against Israel.

In November 1967, the UN passed Resolution 242 calling for all warring nations to recognize one another and make peace and for Israel to withdraw from some of the occupied lands. The Arab nations continued their refusal to recognize Israel, and Israel refused to return territory until it received recognition.

4. *The Yom Kippur War, 1973.* The fourth Arab-Israeli war began on October 6, 1973 (Yom Kippur, the holiest day of the year to Jews), when Egypt attacked Israel by surprise across the Suez Canal. The war, which the Egyptians call "the October War," lasted almost a month, with Egypt gaining a small amount of land in the Sinai. Syrian troops attacked Israel on the Golan Heights but were beaten back. Several other Arab countries sent troops to fight. The Soviet Union increased its arms shipments to the Arabs, hoping to avoid another victory by Israel. To counter the Soviets, the United States sent military help to Israel. Oil-rich Arab nations pressured the United States not to help Israel and began an oil embargo (a refusal to sell oil). Once again, the UN arranged a cease-fire to end the fighting. In 1973 the UN also passed Resolution 338, calling for "negotiations . . . between the parties concerned . . . aimed at establishing . . . peace in the Middle East."

GEOGRAPHY

Use of Geography

Developments Between 1973 and 2000

1. In 1977 Egyptian president Anwar Sadat visited Israel to begin peace talks. He was the first Arab leader to visit Israel. Later in the year, Israeli prime minister Menachem Begin visited Egypt.

2. In 1979, at Camp David near Washington, D.C., an Egyptian-Israeli Peace Treaty was signed by Sadat and Begin. President Jimmy Carter of the United States brought the two leaders together. The peace treaty provided that (1) Egypt and Israel would recognize each other and exchange ambassadors; (2) the state of war that existed between them from 1949 to 1979 was over; (3) Israel would return the Sinai Peninsula to Egypt in stages between 1979 and 1982, and a UN peacekeeping force would be reestablished on the border; and (4) negotiations would begin on the status of the Palestinian Arabs.

3. Many Arab nations were angry at Egypt's actions and broke off relations. In 1981 Muslim extremists assassinated Sadat, and Hosni Mubarak became the new Egyptian president.

4. In 1982 Israel invaded Lebanon in response to repeated terrorist attacks by the Palestine Liberation Organization (PLO)

GEOGRAPHY

Human Systems

and the inability of the Lebanese government to control PLO actions. The PLO claimed to speak on behalf of Palestinian Arabs and was so recognized by most Arab nations. By 1984 the PLO forces had left Lebanon. The Israeli action in Lebanon stirred much controversy among Israelis, and after the 1984 Israeli elections, its army was pulled back from Lebanon except for a small "security zone" in southern Lebanon.

5. Also in 1982, Israel, in compliance with the peace treaty with Egypt, withdrew completely from the Sinai Peninsula.

6. In 1987 an uprising by Palestinians in the West Bank and Gaza Strip began. This uprising, called the Intifada, was a protest against continued Israeli occupation of the land it had won in war. Many Palestinians supported the PLO and its leader, Yasser Arafat, in its goals of overthrowing Israel and establishing a Palestinian state. However, the PLO was branded as a terrorist group by Israel, because it was one of several Arab organizations that had carried out murderous actions against civilians in the Middle East and elsewhere in the world. Consequently, the Israeli government refused to negotiate with the PLO over the status of the occupied territories.

Within Israel the question of what to do with the occupied territories created discussion and divisiveness. Many Israelis wanted to keep the territories because they view a Palestinian state as a military threat, and some claim that a Palestinian state already exists in Jordan. Others wanted to meet some of the Palestinian demands.

7. The Arab boycott (a refusal to buy goods from someone) against Israel continued as an economic weapon. It operates on two levels: (1) all direct trade between Arab states and Israel is forbidden; and (2) Arab countries will not do business with any company that does business with Israel. Therefore, many companies, afraid of losing business with Arabs, will refrain from having contact with Israel. Israel has repeatedly asked for an end of the boycott.

As of 2017, most Arab countries—but not all—supported the boycott. Yet, there are indications that several quietly trade with Israel.

8. The 1991 breakup of the Soviet Union, a longtime supplier of weapons to Arab nations, meant that the flow of arms into the Middle East would be reduced. Another consequence of the breakup was the increased influence the United States, as the world's chief superpower, could now exert in the region. U.S. prestige also increased in some parts of the Arab world based upon the U.S. role, supported by a few Arab nations, in

WORLD ISSUES

Terrorism

GEOGRAPHY

Use of Geography

WORLD ISSUES

Terrorism

GEOGRAPHY

Human Systems

WORLD ISSUES

Determination of Political and Economic Systems

GLOBAL CONCEPTS

Interdependence

CONCEPTS GLOBAL

defeating Iraqi President Saddam Hussein's forces during the 2003 Persian Gulf War.

9. A much more dramatic moment in the quest for Middle East peace occurred on September 13, 1993, in Washington, D.C. On that day, with U.S. president Bill Clinton presiding, Israeli prime minister Yitzhak Rabin and PLO chairman Yasser Arafat shook hands and signed a peace agreement. With millions watching on television, the two former adversaries shook hands on the first-ever pact between Jews and Palestinians to end their conflict. Its key features were: (1) Israelis would withdraw from Gaza and the West Bank city of Jericho by April 1994; (2) a five-year period of Palestinian self-rule would begin in these places; and (3) talks on a permanent agreement would start by December 1995, with the agreement to take effect in December 1998. These features were originally agreed upon at talks in Oslo, Norway.

10. Another historic event affecting the Middle East occurred in 1993. This was the signing in Jerusalem of an agreement between Israel and the Vatican, whereby diplomatic relations would be established for the first time. The Roman Catholic Church would now recognize the state of Israel, reversing its prior policy.

11. Peace in the region received another boost in July 1994. At that time, Prime Minister Yitzhak Rabin of Israel and King Hussein of Jordan signed a peace treaty that ended forty years of war between them.

WORLD ISSUES

Determination
of Political
and Economic
Systems

Arab Views of the Conflict

1. The creation of Israel in 1948 was wrong and was another sign of Western imperialism in the Middle East. Many Arabs view Israel's creation as illegitimate.

2. Israel was established on land that belonged to Arabs. Any housing and settlements built by Israel on land it had after the 1967 war should be removed.

3. Arabs never accepted the UN Partition Plan of 1947.

4. The majority of people in the Middle East are Arabs. Israeli society and culture represent a threat to Arab values.

5. Israel's creation stemmed from European guilt about what happened to Jews during the Holocaust. It is wrong to take out this guilt on the Arabs. A Jewish state should have been created somewhere, but not in the Middle East.

6. Palestinians deserve a land of their own.

7. The UN has condemned Israeli actions in the occupied territories.

8. Jerusalem is a holy city to Muslims, as it contains the Dome of the Rock and the El Aksa Mosque and is the third

holiest city after Makkah (Mecca) and Medina. Jerusalem should be under Muslim authority, not occupied by Israel.

9. Arab sovereignty in Palestine, prior to 1948, was more recent than Jewish sovereignty.

10. Israel seeks to expand beyond its borders.

11. Israel must give back land it gained in wars as a condition for any peace negotiations.

12. The Intifada events showed the wrongfulness of Israeli occupation and the need for a Palestinian state.

Israeli Views of the Conflict

1. Israel is located on land that was the original homeland of the Jewish people and that was promised to them in the Bible.

2. Arabs sold land to Jews prior to 1948; other Arabs fled from the land in the 1948–1949 war.

3. The UN Partition Plan was approved by a majority of the world's nations. Israel is an existing, functioning nation, recognized by 172 of the 193 members of the United Nations.

4. As a small nation of 8 million people, Israel does not represent a threat to the 100 million Arabs in fifteen nations in the region. Arabs who still live in Israel have a high standard of living and live in the only democracy in the Middle East.

5. A Jewish state is needed as a safe place and refuge, because of the centuries of anti-Semitism in Europe and in Arab lands.

6. Jordan exists as a state for Palestinians. It was created illegally by the British in 1922 from 77 percent of the land that Britain held as a mandate from the League of Nations. There is no need or obligation to create a second Palestinian state. Most Jordanians today are Palestinians.

7. UN votes condemning Israel are signs of Arab ill-feeling and reflect Arab pressure on oil-poor countries to vote with the Arabs or face oil embargoes.

8. Jerusalem was the capital of Jewish kingdoms in ancient times and is a holy city to Jews, containing the Western Wall and the sites of the first two temples. These areas were restricted to Jews when Jordan ruled Jerusalem from 1948 to 1967. Today the Israeli government permits the Muslim holy sites to be watched over by members of the Israeli Muslim community. Jerusalem was never an important Arab political center, as was true of Damascus and Baghdad.

9. Jewish sovereignty in Palestine was earlier in history than that of the Arabs.

10. If Israel had not been attacked so often by the Arabs, it would not have any land other than that given to it under the 1947 Partition Plan. Israel has never intentionally tried to

GLOBAL
CONCEPTS

Empathy

CONCEPTS
GLOBAL

GEOGRAPHY

Human Systems

GLOBAL
CONCEPTS

Empathy

CONCEPTS
GLOBAL

GEOGRAPHY

Use of Geography

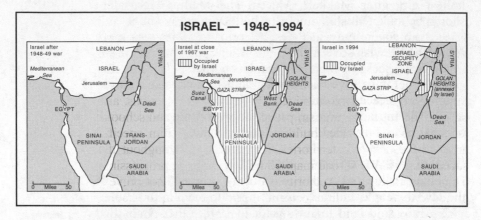

ISRAEL — 1948–1994

take away land from any Arab nation, whereas the Arabs have tried to take away and destroy Israeli land. Israel has the right to build housing and settlements on West Bank land, as that region was never legally controlled by any Arab nation.

11. Israel is willing to negotiate with the Arabs and return land if the Arabs end the war they have waged since 1948. With the exception of Egypt (since 1979) and Jordan (since 1994), no Arab nation recognizes Israel's right to exist. Israel has shown that it is willing to exchange land for peace (for example, the return of the Sinai to Egypt).

12. The two Intifadas were just other phases of the attempt by Arabs since 1948 to destroy Israel.

Developments in Arab-Israeli Relations in the Early 21st Century

A second Intifada emerged in 2000 similar to the one begun in 1987. This showed continued Palestinian resentment against Israel and its perceived occupation and settlement policies. The resentment was seen in deadly terrorist attacks on Jewish civilians. These attacks on innocent people were carried out by homicide bombers (often labeled "suicide bombers" in the media). One Israeli countermeasure was the construction of a barrier, started in 2004, known as the "security wall" or "separation barrier," designed to stop the penetration of homicide bombers from the West Bank. It has had much success in reducing murderous acts. The Israelis also claim that it was necessary since the Palestine Authority has failed to disarm terrorist groups and to prevent their attacks. However, its erection caused bitterness in the Arab world and harsh criticism from several nations outside the Middle East. Critics condemned it as illegal.

A more hopeful sign of calm was a road map plan for peace formulated in 2002. This plan grew out of the Oslo Accords of 1993 and was to be implemented under the guidance of a quartet consisting of the United States, Russia, the United Nations, and the European Union. The goal, as agreed to by Israel and the Palestinians, was to plan for a future Palestinian state. The Palestinians, in the meantime, would adopt democratic reforms, end terrorist actions, and halt the vicious anti-Semitism prevalent in mosques and schools. Israel would stop settler buildups and withdraw from specific areas in the occupied territories. Unfortunately, throughout the succeeding years, the road map did not appear to be progressing. The ruling Palestinian Authority could not or would not prevent armed terrorist groups from committing atrocities against Israelis. Israel, in response to Palestinian violence, carried out house searches, made arrests of suspected terrorists, closed down border crossings, and targeted assassinations of militant leaders. The cycle of attacks and counterattacks resulted in the deaths of many people. The preaching and teaching of anti-Semitism throughout the occupied areas, as well in most of the Arab world, continued unabated. In the last several years, a number of events have occurred in the Middle East that may likely influence the course of future relations between Israel and the Arab Muslim peoples in the Middle East:

1. *The death of Syrian President Hafez al-Assad in 2000.* He was very anti-Israeli and permitted dangerous radical Arab terrorist groups to maintain headquarters in his country. His place was taken by his son, Bashar al-Assad, who refused to grant recognition to Israel and has demanded that Israel return the Golan Heights to Syria. He has also allowed terrorist organizations to remain in his country.

2. *The death of Yasser Arafat in 2004.* As the most significant figure among Palestinians, he was involved in high-level negotiations with Israel, the United States, and many other nations in an attempt to create a Palestinian state and to better the lives of his people. By the time of his death he had failed to accomplish these goals, as he was not seen as trustworthy by the Americans and the Israelis. His place as head of the Palestinian Authority was taken by Mahmoud Abbas, head of the Fatah Party. He faced acute challenges in trying to unify his people and in disarming violent militant groups who want to destroy Israel.

3. *The withdrawal of Israeli settlers from Gaza in 2005.* Under a decision made by Israeli prime minister Ariel Sharon, Israel arranged for the removal of the more than 8,000 Jewish settlers from the Gaza Strip. This entire area would now have

limited self-rule under the Palestinian Authority, with the hope of one day becoming part of a Palestinian state. Although some Israelis were against Sharon's decision to evacuate Gaza, the vast majority of the population supported it and hoped it would be seen as a step toward peace by the Palestinians and their supporters in the Arab world and elsewhere. Although the Israelis left behind some manufacturing and agricultural sites for use by the Palestinians, the Palestinians nevertheless destroyed them. Militant groups among the Palestinians also began to fire missiles and rockets into areas of Israel, causing property damage and civilian casualties.

4. *The threat by Iran's President.* In November 2005, Iran's president called for the eradication and destruction of Israel by any means possible. This was seen as a dangerous pronouncement and a violation of the United Nations Charter. Iran is thought to possess nuclear weapons and has supported radical Islamist groups who have carried out homicide bombings in Israel. Although no Middle East Arab nation condemned Iran's nuclear threat, it was denounced by the United States and many other nations. The threat has continued to the present day. (Iran's nuclear development is also of concern to the United States. In 2015, the U.S. signed an agreement with Iran on this issue, known as the Joint Comprehensive Plan of Action. Iran promised to engage in peaceful nuclear work and to permit verification of such work. In turn, the U.S. agreed to ease many economic sanctions on Iran.)

5. *The impact of Hamas.* The early months of 2006 witnessed some major developments affecting Arab-Israeli relations. In January, the elections held in the Palestinian territories were won by Hamas. This victory was seen, however, as a severe hindrance to the peace process. Labeled as a terrorist group by the United States and the European Union, Hamas has staged several homicide bombings over the years that have killed innocent Israelis and some Westerners. Hamas rejects any negotiations with Israel, refuses to recognize any of Israel's land claims, and vows to destroy Israel. As of April 2006, the quartet (see page 177) stated that financial assistance to the Hamas-controlled Palestinian Authority is likely to suffer. This is because Hamas has not been willing to recognize Israel, renounce violence, and accept previous agreements. Hamas was a Palestinian political party that now controlled Gaza, and disagreed on several issues with the other Palestinian political party, Fatah, which controlled the West Bank area. The continued Hamas firing of missiles and rockets into nearby sections of Israel, as well as the capture of an Israeli soldier, prompted Israel to stage a series of

attacks in Gaza in late 2008 and early 2009. These attacks seek to avoid civilian injuries and are aimed chiefly at Hamas officials and military personnel.

6. *Protection from nuclear attacks.* Concerned about a nuclear confrontation from hostile Muslim nations, Israeli planes destroyed nuclear weapon sites in Iraq in 1981, and in Syria in 2007.

7. *Lebanon War in 2006.* In order to stop attacks from Southern Lebanon, Israel established a "security zone" in the region from 1982 to 2000. Although Israeli forces left the region in 2000, there was continued rocket and sniper attacks from across its northern border. This was mainly by Hezbollah. Hezbollah was a political party, consisting of Islamic extremists and other Arabs, financed by Iran and anti-Western countries dedicated to Israel's destruction. As the Lebanese government could not or would not curtail Hezbollah's activities, the Israeli army and air force crossed into Lebanon in 2006. A 34-day war took place, leading to a cease-fire arranged by the UN. Hezbollah has gained power and prestige in Lebanon and has increased its arms supplies with help from Iran and Syria. Tension still exists along the Israeli-Lebanese border.

8. *Israeli blockade of Gaza.* In an attempt to prevent arms and weapons from reaching Hamas fighters, Israel imposed a naval blockade on Gaza. In May 2010, a flotilla (group) of six vessels attempted to break the blockade. The vessels sailed from Turkey, containing Hamas supporters. When Israeli commandos boarded one of the ships to check for weapons, they were violently attacked by people on the ship. As the commandos fought to protect themselves, several were injured while nine of the attackers were killed. The other ships were escorted peacefully to Israel, where any humanitarian items they carried were sent to Gaza. The UN conducted an investigation and determined that under international law, the blockade was legal.

9. *The appeal by the Palestinian Authority to the UN for statehood, 2011.* In September 2011, Mahmoud Abbas, head of the Palestine Authority, asked the UN to grant statehood to the Palestinians. He hoped that the Security Council would give its approval after studying the request. There were serious problems with this request:

a. President Obama was expected to have the United States veto the request.

b. The UN cannot create a state, but can grant observer status.

c. The Abbas appeal violates previous agreements between the Palestinians and Israel, whereby they would meet by themselves on the statehood issue.

d. The Palestinians are not united and have no fixed boundaries. The Fatah Party controls the West Bank, whereas Hamas controls Gaza.

e. The appeal was rejected.

10. *The Gaza War of 2014.* This conflict was brought on by Hamas. It repeatedly fired missiles and mortars into southern Israel, breaking a promise not to do this. It also dug tunnels under the border with Israeli to enable fighters to enter Israel and cause death and destruction. Hamas had also kidnapped and murdered three Israeli teenagers in the West Bank. Hamas would fire missiles and rockets from civilian sites, such as hospitals, mosques, schools, and heavily populated areas. Such actions were done to present the Israeli military with a difficult ethical challenge: whether to attack such areas. Hamas was using people as human shields. Israel employed an Iron Dome missile defense system that enabled it to destroy rockets and artillery shells. Israel did something very unusual in this conflict. It gave warning to Gaza civilians prior to an attack. The air force would drop leaflets and also use text messages and phone calls to citizens whose houses and areas were to be targeted. A cease-fire was arranged after 50 days of combat.

11. *2017 and after.* As 2017 drew to a close, it was hoped that both the Israelis and the Palestinians would once again meet to discuss vital issues. Israeli prime minister Benjamin Netanyahu has echoed this hope and does not want to have preset conditions for any talks. Palestinian president Abbas, however, has asked for a halt on settlement building by Israel prior to any talks. The key issues center around the settlements, as well as the status of Jerusalem, Arab refugees, Palestinian statehood and boundaries, and Arab recognition of Israel as a Jewish state.

Other Political Developments in the Middle East, 1979–Present

Iran-Islamic Fundamentalism and the War with Iraq. The shah of Iran, Mohammed Reza Pahlavi, introduced many Western and modern practices to his country during the 1960s and 1970s. However, many religious leaders felt that traditional Islamic customs were threatened by Western ideas. These leaders were Islamic fundamentalists, who wanted to keep Islam pure and fundamental, without any "contamination" from the outside world. Known as Islamists, they opposed the shah and were also upset with the dictatorial manner in which he ruled. Riots and demonstrations against the shah forced him to leave Iran in 1979. In his place the country was run by

GLOBAL
CONCEPTS

Empathy

CONCEPTS
GLOBAL

an Islamic Revolutionary Council, led by Ayatollah Ruhollah Khomeini. This Iranian Revolution, also known as the Islamic Revolution, caused concern in other Muslim nations in the Middle East. The Ayatollah's government was anti-Western and held fifty-two Americans as hostages from 1979 to 1981. Although Khomeini died in 1989, the new rulers of Iran have followed similar foreign and domestic policies.

In 1980 war between Iran and Iraq broke out when Iraq, under its leader Saddam Hussein, attacked Iran. Known as the Iran-Iraq War, this conflict had several causes. These included: political causes—each nation wanted to dominate the Persian Gulf area; frequent criticism by Hussein and Khomeini of each other; border disputes existed; social causes—Iraq feared the "export" of the Iranian Revolution; there were great religious differences between the Sunni Muslims of Iraq and the Shi'ite Muslims of Iran; and economic causes—the oil fields of the Persian Gulf area are very valuable; the Persian Gulf itself is the most important route for transporting oil from the Middle East. The fighting ended in 1988 under a UN-supervised agreement, but it caused hundreds of thousands of casualties and hurt the economies of both nations. The war ended as a stalemate.

WORLD ISSUES

War
and
Peace

Today, Iran is tightly run by the Muslim clergy. As a result, strict limits are placed on basic rights and freedoms. Another aspect of contemporary Iran is the expansion of its nuclear program. This is seen as a threat to countries in the Middle East, particularly Israel and Saudi Arabia. It has also increased tensions with the United States. To address Iran's nuclear challenge, the U.S. has used economic sanctions as well as diplomatic strategies. The most significant of these actions was the 2015 nuclear agreement between the two nations. It called for various verification and compliance measures as a means of slowing down and restricting Iran's nuclear weapons capability.

Lebanon—Civil War and Syrian Occupation. A civil war broke out in Lebanon that lasted from 1975 to 1990. It can be explained by examining the country's political and religious history. When the French mandate in Lebanon ended in 1943, a government was created that was supposed to strike a balance between Lebanese Christians and Muslims. Since the Christians were then the majority group, it was decided that most of the top government positions (such as president and armed forces commander) would go to Christians. From the 1940s to the 1970s, Lebanon prospered economically and was peaceful. However, Muslims became the majority group, and they wanted changes in the political structure to give them

GEOGRAPHY

Use of Geography

more power. It was also in this period that Palestinian refugees, including PLO leaders, settled in Lebanon as a result of the Arab-Israeli wars. From these settlements, many Palestinians made terrorist raids into Israel. Frequently, Israeli forces attacked these settlements in retaliation. Lebanese Christians, represented by the Phalange Party, were against the Palestinian presence in Lebanon.

In 1975 Muslims and Christians began to fight each other. In addition, different Muslim groups began to fight one another and different Christian groups also began to fight one another. Each of the groups formed its own private army, or militia. In 1976 Syria, under President Hafez el-Assad, sent in troops as requested by the Arab League (an organization of Arab nations in the Middle East). Although Syria's purpose was to restore order, at various times the Syrians supported different militias in Lebanon. By 1990 there were 40,000 Syrian soldiers in Lebanon, and President Assad began to drop hints of incorporating Lebanon into a "greater Syria."

WORLD ISSUES

Terrorism

Other Middle Eastern nations, such as Iran and Libya, also supported one or more of the warring groups. Some of these groups, such as the Islamic Jihad, carried out terrorist activities against foreigners and other Lebanese in order to focus world attention on their political goals. These terrorist activities included taking citizens of France, the United States, Germany, and the Soviet Union as hostages and sometimes killing them, hijacking a TWA airliner, and killing American and French soldiers in a suicide bomb attack. Tragically, there was no single government in Lebanon acceptable to all its people and able to bring stability to the nation. The civil war resulted in separated enclaves (closed-in areas) in Beirut and elsewhere under the control of whichever militia proved to be the strongest. The Lebanese economy was ruined by the war.

Syria's role changed in 2005 when its forces withdrew from Lebanon. The withdrawal was mainly the result of the Cedar Revolution. This was the name given to a series of demonstrations following the assassination of Lebanese prime minister Rafik Hariri. Today, Lebanon has an elected president and a parliament. However, considerable political power is held by the party known as Hezbollah. (See page 179.) With members in the parliament as well as maintaining its own well-equipped military force, this Shi'ite extremist party is seen as a threat to Israel and to Lebanon's stability. It has been designated as a terrorist organization by several European nations, Israel, the United States, Gulf Arab countries including Saudi Arabia, and the Arab League.

War in Afghanistan (1979–1989). In 1979 a Marxist pro-Soviet government came to power in Afghanistan. It faced opposition by the majority of Afghan people, who began an armed struggle against it. The Soviet Union invaded Afghanistan, claiming that it was reacting to a request by the Afghan government. However, many observers believed that the real reasons for the Soviet actions were to gain access to oil and gas deposits in Afghanistan and possibly to reach through Iran into the Persian Gulf. The Soviets also may have been afraid of the impact of Islamic fundamentalism in Afghanistan and Iran on the Muslim communities in the Soviet Union. The Soviet military action was condemned by nations around the globe and caused controversy in the Soviet Union itself. The Afghan fighters, the Mujahideen, were supplied by the United States and were able to deny the Soviet Union a victory. In 1989 the Soviets retreated from Afghanistan with severe military and political losses.

Afghanistan was not to have political stability, however, as different religious factions fought each other for control. A coup in 1992 was one sign of this instability.

An Islamist government was established by the Taliban. Yet, they experienced difficulty in trying to put down other Afghan groups who were against them.

Operation Desert Storm—the Persian Gulf War of 1991. This war lasted from January 16, 1991, to February 27, 1991. The conflict, whose chief adversaries were Iraq and the United States, had its roots in the Iraqi invasion of Kuwait in August 1990. Iraq, which wanted to take over Kuwait's rich oil fields and have greater access to the Persian Gulf, would probably have then sought to take over Saudi Arabia. Such actions would have given Iraq control over 40 percent of the world's oil reserves. Saddam Hussein refused to leave Kuwait despite UN requests and its eventual imposition of trade sanctions and threat to use force.

As Iraqi troops killed, tortured, and raped thousands of Kuwaitis, destroyed much property, and were poised for an attack on Saudi Arabia, U.S. President George Bush assembled a multinational force of 500,000 troops from twenty-nine countries. This coalition, under the command of American General Norman Schwarzkopf and containing 450,000 U.S. troops, went into action in January under the authority of a UN Security Council Resolution when Iraq failed to meet a deadline to withdraw its troops from Kuwait. With the use of high-tech

WORLD ISSUES

War
and
Peace

GEOGRAPHY

Use of Geography

WORLD ISSUES

War
and
Peace

GEOGRAPHY

Use of Geography

WORLD ISSUES

Human
Rights

weaponry, the U.S.-led coalition defeated the Iraqis and freed Kuwait in five weeks.

The chief consequences of the war for the Middle East were as follows: (1) Saddam Hussein remained in power, still in possession of a large army and many weapons of mass destruction. He frequently failed to cooperate with the UN inspection teams that came to Iraq to check on his weapons program. (2) The ecology of the Persian Gulf area was severely upset by Iraqi soldiers. They burned oil wells and released great amounts of petroleum into the gulf waters. (3) A large split among Arabs occurred. Egypt, Saudi Arabia, Syria, and Kuwait sided with the United States. In support of Iraq, although not sending in any fighters, were Jordan, Yemen, Tunisia, Algeria, Yemen, and the PLO. (4) Kurdish people in Iraq were treated very harshly by Saddam Hussein. Their attempt to break away from Iraqi rule was suppressed, and many were killed or forced to become refugees. Thousands were given "safe haven" areas in northern Iraq under the protection of the United States and the United Nations.

WORLD ISSUES

Environmental
Concerns

The Future of the Kurds. As an ethnic group of approximately 24 million people, the Kurds have spread out during this century to various parts of Turkey, Iran, Iraq, and Syria. Often suffering persecution, they have long wanted to have a nation of their own—to be called Kurdistan. The greatest concentration of Kurds is in Turkey, whose military-dominated government has most frequently and violently persecuted them. This resulted in the creation of the PKK or Kurdistan Workers' Party, which worked to promote Kurdish independence and recruit guerrillas to fight the Turkish authorities. Turkey's poor human rights record with the Kurds has also resulted in international pressure on the Turkish government to reach a peaceful resolution of the conflict.

War in Iraq. In March 2003, the United States attacked Iraq. Although not supported by the United Nations, but with some help from coalition partners such as Great Britain, the United States was able to defeat the forces of Saddam Hussein in less than two months. The fighting was known as Operation Iraqi Freedom as well as the Second Gulf War. Saddam Hussein was arrested in December 2003 and put on trial in 2005. He was executed by hanging in 2006. The invasion of Iraq was said to be for several reasons: Iraq's possession of weapons of mass destruction (WMDs) and its refusal to comply with demands and requests made by UN inspectors over a number of years after the 1991 Persian Gulf War, Iraq's support of terrorist organizations such as Al-Qaeda and its leader Osama bin Laden, and Iraq's possible links to the September 11, 2001, murderous attack on the World Trade Center in New York. Yet, in the two years following Iraq's defeat, several investigations suggested doubt about the WMD issue as well as any link to Al-Qaeda and the 9/11 attack. During those years, the United States and its coalition partners faced increasing isolated fighting from small groups of insurgent Iraqis and other Arabs who slipped into Iraq and were known as jihadists. Although the United States lost more than 1,000 troops during this time, it tried to achieve unity among Iraq's different ethnic groups and to promote democratic reforms in the country as well as better living conditions. A new constitution was written and elections were held to select a governing body. Traditional tensions among Sunni Muslims, Shi'ite Muslims, and Kurds often made these goals difficult to achieve. In late 2005, the United States began to consider the start of gradual troop withdrawals. It was hoped that U.S.-trained Iraqi soldiers and police could help preserve safety and stability. Inside the United States, controversy grew about the American presence in Iraq. U.S. president George W. Bush maintained that the American role in Iraq was vital in the war against global terrorism. In 2007, a U.S. troop surge made an important impact on the war. Iraqi forces took over more of the fighting. Both the American and Iraqi governments finally reached an agreement on a withdrawal of U.S. combat forces by December 2011. President Obama announced that after this date, a few thousand U.S. troops would remain as advisers and trainers.

In 2014, Haider al-Abadi, who is friendly to the United States, became prime minister. In an attempt to support his government, and to help him fight against the threat from ISIS, the U.S. has sent over 5,000 troops to Iraq in the last three years. ISIS is a militant, terrorist, Islamist group that took over large portions of northwestern Iraq and eastern Syria. Also known as ISIL, Daesh, and the Islamic State, it wants to create a caliphate (a huge territory being ruled by a caliph under strict Islamic rules and guidelines).

War in Afghanistan—The American Involvement. The struggle against global terrorism was also a factor responsible for American forces fighting in Afghanistan. Control of that country by the Taliban, beginning in the 1990s, continued into the 2000s. As Islamic fundamentalists, the Taliban government claimed to be anti-American and protected the terrorist group

Al-Qaeda. Al-Qaeda was held responsible by the United States for the horrific aggression in New York, Washington, D.C., and Pennsylvania on September 11, 2001. The United States viewed this unprovoked aggression as an act of war and sent military forces to Afghanistan. The goal was to overthrow the Taliban (who had refused to shut down Al-Qaeda and give up its leader Osama bin Laden), destroy Al-Qaeda, and capture its leaders. With the defeat of the Taliban in December 2001, the United States helped anti-Taliban Afghans to create a government headed by Hamid Karzai. In 2004 Karzai was elected president and a new constitution was adopted. Nevertheless, scattered fighting and homicide bombings by Taliban terrorists continued. These were met by the remaining American forces, supported by troops from some NATO countries and from Pakistan. The hunt for Osama bin Laden continued, however, as he was thought to be hiding in the rugged mountainous region surrounding the Afghan-Pakistani border. Finally, in September 2011, U.S. Navy Seals found and executed bin Laden in a house in Pakistan.

Also in 2011, President Obama ordered the withdrawal of 10,000 troops from Afghanistan by the end of the year, and to withdraw another 23,000 by the summer of 2012, part of what he called "the beginning, but not the end, of our effort to wind down this war." He also noted that "by 2014, this process of transition will be complete, and the Afghan people will be responsible for their own security." The president said his announcement was a fulfillment of a commitment he made in December 2009 when he authorized a surge of 30,000 U.S. forces into Afghanistan.

Although American troops did leave in 2014, the situation in Afghanistan began to decline. Because of corruption, tribal differences among the Afghans, and their poorly skilled army, the Taliban was able to regain territory they had lost previously. U.S. Marines began to return to the country, reaching a total of 8,700 by the summer of 2017. Their goals did not include fighting, but rather mainly further training local forces and thus preventing the Taliban from gaining more land and power. Without setting any specific withdrawal deadline date, the U.S. hopes to persuade the Taliban to stop the war and settle for peace. Accordingly, President Donald Trump has considered sending a few more thousand troops to the region.

The Arab Spring of 2011. The Arab Spring of 2011, also known as the Arab Uprising and Arab Awakening, was a series of political revolts and changes that began in Tunisia. It soon continued to spread throughout the Arab world, from Algeria to Syria. These monumental changes, as with other major events and movements in world history, had causes that were both underlying and immediate. The basic causes were severe unemployment, government oppression, and corruption. The immediate cause was a tragedy in Tunisia in 2010, a tragedy that was to spark uprisings in other nations.

1. *Tunisia.* In December of that year, a street vendor was beaten up and humiliated by a government official for no good reason. Such an occurrence was frequent in that country. Consequently, the vendor set himself on fire and died. Protests and anti-government demonstrations erupted all over the nation. Later in the month, the president, a man who had held office for 23 years, fled the country.

2. *Egypt.* News about the rebellious situation in Tunisia reached Egypt and other Arab nations. In January 2011, thousands of Egyptians, mostly young people, gathered in Tahrir Square in Cairo. They were expressing their anger at the many years of harsh and brutal actions by the government against any political opposition. Their protests became violent at times, striking out at police forces, and reflecting resentment at rising food prices and a denial of basic freedoms. By using social networks such as Facebook and Twitter, angry citizens were able to contact other protesters and thus organize massive demonstrations in Cairo and elsewhere in the country. So effective were these actions that President Hosni Mubarak, who had been in power for 30 years, left the country. Ultimately he returned to Egypt and was put on trial. The chief charge was conspiracy to kill pro-democracy demonstrators whose protests drove him from office. The official death toll was 840.

3. *Syria.* In March 2011, anti-government riots and protests broke out in Syria. The reasons were similar to those that had led to unrest in Egypt. The target of the Syrian uprising was President Bashar al-Assad and his family's repressive 40 years in power. His government's response to the demonstrations was violent and lethal. In Damascus and other cities, Syrian army units fired on unarmed civilians, including women, the elderly, and children. Other crimes included torture and forced disappearances. A rebel group, known as the Free Syrian army, has fought to overthrow Assad. It has the backing of the United States, which has provided air support as well as the training of soldiers. The U.S. is also concerned with halting the spread of ISIS in Syria, even though that group is against Assad. Assad has had military assistance from Russia, Iran, and Hezbollah (an Iranian-supported terrorist militia from Lebanon). The

fighting among all these forces, in what can be called a Syrian civil war, has had a terrible impact upon the civilian population. By 2017, estimates were that over 400,000 people had been killed while almost 5 million had fled as refugees.

4. *Libya*. A movement against the 42 years of harsh dictatorial rule by Colonel Muammar al-Qaddafi began in February 2011. Protesters took up arms and were joined by many soldiers of Libya's armed forces. Libyans who were loyal to Qaddafi fought back. The result was a fierce civil war. In March, air strikes against Qaddafi and his supporters, as authorized by the UN Security Council, were made by European and American warplanes. In October, Libyan rebels tracked down Qaddafi and killed him.

5. *Other Arab nations*. From 2011 onward, protests also occurred in Algeria, Bahrain, Jordan, Morocco, Oman, Saudi Arabia, and Yemen. Except for Yemen, none of these caused as much bloodshed or change as was true in Tunisia, Egypt, Syria, and Libya. Yet, the future political situation in these four nations, as well as the rest of the Arab world, remains uncertain. Possibilities include open elections and other democratic reforms, military dictatorship, control by Islamic extremists, and a return to one-party rule. Whether these or any other developments take place in the next few years, it is clear that 2011 will have proven to be a critical moment in the history of the Middle East.

Current Economic Issues

1. Overpopulation and a growth in cities have put a strain on the economy in some areas. People are demanding that their governments do more to improve living standards. These demands are part of the movement described as a "revolution of rising expectations." They are also some of the reasons for the 2011 protests known as the "Arab Spring."

2. Extensive spending on military weapons, especially in Libya, Egypt, Syria, Iran, and Iraq, has reduced funds needed for economic and social development.

3. Greater regional cooperation could help the nations of the Middle East in finding solutions to common problems. For example, the removal of political barriers between Israel and the Muslim majority nations, as well as barriers between the Muslim nations themselves, could lead to increased trade, reduction of arms spending, and improved desalinization projects. (These projects would make seawater drinkable by removing the salt content.) Desalinization is one method used by Israel to achieve water self-sufficiency. This accomplishment is

all the more remarkable given the fact the land is over 50% desert. Indeed, Israel even sells water to Jordan and the Palestinian Authority.

4. Arab nations such as Saudi Arabia are wealthy from money ("petrodollars") paid to them for their vast amounts of oil. They dominate OPEC (Organization of the Petroleum Exporting Countries), which attempts to exercise some control over the global oil industry. Changes in world oil prices, as well as searches for alternative sources of energy, can affect the incomes of these nations.

5. Energy is also an issue that concerns Turkey's GAP Project. This is a massive hydroelectric plan that would see the construction of 22 dams on the watershed of the Tigris and Euphrates Rivers, whose sources are in Turkey.

6. Israel's economy had improved greatly by the early 2000s, particularly with the growth of high-tech industries. Of significance has been the emigration of Jews from the former Soviet Union, many of whom are highly skilled engineers and scientists. This growth, from what was once an agricultural-based economy, has been described as progressing from "Jaffa to Java" (Jaffa oranges to a computer program).

7. Much of the Arab world faces major challenges, as noted in the United Nations' Arab Human Development Report. Produced in 2005 by a group of Arab scholars led by Egypt, the report concluded that the Arab people suffer from three severe problems: a lack of freedom, a deficit of knowledge, and a lack of women's empowerment.

8. In the last few years, the discovery was made of a potentially abundant source of natural gas in the eastern Mediterranean Sea. Israel, Lebanon, and Turkey, along with Greece and Cyprus, have expressed great interest in developing this source.

Part E: South Asia and Southeast Asia

ECONOMIC STRUCTURE OF SOUTH ASIA

Agriculture

In recent decades, food production in India has increased. Near self-sufficiency has been achieved despite some bad monsoon years. Crop production focuses mainly on rice, wheat, cotton, tea, jute, and sugarcane.

GLOBAL
CONCEPTS

Technology

CONCEPTS
GLOBAL

Much of this agricultural development has resulted from the Green Revolution, the use of modern science and technology to improve agricultural productivity. Examples of modern technology include laboratory-produced fertilizers, insecticides, and improved seeds, which are high-yielding and drought-resistant. A leading figure in this work has been the American agronomist (plant scientist) Dr. Norman Borlaugh (winner of a Nobel Peace Prize in 1970). Critics, however, have noted some negative aspects of the Green Revolution:

1. Resistance among farmers to new planting and landholding patterns.

2. Higher financial costs when using new technology and machinery (more readily used by "agribusiness," or large landholders, rather than small farmers).

3. Need for better nationwide infrastructure, such as storage facilities, dams, and highways.

4. The taste of the food produced is different from that of traditional crops.

WORLD ISSUES

Economic
Growth and
Development

WORLD ISSUES

Environmental
Concerns

Industrial Production

India has some of the world's largest steel mills and is a major producer of bauxite (aluminum ore). Other major industrial products include textiles, machinery, cement, and scientific instruments. Recently, Indian scientists have made advances in nuclear energy and in developing space satellites. India is the most industrially advanced nation on the subcontinent and has one of the world's ten highest GNPs. Like all industrialized societies around the globe, India must find ways of coping with the environmental consequences of industrialization. The massive accidental release of poisonous pesticides at the Union Carbide facility in Bhopal in 1984 caused nearly 4,000 deaths and more than a half million injuries, according to government reports. The Taj Mahal, a mausoleum built of white marble by an Indian emperor in the 17th century, is one of India's historical treasures and most visited tourist attractions. Dust and fossil fuel deposits are progressively discoloring its surface, including the intricately designed and inset semiprecious stones.

Economic Conditions: Decision Making and Planning

Since independence, India has adopted elements of both a free enterprise/capitalist system and a socialist system. This combination is called a mixed economy. Although the government controls certain parts of the economy, it tries to develop strategies to benefit all parts. Since 1947, this process has been based on a series of twelve national economic programs called Five-Year Plans. Directed from the central government in Delhi, overall objectives of these plans included economic growth through the modernization of agriculture and industry, full employment to reduce poverty and inequality in the distribution of income and wealth, and India's economic self-reliance. Key choices involve funds for items such as heavy industry, exportable goods, small-scale cottage industries, and village development schemes. Decision makers must keep in mind two facts about India's population:

1. More than 75 percent of the people live in villages.

2. Population growth can limit economic gains. Though the rate of growth is declining, India's population passed 1.3 billion in 2017. Projections indicate that India will surpass China as the world's most populous nation by 2023.

Although the standard of living in India and its neighboring countries has generally improved since the departure of the British, severe poverty and malnutrition still exist in many areas. These features are evident in such large cities as Calcutta as well as in the villages.

The attempts by nations such as India to raise sharply the standard of living for all citizens, as well as promote economic growth, have necessitated borrowing money from overseas and importing needed goods. Consequently, India continues to face a large foreign debt, which has increased steadily since 1990, and a trade imbalance (where the value of imports exceeds that of exports).

Since the 1990s, India has made significant moves to boost its economy. It has attracted Western support by approving

WORLD ISSUES

Determination of Political and Economic Systems

more foreign investment projects. It privatized some state-controlled companies, cut interest rates, and raised the ceiling on executive pay. The last move was designed to induce talented Indian managers to stay in India, and thereby reduce India's "brain drain" (migration by one nation's skilled and educated people to another nation, where they hope to gain better positions and more money). Frequent scandals and corruption involving some businesspeople and government officials and a vast bureaucracy (large number of offices where permission is needed for commercial ventures) further complicate attempts to achieve economic progress. One economist has commented on how this "license-permit-raj" system can slow down investment and invite bribery.

Since the late 1980s successive Indian administrations have focused on encouraging economic reform and foreign investment, bringing the nation's economy more extensively into the network of world trade. The growing urban middle class provides a large, skilled workforce, fostering growth in fields like information technology and software development in areas like Bangalore's "Silicon Valley," making India a popular choice for international companies seeking to outsource work. All this has turned India's stock market into one of the world's fastest rising indicators of economic progress.

Thus, only a few years after being considered a near "basket case," India occupies an increasingly influential role in the global economy. Severe problems still exist—poverty, ethnic conflict, inequality, environmental degradation, lagging productivity, high tariffs—and continue to hinder improvements in the standard of living for millions.

Each of India's neighboring nations has its own set of strengths and problems. Internal social and political conflict can short-circuit productive economic decision making. Over 40 percent of Pakistan's labor force is employed in agriculture—the nation is a major exporter of rice, for instance. Its textile industry is a major source of foreign exchange. Other significant industrial products include construction materials, pharmaceuticals, and fertilizer. The country is dependent on imports for many other manufactured goods as well as petroleum products. Significant increases in energy output based on hydroelectric and thermal power have contributed to a more useful and efficient infrastructure. The economy of Sri Lanka, a nation recovering from a long and bloody civil war, is built upon agriculture and tourism. Textiles and apparel, tea and spices, precious gems, and rubber products are among its exports. Impoverished Bangladesh is another agriculture-dependent nation. Principal products are rice, jute, tea, wheat, sugarcane, and tobacco. Most heavy industrial and other manufactured goods must be imported.

Political Structure in India

India has existed since independence as the world's largest democracy. It has a parliamentary form of government similar to that of Britain but different from that of the United States.

India has had several important political leaders.

1. Jawaharlal Nehru, the first prime minister (1947–1964). Nehru brought some stability to the new nation and tried to achieve a sense of "unity in diversity." He hoped to build a spirit of nationalism, in spite of the many differences among India's population, including religion, language, and varying loyalties to local states and regions.

2. Indira Gandhi, prime minister (1966–1977, 1980–1984). Mrs. Gandhi, the daughter of Nehru, held power longer than any Indian leader. Although popular when she first took office, she gradually began to govern with an "iron fist" in order to pursue her policies concerning economics, birth control, and other issues. Her proclamation of a "state of emergency" in the 1970s was seen as harming India's democracy and led to her downfall in the 1977 elections. Her successors proved unable to achieve their goals and Mrs. Gandhi returned to power in 1980, faced with severe internal problems such as persistent poverty and the desire by Sikhs to have their own nation in the Punjab region. Her strong actions against Sikh militants provoked a harsh reaction and led to her assassination by two Sikhs in 1984.

3. Rajiv Gandhi, prime minister (1984–1989). Indira Gandhi's son, Rajiv, tried to obtain foreign help for India in meetings with American President Reagan and Soviet Premier Gorbachëv. Although he began his term of office amid much sympathy due to his mother's death, Rajiv proved to be a weak and unpopular leader. He made little progress in solving domestic problems (poverty, Sikh dissension). An Indian politician in an opposition party claimed that the mood of the people was "one of extreme disenchantment." Consequently, in the elections of November 1989, Gandhi and his Congress Party were voted out of office.

4. Vishwanath Pratap Singh, prime minister (1989–1990). V. P. Singh's Janata Dal Party won 141 of the 525 seats up for election in the Lok Sabha in 1989. Other parties supported the Janata Dal and joined with it to form a coalition (a combination formed of different political parties to run a government when no single party has a majority of seats). Singh found it very hard to keep this coalition together. One reason was his

GLOBAL CONCEPTS
Political Systems
CONCEPTS GLOBAL

GLOBAL CONCEPTS
Power
CONCEPTS GLOBAL

GEOGRAPHY

Human Systems

A COMPARISON OF TWO DEMOCRACIES

	United States	India
Basic form	Federal republic; one central government and 50 state governments	Federal republic; one central government and 17 state governments
Legislature	A bicameral system: Congress consists of the Senate and House of Representatives	A bicameral system: Parliament is composed of the Council of States (Rajya Sabha) and House of the People (Lok Sabha)
Executive	A president indirectly elected by the public (presidential form)	A prime minister elected by the legislature (parliamentary form; the prime minister usually is head of the majority party in the Parliament)
Governing document	Constitution of 1787 with subsequent amendments	Constitution of 1950 with subsequent amendments
	Both documents describe the political structure, protect civil rights and liberties, and were influenced by British legal traditions.	
Political parties	Two main parties: Democrat and Republican	Several parties: Congress, Janata Dal, Bharatiya Janata

support of a report recommending that up to 49 percent of jobs in government and public works be reserved for untouchables and members of low-ranking castes. Singh's decision led to riots and to the withdrawal of the BJP (Bharatiya Janata Party), a right-wing party supported mostly by upper-caste Hindus. As opposition to Singh increased, the coalition government fell apart and new elections were scheduled for 1991.

5. P. V. Narasimha Rao, prime minister (1991–1996). Although six political parties entered the 1991 elections, most people believed that the Congress Party would emerge as the winner, with its leader, Rajiv Gandhi, regaining the prime minister post. However, Gandhi was assassinated in May 1991. The Congress Party won the election and P. V. Narasimha Rao became prime minister. However, since the Congress Party did not win a majority of seats, Rao had to form a coalition government to run the country. The government made some progress in boosting India's economy by creating more of a free market system.

6. By 1996 Rao's Congress Party, dominant for more than 40 years, had proven unable to govern effectively. After two years of a chaotic coalition, the strongly Hindu-supported Bharatiya Janata Party (BJP), promoting conservative social and economic ideas and nationalism, won the election. Atal Behari Vajpayee, the new prime minister, began his term in office by flexing India's military muscle. In 1998, India conducted nuclear tests, shocking and surprising the world. Vajpayee's popularity and the BJP's prestige rose meteorically, even though India received immense criticism and a decline in foreign investment and trade occurred. His government also fostered modernization of and spending on defense and introduced many important economic reforms, encouraging the private sector and foreign investment. Early in the new century these reforms helped to accelerate GDP growth at record levels. The modernization of public and industrial infrastructures, job creation, and a vigorous high-tech industry raised India's international profile and prestige. Good crop harvests, expanded irrigation and housing programs, and strong industrial expansion increased the confidence of Indians and outside investors alike.

Not all activities of the BJP administration were deemed positive. Vajpayee and his government angered many unionized workers groups and public employees with an aggressive campaign of privatization of government corporations. The BJP was also accused of "Hinduizing" the official state educational system and curriculum. The murder of Christian missionaries by Hindu fundamentalists seemed to some to signal government laxness on the issue of religious extremism. In 2001 communal violence between Hindus and Muslims killed thousands over the issue of a holy place in Northern India. After a terrorist attack on the Parliament building in Delhi, Parliament passed the Prevention of Terrorism Act, allowing police and security forces extraordinary powers to detain and question suspects for indefinite periods and expanding government authority over freedom of speech, assembly, and other fundamental liberties. Human rights activists, minority rights groups, the Congress Party, and others strongly attacked it as a rash, discriminatory, totalitarian law.

7. In India's 2004 elections, the BJP was ousted by a comeback of both the Congress Party and its Gandhi "dynasty" under the leadership of the Italian-born widow of former Prime Minister Rajiv Gandhi. Sonia Gandhi, however, declined the prime ministership, instead, asking former Finance Minister Manmohan Singh to lead the new government. As a rather low-key politician, Singh's image was "squeaky clean" and he was

a widely respected economist. He has been credited by many with overseeing the beginnings of India's early 1990s economic liberalization that averted a major financial crisis. Singh and the Congress Party had campaigned on a platform of creating jobs in government-owned companies. The election result created optimism that the pace and nature of reforms would continue and even increase.

Singh pursued an aggressively positive foreign policy, exchanging visits with leaders of China, Afghanistan, and the United States in addition to actively participating in and frequently serving in informal leadership roles in international economic summit meetings.

In 2007 India celebrated the sixtieth anniversary of its independence from Britain. That same year India experienced its highest ever economic growth rate, evidence of its role as an emerging productive and commercial power. The Singh government, reelected in 2009, continued to pursue globalization of the economy, promoting India's vast labor force as a tool for increasing production of export goods to help relieve the country's widespread poverty. Grass roots efforts included the building of numerous new higher-educational institutions in the technical and management sectors, establishment of extensive rural health and employment initiatives, and providing broadened opportunities for "disadvantaged classes" such as untouchables (officially referred to as Scheduled Castes).

India's political pendulum swung away from the Congress Party and the influence of the Nehru–Gandhi "dynasty" once again in 2014. A resurgence of fervent Hindu nationalism swept Narendra Modi to the office of prime minister in the parliamentary election. For the first time in decades, one party, the Bharatiya Janata Party (BJP), won an absolute ruling majority in the Lok Sabha, India's lower parliamentary chamber. Basing his appeal on his record of promoting economic success as leader of the state of Gujarat, Modi appealed to the electorate's disgust with the slow economic growth, the rampant corruption, and the crumbling infrastructure with a very tech-savvy campaign (even using holography) directed especially at the nation's opportunity-seeking younger voters. Nevertheless, the new government worried many voters because of the prime minister's perceived "soft" stance on anti-Muslim violence. Initially, robust economic growth, an increase in foreign investments in some areas, and tax code reform resulted in increased confidence in India's economy. A chaotic attempt to stifle India's illegal "black economy" of money hoarding, tax evasion, and counterfeiting, by temporarily withdrawing all large denominations of paper money from circulation in 2016, drew widespread criticism. Statistics seemed to indicate an economic slowdown at least in the short term (through mid-2017) although Modi's government and some analysts foresaw a sensible adjustment and longer-term growth.

Political Structure in Pakistan and Bangladesh

Although Pakistan today can be described as a parliamentary democracy with a constitution, its first years after partition were very unstable with frequent instances of divisiveness and "strong-man" rule in Pakistan since independence in 1947.

Mohammed Ali Jinnah's death in 1948 was a severe blow to the young nation. The ineffective political struggles for power by civilians ended when the military suspended the constitution in 1958 and declared martial law. General Mohammed Ayub Khan ruled the country until 1969. Another example of dictatorial rule by the military occurred in 1977, when General Mohammed Zia took power away from the civilian-elected prime minister, Zulfikar Ali Bhutto. General Zia's rule ended with his death in a plane crash in August 1988. In that year, voters put into power the Pakistan People's Party and its leader, Benazir Bhutto. As the daughter of a former prime minister, Bhutto became the second woman after India's Indira Gandhi to head a government on the subcontinent and at that time was the only woman ever to govern a Muslim nation. In August 1990 the president of Pakistan dismissed the government of Bhutto, accusing it of corruption and nepotism (favoring relatives for jobs). Bhutto claimed, however, that democratic reforms she tried to institute had angered many army officials. It was they who supposedly caused her downfall.

In October 1990 Mian Nawaz Sharif became prime minister of Pakistan. He helped to boost the nation's economy but was unsuccessful in foreign dealings with India and the United States. Antigovernment demonstrations increased, leading to new elections in 1993, and Benazir Bhutto returned to power as prime minister. Her chief problems involved poverty, corruption, education, and Islamic fundamentalism. Eventually, Sharif returned to power. Sharif himself was deposed in a military coup in 1999. Leader of the coup and subsequently self-appointed president was Army General Pervez Musharraf. Considered a moderate leader by Western governments, Musharraf spoke of "enlightened moderation" and criticized the idea of the inevitability of a "clash of civilizations" between the Islamic and Western worlds. After the 9/11 attacks and the American ouster of the Taliban in Afghanistan, he was forced to strike a balance between Islamic fundamentalists in Pakistan

WORLD ISSUES

Determination of Political and Economic Systems

GLOBAL CONCEPTS

Power

CONCEPTS GLOBAL

197

and Western governments pressuring him to aid in the "war on terror." He survived a number of assassination attempts and polls seemed to confirm his popularity among Pakistan's population. Criticism from international sources and domestic women's organizations has been directed against the government's perceived failure to deal with the issue of violence against women, particularly gang rapes and so-called honor killings of women and girls who do not adhere to strict social conventions. The Musharraf administration failed to repeal the harsh Islamic penal code in which a woman's testimony is weighed at half that of a man. Women's rights continue to be an issue in Pakistan.

The return of the popular Benazir Bhutto to Pakistan in 2007 created another period of political turmoil. In spite of death threats from radical Islamists she planned to campaign for the election scheduled for January 2008. Enthusiastic crowds and an attempted assassination greeted her arrival—she survived but over a hundred in the crowd were killed. A second suicide bomber's attempt succeeded, however, and fomented further political instability. Victory by her Pakistan Peoples Party in the 2008 election became her legacy, as her husband Asif Ali Zardari became president. The early years of Zardari's presidency proved turbulent—allegations of corruption and favoritism, the fragility of his ruling coalition, and the issuance of an arrest warrant for former president Musharraf, accused of involvement in the assassination of Bhutto. Perhaps most damaging were criticisms that his administration did not prevent the American raid and capture of Osama bin Laden in 2011.

As the 21st century headed into its second decade, religiously based disputes and violence continued to bedevil Pakistani politics and life. Suicide bombings and political killings by Muslim militants included assassinations of politicians and targeting of businesses, commercial areas, schools, and universities. Radical Islamists targeted those they considered "blasphemers," including Christians, Hindus, and activist women. In one instance of sectarian violence, Taliban gunmen seriously injured 14-year-old campaigner for girls' rights, Malala Yousafzai, whom they accused of "promoting secularism." Yousafzai's 2012 ordeal turned into an ironic "black eye" for her attackers, sparking a wave of anger and disgust with the militants, both within Pakistan and abroad. She has become an international spokesperson for women's rights and education and a celebrated activist and author. Among her many awards, she won a share of the 2014 Nobel Peace Prize for her struggle against the suppression of women, children, and young people.

As in other South Asian nations and elsewhere, corruption in government and business has led to controversy, especially over attempts to deal with prosecutions of prominent politicians, such as former president and military strongman General Pervez Musharraf, and even Prime Minister Raja Pervez Ashraf. Anti-government protests over corruption and sectarian violence in the capital of Islamabad prompted the arrest of dozens of activists in 2014. By 2017, Islamic State (ISIS) terrorism added to Pakistan's reign of violence—a suicide bombing killed nearly 90 people at a religious shrine.

Bangladesh came into existence in 1971. Previously it had been the part of Pakistan known as East Pakistan. It was separated from the western part of Pakistan by 1,000 miles. Political, religious, and economic tensions led to a rebellion by East Pakistan in 1971. A war broke out in which India sided with the East Pakistanis. By December the rebellion was a success, and the nation of Bangladesh was declared.

Bangladesh's first prime minister, Sheik Mujibur Rahman, had led the struggle for independence. His inability to deal with food riots and a growing population as well as a growing perception of corruption were some of the reasons for his assassination. After his death, the country experienced several coups. One of these was led by Lt. General Hussain Mohammed Ershad, who ruled as a military dictator from 1982 to 1990. His resignation was brought on by a series of protests and demonstrations and was followed by elections in February 1991. Begum Khaleda Zia, only the second woman to rule a Muslim nation, became prime minister, as her BNP party (Bangladesh Nationalist Party) emerged victorious. A change in the nation's constitution gave her greater power than that of any former prime minister. After being out of office as a result of losing in 1996, the BNP won the 2001 election with a two-thirds majority and Khaleda Zia was once again sworn in as the prime minister. Her administration focused on education, introducing compulsory free primary education, free education for girls up to the tenth grade, stipends for female students, and food for education programs. Corruption issues dogged Khaleda Zia's second term and continued after she stepped down in 2006. Both she and her opponent, Sheikh Hasina Wazed, daughter of Sheikh Mujibur Rahman and leader of the Awami League Party, spent time in jail on corruption charges. In the 2008 election following their release, Hasina became prime minister; her government focused on bringing to justice those involved in her father's 1975 assassination and trying war crimes cases from the 1971 independence struggle. After a brief period out of

GLOBAL
CONCEPTS

Change

CONCEPTS
GLOBAL

GEOGRAPHY

Use of Geography

office, Sheikh Hasina became prime minister again, ushering in a period of relatively high economic growth. Her government put down an attempted coup by military officers in 2012, but the next two years saw increasingly widespread political unrest and violence in the form of strikes, riots, and acts of vandalism, which led to massive property damages, economic losses, and the deaths of many ordinary citizens. In the election of 2014, voters faced harassment, physical violence, and a mass boycott of Hasina's Awami League opponents. Her electoral victory seemed to restore political stability. Unfortunately, Islamist extremism, perhaps fomented or at least inspired by ISIS, visited Bangladesh in the form of massacres in an upscale area of the capital, Dhaka, and another at a massive religious gathering.

The constant political turmoil of the first 41 years of Bangladesh's existence has had little bearing on the nation's many basic handicaps. There are enormous problems in governing a country plagued by overpopulation, severe natural diasters such as floods, and a declining world market for jute—the country's chief product.

GEOGRAPHY

Use of Geography

Current Political Issues in South Asia

Separatist (secessionist) movements were the most dangerous political issues facing India and Sri Lanka in the 1990s. Different groups in both nations have grievances against the national governments and want to break away.

GLOBAL CONCEPTS

Identity

CONCEPTS GLOBAL

In India's Punjab state, Sikhs wanted to form their own nation—Khalistan. Resentment against the central government in New Delhi was fueled in 1984 when Mrs. Gandhi sent troops to attack Sikh militant separatists in the Golden Temple at Amritsar, the holiest shrine to Sikhs. Continued violence by both Sikh terrorists and government forces resulted in many deaths, with over 5,000 people killed in 1991. With an increased police and military presence by the Indian government and a diminished desire for independence, the Sikh rebellion seemed to be over by 1994.

GLOBAL CONCEPTS

Diversity

CONCEPTS GLOBAL

India was also concerned about growing unrest by the Muslim majority in the northern state of Kashmir. Kashmir is the larger part of an area that was taken over by India after the 1947 partition. However, Pakistan has challenged India's claims to the state, especially as Muslims are in the majority. Early in 1990, efforts by the Jammu and the Kashmir Liberation Front to secede from India led to riots and violence. India has claimed that Pakistan has been behind these activities. India has also been bothered by anti-government activity by tribal groups, such as the Assamese in the northeast. In the

GEOGRAPHY

Human Systems

late 1990s, India and Pakistan exchanged artillery fire in the area. An infiltration of Islamic militants and a renewed terrorism campaign has continued to increase since 2009.

In 2016, Indian security forces killed the leader of a Kashmiri Muslim activist (or terrorist) group, sparking province-wide protests and attacks on security forces and public properties. Police and Indian paramilitary forces used pellet guns, tear gas shells, rubber bullets, and assault rifles, resulting in the deaths of more than 90 civilians, with over 15,000 civilians and 4,000 security personnel injured. Fractious relations between the Indian and Pakistani governments remain fixed in their policies regarding possession of Kashmir, with no resolution in sight.

In Sri Lanka, the Tamil people, who are of Indian origin, want to have their own state. From the 1970s into the present century, the Sri Lankan government has had difficulty putting down terrorist actions by Tamils against members of the majority Sinhalese community. Many Sri Lankans think that people in South India helped the terrorists. The Colombo government nevertheless welcomed the presence of Indian troops to help keep the peace from 1987 to 1989. The campaign against the Sri Lankan military and leadership, as well as the Indian government, by the insurgent group, the Tamil Tigers, was highlighted by the suicide-bomber assassinations of a Sri Lankan president and an Indian prime minister. Through the late 1990s government troops slowly pushed the Tigers into smaller areas in the north. A 2001 cease-fire and a period of sporadic negotiations ended with the election of a new Sri Lankan government in 2006, as it undertook a renewed campaign to eliminate the separatists. By 2009, the remnant of the Tamil Tigers either surrendered or fled the country, and by 2011, most of the former insurgents had been "reintegrated" into Sri Lankan society.

Communalism (ethnic tension between Hindus and Muslims) has been a frequent source of irritation in India. Part of this tension stems from the partition of the subcontinent in 1947. Much bloodshed broke out between the two groups, as some Muslims in India wished to migrate to Pakistan, while some Hindus in Pakistan wished to migrate to India. Religious differences between the two groups have been another source of friction. The worst case of communalism in recent years occurred in late 1992 and early 1993, and stemmed from an incident in Ayodhya. Located in north India, this site contained a mosque built in the 16th century by a Mughal ruler. Hindus have claimed, however, that the site is the birthplace of Lord Rama and that the mosque should be replaced with a Hindu temple. After unsuccessful marches on the site in 1989 and 1990, Hindu extremists tore

WORLD ISSUES

Terrorism

WORLD ISSUES

Politics and
Economic
Refugees

down the mosque in 1992. This led to terrible Hindu-Muslim riots in Bombay and elsewhere in India. Within two months over 3,000 people had been killed and many homes had been destroyed. Massive violence again erupted relative to this issue in 2001 and 2002.

In 2006, a three-day terrorist rampage of gun battles and bombings in the western Indian port of Mumbai was carried out by Islamist militants. Allegations that the perpetrators had received support from elements of the Pakistani security agency further soured relations.

Wars have been fought three times between India and Pakistan. While the two nations are now at peace, it remains to be seen whether they can permanently overcome problems over borders, distrust, communalism, and nuclear arms. The growth and testing of nuclear weapons by both India and Pakistan in 1999 made for a very tense situation. Each nation felt it had to maintain a strong military stance. Shortly thereafter, the two nations initiated a peace process to permanently resolve the dispute over Kashmir and other conflicts, symbolized by the opening of a first-ever bus service between the Indian capital of Delhi and Lahore in Eastern Pakistan.

During the Cold War between the United States and the Soviet Union, India tried to follow a policy of nonalignment. In doing so, India hoped to establish itself as a leader of the so-called Third World nations. This policy has come into question, however, since India fought a war with China over a border dispute and had been more friendly toward the former Soviet Union than toward the United States. India was not as alarmed as was Pakistan during 1979–1989, when Russian soldiers were fighting rebels in Afghanistan. Today, however, with the Soviet Union gone, India realizes the importance of establishing better relations with the United States.

GEOGRAPHY

Use of Geography

The history of South Asia has been carved by its native inhabitants as well as by outsiders. The British dream of having the colony of India become one united nation upon independence did not materialize. The internal (national) and external (international) problems facing South Asian nations will take time to overcome. It should be remembered, nevertheless, that they have done much to improve themselves since independence.

ECONOMIC STRUCTURE OF SOUTHEAST ASIA

Agriculture

Due to the amount of rainfall and kind of soil, rice is the major crop grown in Southeast Asia. For many years, in fact, Myanmar was the world's largest exporter of rice. From the rich forest lands come teak and ebony. Farming is the occupation of well over half the people of the region. Although famine has never been a problem, nations of the region still look for ways to increase food production. Increases can come from using more modern farming methods as well as from the Green Revolution. Much hope also rests with the Mekong River development project. This project includes the construction of several dams along the Mekong River. It is expected that these dams will control floods, provide water for irrigation, and be a source of electricity.

GLOBAL CONCEPTS

Environment

CONCEPTS GLOBAL

GEOGRAPHY

Human Systems

Industrial Production

The region is rich in natural resources. Chief among these are tin, iron ore, and petroleum. Several nations (Brunei, Indonesia, and Malaysia) have significant reserves of oil and natural gas; petroleum and petrochemical products aid in the economic development of these nations. In these countries and others, particularly Thailand, Singapore, and the Philippines, the textile (clothing), plastics, electronics, and even automotive (Thailand has begun manufacturing vehicles) industries promote modernization and help raise skill and educational levels. These manufacturing sectors, along with more traditional industries based on renewable resources in agriculture (rubber, sugarcane, lumber) and aquaculture (fishing), have enhanced the standing of Southeast Asian countries in the world economy. Expansion of tourism, given the region's natural features and historic sites, has also served to generate income.

WORLD ISSUES

Economic
Growth and
Development

These nations, along with several other strong Asian economies, have been referred to as "Economic Tigers," reflecting their rapidly growing industrial and export sectors and increasingly significant role in world trade. Growth rates in these "Tiger" economies reached 6 percent from the 1960s through the 1990s, raising standards of living but creating new issues for their governments to deal with. Nations depending on only a few export products are vulnerable to changes in global demand, overuse of agricultural land, and careless industrial development causing degradation of the environment. Political and social issues can arise over competing land use demands.

ASEAN

The Association of Southeast Asian Nations was formed in 1967 to promote cooperative economic advancement. It seeks to increase exports and gain more help from nations such as Japan.

Economic Decision Making

Different economic systems are found in the countries of Southeast Asia. Capitalist features predominate in early members Singapore, Thailand, Brunei, Indonesia, Malaysia, and the Philippines. Greater centralized control of the economy was found in countries admitted in the 1990s: Myanmar, Laos, Cambodia, and Vietnam.

In 2004, ASEAN nations signed an accord with China aimed at creating the world's largest free trade area by 2010. The agreement seemed to signal ASEAN's intention to create a unified economy similar to the European Union. It also gave China access to new markets that would reduce, and possibly eventually challenge, the influence of the United States in Asia. Japan has also explored "heightened partnerships" with ASEAN and its member nations in trade, investment, and disaster prevention and relief.

In 2015, the ten member nations initiated the ASEAN Economic Community (AEC) with the goal of transforming the area into a single economy, making it the fourth-largest in the world. Among the projected benefits are:

- The formation of a single market with over 600 million potential customers
- Promoting lower trade barriers and higher trade amounts
- Attracting foreign investment
- Job creation
- Boosting household income
- Developing a larger middle class
- Increasing consumption of goods and services

The middle years of the 21st century's second decade featured examples of growth throughout the region. In Laos, investments in the energy-production sector fueled growth figures in the 7 percent range. The Philippine economy benefited from tax reform and infrastructure spending. Foreign investment in Cambodia's clothing industry and construction projects created jobs. A young workforce, investment in natural resources, and pro-business government policies were bringing Myanmar increasingly into the region's economic web.

Political Developments

Nationalistic, anticolonial movements began in Southeast Asia in the 19th century and gained strength after World War II. The war was of importance for these nationalistic movements for several reasons: (1) Between 1942 and 1945, the European colonial powers lost much of their territorial control to the Japanese. (2) The Japanese, who took over the colonies, were hated as much as the European colonial powers, and the Southeast Asian people rose up to fight for independence. (3) At the war's end, some of the former European colonial powers took back control of their colonies, but they were weary and drained from the war. They sought to comply with the aims of the United Nations charter, and therefore were willing to grant independence. (4) Other colonial powers who took back control of their former colonies were unwilling to grant independence, and they were confronted by native leaders who had fought against the Japanese.

A peaceful transition to independence occurred in these nations: Myanmar (then Burma), Malaysia, Singapore, and Brunei—from England; and the Philippines—from the United States. (The United States gained control from Spain in 1898, after the Spanish-American War.)

Bloody transitions to independence occurred in Indonesia, Cambodia, Laos, and North and South Vietnam. Indonesia, under the nationalist leader Ahmed Sukarno, fought against the Dutch from 1945 to 1949. Cambodia, Laos, and North and South Vietnam were created in 1954, after these nations fought the French for eight years. The major forces defeating France were the Vietnamese Communists, led by Ho Chi Minh. After the French defeat in the battle at Dien Bien Phu, the Geneva Accords were signed. They brought the war to an end and provided for French withdrawal from Indochina.

In the early 1960s fighting broke out in South Vietnam, as North Vietnam attempted to establish one unified nation of Vietnam. Fighting against the South Vietnamese government were the Viet Cong (South Vietnamese Communists) and ultimately the army of North Vietnam. The Viet Cong and North Vietnamese received material assistance from China and the Soviet Union. South Vietnam received help from the United States in the form of material as well as over 500,000 combat troops. In 1973 President Richard Nixon withdrew U.S. forces in the hope that both North and South Vietnam could work out their differences peacefully. The South Vietnamese government, under President Nguyen Van Thieu, grew weak and very unpopular. Fighting resumed, resulting in a North Vietnamese takeover in

1975 and the proclamation in 1976 of a united country. Hanoi became the country's capital, while Saigon, the former capital of South Vietnam, had its name changed to Ho Chi Minh City.

Independence Period (1963–Present)

The political structures that have evolved since independence reflect the varied backgrounds of the nations in Southeast Asia. Therefore, it is not surprising to find different forms of government.

Nation	Form of Government	Current Leader*
Brunei	Monarchy	Sultan Sir Hassanal Bolkiah
Cambodia	Constitutional monarchy	King Norodom Sihamoni; Prime Minister Hun Sen
Indonesia	Republic	President Joko Widodo
Laos	Communist state	President Bounnyang Vorachit
Malaysia	Constitutional monarchy	Prime Minister Najib Razak
Myanmar (Burma)	Parliamentary republic	President Htin Kyaw
Philippines	Federal republic	President Rodrigo Duterte
Singapore	Parliamentary republic	Prime Minister Lee Hsien Loong
Thailand	Constitutional monarchy	Prime Minister General Prayut Chan-o-cha; King Maha Vajiralongkorn
Vietnam	Communist state	President Nguyên Xuân Phúc

*Given the instability in Southeast Asian politics, these leaders may hold office only for a short time. Each was his nation's leader in 2017.

Key Issues Since Independence

GLOBAL CONCEPTS

Human Rights

CONCEPTS GLOBAL

Local versus central control has been a problem in Myanmar, also called Burma, where local tribal groups (Karens) in rural remote areas have refused to obey decisions of the national government in Yangon (Rangoon). In the 1990 elections, Aung San Suu Kyi and her National League for Democracy Party emerged as victors. However, these results were nullified by the military leaders of the State Law and Order Restoration Council (SLORC). Although Aung San Suu Kyi was awarded the 1991 Nobel Peace Prize, she was placed under house arrest and has been in and out of detention since.

The military junta has exercised a restrictive domestic control and kept the nation isolated internationally in spite of widespread pro-democracy demonstrations, ethnic unrest, and occasional violence. In response to this and the international attention bestowed upon Suu Kyi's peaceful opposition, the regime secretly relocated the government from the traditional capital of Rangoon (or Yangon) to an interior isolated mountain compound. Attempts at reform resulted primarily in increased military control and limitations on political parties. Mismanagement of foreign aid following a destructive 2008 cyclone, continued detention of political prisoners, lack of attention to a rampant AIDS epidemic, closed-down universities—these seemed to be the chief "accomplishments" of a military regime funded and empowered by its control of the lucrative heroin trade.

Sustained diplomatic pressure from a variety of nations—Asian as well as Western—led Myanmar's military leaders to relax political restrictions and plan for elections to be held in late 2010. Though not permitted to participate as a candidate, Suu Kyi was released from detention shortly afterward and in the following months conferred with several prominant world leaders, including American Secretary of State Hillary Clinton. A special parliamentary election scheduled for April 2012 was to include candidates from Suu Kyi's political party, the National Democracy League, with Suu Kyi herself registered as a candidate.

GEOGRAPHY

Human Systems

The National Democracy League (NDL) won a resounding victory, sweeping nearly all the open seats in Myanmar's legislature, leading Aung San Suu Kyi to hope "this will be the beginning of a new era." Another resounding electoral landslide in 2015 furthered hope for an even more rapid turn in the direction of greater democracy, even though the military still wielded much power and influence. A legal technicality prevented the inspirational crusader for political rights from becoming president, but her appointment as "state counselor" in 2016 granted Aung San Suu Kyi virtual prime minister status. She has, however, come under fire since because of reports that human rights abuses and ethnic cleansing has taken place against the country's Rohingya Muslim ethnic minority in Myanmar's northwest, allegedly carried out by the military.

Civil war and invasions have plagued Cambodia since Prince Norodom Sihanouk was overthrown in 1970. The military rulers who took over were unable to defeat the Khmer Rouge, a communist force backed by Vietnam. By 1976 the Khmer Rouge, under its leader Pol Pot, controlled the nation and changed the official name to Kampuchea. (However, the country today is commonly referred to as Cambodia.) The Pol Pot government proved to be harsh and genocidal, killing thousands of people. It tried to impose a drastic social and economic restructure of society between 1975 and 1978. Its actions were the basis for a feature movie titled *The Killing Fields*. The Pol Pot government

GLOBAL
CONCEPTS
Political Systems
CONCEPTS
GLOBAL

angered Vietnam, which had long wished to take over the territory. (Historically, the people of Kampuchea, or Cambodia, and Vietnam have been enemies.) With Soviet encouragement and material aid, Vietnam conquered Cambodia in 1978 and installed a government headed by a native figure, Hun Sen. This government faced a rebellion by Khmer Rouge forces, backed by China. With Vietnamese forces withdrawing in 1989, a coalition government was established that sought to bring together the Khmer Rouge and other warring groups.

A UN-supervised cease-fire agreement was signed in 1991, providing for a UN peacekeeping force and UN-sponsored elections. The elections, held in May 1993, produced a 120-member National Assembly, which promptly drew up a new constitution and provided for the return of Norodom Sihanouk as king. In September 1993, Sihanouk ascended to the throne in an elaborate ceremony. His new government was immediately recognized by the United States. His biggest political problem has been trying to put down the armed resistance of the Khmer Rouge. Although they were a party to the 1991 agreement, the Khmer Rouge boycotted the 1993 elections and have been upset with some of Sihanouk's political actions since he became king. Sihanouk abdicated in 2004 and was replaced by his son Norodom Sihamoni. Trials of former Khmer Rouge leaders commenced in 2006 and ongoing tensions between Cambodia and Thailand regarding control of an ancient Hindu temple complex resulted in it being declared a World Heritage site in 2008. A disputed 2009 election extended the rule of the Cambodia People's Party led by Prime Minister Hun Sen.

Hun Sen, the former Khmer Rouge soldier turned politician, was reappointed by parliament in September 2013 for a five-year term, in spite of mass demonstrations and allegations of election fraud. Opposition parties have routinely boycotted elections, citing threats from the ruling group and prosecution for criticizing them. The current economy is dominated by the garment industry and tourism. (Cambodia is also home to the World Heritage site at Angkor Wat, where each year over one million tourists visit the complex of ancient Hindu temples.) Both these job sectors offer expanding sources of income. There is also the possibility of tapping into offshore oil and gas reserves and attracting overseas investments to replace aid. However, corruption has consistently been a major drawback, and Cambodia continues to be one of the world's poorest nations. A large percentage of the workforce continues to be employed in subsistence farming.

Instability and corruption are features in many parts of Southeast Asia. However, they erupted into a striking change of government in the Philippines in 1986. Ferdinand Marcos, who had ruled with strong military backing since 1965, was an unpopular ruler who enriched himself and did little to help the masses of people. Widespread demonstrations, a controversial election, and a declining military enabled Corazon Aquino to come to power in 1986, as Marcos fled into exile. He died in 1989, while in Hawaii. As president from 1986 to 1992, Mrs. Aquino was unsuccessful in dealing with problems concerning hostility from Communist and Muslim groups, corruption in government, and a declining economy. A significant foreign policy decision of her government was to refuse to renew the lease on the naval base at Subic Bay. She did not run for reelection in 1992. Fidel Ramos was the winner in that election, decisively defeating former Filipino first lady Imelda Marcos. During his administration, Ramos began implementing economic reforms intended to open up the once-closed national economy, encourage private enterprise, invite more foreign and domestic investment, and reduce corruption. However, Ramos was himself accused of corruption, and when he proposed an amendment of the constitution to allow him to run for a second term, voters rejected him in favor of Joseph Estrada. He, too, was accused of corruption, and impeachment proceedings were initiated. When supporters attempted to undermine the process, the armed forces threw their support to Vice President Gloria Macapagal-Arroyo, daughter of a former president. Despite protests and attempted rebellions questioning the legitimacy of her ascension to the presidency and charges of corruption against her husband, she was elected to a new term in 2004. Concerns about election rigging quickly led to an attempt at impeachment. In 2005 renewed Islamic militancy wracked areas of the southern islands. A coup plot and resultant state emergency in 2006 resulted in the deaths of several hundred political activists allegedly killed by the military. With Mrs. Macapagal-Arroyo constitutionally barred from another term, another "dynastic inheritor" was victorious in the election of 2010: Benigno Aquino III, son of Corazon, and the fourth generation of his family to hold high office under the banner of the Liberal Party, assumed the presidency.

Almost from the start, the Aquino administration had to contend with rising opposition. Criticism focused on inadequate government responses to disasters (a typhoon and an earthquake in 2013), cases of misuse of government funds, and political patronage and other instances of corruption. Ongoing frustrations with poor public services and perceptions of

GLOBAL
CONCEPTS
Political Systems
CONCEPTS
GLOBAL

Human Systems

increased inequality and rising crime led to a populist electoral revolution in 2016.

Rodrigo Duterte, plain-speaking, occasionally foul-mouthed, and often politically incorrect (some might say misogynist), overwhelmingly rode to the presidency via promises of zero tolerance of crime and the elimination of the "drug menace." Duterte has increasingly acted to distance himself from the United States, the Philippines' closest ally. The U.S. military presence has been the most divisive issue. Duterte has an 86 percent approval rating in the Philippines, but his break with America has created controversy. Many of his actions seem to challenge the liberal Western values enshrined in the Philippine constitution. To Filipinos frustrated by poverty and inequality, Duterte's strident nationalism coincides with their distrust of Western institutions and the elitism of the Philippine government and the business establishment.

There are other tensions that have existed in the region in the post-independence period. They include:

1. Indonesia has had disagreements with Malaysia. It also had riots that caused the deaths of many Chinese in 1965 in the midst of a strong anticommunist policy and scattered anti-Chinese prejudice. Indonesia has been condemned for its human rights violations, based upon its actions in dealing with protests in East Timor. East Timor, after bloodshed and a vote, was granted independence. In addition, the end of Indonesian President Suharto's one man rule was seen as a welcome sign. An election in 1999 was peaceful, with the selection of a new president, Wahid. Under Wahid and the short administration of his predecessor, Habibie, a process of democratic reform was begun. This continued, in fits and starts, following the 2001 election of Indonesia's first woman president, Megawati. Daughter of former strong man Sukarno (some media call her "Sukarnoputri," indicating that aspect of her status), she appeared to see her role mainly as a symbol of national unity. Former military reformer Susilo Bambang Yudhoyono's reputation for integrity, strong personality appeal, and excellent communication skills enabled him to replace Megawati in the election of 2004. Known as the "thinking general" and popular for his investigation of the 2002 extremist bombing in Bali, he faced further Islamist issues, separatist movements in Aceh to the west and Papua New Guinea to the east, as well as problems caused by the 2004 tsunami in Sumatra. As a result of its position on the Pacific Rim's tectonically active "Ring of Fire," Indonesia suffered through destructive earthquakes in 2005 and 2007. Heavy rains causing massive flooding displaced over 400,000

people in 2007. The controversy-free presidential election of 2009 returned Yudhoyono to the office, solidifying Indonesia's reputation as a stable democracy. The nation also increased its leadership role in regional and global affairs, and economic growth continued to reduce poverty levels and limit inflation. Slow-paced anticorruption political reform and increasing religiously motivated violence were Yudoyono's most trying challenges.

Indonesia's constitution limits its president to two terms in office, and the 2014 election featured a pair of candidates representing very different political interests. A standard-bearer, representing the nation's traditional political and military elites, was defeated by a more populist figure, former furniture maker, Joko Widodo (or Jokowi). Viewed as an uncorrupted politician from a humble background, Jokowi's victory was seen as partly due to his popularity with young people in both urban and rural areas. His election fueled anticipation of a new era in the world's third-largest democracy, but it has been a struggle to achieve a significant reform program in a country still dominated by political operatives from the military and upper classes.

Jokowi's rise also illustrates the continued dominance of Indonesian politics by parties dedicated to secularism and nationalism. The former focus distresses some segments of the Muslim population (87% of the nation), and, since 2000, has created some Islamic terrorist incidents including vicious bomb attacks by several home-grown radical groups. In the case of nationalism, suspicion of the often more well-to-do citizens of Chinese ancestry has minimized their political influence. Most Indonesians seem to view corruption as very prevalent among government officials. Military, police, and customs agency involvement in smuggling, extortion, and other crimes may result in a major loss of trust in government by Indonesia's citizens. These are the very institutions that should be protecting the populace. The economic growth surge of 2010 to 2014 has slowed, but there would seem to be an opportunity for Jokowi's administration to deliver on the promises of financial reform, especially in the taxation system.

2. Chinese and Vietnamese antagonism surfaced in 1979 with a short-lived border war. Vietnam's withdrawal from Cambodia in 1989 after the ousting of the violent Khmer Rouge soothed Chinese-Vietnamese relations. But there have been renewed tensions over control of small island groups in the South China Sea. But on this and other issues, relations between the two countries have improved significantly in recent

years. The two countries are bound by culture—and increasingly by economics. Trade is growing rapidly, and Vietnam has become a popular vacation spot for Chinese tourists. And the Vietnamese Communist Party looks to the Chinese Communist Party as a model for opening up its economy while maintaining tight control over politics.

3. Thailand has been worried about the spread of communism from Vietnam, as well as the problem of coping with refugees from the fighting in Cambodia. Instability caused by corruption and political infighting led to a military-dominated government from 1990 to 1992. In October 1992 a civilian-led government was installed in Thailand for the first time in sixty years. Subsequent elections resulted in several coalition governments emphasizing prudent economic management and political reforms. A new 1997 constitution mandated political change. In the January 2001 elections, telecommunications multimillionaire Thaksin Shinawatra and his Thai Rak Thai Party (TRT) won an overwhelming victory on a populist platform of economic growth and development. After winning an unprecedented second term in 2005, Shinawatra has promised to eradicate poverty by spending $60 billion on new infrastructure and continuing privatization of state firms despite strong opposition from unions. The TRT has also advocated low-interest loans and subsidized health care for Thailand's rural poor. A massive tax-free stock sale of a business in 2006 by family members resulted in antigovernment protests and eventually charges of tax evasion against Shinawatra's wife and children. Removed by a military coup and subject to government-imposed taxes, fines, asset seizure, and arrest, the family fled into exile. Popular opposition to the replacement government led to street protests and a "Million Person March" in 2010; government troops cracked down violently on the demonstrators in what the Thai media labeled "Cruel April" followed by "Savage May." When the military finally permitted elections in 2011, the populist Pheu Thia Party's challenge to the established power elite legitimized the earlier protests. Ironically, the new prime minister was Yingluck Shinawatra, younger sister of the ousted former leader. Suspicion that she would be a mere puppet of her exiled brother seemed likely to be the most significant roadblock to her possible success in uniting the fractious elements of Thai society. Shinawatra's administration had to cope with Islamic fundamentalism among the Muslim minority in the southwest, which has created antigovernment violence. In recent years, it has been concerned with an alarming spread of HIV/AIDS among the urban population.

WORLD ISSUES

Political and Economic Refugees

Thailand's political unrest continued as a result of several issues: a proposed bill promoting reconciliation that many felt would provide amnesty for the prime minister's exiled brother, government cuts in subsidies for rice farmers, and murder charges against a former prime minister for his actions during earlier protest marches. Yingluck Shinawatra announced an election for 2014, but refused demands for to her to step down immediately. Elections held in February were declared unconstitutional, and the army seized power via a coup in May of 2014. After 70 years on the throne, Thailand's King Bhumibol Adulyadej, the world's longest-reigning monarch, died at the age of 88 in October 2016. His son, Crown Prince Vajiralongkorn, was proclaimed king and signed the new constitution drafted by the military, providing a path for a return to democracy. Bangkok was the site of a bombing at a hospital in 2017 on the third anniversary of the military coup, echoing earlier incidents. A previous similar attack at a tourist attraction in 2015 had caused 20 deaths. Thai officials did not identify any groups as being responsible.

4. Singapore, which is inhabited mostly by people of Chinese ancestry (74%), strives to maintain good relations with its two large Malay-dominated neighbors, Indonesia and Malaysia. (The Malays are the majority ethnic groups in these nations.) This stable and prosperous "city-state" is located on one of the world's busiest maritime shipping routes, making it a major commercial, financial, and transportation hub. Along with its high standard of living compared to its neighbors, it ranks as the world's third-largest foreign exchange market and financial center, is also number three in oil refining and trade, and is the second-busiest container port.

Developments in Vietnam into the 21st Century

Severe economic conditions in Vietnam brought about significant changes in government policy. (1) Many years of fighting within and without the country had drained the treasury. (2) The collapse of the Soviet Union in 1991 led to a drastic reduction in the foreign aid that had long maintained the Vietnamese economy. (3) Centralized planning and a refusal to make needed changes hurt productivity.

High-level contacts with the United States were begun in 1990, stemming mostly from the economic factors described above. Americans have agreed to talks based upon Vietnam's willingness to seek peace with its neighbors and to account more fully for U.S. MIA/POWs (missing-in-action/prisoner-of-war servicemen and women). In 1993 and 1994 American businesspeople and politicians visited Vietnam; normalizing relations between the two former enemies eventually occurred.

Since 2001, Vietnamese authorities have committed to economic liberalization and enacted structural reforms needed to modernize the economy. The goal is to produce more competitive, export-driven industries, making the nation a more integrated member of the international economic community. Vietnam's membership in the ASEAN Free Trade Area (AFTA) and entry into the U.S.-Vietnam Bilateral Trade in December 2001 have led to even more rapid changes in Vietnam's trade and economic regime. Vietnam's exports to the United States doubled in 2002 and again in 2003.

Like that of many nations ruled by a single political party, Vietnam's government faced the challenge of maintaining power in an age of dynamic expansion of communication and information technology. A more open system offered many of the country's citizens an escape from the cycle of poverty, the economy as a whole to continue its rapid growth, and the newly expanded urban middle class to experience a rise in living standards. These trends were somewhat slowed by the global economic downturn of the years after 2008 that resulted in an escalating rate of inflation. Internationally, Vietnam successfully served a term on the UN Security Council and acted as chair nation of ASEAN in 2010.

A "more open" Vietnam did not open the door to wider leeway for freedom of expression for its citizens. Since 2010, activists have been jailed, the government has been accused of clamping down on criticism, a decree banned online discussions of current affairs, bloggers were jailed for infringing on the "interests of (the) state," and a newspaper's license was revoked for articles "abusing freedom and democratic rights." During the early years of the 21st century's second decade, Vietnam was called "Asia's Economic Icon" for its robust, export-led economy. Growth in manufacturing, from steel to smartphones, and from clothing to computer components, fostered job growth, boosted the middle class, and stimulated conspicuous consumption. By 2017, though, slippages in mining production and manufacturing output, coupled with a massive coastal fish kill caused by a toxic industrial spill, painted a less favorable picture of Vietnam's economy.

Part F: East Asia

SECTION 1: CHINA

Long March of the Communist Forces

After Chiang's purge of the Communists in 1927, Mao Zedong, one of the founders of the Chinese Communist Party in 1921, escaped to southeastern China. Mao built up a following among the peasants and organized a guerrilla force called the Red Army.

GEOGRAPHY

Use of Geography

In 1931, the same year Japan conquered Manchuria, Chiang decided to eliminate the Communists. Finally, in 1934 Chiang's Nationalist Army had the Communists surrounded and blockaded. However, Mao organized his followers, broke through the Nationalist lines, and the Communists began the "Long March." Approximately 100,000 Communists began a 5,000- to 6,000-mile march across some of the most rugged terrain in China. Twenty thousand reached northern China in 1935.

The Communist Victory

With the Japanese attack in 1937, both the Communists and Nationalists found themselves resisting further Japanese aggression. From 1940 on, however, as the Nationalists fought the Japanese, the Communists extended their influence in China. Mao concentrated on building up the Red Army and extending its control. In the areas of China under Communist control, economic and social reforms were introduced. Land rentals were reduced and education programs were begun.

When World War II ended, both the Nationalists and Communists tried to regain control of the areas in eastern China that had been under Japanese control.

In 1947 the Communists and Nationalists battled for control of Manchuria. After the Communists won, they began to push the Nationalists southward. In 1949 the Nationalists could no longer hold the country, and they fled to Taiwan, an island off the coast of mainland China. They established a government called the Republic of China, with Chiang Kai-shek as president, and claimed that the mainland, which they considered part of their country, was in rebellion.

GEOGRAPHY

Use of Geography

On October 1, 1949, the Communists established the People's Republic of China, with Mao Zedong as the chairman of the Chinese Communist Party and Zhou Enlai (Chou En-lai) as premier. The capital was established at Peiping, and the city was renamed Peking (now Beijing).

Why the Nationalists Lost the Civil War

One of the most important reasons the Nationalists lost the war was that the Communists were supported by the peasants. When the Nationalists ruled, they did little to relieve the burden of the Chinese peasants (80 percent of the population). Mao and the Communists promised an extensive program of land reform and reduced land rents in the areas under their control.

GEOGRAPHY

Human Systems

The Communist forces did little actual fighting against the Japanese during World War II. Instead, they used the war to spread their influence throughout northern and central China. When the war ended, the Communist forces were strong, fresh, and ready. The Nationalist Army, on the other hand, was war-weary and demoralized. The Communist leaders who survived the Long March had suffered with their people and were seen as popular folk heroes. They were hardened and disciplined. Moreover, the leaders of the Communists—Mao Zedong, Zhu De (Chu Teh), and Zhou Enlai—knew how to appeal to the Chinese people, who were tired of inflation, war, and corruption and blamed Chiang and the Nationalists.

Goals of the People's Republic of China in 1949

The three major goals of the Communists in 1949 were to reestablish China's world prominence, to push economic development, and to improve life for the Chinese people. To reestablish their prominence, the Chinese had to control China again and remove the foreign imperialists. Industries owned and operated by foreigners were nationalized, Christianity was banned, and Christian missionaries were expelled from China. The Communists brought under Chinese control border areas that had at one time been part of the Chinese empire or tributary states. Such areas included Xinjiang (Sinkiang), Manchuria, Inner Mongolia, and Xizang (Tibet).

GEOGRAPHY

Human Systems

To achieve world prominence, the Communists realized that China must be capable of competing with the Western powers both economically and militarily. Consequently, their early economic goal was to industrialize China as rapidly as possible. They employed five-year plans, which stressed industrial production at the expense of agriculture.

The most widespread plan was called The Great Leap Forward. Initiated by Mao in 1959, it was designed mainly to have farms become more productive. The key feature was the establishment of communes, groups of people who lived and worked together. The land they worked on was not owned by them, as Mao's form of communism did not allow for any private ownership of property. Title to the land was held by the commune, whose Communist Party members made all the key economic decisions. The commune also regulated peoples' social lives with regard to such issues as marriage, raising children, housing, and so on. The results of all these efforts were disastrous. Millions died of famine because of poor planning, unrealistic regulations, peasant resistance, and drought.

After the death of Mao in 1976, Deng Xiaoping became the most powerful person in China and in the Communist Party until his death in 1997. The "paramount leader," as he was known, introduced the "Four Modernizations," a program designed to make changes in agriculture, industry, defense, and science and technology. To carry out this program, he introduced elements of capitalism and, as a result, China became a mixed economy rather than a strict command economy.

Beginning in 1979, the communes were dismantled and the "responsibility system" was started. Under this system, the state still owned the land, but individual families could lease it. The families would contract with the state for a certain amount of their produce and they could do as they wanted with any surplus. Free markets were established to sell these surpluses, and production in China increased.

In 1984, the responsibility system was extended to state-owned industries. Managers were allowed to make production decisions. As with the farmers, they had to provide a quota set by the state, but they could decide what to do with surplus production.

Some private enterprise has been encouraged. The government has offered tax breaks and low-interest loans to small businesses such as fast food, beauty shops, carpentry, and so on. The number of workers who can be employed in these small businesses is limited by the state. The production of consumer goods has been stressed as well. There has been much greater production of radios, televisions, cameras, clothing, and so forth. Joint ventures between the Chinese and foreigners have also been encouraged. Foreign companies have also been encouraged to locate in "special economic zones" in the coastal areas of southeastern China. These zones are areas where restrictions that are usually placed on Chinese businesses do not apply, and private enterprise is encouraged.

By 2015, China had the largest GDP (gross domestic product) in the world. China's industries, exports, and oil demand have increased. China is the largest producer and consumer of coal. The burning of fossil fuels has caused severe air pollution in China. It is not unusual, at any given time, to see residents of the Chinese industrial cities wearing face masks to protect themselves from the pollution.

To achieve their goals, the Communists had to transform Chinese society and win the loyalty of the Chinese people. To suppress Confucianism and turn the Chinese into supporters of the Communist state, the Communists were determined to replace family loyalty with loyalty to the state and party. The Communists used the education system to do this. The legal system was used to improve the position of women. New marriage laws prevented families from forcing girls to accept arranged marriages. Divorce laws gave women equal rights. Women were employed in all occupations. The Communists also undertook mass campaigns to improve health and sanitation. Rural "doctors" were trained in the combined use of traditional Chinese medicine and Western medical practices.

A thought-reform movement was established to eradicate the influence of traditional Chinese ideas and replace them with socialist ideology and the cult of Maoism. Former owners of industries, the intelligentsia, businesspeople, and others were subjected to stringent retraining sessions and indoctrinated in socialist ideology. Mao's "Red Book"—*The Thought of Mao Zedong*—became required reading in schools, factory study sessions, peasant study sessions, and so on.

The Cultural Revolution

In the late 1950s, Mao's almost complete control of events in China was challenged for the first time. Conservative party leaders questioned Mao's revolutionary domestic and foreign policies. Mao's opponents, called reactionaries or counter-revolutionaries, were led by Liu Shaoqi (Liu Hsao Ch'i). In 1965 their differences became an actual power struggle. Because the conflict was over economic, educational, scientific, political, and social programs, it became known as the Cultural Revolution.

Mao closed the schools and sent high school and college students into the streets to rout out reactionaries. The students, who were known as Red Guards, attacked, intimidated, and humiliated Mao's opponents and anyone they suspected of being reactionary or influenced by Western ideas. They plunged China into chaos. Factories closed, industrial production fell, and transportation facilities were disrupted. Estimates of the number of

GLOBAL
CONCEPTS
Political Systems
CONCEPTS
GLOBAL

GLOBAL
CONCEPTS
Power
CONCEPTS
GLOBAL

GLOBAL
CONCEPTS
Human Rights
CONCEPTS
GLOBAL

people who died ran into the hundreds of thousands. The chaos eventually led to a military crackdown, and by 1969 the Cultural Revolution was over. Mao appeared to have won the struggle.

Policies Pursued Since Mao's Death

Following the Cultural Revolution, a power struggle emerged between the moderates led by Zhou Enlai, premier of the People's Republic since 1949, and the radicals, led by Jiang Qing (Chiang Ch'ing), Mao's wife.

After Mao's death in 1976, Jiang Qing and three of her strongest allies, who became known as the Gang of Four, tried to take power. However, they were arrested, charged with plotting to seize power, as well as crimes against the people and the party, during the Cultural Revolution. In 1980 they were tried. All four were found guilty, and Jiang was given a death penalty (which was commuted to life imprisonment in 1983). One of the purposes of the trial was to punish the Gang of Four for the way they treated members of the Chinese leadership during the Cultural Revolution. Another was to decrease the esteem in which Mao was held by the Chinese people. Deng Xiaoping, the real ruler of China after Mao's death, felt it was necessary to remove the cult of Mao to effectively carry out his policies. Mao's support for the Gang of Four was revealed during the trial, and it showed the Chinese people that Mao's policies in his old age were in error.

United States–China Relations, 1949 to 2000

GEOGRAPHY

Use of Geography

In 1949 the United States refused to recognize the People's Republic of China as the legitimate government of China. Instead, it recognized the Nationalist Chinese government in Taiwan, under the leadership of Chiang Kai-shek. In 1950 the Communists seized U.S. consular buildings in China, and all direct diplomatic ties were broken off.

The Korean War broke out in June 1950 when North Korean troops invaded South Korea. UN forces were rushed to Korea to support the South Koreans. By autumn of 1950, United Nations and South Korean forces had pushed north to the Yalu River, the boundary between North Korea and China. Fearing an invasion of Manchuria, Mao sent Chinese forces across the Yalu, and fighting raged until 1953, when an armistice was finally signed reestablishing the Korean border along the 38th parallel. United States troops fought under the UN command.

WORLD ISSUES

War
and
Peace

GEOGRAPHY

Use of Geography

As a result of the Korean War, the United States recognized Nationalist China (Taiwan) as the legitimate government of all China and resisted all attempts to seat representatives of the

Chinese Communist government in the United Nations. The Taiwan policy of the United States was considered by Mao as another humiliating blow from a Western imperialist power.

In October 1971 the United States ended its objection to seating the People's Republic in the UN, arguing instead that both Chinas should be seated. However, Communist China was seated and Nationalist China was expelled from the world organization in 1971. The People's Republic of China was given the permanent seat on the UN Security Council previously held by Taiwan.

Another region in Asia that caused friction between the United States and Communist China was Vietnam. When the Communists began to make inroads in South Vietnam through the activities of guerrillas known as Viet Cong, the United States increased its military aid and sent military advisers. In 1965 the United States began to send combat forces to Vietnam. The Viet Cong were assisted and reinforced by the North Vietnamese, who in turn received aid from the former Soviet Union and Communist China. China objected strenuously to the U.S. role in Vietnam and its invasions of Cambodia and Laos.

Use of Geography

In 1971 relations between the United States and Communist China improved when an American Ping-Pong team was invited to China. This was the first time in over twenty years that an American group had been invited to China. In 1972 President Richard Nixon made a state trip to China, and the two nations agreed to reciprocal contact and exchange, and they also agreed to expand trade. In 1973 missions of the two nations were established, and in January 1979 full diplomatic relations were established.

Taiwan continues to be an area of discord. The United States withdrew its diplomatic representation from Taiwan when it recognized the People's Republic. However, the United States still maintains unofficial representation in Taiwan through an American Institute. Both Taiwan and China consider Taiwan a part of China. Their disagreement is over who actually should control China. In recent years, the relationship between the two countries has seen some improvement, in spite of the fact that Taiwan refuses to consider any suggestions from China concerning reunification.

Use of Geography

Trade relations between the United States and China were expanded considerably after diplomatic recognition in the 1970s. In fact, Japan and the United States rank as China's top two trading partners. Diplomatic and trade relations between the United States and China were strained by the government's brutal crackdown on the democracy demonstrators in Tiananmen

Human Systems

Square in 1989. The United States objected to both the actual crackdown and the arrest and subsequent incarceration of thousands of young Chinese. China now enjoys most favored nation (MFN) status with the United States. The Clinton administration had considered tying the renewal of that status to the question of human rights abuses in China. The United States also had demanded that China stop exporting goods produced by prison inmates who were used as forced labor, that an agreement of some sort be reached concerning political prisoners, and that the Chinese adhere to the UN Universal Declaration of Human Rights, among other things. Although China made only some minor concessions in these areas, President Clinton decided to renew China's MFN status. He felt that the continuation of this status would help the American economy and would ultimately improve human rights conditions in China. It was also considered that China's cooperation is critical in dealing with North Korea and in the area of nuclear nonproliferation and in controlling the spread of nuclear weapons. Clinton's action in renewing MNF, however, was criticized by many members of Congress and Chinese human rights advocates. There are indications China has been selling nuclear weapons technology to some Third World nations. The United States has also voiced very strong objections to these actions.

GEOGRAPHY

Use of Geography

In the spring of 1999, charges that the Chinese had not only spied on U.S. nuclear facilities, but that they had actually stolen U.S. technology secrets, came to light. The then Chinese leaders, Jiang Zemin, the president and general secretary of the Communist Party, and Zhu Rongji, the premier, both deny that the Chinese stole anything. Zhu Rongji visited the United States in the spring of 1999 to hold talks with President Clinton in an effort to improve trade relations and gain membership in the World Trade Organization (WTO). The talks were largely unsuccessful, though China did agree to drop bans on U.S. wheat and citrus. Other agreements on further trade concessions and on human rights could not be reached. In December of 1999, the island of Macao was returned to China from Portugal. In 2007 China exported many hazardous products, including pet products, toothpaste, tires, and toys. This brought attention to the lack of quality control in Chinese factories and the head of the food and drug committee was executed.

GEOGRAPHY

Human Systems

Xi Jinping has been the president of China since 2013. Li Keqiang has been the premier since 2013. Xi met with U.S. President Donald Trump early in 2017 at Trump's estate in Florida.

China hosted the Summer Olympics in August 2008 and put on spectacular opening and closing displays for the world. A powerful earthquake in the Sichuan province in 2008 killed over 69,000 and left over 17,000 missing. The earthquake revealed shoddy construction of schools during the early days of the Communist era and those who reported the poor construction were imprisoned.

Liu Xiaobo, a human rights activist, died in July 2017. Liu had been prominent in the Tiananmen Square protests of 1989. At that time, he was jailed for 21 months. He was an academic and an author who was not silenced by this sentence; he wrote a petition calling for democracy and a new constitution. He was imprisoned in 2009 with a sentence of 11 years. Liu was diagnosed with liver cancer in May 2017 while still in prison. He was relocated to a civilian hospital, but was still held as a prisoner. His family requested that he be released to seek treatment abroad. The government refused. He died from cancer on July 13, 2017 at the age of 61. Liu received the Nobel Peace Prize in October 2010 while he was imprisoned. He was not allowed to accept the award and the Chinese government chastised the government of Norway for giving him the award, even though the Norwegian government plays no role in the awarding of Nobel Prizes.

Relations Between the People's Republic and the Third World

Communist China saw itself as the example of revolutionary change for the former colonies of Western powers and also as the leader of the Third World nations. It supported Marxist revolutions in Third World nations, provided technical and financial assistance, and set up cultural exchanges with nations in Africa and Asia.

GEOGRAPHY

Human Systems

Sino-Soviet Relations

The Sino-Soviet Treaty of Friendship of 1950 seemed to indicate that a long-lasting supportive relationship between China and the Soviet Union had begun. The Soviet Union agreed to assist China against aggressive attacks and provide economic and military assistance. By 1960, however, the Soviet Union had cut off its assistance.

Reasons for the split between China and the Soviet Union included:

1. *Khrushchev's attacks on Stalin.* Mao was a great admirer of Stalin.

2. *Peaceful coexistence.* Khrushchev believed that through peaceful coexistence, the world's people would see the superiority of the communist system, and communism would spread worldwide. Mao believed war and revolution were necessary.

3. *Leadership.* The Soviet Union considered itself the leader of the world communist movement. Mao disputed its claim to leadership.

4. *Soviet support for India.* In 1962, when Indian and Chinese forces clashed over territory, the Soviet Union assisted India.

5. *Border disputes.* The Soviets hold territory in Central Asia and northeastern China that China claims. There have been occasional outbreaks of fighting between troops stationed on the borders.

6. *Afghanistan.* China objected to the Soviet invasion in 1979. Mikhail Gorbachëv's trip to China in May 1989 was intended to normalize relations, but his visit was upstaged by the student rebellion in Tiananmen Square. In spite of all their differences, China and Russia signed a 20-year Friendship Treaty in 2001, pledging a peaceful settlement of border disputes and coordination against threats of aggression from others.

China's New Status in the Pacific

GLOBAL CONCEPTS
Interdependence
CONCEPTS GLOBAL

Chinese diplomatic relations with Japan were reestablished following President Nixon's trip to China in 1972. Since then, the two countries have signed trade agreements, and Japan has become one of China's largest trading partners. Japan imports China's agricultural products and petroleum, and China imports Japanese machinery and technology. Japan has given China millions of dollars in loans for development.

GEOGRAPHY

Human Systems

In 1984 Great Britain and China reached an agreement to return the island of Hong Kong (Xianggang) to Chinese control in 1997 and that return, in fact, did take place on July 1 of that year. Hong Kong became a Special Administrative Region of China. Under the agreement reached in 1984 Hong Kong was to be allowed to maintain its capitalist system for 50 years. In 1996 Tung Chee Hwa was elected by a selection committee to be the first chief executive of Hong Kong. Restrictions have been imposed on demonstrations and voting rights. In July 2004 citizens of Hong Kong protested Beijing's refusal to allow greater freedom. Leung Chun-ying was elected Chief Executive of Hong Kong in 2012.

Large pro-democracy demonstrations took place in 2014. Demonstrators were opposed to a Chinese plan to restrict candidate selection for a proposed direct election of the Chief Executive in 2017. In 2015, Hong Kong's Legislative Council postponed direct elections in 2017 because of the limitations on candidate selection. An election was held in 2016. Pro-China candidates did win 40 seats, but 6 members of the 2014 protests were elected to the Legislative Council, including Nathan Law, the youngest member ever to be elected to the Legislative Council and a leader of the 2014 protests.

GLOBAL
CONCEPTS

Human Rights

CONCEPTS
GLOBAL

Human Systems

China After Tiananmen

In the aftermath of the pro-democracy movement and the military crackdown in 1989, the Chinese government reverted to many policies that seemed to be a reminder of the more authoritarian times of Mao. There were more restrictions on the press, there were political study sessions for workers, films and music were banned, and so on. But these restrictions seem to be loosening again. It appears that the economic changes that the government deems necessary to maintain growth and prosperity cannot be achieved under the social and political restrictions that the hard-liners would like to impose.

The pace of growth of the Internet and the number of users in China has increased enormously. The government struggles to stay ahead of Internet developments and to limit the information that can be accessed and shared by Internet users. The Internet Affairs Bureau of the State Council's Information Office is charged with controlling Chinese Internet users' access to unwanted information while still allowing access to desired information. Google has left China completely after blaming hackers in China for cyberattacks on its system.

A historic meeting was held in 2016 between Chinese President Xi Jinping and Taiwanese President Ma Ying-jeou. This was the first direct meeting between the leaders of these two nations since 1945. No significant agreements were reached concerning Taiwan's sovereignty, but the two nations did agree to establish a telephone hotline between the two governments.

Developments in the 21st Century

On the domestic front, the most significant development has been the extraordinary growth of China's economy. China has become the most productive economic force in East Asia, outstripping Japan. China's admission into the World Trade Organization (WTO) in 2001 marked a vital milestone. Nevertheless, protests against this admission were held by several human rights and labor organizations throughout the world.

Other post-2000 domestic issues are as follows:

1. Several health trends have caused alarm throughout China. HIV/AIDS has been increasing at a terrible rate. In 2002, China

suffered an epidemic of severe acute respiratory syndrome (SARS), and hundreds died as a result. In 2004–2005, an outbreak of avian bird flu virus worried medical officials. Thousands of birds and chickens were slaughtered in an effort to contain the contagion.

2. Space exploration was evidenced by a major achievement. In August 2003, China became the third nation, after the United States and Russia, to send a man into space. China landed the unmanned Yutu rover on the moon in 2013.

3. Industrial disasters have accompanied China's economic advancement. These have been due mainly to inadequate regulation, corruption, and human error. Examples can be seen in a gas well explosion in South Central China that killed 233 people. A benzene runoff polluted a river near Harbin, in the north, in 2005, leaving millions without drinkable water for several days.

4. China's treatment of two large minority groups has raised issues of prejudicial and abusive treatment. Tibetans came under Chinese occupation in 1951, with a communist government being installed in 1953. The Buddhist religion was repressed, as 100,000 Tibetans fled to India with their spiritual leader, the Dalai Lama. Muslims living in the northwest, in Xinjiang, fear crackdowns on their rights and freedoms and have considered separating themselves from China.

In the area of international relations, the post-2000 period has been marked by these developments:

1. Relations with Russia have been improving. In November 2005, Russian President Vladimir Putin announced that Russia would build a pipeline carrying oil into China. Russia is the world's second largest oil exporter after Saudi Arabia. Russian trade with China was approaching record levels in 2006.

2. Chinese pride was bolstered in 2001 by two noteworthy international acts of recognition. China was admitted into the WTO and was awarded the Olympic Games for the year 2008.

3. China has taken a larger diplomatic role with regard to situations on the Korean peninsula. She has hosted talks and acted as an intermediary on issues relating to North Korea's nuclear weapons program.

REVIEW QUESTIONS

Multiple Choice. Select the letter of the answer that correctly completes
each statement.

1. The unequal treaties were the result of a war fought against
   A. Japan
   B. Britain
   C. Russia
   D. Vietnam

2. The Chinese considered foreigners to be barbarians. This attitude was an example of
   A. ethnocentrism
   B. cultural diffusion
   C. empathy
   D. interdependence

3. During the 19th century, Western nations were able to gain control over parts of China mainly because
   A. the Chinese had a strong tradition of nonviolence
   B. China lacked the military technology needed to stop these ventures
   C. China was promised aid for its industries
   D. the Chinese lacked a strong cultural identity

4. During the Communist Revolution in China, many farmers supported the Communists because they promised
   A. land reform
   B. a peace treaty with Japan
   C. a federal republic
   D. aid from the industrial nations

5. After gaining control of the Kuomintang (Nationalist Party), Chiang Kai-shek's most important goal in the 1920s was
   A. land reform to assist the peasants
   B. destruction of the Communists
   C. the invasion of Korea
   D. assisting Ho Chi Minh in overthrowing the French

6. Hong Kong
   A. is a British Crown Colony
   B. was returned to the Chinese in 1997
   C. has an economy based on agriculture
   D. was won by the Japanese in the Sino-Japanese War

7. The Communist victory in the Chinese Civil War was a result of all the following *except*
   A. the inability of the Nationalists to stabilize the economy
   B. the lack of U.S. aid to the Communists
   C. peasant dissatisfaction with the Nationalist regime
   D. the effective use of propaganda and guerrilla warfare by the Communists

8. A study of the history of China would reveal that
   A. there has always been strong central government in China
   B. until modern times a single dynasty ruled China
   C. periods of strong central government alternated with periods of internal disturbance, foreign invasion, and government corruption
   D. foreigners ruled China for far longer periods than native Chinese

9. During the early 1800s the relationship between China and the Western nations was strained because
   A. the Western nations did not wish to purchase Chinese goods
   B. China insisted it be dealt with through the tribute system
   C. the Western nations wished to purchase opium and the Chinese refused
   D. China wished to buy Western armaments and other manufactured goods and was rebuffed

10. A country with an unfavorable balance of trade
   A. exports goods of greater value than it imports
   B. imports goods of greater value than it exports
   C. exports natural resources and imports manufactured goods
   D. imports manufactured goods and exports textiles

11. Which form of government is most likely to suppress human rights?
   A. constitutional monarchy
   B. democratic republic
   C. parliamentary system
   D. totalitarian regime

12. The ethnocentric attitude of the Chinese
   A. resulted in a reluctance to adopt aspects of other cultures
   B. led to periods of internal strife during famine
   C. prevented the Chinese from expanding their territory
   D. caused student rebellions in the 1980s

13. The 19th century was China's Age of Humiliation for all the following reasons *except*
    A. China was conquered by the Mongols
    B. the unequal treaties
    C. China's defeat in the Opium War
    D. the granting of spheres of influence to Western nations

14. In the late 1880s Confucian scholars resisted government reform and economic change because
    A. the Empress Dowager wished to hand the reins of government to the peasants
    B. they feared it would erode their own political influence
    C. the Russians threatened to withdraw financial aid if the changes took place
    D. Japan had agreed to help them maintain an isolationist policy

15. During the Manchu Dynasty in China the tribute or tributary system
    A. required foreigners to bring gifts to the Chinese emperor and recognize China's superiority
    B. was used to build irrigation systems in the North China Plain
    C. allowed the Chinese to assimilate the culture of the Manchus
    D. granted extraterritorial rights to the European traders in Hong Kong

16. Sun Yat-sen's Three Principles of the People were designed to do all the following *except*
    A. rid China of foreign influence
    B. establish democratic government
    C. break up large estates and provide peasants with land
    D. bring all industry and mining under government monopoly

SECTION 2: JAPAN

United States Occupation of Japan (1945–1952)

The U.S. occupation of Japan led to the diffusion of some American ideas and practices into Japanese culture. United States armed forces, under the leadership of General Douglas MacArthur, the Supreme Commander of the Allied Powers (SCAP), occupied Japan from 1945 to 1952. Japan was stripped of its military conquests, and its territory was restricted to the four main islands. Its armed forces were disbanded and weapons factories were closed. Government and military leaders accused of war crimes were brought to trial, and those who had played a role in Japan's military expansion were removed from positions of power. The emperor renounced his divinity. Nationalistic organizations were banned. MacArthur had a new constitution written for Japan, which went into effect in 1947. It is one of the world's most democratic documents.

GEOGRAPHY

Use of Geography

The American occupation of Japan also brought a number of economic and social reforms. The zaibatsu were broken up; a land-reform program required landlords to sell land cheaply to their tenants; all titles of nobility were abolished; the legal authority of the head of the family over other family members was abolished; and compulsory education was extended for three more years.

GLOBAL
CONCEPTS

Change

CONCEPTS
GLOBAL

The Impact of the Atomic Bombs of 1945

Japan, the only nation in the world ever to have been attacked by nuclear weapons, is opposed to their development and stockpiling. Major demonstrations have occurred in Japan protesting American storage of missiles and the arrival of American nuclear submarines. Similarly, the Japanese protest the testing of nuclear weapons by all nations.

GEOGRAPHY

Human Systems

To allay Japanese fears, the United States–Japanese Mutual Security Pact was revised in 1960 to include a clause stating that the United States could not bring nuclear weapons into Japan without the knowledge of the Japanese government, nor could it use its forces based in Japan in military action without the approval of the Japanese government. Japan has developed the peaceful use of nuclear power, but many Japanese also protest the opening of nuclear power plants.

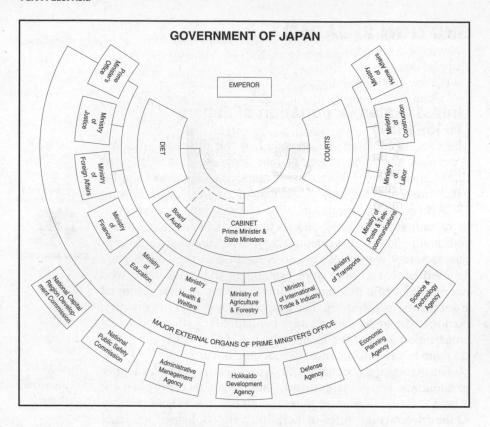

GOVERNMENT OF JAPAN

GLOBAL CONCEPTS

Political Systems

CONCEPTS GLOBAL

GLOBAL CONCEPTS

Human Rights

CONCEPTS GLOBAL

GLOBAL CONCEPTS

Citizenship

CONCEPTS GLOBAL

Democratic System of Government

The 1947 constitution created a parliamentary system with a two-house parliament called the National Diet. The lower house, the House of Representatives, is the more important. The prime minister is elected by the House and is responsible to it. The prime minister and his cabinet can be removed by a "no-confidence" vote, in which case elections will be held for a new house, which then elects a new prime minister. The constitution lists the rights of the Japanese people, which are much like the rights contained in the U.S. Bill of Rights but also include equal rights of women, collective bargaining, equal education, and so on. The right to vote was granted to all citizens over the age of twenty. One of the most well-known provisions of the constitution is Article IX, which renounces the use of war and the "maintenance of land, sea and air forces, as well as other war potential." It does allow the maintenance of defense forces or forces necessary to maintain internal peace.

According to the constitution the emperor is the symbolic head of state and a symbol of the unity of the Japanese people.

His is a ceremonial, not a governing, role. The present emperor, Akihito, came to the throne in 1989 upon the death of his father, Hirohito.

Politics in Japan since World War II has been dominated by the Liberal Democratic Party (LDP). The LDP is closely allied with big business and receives much of its support from rural villages, towns, and small cities. The LDP's major opposition comes from the Socialists, the Democratic Socialists, and the Communists. Supporters of these parties tend to be concentrated in the major urban areas. Their major disagreements with the LDP have been over Japanese–United States relations. Trade unions tend to support these parties.

National politics centers on factions of the LDP within the parliament, with each faction having a leader in the Diet. Legislation is usually passed by consensus, with compromises having been worked out before a bill is actually presented for passage. Until 1993 the LDP managed to maintain political control by forming coalitions with minority parties when necessary. In August 1993 a new coalition of seven minority parties was formed with Morihiro Hosokawa as its leader, and for the first time since the LDP was formed in 1955 it lost control of the government. The Socialist Party gained control of the government in 1994, due in large part to political and financial scandal, but lost power to the LDP in 1996.

The LDP led Japan until 2009 when the country was hard hit by the worldwide recession. The LDP suffered a defeat in the elections, and the Democratic Party of Japan (DPJ) gained control of the Diet. In late 2012, elections swept the LDP into power and former prime minister, Shinzō Abe, became prime minister again.

Present Military Status of Japan

In spite of the provisions of Article IX of the constitution, Japan does maintain forces for the defense of the Japanese islands. These self-defense forces originated in 1950 when U.S. occupation forces were withdrawn from Japan. They were limited to 250,000 men, and service was voluntary. Japan has sent troops into other areas in nonmilitary roles.

Treaty of Mutual Cooperation and Security Between the United States and Japan

According to the terms of the mutual security treaty between the United States and Japan, the United States agrees to take the major responsibility for defending Japan against aggressors. Many Japanese oppose this treaty because they fear that Japan could be drawn into a United States war against its will

GEOGRAPHY

Human Systems

and that the presence of U.S. forces in Japan might even provoke an attack on Japan. Japan's military forces have been steadily built up since 1954, but the government maintains that they are only for purposes of self-defense. In recent years Japan has been pressured by the United States to spend more on its own defense. The Japanese people remain opposed to more spending.

Recovery of the Japanese Economy After World War II

Japan's economic recovery was aided by:

- *Its People*. The Japanese people were disciplined and hard-working. The labor force was highly skilled, receptive to on-the-job training, and well educated. For many years, the people accepted low wages, which gave Japanese industry a competitive edge in the world market.
- *Technology*. When industry was rebuilt after World War II, the latest technologies were used. This allowed the Japanese to use more efficient methods than countries with older factories, giving Japan a competitive edge.
- *U.S. Assistance*. The United States provided the Japanese with millions of dollars of aid, assistance, and loans to rebuild its economy because it wanted a strong economic ally in Asia.
- *Restrictions on the Military*. Japan does not have the enormous cost of maintaining large military forces. Instead, the United States is committed to defending the country. Japan spends less than 1% of its GDP on the military, while the United States spends nearly 4%, and President Trump is looking to increase that amount.
- *Government Assistance*. Businesses in Japan are assisted by the government through low-interest loans, subsidies for new businesses, favorable trade agreements with other nations, and tariffs to protect Japanese industries.

Continuing Needs and Problems Facing the Japanese Economy

Japan's scarcity of raw materials and oil has affected its pattern of economic development. Japan must import almost all the minerals it needs for industry, such as copper, iron ore, lead, coal, zinc, and all its petroleum. The Japanese import oil from China and the Middle East and are looking forward to an oil pipeline being built by Russia that would bring oil to the Sea of Japan. Japan's economic life depends on importing raw materials and exporting finished products to pay for those imports. Although arable land in Japan is scarce, by making use of the advanced farming technologies of the Green Revolution, Japanese farmers provide about 70% of the nation's food supply. Most of the rest comes from the United States, China, Australia, and Canada.

Japan's Role in World Organizations

Japan's role in the United Nations has been affected by Russia's distrust of Japanese-American defense arrangements. Relations between Russia and Japan have sometimes been strained by the presence of American bases in Japan and the close military alliance of the United States with Japan. A dispute over the southern portion of the Kurile Islands and the uneasiness the Russians feel over Japan's close military alliance with the United States caused Russia to block Japan's admission to the United Nations from 1952 to 1956. In 1956 the two nations resumed diplomatic relations, and Japan was admitted to the world organization in 1956.

GLOBAL
CONCEPTS

Change

CONCEPTS
GLOBAL

Japanese Relations with Other Asian Nations

Many of the nations of Southeast Asia have found it difficult to throw off the image of Japan as the militaristic/imperialist nation that invaded, conquered, and exploited their territories during World War II. Some of the nations feel Japan is still exploiting them economically through trade. To create goodwill in Southeast Asia, Japan paid war reparations to the countries that suffered from Japanese aggression. Japan has also provided economic and technical assistance to developing nations and has contributed large amounts to the Asian Development Bank. Japanese industries have been developed in many areas.

In 1972 the People's Republic of China and Japan signed an agreement. Japan recognized the People's Republic as the official government of China and cut its diplomatic ties with Taiwan. This led to a treaty ending World War II between China and Japan and also to trade agreements.

Increasingly, other Asian nations (South Korea, Taiwan, Singapore, China) are competing with Japan in the world market in such areas as textiles, cameras, electronics, and even cars.

Japan became increasingly worried in 1999 about North Korea's hostile nuclear threats. Consequently, many Japanese began to consider the repeal of Article IX of the constitution. South Korea, also worried about North Korea's nuclear capacity, sought to consult Japan about this. An historic moment occurred in the summer of 1999 when Japan and South Korea held joint naval exercises.

WORLD ISSUES

| War |
| and |
| Peace |

GEOGRAPHY

Use of Geography

Developments in the 21st Century

On the domestic front, the event with the single-most important impact on the average Japanese citizen in the early 21st century has to be the 9.0 earthquake that hit northern Japan on March 11, 2011, and the ensuing tsunami. Tens of thousands were dead or missing and nearly 400,000 were left homeless. In addition, the damage to the Fukushima Daiichi nuclear power plant caused radiation levels to rise as far south as Tokyo and to spike at twenty-three times the normal level. The Japanese have faced this disaster as they have faced other natural and man-made disasters in the past, with resilience and fortitude. They have begun the reconstruction of the area and have thus far contained the damage at the power plant as well as could be done under the circumstances. World donations to relief funds were slow in coming, probably due to a perception that the Japanese economy was strong enough that they could take care of themselves. The people of Japan have also perceived their own government as being slow to react and were severely displeased with the lack of response from Prime Minister Naoto Kan. Kan resigned in August 2011 and was succeeded by Yoshiko Noda, who was swept out of power in the 2012 elections.

The roaring Japanese economy suffered a slump and slowdown in the early 1990s leading to several changes in parliamentary leadership in rapid succession. In the mid-nineties the government reaction to an earthquake in Kobe led to accusations against the government for ineffective rescue and relief efforts. In the late nineties the Japanese economy was again severely affected by slowdown and instability and continued to grow worse through the early 2000s. In 2004 the economy rebounded with extensive foreign investment, but in 2008–2009, Japan, dependent on exports, suffered greatly in the worldwide recession when its exports fell by 5 percent. Japan has been replaced by China as the world's second-greatest economic power.

In the field of international relations, Japan has been the focus of many closely watched developments.

1. In November 2003, after the U.S. attack on Iraq in March, the Japanese cabinet approved the deployment of more than 500 noncombatant troops to aid in reconstruction efforts in that country. This was the first time that Japanese soldiers were sent to a combat zone since World War II. The move provoked controversy in Japan, as some feared this might lead to a military right-wing resurgence. Prime Minister Koizumi defended the move as one that was needed to show Japan's importance as a major nation and global power player. Conservatives supported the move and also spoke of rescinding Article IX. Their efforts received some recognition because of the harsh military stance taken by North Korea. That nation has claimed to have nuclear capabilities and has threatened Japan. Very alarming was the

firing by North Korea of a missile over Japan in August 1998, and a missile shot into the Sea of Japan in May 2005. Prime Minister Koizumi has hinted at some form of retaliation should a North Korean missile actually hit Japan. In July 2017, North Korea fired an intercontinental ballistic missile (ICBM), not only capable of reaching Japan, but according to some missile experts, capable of reaching the western coast of the United States (i.e., San Diego, California), and possibly as far in as Denver, Colorado.

2. The Chinese are upset, as are the Koreans, about the alleged misrepresentations in Japanese history school textbooks of Japan's role in East Asia during World War II. The war, also called the Pacific War in Asia, is not accurately described, as narrations about it fail to mention many of the Japanese atrocities that took place in China and Korea between 1931 and 1945. Chinese demonstrations against the publication of these government-approved books took place in China and South Korea in 2005.

3. A continuing source of tension between Japan and Russia is Russia's refusal to return the Kuril Islands to Japan. The Kuril Islands, "discovered" by the Dutch during Europe's Age of Discovery, were ceded to the Japanese by the Russians in 1875. In exchange, Russia was given Sakhalin by the Japanese. At the end of World War II, the Allies gave both Sakhalin and the Kurils to the Soviet Union, the name by which Russia and several other small republics under Russian control were known during the era of communist rule (1917–1991). When the Soviet Union broke up in 1991 and its communist government collapsed, Russia—as the dominant power within the former Soviet Union—retained the international rights and obligations previously held by the Soviets. These rights included possession of Sakhalin and the Kurils. Today Japan still seeks the return of the Kuril Islands, which Russia refuses to cede. Nevertheless, in spite of these tensions, in November 2005, Japan was given a promise by Russian President Vladimir Putin to construct a pipeline that would carry Siberian oil to the Sea of Japan. As Japan has no oil resources, such a promise bodes well for her future energy needs.

4. One positive development affecting Japanese and Koreans occurred in 2002. Japan and South Korea cohosted the international soccer competition known as the World Cup. Previously, Japan had been recognized as the site for international sports competition. Japan had hosted the Winter Games on three occasions. In 1964, Tokyo was host to the Summer Games. Osaka, while never hosting Olympic competition, was host to EXPO '70, the 1970 World's Fair. This was the first time that a world exhibition had been held in Asia.

REVIEW QUESTIONS

Multiple Choice. Select the letter of the answer that correctly completes each statement.

1. After World War II, Japan was occupied by and aided in its recovery by
   A. China
   B. Russia
   C. Korea
   D. the United States

2. The Tokugawa shogunate was best known for its policy of
   A. isolation
   B. interdependence
   C. education
   D. imperialism

3. The Meiji Restoration was significant for its
   A. military conquest of Korea
   B. enlightened approach to modernization
   C. victory over Russia
   D. return to a policy of feudalism

4. Since the early 1970s, Japan's foreign policy has become more independent of U.S. policies because
   A. Japan opposed the U.S. policy of ending the Cold War with Russia
   B. Japan has grown as an economic superpower
   C. the United States has failed to honor its commitments to Japan
   D. Japan is so strong militarily that it no longer needs the United States to protect it

5. The Diet is Japan's
   A. royal family
   B. legislature
   C. economic control board
   D. army

6. The real power of the Japanese emperors has often been usurped by others, but the imperial family has never been dethroned. A major reason for this has been
   A. the Japanese emperor was revered as a god
   B. the military was controlled by the imperial family
   C. shoguns never remained in power long enough to make important decisions
   D. the strong cultural influence of the Chinese

7. During the 1930s and 1940s Japan practiced a policy of imperialism
   in order to gain control of the resources necessary to support its
   industrialization. An example of this was the
   A. opening of trade with the United States
   B. invasion of Manchuria in 1931
   C. signing of the Portsmouth Treaty
   D. expansion of the zaibatsu

8. Which of the following statements about the Japanese imperial family
   is true?
   A. They have most often ruled in name only.
   B. They gained their legitimacy from the shogun.
   C. They control politics in Japan today.
   D. They still claim descent from the gods.

9. Japan's long period of isolation was ended in the 1850s
   A. by the expedition of Commodore Matthew Perry
   B. because the Japanese wanted to renew contact with the European
      colonial powers
   C. by the occupation by the Allied Powers
   D. in order to gain international relief for earthquake victims in Tokyo

10. After the Japanese occupation of Manchuria in 1931
    A. the United States placed an embargo on trade with Japan
    B. the League of Nations condemned the attack
    C. China surrendered to Japan
    D. American and British objections forced the Japanese to withdraw
       from the Asian mainland

11. Japan adopted imperialist policies in the 20th century in order to
    A. control the East Asian sea lanes
    B. gain resources for industrialization and militarization
    C. free the Filipinos from U.S. control
    D. maintain its policy of isolation begun under the Tokugawa shoguns

SECTION 3: KOREA

At the close of World War II, according to an agreement worked out at the Potsdam Conference, the Soviet Union accepted surrender from Japanese troops north of the 38th parallel in Korea, and the United States accepted surrender south of the 38th parallel. Elections for a government of a united Korea were supposed to be held, but efforts to hold the elections were resisted by the Soviet Union, and in 1948 a communist regime was declared in the north with Kim Il-Sung at its helm, and a republic was established in the south with Syngman Rhee as the elected president.

The Korean War

On June 25, 1950, the North Koreans, led by Kim Il-Sung, launched an unprovoked attack on the South. The South Koreans suffered terrible losses. Seoul fell in three days. Almost all of Korea, except for a small area in the southeast, called the Pusan perimeter, was overrun in a month. The UN General Assembly decided to send troops to help the South, under the command of U.S. General Douglas MacArthur. They soon forced North Korean soldiers northward, near the Chinese border. China now intervened with her own forces compelling the UN soldiers to retreat. An armistice was signed in July 1953, near the 38th parallel, in Panmunjom. A demilitarized zone (DMZ) separates the two Koreas to this day.

The war led to mistrust and hatred between people on both sides. The division of the peninsula has increased political and cultural differences. Millions of people became refugees, separated from their families. In the last 50 years, contact between the two Koreas have been rare. Some family exchanges have occurred; a joint South-North Korean women's Ping-Pong team captured the world title in the 1980s. However, North Korea refused to send athletes to the 1988 Olympic Games in Seoul. Unification has been a controversial issue. The first round of high-level talks between both Koreas on this issue was held in Seoul in 1990.

Recent Political Developments

In September 1987 South Korea's constitution was amended to provide for the direct election of a president. In December 1987 the first civilian president of South Korea, Roh Tae Woo, was elected, and he took office in 1988. A second peaceful, democratic election took place in 1992, where Kim Young Sam was chosen president. A continuing sign of political stability occurred with the 1997 election of Kim Dae-Jung as president. Lee Myung Bak won the presidential election in 2007.

Conservative Park Geun-hye became South Korea's first female president in the December 2012 elections. In March of 2017, she was impeached and removed from office by the Constitutional Court over a corruption scandal. She was accused of collusion with longtime confidants to extort millions of dollars from businesses, along with other crimes involving her friend Choi Soon-sil.

Moon Jae-in took office as the new president of South Korea in May 2017. He met with U.S. President Donald Trump in July 2017. At this meeting, President Trump insisted that South Korea renegotiate the trade pact of 2012. President Trump pointed out the imbalance of trade between the two nations in which the U.S. ran a $17 billion deficit in 2016. South Korea is the seventh-largest market for United States exported goods and the sixth-largest supplier of U.S. imported goods.

In 1993 North Korea threatened to withdraw from the nuclear nonproliferation treaty it had signed nearly ten years before and refused to allow inspection of its nuclear facilities. In mid-February 1994 North Korea agreed to the inspection of its facilities by the International Atomic Energy Agency, but refused to let them inspect the facility at Yongbyon, which has the capacity to produce the enriched plutonium that can be used in the production of nuclear weapons. North Korea maintained that it should establish the boundaries of the inspections. In inspections in other countries, the United Nations has established the boundaries. A CIA report in April 1994 indicated that North Korea might already have at least two nuclear weapons. The United States wished to prevent further development of any nuclear weapons on the Korean Peninsula, and called for a UN resolution threatening sanctions against North Korea. China's plan called for issuing a statement encouraging North Korea to allow inspection of its nuclear sites instead, with the possible use of sanctions later. The Chinese plan had the support of other UN members, even South Korea.

In 2002, North Korea admitted it was engaged in a secret attempt to develop nuclear weapons. China sponsored talks to convince North Korea to end its nuclear weapons program until 2009 when North Korea withdrew from the talks and expelled the International Atomic Energy Agency (IAEA) inspectors. It then tested several missiles and apparently tested two nuclear devices undergound. As a result, the UN Security Council threatened sanctions against North Korea.

GEOGRAPHY

Use of Geography

In March 2010 a South Korean ship was hit by a torpedo, killing forty-six sailors. South Korea eventually claimed that the attack was at the hands of the North Korean government. In August that same year the United States joined with the South Koreans in military exercises to show their support of South Korea.

In late March and early April of 1994 the armies of both North and South Korea were put on alert, and the United States offered to deploy Patriot missile launchers to help South Korea defend against possible North Korean attack. Kim Il Sung, who had led North Korea since 1946, threatened that the peninsula was "on the brink of war."

South Korea maintains a military defense treaty with the United States, and the U.S. military has over 36,000 troops stationed in South Korea. These U.S. troops were put on a high alert in the late 1990s due to increasing hostile threat on the part of North Korea.

The most dramatic event to occur in Korea in mid-1994 was the death of North Korean leader Kim Il Sung. Known as the "Great Leader," he designated his son Kim Jong Il, known as the "Dear Leader," as his successor. North Korea's economy declined and its people suffered from severe food shortages under Kim Jong Il's command. Kim Jong Il died in December 2011. He was succeeded by his youngest son Kim Jong Un. In 2013, Kim ordered the execution of his uncle, Jang Song-thaek, in an apparent move to consolidate his own power. Kim's half-brother was killed in Malaysia by assassins who used a nerve agent. North Korea denied any role in the assassination, but it was speculated that Kim had ordered the assassination, again, to consolidate his own power.

Under Kim's rule, North Korea has conducted a number of nuclear and missile tests. In March 2017, North Korea test-fired four banned ballistic missiles over the Sea of Japan, three of which landed in waters that Japan claims as its own exclusive economic zone. In July 2017, North Korea test-fired an intercontinental ballistic missile that some missile experts believe could be capable of carrying a nuclear warhead and capable of reaching the West Coast of the United States and possibly as far in as the central United States.

Developments in the 21st Century

The new century began on a high note for South Korea. Its President, Kim Dae Jung, met North Korean leader Kim Jong Il in June 2000. At this unprecedented meeting in Pyongyang, North Korea's capital, they agreed to seek reconciliation and unification for their countries. In October of that year, President Jung was awarded the Nobel Peace Prize.

To support the U.S. military role in Iraq, South Korea sent 3,000 troops there in 2004. Although South Korea's military was mainly concerned about the actions of North Korea, President Roh's government was less fearful of future hostility from North Korea than was the United States. The South's "sunshine policy" toward the North and its attempt to relieve food shortages there by sending shipments of grain and other goods are examples. The United States would adopt a stronger stand toward the North and was more worried about North Korea's potential for nuclear aggression. In 2002, President Bush accused North Korea, along with Iran and Iraq, of being an "axis of evil." That same year North Korea admitted to maintaining a secret nuclear weapons program, an activity that was a violation of past agreements. In the following year, North Korea withdrew from the Nuclear Nonproliferation Treaty. Although the United States then insisted that the North dismantle its nuclear weapons program, the North demanded a nonaggression treaty and economic aid from the United States. Six-nation talks sponsored by China, beginning in 2003, have failed to result in any agreement on the nuclear weapons issue. These talks ended in 2009.

Economic Geography of Korea

Traditionally, agriculture was the chief economic activity in Korea. Industrial activity was on a low level and was severely hurt during the Korean War (1950–1953). However, since the war, both North and South Korea have made significant economic strides. South Korea's GDP grows by more than 2% annually. Its per capita GDP is over $36,000. Nearly 96% of its people are employed in industry and services. North Korea's GDP is approximately $40 billion; its growth rate is about 1%. About 63% of its people are engaged in industry and services and about 37% are engaged in agriculture.

REVIEW QUESTIONS

Multiple Choice. Select the letter of the answer that correctly completes each statement.

1. South Korea
   A. has a communist government
   B. has more natural resources than North Korea
   C. has had greater economic success than North Korea
   D. signed a mutual defense treaty with China

2. Korea is
   A. a peninsula
   B. an island
   C. a subcontinent
   D. an archipelago

3. The man who controlled North Korea from 1946 to 1994 was
   A. Kim Jong Il
   B. Kim Young Sam
   C. Kim Il Sung
   D. Chu Chang Chun

4. Korea has been divided at the 38th parallel since
   A. World War I
   B. World War II
   C. the Korean War
   D. the Russo-Japanese War

5. Today the majority of Koreans make their living in
   A. agriculture
   B. fishing
   C. manufacturing and services
   D. lumbering

Part G: Africa

African Nationalism and Pan-Africanism

The nationalist movements in Africa varied from region to region and colony to colony. However, for Africans of all colonies, nationalism meant that they wanted to rule themselves and to decide what form that rule would take.

During World War II, many Africans served in the armies of their colonial rulers in Asia, Europe, and Africa. Many others moved to the cities to work in wartime industries for comparatively high wages. In the cities they acquired new skills, learned about life in other parts of the world, joined labor unions and political organizations, and came into contact with the ideas of young nationalists. They began to see that a unified nation might be built and began to transfer their loyalties from traditional groups and authority to these new groups and the idea of a modern nation state.

GEOGRAPHY

Human Systems

When the war ended, many of the colonies in Asia achieved independence. Successful independence movements in Asia encouraged the Africans to seek their own independence. Some African nationalists employed the nonviolent methods of Mahatma Gandhi and used passive resistance. Others employed guerrilla tactics. The Europeans, struggling to repair their own economies, industries, and societies, could not afford a prolonged struggle in Africa. They began to prepare their colonies for independence.

GLOBAL
CONCEPTS

Change

CONCEPTS
GLOBAL

In 1957 the Gold Coast gained its independence from Great Britain. It changed its name to Ghana. Guinea gained its independence from France the following year. By 1977 there were more than forty independent nations in Africa. The era of African colonialism was over.

GLOBAL
CONCEPTS

Power

CONCEPTS
GLOBAL

The colonial legacy left a major problem for the newly independent African nations to deal with—rivalries among the many ethnic groups inhabiting their nations. The new African nations must try to unite people with diverse languages, religions, and customs. Many African leaders have met this challenge by outlawing all but one political party and creating single-party states. Most leaders do not see this as undemocratic, because membership in the one party is open to all, and they feel that a single party will ensure a more stable government. Some African nations have approached the problem by not holding elections. In others, elections are so corrupt that they are meaningless.

WORLD ISSUES

Determination
of Political
and Economic
Systems

In many African nations, the military staged a coup d'etat (overthrow of the government). Sometimes the coup was to overthrow leaders who were thought to be bad, ineffective, or corrupt. Sometimes it was in an effort to improve economic conditions or to subdue rival political factions that had built up their own military. Sometimes it was simply the desire of military leaders for more power.

Use of Geography

GLOBAL
CONCEPTS
Identity
CONCEPTS
GLOBAL

In about 1960 there was a call for pan-Africanism, a joining together of African nations to improve conditions for all African peoples. The goals of pan-Africanism are to improve economic, political, and social conditions for all Africans. Nationalist feelings in the various African nations have been a stumbling block to pan-Africanism, however.

In 1963 the Organization of African Unity was created to try to foster cooperation and unity in order to achieve progress. It was disbanded in 2002 and replaced by the African Union with a membership of fifty-three nations.

South Africa

The Dutch established a supply station at the Cape of Good Hope in 1652. Before long, Dutch settlers began to arrive, and the supply station became Cape Colony. (The Dutch settlers and their descendants are known as Afrikaaners. The Dutch farmers were known as Boers.) The Hottentots and Bushmen were pushed north as the settlers took more land for farms. The farmers (Boers) employed black slave labor.

GEOGRAPHY

Use of Geography

In the late 18th century, the British came to establish their own supply stations, and in 1806 they seized the Cape Colony. In 1836 several thousand Boers began the "great trek" northeast-ward to escape British rule and preserve their Afrikaaner culture. They were resisted by the Zulu (Bantus), who were defeated at the Battle of Blood River in 1838. By the 1850s the Boers had established two republics in the interior: the Transvaal and the Orange Free State. However, when diamonds were discovered in the Orange Free State in 1871 and gold in the Transvaal in 1886, British miners and businesspeople began to arrive.

Hostilities between the Afrikaaners and the British increased until the Boer War of 1899 to 1902, in which the Afrikaaners were defeated. In 1910 the British united the two Boer republics, Cape Colony and Natal, into the Union of South Africa, which became a self-governing country of the British Empire in 1934.

African and Asian (mostly from the British colony in India) workers were recruited for work in the mines and associated industries. Many Afrikaaners believed in the superiority of the white race and its culture, and the British did little to prevent this attitude or the resulting discrimination and segregation.

In 1948 the Afrikaaner Nationalist Party gained control of the government and began the policy of apartheid (Afrikaans word meaning "separateness"). This policy rigidly defined four racial groups: white, black, Asian, and colored. Under this policy each group was to have its own living areas and develop its own political institutions. Black Africans had to carry passbooks containing information on where they lived and worked and where they could travel. Intermarriage was forbidden, separate education was provided, strikes by black workers were outlawed, jobs were restricted to racial groups, separate facilities had to be maintained, and blacks could not own land outside reservations. Blacks had no vote and no representation in government. They were denied basic human rights. The Bantu Authorities Act of 1951 established ten Bantustans (homelands) for the blacks. Until 1985 a policy of forced relocation of unemployed blacks to the homelands was followed. The blacks were to be allowed "separate but equal" development on these homelands. They were to become independent countries with their own governments and economies.

GLOBAL CONCEPTS
Human Rights
CONCEPTS GLOBAL

GLOBAL CONCEPTS
Justice
CONCEPTS GLOBAL

POPULATION OF SOUTH AFRICA

Official Category	Number of People (millions)	% of Total Population
Black	23.9	67.7
White	4.8	18.3
Colored	3	10.6
Asian	1	3.4

In 1912 the African National Congress (ANC), an organization to unite the South African blacks, to end segregation and to work for the right to take part in government, was created. The ANC was originally a nonviolent organization. They used strikes and employed many of the same methods used by Mahatma Gandhi. After the Sharpeville Massacre in 1960, the ANC turned to the use of sabotage. They blew up power lines and refineries to undermine confidence in the government, disrupt the economy, and bring international attention to their plight. The government banned the ANC and arrested its leaders, including Nelson Mandela.

Beginning with the Soweto riots in 1976, activity against the policy of apartheid increased in South Africa. As more and more nations condemned the policy, some restrictions were relaxed.

Petty apartheid (separate facilities) was largely dropped, though some beaches remain restricted. Blacks were allowed to form labor unions, but they still had no voice in government.

As protests and violence escalated, international pressure on South Africa to change its policies increased. The government, under the leadership of P. W. Botha, repealed the pass laws and the Mixed Marriages Act. Many black prisoners were released.

In 1974 South Africa lost its voting privileges in the United Nations. In 1986 the U.S. Congress passed sanctions against South Africa. Most American companies sold their interests and left South Africa. The British Commonwealth nations also voted for sanctions.

F. W. de Klerk became president of South Africa in 1989. In 1990 he lifted the ban on the ANC and released Nelson Mandela from prison. By June 1991 the last of the apartheid laws, the race registration law, was repealed, and talks between the white government and representatives of the ANC—including, of course, Nelson Mandela—were begun. In June 1993 the representatives agreed on a date in April 1994 for the first election, in which all people in South Africa would be eligible to vote for a legislature, which would write a new constitution for the country. In September 1993 Nelson Mandela told world leaders that enough progress had been made with the government in South Africa and that the economic sanctions imposed by other nations could and should be lifted.

Proposals for the new constitution included guarantees of freedom of speech and fair trial, freedom to choose where to live, freedom from torture, limits on the president's power to declare a state of emergency, and guarantees against the loss of citizenship. In addition, it had been agreed that the homelands would be abolished immediately after the elections.

There were a number of groups that condemned the agreements. They included conservative Afrikaaners who did not wish to see any change in the government at all and other white groups that demanded that territory be set aside as a white homeland that would no longer be part of South Africa. There were also black groups that were against the agreements. They included the Inkhatha Freedom Party, which represents the Zulu ethnic group, numbering more than 8 million. Nelson Mandela went on to win the presidential election in April 1994.

In spite of all the objections, enormous steps have been taken to end the system of apartheid in South Africa and to finally provide political representation for the majority of its people.

In December 1993 Nelson Mandela and F. W. de Klerk jointly received the Nobel Peace Prize for their efforts to work out a plan for the peaceful transition to majority rule and to bring about the end of apartheid in South Africa. The 1994 elections were generally peaceful, and resulted in a multiparty legislature. Nelson Mandela became the nation's new leader in an historic inauguration.

In 1995 President Nelson Mandela appointed a Truth and Reconciliation Commission under the leadership of Desmond Tutu to investigate murders and other human rights abuses under the apartheid government. Elections for a new government were held in the spring of 1999, but Nelson Mandela had no intention of running for office again. His successor proved to be Thabo Mbeki. In 2004, the African National Congress (ANC) won another landslide victory, and Mbeki was sworn in for another term. South Africa has an extremely high percentage of HIV-positive people (more than 5 million) among its population. Mbeki long denied the link between HIV and AIDS but in 2003 reversed his policy and the government approved a plan to distribute AIDS drugs free of charge. Mbeki resigned in 2008 and Jacob Zuma was elected president in April 2009. Nelson Mandela died in 2013. The ANC won 54% of the 2016 national vote—a large drop in their majority. They also lost municipal votes in Pretoria and Port Elizabeth in 2016. These losses were largely due to economic reasons. South Africa suffered an economic setback from the world recession in 2009, but remains the world's largest producer of gold and gem-quality diamonds. In 2010 South Africa gained some international prestige as the first African nation to host the World Cup Soccer Tournament.

Kenya

In the late 19th century, Kenya came under the control of the British government as part of the East Africa Protectorate. Before long, British settlers came.

The nationalist movement in Kenya began in the early 20th century. Jomo Kenyatta, the leader of the nationalist movement, became president of the Kenya African Union in 1947. Its major goals were to regain control of the land lost to the Europeans, to halt exploitation of Africans by Europeans, and to gain basic civil rights for Africans.

An organization known as the Mau Mau was created in 1952, which used terrorist and guerrilla activities to free Kenya. The British declared a state of emergency and placed thousands in detention camps.

In 1956 the British began gradual reforms and Africans were allowed some participation in government. However, Africans

GEOGRAPHY

Human Systems

demanded independence, and in 1963 Kenya was granted independence. In 1964 Kenya became a republic in the British Commonwealth of Nations and Jomo Kenyatta its first president.

There were many problems in Kenya as a result of differences among the many ethnic groups (the Kikuyu, the Luo, the Masai, the Kalenjin, and so on). Kenyatta, a Kikuyu, urged his people to forget their ethnic loyalties and accept a principle he called harambee (pulling together). Kenyatta died in 1978 and was succeeded by Daniel Arap Moi.

WORLD ISSUES

Determination
of Political
and Economic
Systems

Because the major political parties in Kenya represented the major ethnic groups and helped prolong the ethnic rivalries, Kenya was declared a one-party state in 1982. The only legal political party is KANU (Kenya African National Union). In 1991 a constitutional amendment established a multiparty system. Several new parties have emerged since then, but there is much factionalism, and elections have been plagued by electoral fraud. Moi was elected to his fourth term of office December 1992, and in January 1993 he dissolved the multiparty legislature, probably because he feared the legislature would introduce legislation that would limit presidential powers. Moi was re-elected in 1999. Moi was prohibited by the constitution from running for office in 2002. The opposition leader, Mwai Kibaki, won that election. He promised to put an end to corruption but made little progress toward that goal. A new constitution won approval in August 2010. It limited presidential power. In March 2013, Uhuru Kenyatta (Jomo Kenyatta's son) won the presidential election and is still in office. Kenya is considered one of the top human rights violators in the world, and in recent years American tourists have been cautioned about traveling in Kenya because of the strife and ethnic conflicts.

GLOBAL
CONCEPTS
Human Rights
CONCEPTS
GLOBAL

The government began a program to Africanize Kenyan life and economics. Asians were required to obtain work permits and could not be employed unless there were no Kenyans suitable for the job or they had special talents. Many Asians emigrated to Great Britain. In 1968 Britain limited immigration, and the remaining Asians have suffered economically and socially. As part of the program to Africanize Kenya, European ownership of land has also been reduced.

WORLD ISSUES

Political and
Economic
Refugees

Most of Kenya's people make a living in agriculture, although fertile land is scarce. Kenya has one of the most rapidly increasing populations in the world. The annual per capita income is about $2,200. Major exports are cash crops such as coffee, tea, and sisal. Industrial development is limited, and the unemployment rate is high. The country has two official languages, English and Swahili, and many ethnic languages are spoken by the groups inhabiting the country.

GEOGRAPHY

Human Systems

The global recession in 2009 and one of the worst droughts to hit East Africa in the last 60 years combined to cause a decline in GDP growth of 3.5 percent. Cattle deaths in the north caused by the drought led to widespread hunger and ethnic conflict. Relief for Kenyans suffering from hunger and homelessness was slow in coming. The situation was made even worse by an influx of Somalian refugees also affected by the drought. The Dadaab refugee camp in northern Kenya was housing more than four times the number it was designed for. Nearly 1,400 Somali refugees per day were arriving in the spring of 2011. In 2016, the government announced plans to close the camp over time.

Nigeria

Over 200 different ethnic groups live in Nigeria, but the four largest and most politically dominant are the Hausa and Fulani in the north, the Ibo in the southeast, and the Yoruba in the southwest.

In the mid-19th century, the British began their expansion into Nigeria. By 1914 all of Nigeria was a British colony. After World War I a nationalist movement arose. The British gradually allowed more African participation in government until in 1954 a constitution creating a federal union, ensuring the power of the three major regions—the east, the west, and the north—was accepted. Independence was finally granted in 1960.

Almost immediately, regional differences became obvious. The northern region, with the largest population, controlled the federal government. In 1966 there was a coup led by Ibo military officers, and General Ironsi took control of the government. Later in 1966 violence broke out against Ibo living in the north, and General Ironsi was killed by Hausa soldiers and replaced by Yakuba Gowon, a northerner. General Ojukwu, the leader of the Ibo region, declared eastern Nigeria independent as the Republic of Biafra.

GEOGRAPHY

Human Systems

Civil war broke out about two months later. Biafra was unable to hold back the Nigerian troops or to feed its people. An estimated one million Biafrans died as a result of military action or starvation. Early in 1970 Biafra surrendered.

Military coups have occurred frequently in Nigeria since 1970. The country has been under military rule for most of the years since independence. It has been divided into nineteen states, each having its own governor. From 1983 to 1989 all political parties were banned. In 1989 political parties were again allowed to register. Later in 1989 the incumbent president, General Ibrahim Babangida, announced that the government would create two new political parties because, he said, other political parties were

WORLD ISSUES

Determination
of Political
and Economic
Systems

linked to discredited groups and had also failed to fulfill registration requirements. Elections were held in the summer of 1993, but the results were voided by Babangida. In August 1993, after much turmoil in the nation, Babangida resigned, and an interim government was named. That government was overthrown by General Sani Abacha, who died in 1998. The new government was headed by General Abdul Salam Abubakar. In 1999, Nigeria returned to civilian government with democratic elections. Olusegun Obasanjo was chosen president. Obasanjo promised reform, but within two years it was obvious they were empty promises. He was, however, reelected in 2003.

Obasanjo's chosen successor, Umaru Musa Yar'Adua, won the election in 2007. He died in 2010 and was succeeded by Goodluck Jonathan, his vice president. Jonathan won the election over Muhammadu Buhari in 2011. This led to widespread riots in the north (Jonathan was a southern Christian, while Buhari was a northern Muslim).

Nigeria made a rapid recovery from the civil war, largely because of oil revenues. However, mismanagement and overspending of funds led to an economic decline in the early 1980s. In 1987 the government announced plans for economic austerity and began to encourage a birth-control program. Today Nigeria's stability is threatened by the spread of Islamic law (sharia) across the northern region, which is heavily Muslim. This has caused fighting between fundamentalist Muslims and Christians. Besides petroleum, exports include cash crops such as rubber, palm products, and timber. The annual per capita GDP is less than $800. In 1994, labor disputes continued to weaken Nigeria's economy.

Violent communal conflict spread throughout much of Nigeria in the late 2000s. The government moved against rebel groups in the Niger delta in 2009, killing hundreds, but it did not prevent the rebel groups from expanding their resistance to Lagos, where they set fire to an oil depot and several tanker ships. Christians and Muslims attacked each other in the city of Bauchi. A Muslim militant group called the Boko Haram came under attack by government forces, killing at least 800. In 2010, Muslim herders were attacked in Jos and they retaliated by killing farmers in surrounding villages. Much of the conflict in Nigeria is ethnic and religious and, for the most part, caused by rivalry over distribution of resources and income.

Boko Haram declared it was a part of ISIS in 2015. Boko Haram had kidnapped 276 schoolgirls from the town of Chibok in 2014. Some of them were released in October 2016, and more girls were released in May of 2017. They were exchanged for five Boko Haram commanders who were released by the government of Muhammadu Buhari. The freed girls are in the custody of the government while they are receiving medical attention, trauma counseling, and rehabilitation. Some girls are still being held.

Ghana

Several civilizations once existed in the area of what is now Ghana. The country's name comes from the ancient empire of Ghana, which was located to the northwest of what is now the modern African country of Ghana. The Ashanti Empire flourished in the area in the 18th and 19th centuries.

British rule in the region was established in 1901, and Ghana became a republic in 1960. President Kwame Nkrumah built hospitals and schools and promoted developmental projects. However, he ran the country into debt, jailed his opponents, and was accused of corruption. Nkrumah was given dictatorial powers in 1964 and created a one-party socialist state. In 1966, he was overthrown by a military coup, and a series of military coups followed. Several of these coups were engineered and led by Jerry Rawlings. Rawlings suspended the constitution and instituted austerity programs that decreased the deficit over the next ten years. In 1992, he returned the country to civilian rule and elections were held. Rawlings was elected president in 1992 and 1996. In 2001, John Agyekum Kufuor was elected president. He set up a National Reconciliation Commission to review human rights abuses during military rule. He was reelected in 2004. In 2008, John Atta Mills won the election to the presidency. He died in 2012 and was replaced with Vice President John Dramani Mahama, who won a full term in the 2012 elections.

Ghana's major exports are cocoa and gold.

Africa in the Global Context

For the most part, after independence African nations chose to remain nonaligned (choosing to be neither pro-Soviet nor pro-United States). African leaders also feared neocolonialism. For this reason, many were reluctant to maintain strong relationships with their former colonial rulers or with any industrialized Western nation. Others were economically so weak that they had to allow colonial banks and industries to remain in place. In addition, many nations that avoided foreign involvement immediately following independence have since been forced by economic and political crises to accept the presence of multinational corporations.

WORLD ISSUES

Determination of Political and Economic Systems

International Organizations

Many African nations have joined a number of international organizations to promote African unity, improve economics, and strengthen their influence in world markets and world events.

1. *The United Nations.* The African nations now have the most powerful voting bloc in the United Nations General Assembly, with about fifty members, and can influence UN decisions and policies. African nations have received much aid and assistance through various UN agencies.

2. *The World Bank.* The bank, a specialized agency associated with the UN, provides loans and technical assistance to developing nations.

3. *The International Monetary Fund.* The IMF, another specialized agency of the UN, provides loans to members with balance-of-payments problems and provides technical assistance.

4. *The Commonwealth of Nations.* Many of the former colonies of Great Britain belong. It was organized to promote economic cooperation and to coordinate scientific, military, and educational affairs.

5. *The Lome Convention.* In 1975 a number of African, Caribbean, and Pacific nations voted to associate themselves with the European Economic Community to gain economic benefits through trade and tariff agreements.

6. *Organization of Petroleum Exporting Countries.* OPEC, designed to control world oil prices by coordinating and controlling production, has four African member states: Algeria, Gabon, Libya, and Nigeria.

7. *Organization of African Unity.* The OAU was founded in 1963 to promote unity, solidarity, and cooperation among African states. It had little power beyond talking and trying to encourage cooperation. It has enjoyed some success in settling boundary disputes and developing energy sources. The OAU was disbanded in 2002 and replaced by the African Union, which has the same fifty-three members as the OAU. These members include all the African nations except Morocco.

Foreign Intervention

In certain instances African countries or groups within those countries have been forced to ask for, or have been unable to prevent, foreign intervention in their internal affairs.

1. *The Congo in the 1960s.* After the Belgian Congo became independent in June 1960, the Province of Katanga, under the leadership of Moise Tshombe, seceded and declared its independence. Belgium sent troops to end the rebellions. The prime

minister (Patrice Lumumba) of the Congo appealed for Soviet aid, and the Soviets sent weapons, transport equipment, technicians, and advisers. Soviet influence alarmed some Congolese and most Western nations, who encouraged the president of the Congo (Kasavubu) to dismiss Lumumba. An army leader, Joseph Mobutu, ordered the Soviets to leave the country, and in 1961 Lumumba was assassinated. Meanwhile, the Katanga rebellion continued, with Tshombe employing European and South African mercenaries to resist a United Nations peacekeeping force that had been sent into the region. An agreement to end the secessionist movement was finally reached, and UN troops left the Congo in 1964. Tshombe was elected president, but in 1965 he was overthrown in a military coup led by Mobutu. In 1971 Mobutu changed the name of the country to Zaire. Foreign investors were invited back into the country (most fled during the terrorism of the rebellions), but continued conflict in the country has discouraged them. Throughout the 1980s and 1990s, government corruption and economic decline grew worse and worse. Rwandan refugees flooded eastern Zaire in 1994. Rebels from Rwanda attacked the refugee camps in Zaire, and Zairian government troops became involved in the turmoil. Mobutu spent many months in 1996 out of the country for medical care. Meanwhile, a rebel leader, Laurent Kabila, an enemy of Mobutu, began to build up his power and to move toward Kinshasha, the capital. Mobutu returned to Zaire to negotiate with Kabila but was unsuccessful. He went into exile, and Kabila took control of the country and renamed it Congo. Mobutu died in the fall of 1997.

2. *French military involvement in Chad*. Chad gained independence from France in 1960. Chad has a sparse population (being located mostly in the regions of the Sahara and the Sahel). The population is divided between the Christian south and the Muslim north, and tribal differences are also a problem. In 1960 a southerner, Francois Tombalbaye, became president. A rebellion broke out in the northern and eastern sections in 1965 and resulted in civil war. In 1975 a military coup overthrew Tombalbaye's government, but another southerner took control of the government. The conflict between the north and south continued, with France supporting the southern government. Northern forces called on Libya for assistance, and Muammar Qaddafi sent Libyan troops. In 1981 foreign troops were withdrawn, but in 1982 civil war broke out again. Libyan forces entered the war in support of the north, and French and Zairian forces entered the war in support of the south. In 1984 France and Libya agreed to remove their forces, but Libyan troops remained in the north in violation of the agreement. In 1987

GEOGRAPHY

Use of Geography

the government launched an attack against the northern and Libyan forces and regained control of all but a small strip of land where Libya has an air base. In 1990 a Libyan-supported group overthrew the government, and their leader became president. Libyan troops were said to have withdrawn in May of 1994, and a new constitution was approved in 1996, leading to Chad's first multiparty presidential election.

3. *Superpower rivalry in Ethiopia and Angola.* Except for a short time during World War II when it was occupied by Italian forces, Ethiopia was one of the only two African nations that maintained their independence. Emperor Haille Selassie ruled Ethiopia from 1916 to 1974. The United States provided the emperor with aid and assistance partly because of the country's strategic location on the Red Sea. In 1974 he was overthrown, and the army began making socialist reforms—land was taken from landowners and turned over to peasant associations. In 1976 a military agreement was reached with the Soviet Union, and United States military advisers were expelled. Ethiopia and Somalia have had border disputes since Somalia became independent in 1960. Because the Soviet Union was supporting Ethiopia, Somalia turned over a military base to the United States.

Angola received its independence in 1975. After independence, three rival groups fought for control and there was a civil war. The MPLA (Popular Movement for the Liberation of Angola) was supported by the Soviet Union and Cuba; the FNLA (National Front for the Liberation of Angola) was supported by the United States, France, and Zaire; and UNITA (National Union for the Total Independence of Angola) was supported by Portugal, China, South Africa, and white Angolans. By 1976 the MPLA had achieved victory. The MPLA established a Marxist state with Soviet backing and Cuban support troops. The United States continued to provide assistance to UNITA rebels, so conflict continued. In 1991, according to the terms of an agreement worked out by President Mobutu of Zaire, the last Cuban troops were withdrawn from Angola. Later that same year UNITA signed a treaty with the government to end the civil war that had gone on for 16 years. UNITA rejected election results in 1992, and fighting broke out again. In 1993 the United States recognized the government of Angola for the first time since its independence in 1975.

4. *Ethnic clashes in Rwanda.* Lingering tensions between the Hutus and the Tutsis in Rwanda exploded in 1994 when the country's Hutu president died in a mysterious plane crash. Hutus blamed the Tutsis. The resulting fighting caused over 500,000 deaths. Refugees seeking to escape Zaire were faced with food

GEOGRAPHY

Use of Geography

GLOBAL
CONCEPTS

Change

CONCEPTS
GLOBAL

shortages and outbreaks of cholera and dysentary. France sent troops to try to stop the fighting and to restore political stability.

United States–African Relationships

As part of its policy to contain the spread of communism in the 1960s, the United States began to provide aid and assistance to many African nations.

Americans (government and private citizens) have provided assistance (medical, food, volunteers) to drought-stricken and famine-ridden regions of Africa. Starting in the 1960s, the Peace Corps has helped to develop rural Africa—teaching agricultural techniques, establishing schools, and carrying out many other programs.

The American government has provided millions of dollars in military loans and grants. American multinational corporations have established branches in many African nations, providing employment and infusing some money into the local economy. The United States has on occasion maintained military bases in Kenya, Somalia, and Liberia.

In the past, black African nations have had difficulty reconciling American ideals on human rights with the reality of racial prejudice and inequality in the United States. However, the civil rights gains of the 1960s and the recent change in American policy from constructive engagement to divestment and sanctions against the government of South Africa have done much to improve this situation. The trips to Africa taken by President Clinton in 1998 and Secretary of State Albright in 1999 were signs of continuing U.S. interest in Africa.

Somalia and the United States

The Somali Republic became independent in 1960. As a result of a coup in 1969 Somalia came under the rule of General Muhammad Siyad Barrah. In 1991 Barrah fled the country, and there was intense fighting between rival clans to gain control of the country. By the late fall of 1992 thousands of people were in peril. Civil war, drought, and famine had already taken the lives of thousands, and the lives of thousands more were threatened. The rival clans interfered with international efforts to relieve the famine by keeping relief supplies from reaching their enemies and also to make the people dependent on them for the supplies. By November 1992 the Bush administration felt that conditions in Somalia had deteriorated to the point where U.S. intervention was necessary. He volunteered U.S. troops for the UN force in Somalia to protect the relief workers, supply routes, and humanitarian-aid distribution points. The UN authorized the U.S.

forces to use all means necessary to deliver the relief supplies to the needy. The pressure from the UN and U.S. forces resulted in the signing of a peace treaty by the two most powerful clan leaders in December 1992. Early in 1993, shortly after the agreement was reached, it was broken, and clan fighting broke out again. In June 1993 Pakistani members of the UN peacekeeping forces were killed; General Mohammed Farah Aidid, one of the most powerful clan leaders in Mogadishu, the capital, was considered responsible. Subsequently, several attacks were carried out against Aidid's weapons caches and his supporters' holdings. Aidid was targeted for capture, but he was not caught. In October several members of the peacekeeping forces were killed, including eighteen Americans. Another American was taken captive and interrogated by Aidid's forces, and video excerpts from the interrogation were broadcast worldwide. More American forces and equipment were ordered to Somalia, but it was also announced that all American forces would be withdrawn by March 1994. This was done, amidst concern for the future of Somalia.

By 2011 Somalia had been without a central government for 20 years. One sign of the lawlessness rampant in Somalia is the existence of Somalian pirates who prey on ships in the Indian Ocean. Another was the rise of several Islamist groups that advocate strict Shari'a. One of these groups is the al-Shabab (youth). The al-Shabab has fought the Transitional Federal Government (TFG). The United States has used several means to destroy al-Shabab leaders as they have ties to Al-Qaeda. The United States declared al-Shabab a terrorist organization. As a result, it became a crime to aid and abet al-Shabab and the United States begin withholding economic and food aid from areas controlled by al-Shabab. These areas are now the areas of Somalia that suffer the most from the drought and famine in Somalia.

Sudan

On January 9, 2011, a referendum was held in Sudan to determine independence for southern Sudan. The southern Sudanese voted overwhelmingly for independence. On July 9, 2011, South Sudan celebrated its first independence day. After years and years of civil war and atrocities between northern and southern Sudanese, it remains to be seen if Sudan and South Sudan can coexist without warfare and strife. There is hope; South Sudan has resources, but North Sudan has the infrastructure to transport those resources. Perhaps they can create a relationship based on common economics, and end the years of strife. In any case, the newest nation in the world is South Sudan, carved out of the largest nation in Africa.

Part H: Latin America

Political Revolutions

The 20th century led to important political changes in many nations in Latin America. Democratically elected governments replaced military-led governments throughout the region. In addition, Mexico experienced a political revolution when the candidate of the ruling party was defeated in the presidential elections of 2000. The long-term effects of all the political changes are not clear yet. However, Latin American and Caribbean nations are faced with increasingly social and economic problems brought on by demographic changes and an unequal distribution of wealth, land, and opportunities for an education and in general a better life.

Mexico

The Mexican Revolution of 1911 led to important changes in that nation. After the fall of Díaz, military leaders succeeded one another as president and created a constitutional government based on a one-party political system. The Roman Catholic Church lost much of its influence and power. The Mexican labor movement was allowed to develop and became an important force. The labor unions competed with the new developing industrial oligarchy to influence the government.

GEOGRAPHY

Environment and Society

Mexico became more nationalistic, and the nationalization of the petroleum industry in the 1930s by Lazaro Cardenas symbolized the nation's change of direction. In the years after 1940, the leaders of the ruling political party, the PRI, sought to create political stability by allowing a middle class to develop and by encouraging economic change. However, the PRI has continued to hold power despite growing political opposition.

In 1988 Carlos Salinas de Gotari was chosen by the PRI as its official candidate and took office after a disputed presidential election. President Salinas made a number of painful budgetary reductions. There were cuts in spending on education, health care, and other social services. Thousands of government workers were laid off and state-owned industries were sold to private investors. President Salinas also moved toward freer trade, and the Mexican government ratified NAFTA.

GEOGRAPHY

Human Systems

In 1994, President Salinas hand picked Ernest Zedillo as PRI's presidential candidate after the original candidate Luis Donaldo Colosio was assassinated. President Zedillo was elected in August 1994 for a six-year term. Salinas promised that the PRI, in power for more than six decades, would not resort to fraud or irregularities to win the scheduled August 1994 elections. In early 1994, a rebellion took place in Chiapas, a poor state in southern Mexico where descendants of the Maya live mostly in poverty. This rebellion is further indication that political, economic, and social reforms are needed. As Mexico entered the millennium the demands of the Zapatistas were still not met by the national government.

In 2000, the free and fair election of Vincente Fox of the National Action Party (PAN) as president for a six-year term ended 71 years of uninterrupted rule by the Institutional Revolutionary Party (PRI). Even though the Mexican two-house legislature remained under PRI control, the fact that the president who was elected was not the PRI candidate was a hopeful democratic sign in Mexico. The Mexican people are increasingly demanding open and fairer elections. The question remains whether a democratically elected government in Mexico can solve problems such as political corruption, drug trafficking, lack of adequate employment, and illegal immigration to the United States. In 2006, Felipe Calderon, the PRI candidate, was elected president of Mexico. President Calderon used the Mexican military to combat narco-terrorism. His term in office ended in 2012 without any clear-cut success against the drug trade cartels, despite the use of the Mexican military.

Enrique Peña Nieto was elected president in 2012. His election returned the PRI to power after 12 years of PAN presidents. President Peña Nieto has had to confront the same problems as his predecessors. The Mexican economy, the second-largest in Latin America, has not provided enough jobs for the growing Mexican population. Reduced employment opportunities continue to be the major reason for Mexicans trying to enter the U.S. legally and illegally. Corruption continues to damage and reduce confidence in the Mexican economy and the judicial system. Despite some success in capturing or eliminating cartel leaders, the drug cartels continue to be a serious problem that defies a solution. Illegal immigration, drug use, and smuggling are everyday problems that affect the quality of life of the Mexican people and have caused tensions between the United States and Mexico. President Donald Trump, elected in 2016, has promised to build a wall to curb illegal immigration, eliminate drug trafficking from Mexico, and renegotiate the NAFTA agreement. These are some of the very important issues that have led to increasing friction between the two nations.

Cuba

Cuba remained a Spanish colony until 1898 when independence was established as part of the treaty that settled the Spanish-American War. The U.S. influence in Cuba continued after its military occupation ended in 1902. Between 1933 and 1959 Fulgencio Batista dominated, and although he provided political stability, economic problems led to increased suffering. A rebellion supported by young professionals, students, urban workers, and some farmers was led by Fidel Castro. By 1959 Castro's military forces had defeated Batista's army and seized power.

Castro brought about great political, social, and economic changes. He turned to the communist nations, especially the former Soviet Union, for economic support and protection from the United States. By 1965 Castro's socialist state was officially ruled by the Cuban Communist Party and guided by the principles of Marxism-Leninism.

Castro sought to export the Cuban Revolution by supporting guerrilla movements in Bolivia, Colombia, Nicaragua, El Salvador, and elsewhere. This forced the United States to pay greater attention to the social and economic problems in Latin America. Starting in the 1960s, the United States began to work to isolate Cuba politically and economically.

During the 1990s, the United States continued its trade embargo against Cuba despite opposition from many Latin American and European countries. In the 1980s, the collapse of communism in Europe had ended the massive support of the former Soviet Union and Eastern European nations for Cuba. By the early 1990s, Cuba increasingly experienced economic and social problems. In 1994, Cuba and the United States reached an agreement concerning increased Cuban immigration after another wave of Cubans left the island nation for the United States to escape the harsh economic conditions. Throughout the 1990s, the United States insisted that Cuba make political reforms if it wanted to have the trade embargo lifted. As the new millennium began, Fidel Castro increasingly faced difficult choices as the Cuban economy continued to deteriorate. In 2007, Fidel Castro became ill. Fidel was replaced as president in February 2008 by Cuba's Parliament. In August 2015, the United States reestablished diplomatic relations with Cuba and opened its embassy in Havana.

During the administration of President Barack Obama, U.S. and Cuban relations improved. Tourism and some exchanges of trade goods and services increased. More Americans took advantage of the relaxed travel rules to visit Cuba. President Raul Castro has allowed more private enterprise to exist within the mostly government-run, socialist economy. Increased tourism, currency reforms, and growing private-enterprise opportunities have led to improvements in the quality of life of a large percentage of the Cuban people.

The death of Fidel Castro in 2016, in a sense, signaled the passing of the Cuban Revolution despite the fact that the Cuban government remains under the control of the country's Communist Party. The election of President Donald Trump has led to a renewed atmosphere of tension between the two nations. President Trump has called for a more open political and election system and an economy less directed by the government.

Nicaragua

The U.S. interest in Nicaragua dates from the late 1840s when the American government contested British supremacy in Central America. The United States began a military occupation of the nation in 1912, which lasted until 1933. In the mid-1930s, the national guard, trained by U.S. military officers, took responsibility for maintaining order. The national guard was the instrument for the rise of the Somoza dictatorship, which ruled Nicaragua from 1936 through most of the 1970s. Although there was economic progress under Somoza in agricultural production and then in the industrial sector, there was little real distribution of income.

The assassination of Pedro Chamorro, the publisher of an opposition newspaper, in 1978 sparked an uprising that toppled the Somoza dictatorship and brought the Sandinista Front to power in 1979. The Sandinistas sought to create a socialist-type state in Nicaragua, and Daniel Ortega became the nation's leader. The Sandinistas soon faced opposition from the United States. Moreover, the Sandinista government faced serious economic problems brought on by alienating important segments of the agricultural and industrial sectors.

Hostility toward the Sandinista government because of its ties to Castro's Cuba, the former Soviet Union, and the insurgency in El Salvador led the United States to support the Contra military forces, which were seeking to overthrow the Sandinistas. The costly civil war in Nicaragua led to large numbers of casualties, increased emigration, and a further deterioration of the Nicaraguan economy.

GEOGRAPHY

Human Systems

In 1990, a democratically elected government headed by Violeta Chamorro, the wife of Pedro Chamorro, took power. The Sandinistas peacefully gave up power but continued as part of the government. In the mid-1990s another presidential election was held and once again the Sandinista Party lost. President Aleman continued the policy of national reconciliation initiated by the previous government. Presidential elections were held in 2001. Enrique Bolanos of the Liberal Constitutionalist Party was elected to the Nicaraguan presidency, defeating the Sandinista candidate Daniel Ortega. President Bolanos promised to reinvigorate the economy, create jobs, fight corruption, and support the war against terrorism. Bolanos took office in 2002. In Nicaragua, political, social, and economic problems remain, but it is hoped that they can continue to be peacefully resolved. In 2006, Daniel Ortega was elected president of Nicaragua. Daniel Ortega was reelected in 2011 for another five-year term of office. He has continued to promote socialist economic policies and to align Nicaragua with like-minded nations in Latin America. Under his political leadership, Nicaragua has become more moderate in its actions than it was during the Sandinista period.

Brazil

Getulio Vargas came to power as a result of the Revolution of 1930. Vargas ruled Brazil from 1930 to 1945 and set up programs to promote industrial growth. In the 1950s, Juscelino Kubitschek was elected president. Kubitschek created the new capital city, Brasilia, in the interior of the country. He also began programs to develop Brazil's highways, universities, airports, factories, and hydroelectric plants.

In 1964, the military overthrew President Joao Goulart after the economy faltered and as a result of political disagreements. The military governments that ruled Brazil to the end of the 1980s banned political parties and encouraged economic growth. The generals encouraged foreign investment, and in the 1970s, an economic boom called the Brazilian miracle took place. The upper and middle classes obtained most of the benefits during this time of greater prosperity.

By the late 1980s, Brazil's staggering debt of $110 billion and widespread economic and social problems forced the military to give up power slowly to the politicians. In 1990, Fernando Collor de Mello was elected president. President Collor began a series of drastic economic reforms to control Brazil's spiraling inflation.

In 1993 President Collor was removed from office because of corruption. The vice president, Itamar Franco, took over the presidency. In the 1990s Brazil's leaders tried to find solutions to the problems of high inflation, widespread poverty, malnutrition, lack of adequate health care, and crime in the western hemisphere's second largest nation in terms of territory, population, and economy.

In 1994, Brazil placed its hope in Fernando Henrique Cardoso, the newly elected president, to resolve its many problems. By the 1990s, Brazil had one of the top ten economies of the world. Despite Brazil's economic growth, the problem of inflation made Brazilians live in constant fear that money earned today would be worth much less tomorrow. Cardoso worked to stabilize the Brazilian currency during his first term in office. Brazil became a more reliable trading partner in the expanding global economy, and the nation was able to pay back some of its huge foreign loan debt without devaluing its currency.

Cardoso was reelected in 1998. In his second term in office, Cardoso faced renewed economic problems. The financial crisis that developed in Asia threatened to spread to Brazil. Brazil made an important agreement with the IMF to curtail its budgetary expenses by cutting government employment and eliminating many of the corrupt political practices that made doing business in Brazil so costly. The Brazilian Congress and state governments resisted the call for this type of economic reform, but President Cardoso pushed ahead to bring about needed change.

In the presidential elections of 2002, the Workers Party candidate, Luis Ignacio da Silva ("Lula") was elected to the Brazilian presidency. Lula's election to a four-year presidential term was seen as another step in promoting real democracy in Latin America's largest and most populous nation. Lula was considered to be a man of the people and was a trade union leader and worker. As president, Lula worked to maintain a balance between his Workers Party supporters and the opposition, which was more procapitalist and favored the idea of economic globalization. This delicate balance was complicated by the fact that resource-rich Brazil with its growing trade-oriented economy has a very unequal distribution of wealth and income.

In 2005, a political scandal erupted in Brazil, and the Workers Party was accused of corrupt political practices. The outcome of the scandal severely weakened President Lula's ability to govern effectively. As the 21st century develops, it is still hoped that Brazilian leaders will make their nation a land where political promises become a reality for all the

Brazilian people. Brazilian leaders must find solutions that will allow the vast majority of its citizens to live better lives than they do today. In January 2011, Dilma Rousseff took office as the first female president of Brazil. Brazil hosted the summer Olympic games in 2016, which was recognition of the country's increasing political influence and economic importance as one of the rising BRIC nations.

Dilma Rousseff was reelected President of Brazil in 2014. Her second term in office was not completed because she was impeached and removed from office. A corruption scandal involving the Brazilian oil company, Petrobras, which involved bribes and payoffs to many Brazilian politicians, was the primary cause of her downfall. The slowing Brazilian economy in the post–world recession years after 2007–2008 and the alarming crime rate were additional issues that led to her impeachment by the Brazilian Senate. Vice President Michel Temer took over as president, but the political turmoil continues in Brazil with President Temer also being accused of corruption. Brazil still suffers from an unequal distribution of wealth, land, and income and is again experiencing increasing poverty and declining living standards despite being a nation that has an increasing GDP and is ranked in the top ten of the world's economies.

Argentina

The landed elite, primarily cattle ranchers, were the real source of power in Argentina. Argentinean nationalism developed during the rule of the caudillo tyrant Juan Manuel de Rosas. Rosas ignored the constitution and often used his military power to persecute and terrorize his enemies. Although the provinces of Argentina remained loosely associated under Rosa's federalist control, by the time of his overthrow in 1852, he had, to a large measure, forged national unity. However, the establishment of democratic traditions did not come until later in the 1800s.

In the 1940s a military officer, Juan D. Perón, rose to power. Perón was a populist who used the democratic process to promote a program that favored the middle and labor sectors of society. Perón was elected president twice. Juan Perón and his first wife, Eva Perón, relied on the support of the workers. His program, *Justicialismo*, sought a balance between society's opposing forces. Perón was overthrown in 1955 by the military, with the support of the traditional elite who found his programs threatening. However, Perónism continued to be a political force. In 1973, Perón and his new wife Isabel were chosen as the presidential and vice presidential candidates by the Perónist Party. Perón was reelected but died shortly there-after. Isabel Perón succeeded him but soon was overthrown by a military coup d'état. A period of harsh military rule followed.

In 1976, as terrorist attacks worsened, the military started a brutal campaign known as the dirty war. As many as 25,000 people, mainly students and workers, were killed or "disap-peared" during this time. In 1982 the military launched a cam-paign to gain control of the Malvinas Islands, also called the Falkland Islands, about 300 miles off the coast of Argentina. These islands had been ruled by the British since the 1830s. The British refused to recognize the Argentine claim and soundly defeated the Argentine military. With this defeat, the military lost all credibility and popular support.

In 1983 voters elected a new president, Carlos Menem. President Menem, who ran for the presidency as a candidate of the Perónist Party, instituted drastic economic reforms, which resulted in curbing a high rate of inflation, pegging the national currency to the dollar to safeguard its value, and selling off government-owned national companies that were inefficient and losing money. Argentina's constitution was amended in 1993 to allow Menem to run for a second term. In the 1990s, President Menem brought political stability and economic growth to Argentina. In 1999, President Menem sought to amend the nation's constitution to be able to run for the presi-dency a third time; however, the Argentine judiciary refused to sanction this constitutional change.

In 1999, Fernando de la Rua was elected president of Argentina. However, by 2001, he was forced to give up his office because of mounting economic problems that led to increasing social unrest. Argentina's economic situation wors-ened to the point where its dollar-based currency lost most of its value. In 2002, Eduardo Duhalde became the president, but he too could not reverse Argentina's deepening socioeconomic crises. In less than a year new presidential elections were held.

In 2003, Nestor Kirchner was elected president of Argentina. Since his election, Kirchner has won support from the Argentine people for his nationalist economic policies and his decision to legally pursue the former military leaders responsible for the crimes committed during the period of political repression fol-lowing the death of Juan Perón.

In 2007, Cristina Fernandez de Kirchner succeeded her hus-band as president of Argentina. She served as president until 2015. Argentina was severely affected by the economic recession crisis that shook the world's economies starting in 2007–2008. President Kirchner's highly politicized effort to establish currency controls, introduce a new tax system for agricultural exports, and resolve problems concerning Argentina's international debt led to increasing tensions during her two terms in office. The proposed tax system was finally rejected by the Argentinian Senate. In the presidential election of 2015, Mauricio Macri was elected president of Argentina. Macri has pursued more of a middle-of-the-road capitalist economic program as a way to improve Argentina's economy.

Venezuela

Following independence in 1821, most of Venezuela's 19th century history was characterized by periods of political instability, dictatorial rule, and revolutionary activities. In the first half of the 20th century, political authoritarian governments and dictatorships continued to follow one after the other. During the post–World War II years, the Venezuelan economy changed from being primarily agricultural to an economy centered on petroleum production and exportation.

After the overthrow of General Marcos Jimenez in 1958 and withdrawal of the military from direct involvement in national politics, Venezuela began a period of unbroken civilian democratic rule. Until the elections of 1998, the Democratic Action Party (AD) and the Christian Democratic Party (COPEI) dominated political elections and offices on both the national and state levels. Venezuela became one of the more stable democracies in Latin America.

This political calm began to come to an end starting in 1989, when Venezuela experienced riots, the so-called Caracazo, in response to an economic austerity program launched by its then president Carlos Andres Perez. In 1992, a group of army officers led by future president Hugo Chavez tried unsuccessfully to overthrow the government in a military coup. A year later Perez was impeached on corruption charges.

Political instability increased throughout the 1990s, as popular dissatisfaction with the traditional political parties and economic frustrations continued to cause unhappiness and disorder. In the presidential elections in 1998, Hugo Chavez won the presidency after campaigning for broad reform, constitutional change, and a crackdown on corruption.

In another election in 2000, Hugo Chavez and his Fifth Republican Movement (MVR) won control of the national legislature. Chavez now had the power and votes to bring about the political changes that he had promised in 1998. The traditional elites who had ruled the nation organized opposition to what they called Chavez's socialist policies.

GEOGRAPHY

Use of Geography

The years since 2000 have seen continued political strife. Venezuelans are divided into two political camps. They are either pro- or anti-Chavez. The anti-Chavez forces tried to have the president removed from office by means of a recall vote. In 2002, the opposition to Chavez began a national work stoppage centering on the petroleum industry. The political situation became so heated that the Organization of American States (OAS) created a Group of Friends of the OAS—Brazil, Chile, Spain, Portugal, Mexico, and the United States—to find a peaceful solution to the growing crisis, which threatened civil war.

In 2004, after long negotiations, a recall vote, which was allowed by the Venezuelan constitution, was agreed on. In the recall vote Chavez was supported by the majority of the Venezuelan people, particularly the lower socioeconomic groups, and held on to his office until his death in 2013. After his electoral victory in the recall, and re-election in 2006, Chavez continued to pursue his economic program, which was designed to assist Venezuela's poorest classes. Venezuela continued to experience difficulties in its relations with the United States, which opposed Chavez's friendly relations with the Fidel Castro government in Cuba and his ideas about making the nation's petroleum industry more profitable for the Venezuelan government and people by raising crude oil prices.

In 2013, Vice President Nicolás Maduro succeeded Hugo Chávez as president of Venezuela. Maduro narrowly won a highly contested special presidential election in 2013. Since becoming president, Maduro has mostly ruled by decree and has sought to prevent the political opposition from changing the nation's socialist economic system and removing him from office. Growing numbers of the Venezuelan people are now in favor of a more capitalist program to relaunch the nation's ailing economy and improve the average living standards, which have deteriorated in recent years. The severe fall in the price of oil, which is Venezuela's chief export earner, has reduced available government revenues. Increased poverty, a rising crime rate, and growing hunger are problems that need immediate attention in today's Venezuela.

Political Integration

In 1823, when Spain threatened to try to regain its colonial empire in Latin America, the United States responded with the Monroe Doctrine. President James Monroe in a statement issued to Congress declared that the American continents were henceforth not to be considered as subjects for future colonization by European nations. The statement also said that any attempt by European powers to extend their system to this hemisphere would be considered dangerous to the peace and safety of the United States. In addition, the United States declared that it would not interfere in European affairs.

The Monroe Doctrine was favorably received by the Latin American nations. Although the United States did not possess the military force to back up this bold statement, it knew that the British navy would protect Latin America because of Britain's commercial interests in the region.

Prior to the 1860s, the United States had done little to protect Latin America from European intrusions. However, in the late 1800s the United States began to play a greater role in the affairs of Latin America. In 1898 the United States defeated Spain in the Spanish-American War and gained control of Puerto Rico and Cuba. Cuba soon gained its independence, but the era of U.S. domination of much of Latin America, especially Central America and the Caribbean, had begun.

President Theodore Roosevelt changed the role of the United States in Latin America from protector to that of an international police power. In 1904 the Roosevelt Corollary to the Monroe Doctrine stated that if the Latin American nations failed to properly maintain their political and financial affairs, the United States would intervene to restore order. This corollary led to interventions in the Dominican Republic, Nicaragua, Haiti, and elsewhere. In addition, the U.S. desire to build a canal to connect the Atlantic and Pacific oceans led it to defend Panama's secession from Colombia in 1903. The Hay-Bunau-Varilla Treaty negotiated with the newly independent nation to build the Panama Canal was very favorable to U.S. interests.

GEOGRAPHY

Human Systems

This policy of interference in Latin American affairs caused a growing resentment in the region toward the "colossus of the north" as other presidents continued Theodore Roosevelt's aggressive policy. President Taft supported dollar diplomacy, which encouraged American bankers to make loans to Central America and the Caribbean nations. This led to intervention to protect American creditors.

During the 1930s President Franklin D. Roosevelt sought to modify U.S. policy toward Latin America in his Good Neighbor policy. Under Roosevelt, the United States succeeded in its economic and security objectives, but the Good Neighbor policy did little to resolve Latin America's fundamental political, social, and economic problems or reduce the region's distrust of the United States.

After World War II, a new inter-American system, known as the Organization of American States (OAS), was established.

At first, it included twenty Latin American nations and the United States, but it has since admitted Canada, Trinidad and Tobago, Barbados, and Jamaica. The charter of the OAS provides a legal framework for a permanent inter-American organization. In 1967 a series of changes amended the charter. A general assembly of member nations that meets annually was established, and a secretary general elected to a five-year term was approved. The amended charter stresses economic development, social justice, and regional integration.

The OAS record of preserving hemispheric peace has been mixed. The United States has sought to involve the OAS in its attempts to regulate Latin American political affairs. The American-sponsored Bay of Pigs invasion of Cuba in 1961 and the United States' military occupation of the Dominican Republic in 1965 were seen as violations of the OAS charter by many Latin American nations. However, Latin America did support the United States by voting to exclude Cuba from the OAS in the early 1960s.

In the 1980s the United States invaded Grenada and Panama to overthrow dictatorships. The Latin American nations resent these interventions and favor a legal channel for solving international disputes. The Latin American nations also opposed U.S. intervention in Nicaragua. The Contadora peace plan drafted by a group of Latin American nations, most notably Costa Rica, was an attempt to stop armed conflict and to establish regional peace in Central America. The Nicaraguan election in February 1990, won by Violeta Chamorro who ran against the Sandinista candidate Daniel Ortega, was the first hopeful sign that electoral politics would replace armed conflict in Central America. During the 1990s, there were peaceful resolutions of the armed conflicts in the nations of Guatemala and El Salvador. The trend towards electoral politics in these nations is another indication that the devastating civil wars that lasted from the 1950s and impacted mostly on helpless civilian populations are a thing of the past in Central America. Today, democratically elected governments rule throughout Latin America.

Puerto Rico

GEOGRAPHY

Human Systems

The U.S. rule over Puerto Rico has changed since the Spanish-American War. This evolutionary process transformed the original military government in 1898 into a civilian government under the Foraker Act of 1900. The Jones Act of 1917 allowed the popular election of both houses of the bicameral legislature and a voice in appointing the governor's cabinet.

The Muñoz Rivera and Muñoz Marín political dynasty that dominated Puerto Rican politics from 1900 to the mid-1960s was supported by the United States. The idea of independence did not have much political support in this period. Under Public Law 600 in 1952, Puerto Rico became an associated free state with full autonomy in internal matters and its own constitution. As citizens of the United States, Puerto Ricans share a common currency and the right to defense by the U.S. government. In 1967, a plebiscite (vote) resulted in a large majority favoring commonwealth status rather than statehood. Less than 1 percent of the people voted for independence. In recent years, although some favor independence, the vast majority of the Puerto Rican people favor either statehood or commonwealth status.

In the 1950s reforms initiated by Muñoz Marín led to the development of industry and the growth of tourism on the island. Operation Bootstrap, a United States–sponsored program, offered companies tax savings to build plants in Puerto Rico. Despite economic progress, unemployment in Puerto Rico remained high throughout the past decades. After a vote in 1993, Puerto Rico's political future was determined when the results ended in a victory for the supporters of commonwealth status. In 1998, the issue of whether Puerto Ricans really favored statehood, commonwealth status, or independence was once again put to a vote. The Puerto Rican people reaffirmed their desire to maintain their commonwealth status.

Puerto Rico experienced severe economic problems in the first decades of the 21st century. The Commonwealth of Puerto Rico's economy basically has been in a deep recession in recent years, which has resulted in increased poverty, rising unemployment, and a problematic crime rate. In 2017, Puerto Rico was threatened with bankruptcy. The problems the Puerto Rican people now face led to a vote in 2017 that demonstrated that most Puerto Ricans now favor statehood.

In September 2017, Hurricane Maria, a Category 5 hurricane, devastated Puerto Rico and caused catastrophic damage, including an almost complete destruction of the island's electrical network. The widespread damage all over the island has resulted in a major humanitarian crisis. Despite federal government assistance, Puerto Rico faces a long road to recovery, which will also influence the island's residents as to the political status that they will seek in the future.

REVIEW QUESTIONS

Multiple Choice. Select the letter of the answer that correctly completes each statement.

1. The continent that was most affected by the breakup of the European colonial empires after World War II was
   A. Africa
   B. Asia
   C. Latin America
   D. Europe

2. Which of the following was not the result of the Cold War?
   A. NATO
   B. SEATO
   C. United Nations
   D. Warsaw Pact

3. Which of the following national leaders adopted a different strategy for winning independence from European colonialism than the others?
   A. Jomo Kenyatta
   B. Ahmed Bon Bella
   C. Mustafa Kemal
   D. Mohandas K. Gandhi

4. All the following areas have experienced civil wars in the 20th century during the process of becoming independent nations *except*
   A. Western Europe
   B. Indian subcontinent
   C. sub-Saharan Africa
   D. Southeast Asia

5. Select the correct Cold War relationship that shows benefactor and recipient.
   A. U.S.S.R. and Greece
   B. U.S.S.R. and Congo
   C. Communist China and Japan
   D. Communist China and South Korea

6. The nation that had become independent of European colonial rule before World War II was
   A. South Africa
   B. Israel
   C. India
   D. Vietnam

7. NATO includes the following nations *except*
   A. Great Britain
   B. France
   C. Finland
   D. Canada

8. Identify the leader who is incorrectly paired with his political affiliation.
   A. Mao Zedong/Kuomintang
   B. Yasser Arafat/Palestine Liberation Organization
   C. Jawaharlal Nehru/Congress Party
   D. Jomo Kenyata/Mau Mau

9. Identify the leader who is incorrectly paired with his policy.
   A. Mikhail Gorbachëv/Perestroika
   B. Sun Yat-sen/Three Principles of the People
   C. Nelson Mandela/Apartheid
   D. Ayatollah Ruhollah Khomeini/Islamic Fundamentalism

10. The European Union includes the following nations *except*
   A. Ireland
   B. Spain
   C. Italy
   D. Turkey

THEMATIC ESSAYS

Essay #1 Theme: Independence

In the second part of the 20th century, many nations became independent. Some fought for freedom from European colonial empires after World War II while others became independent after the fall of Soviet communism as a result of the Cold War.

Task:

1. Define the term "independence."
2. Select one nation you have studied and give one specific historical example showing how that nation became independent.
3. Assess whether independence was either positive or negative for that nation.

Essay #2 Theme: Globalization

The rapid advance of science and technology since World War II has forced nations increasingly to view the world as a "global village." Globalization poses new challenges and demands.

Task:

1. Define the term "globalization."
2. Select one nation you have studied and give one specific historical example showing how globalization has influenced the development of that nation.
3. Assess whether globalization has either been positive or negative for that nation.

Essay #1
This task is based on the accompanying documents (Documents 1–4). Some of these documents have been edited for the purposes of this task. The essay is designed to test your ability to work with historical documents. As you analyze the documents, take into account both the source of each document and the author's point of view.

Historical Context: The second half of the 20th century saw the independence of many nations. Some came from European colonial empires after World War II while others became independent after the collapse of Soviet communism as a result of the Cold War. The documents below relate the approaches of various national leaders to independence in the 20th century.

Task: Analyze the beliefs expressed in each document in order to evaluate the approach each leader took in shaping his new nation.

Part A: The documents below relate the beliefs of four national leaders of countries that became independent from European colonial empires after World War II or Soviet communist rule as a result of the Cold War. Examine each document carefully and answer the question that follows.

Part B: Write a well-organized essay that includes an introduction with a thesis statement, several paragraphs explaining the thesis, and a conclusion. Use evidence from the documents to support your position. Do not simply repeat the contents of the documents. You should also include specific related outside information based on your study of history.

DOCUMENT 1

"The All Indian Congressional Committee firmly believes in the policy and practice of non-violence, not only in the struggle for independence, but also, in so far as this may be possible of application, in Free India. . . . A Free India would, therefore, throw all her weight in favor of world disarmament, and should herself be prepared to give a lead in this to the world. . . . Effective disarmament and the establishment of world peace by the ending of national wars depend ultimately on the removal of the causes of wars and national conflicts. . . . To that end India will peacefully labor."

—Jawaharlal Nehru (1944)

According to the text, how does the AICC's plan for an independent India reflect the idealism of Gandhi's philosophy?

_____

_____

_____

DOCUMENT 2

"I blame the Government because—knowing that the Africans have grievances—they did not go into these grievances: shortage of houses in places like Nairobi, land shortage, and the poverty of the African people both in the town and the Reserves. I believe if the Government had looked into the economic and social conditions of the people, they could have done much good. . . . They wanted—I think—not to eliminate Mau Mau, but to eliminate the only political organization, the KAU, which fights constitutionally for the rights of the African people, just as the Electors Union fights for the rights of the Europeans and the Indian National Congress for the rights of the Asians."

—Jomo Kenyatta (1968),
Suffering Without Bitterness

According to the reading, how does Kenyatta justify the struggle against European imperialism?

_____

_____

_____

DOCUMENT 3

"The previous (Communist) regime, armed with a proud and intolerant ideology, reduced people into the means of production, and nature into its tools. . . . Out of talented and responsible people, ingeniously husbanding their land, it made cogs of some sort of great, monstrous, thudding machine, with an unclear purpose. . . . For all of us have grown used to the totalitarian system and accepted it as an immutable fact, and thereby actually helped keep it going. None of us are only its victims, we are all also responsible for it. . . . If we realize this, then all the horrors that the new Czechoslovak democracy inherited cease to be so horrific."

—Vaclav Havel (1990),
New Year's Day Address

According to the text, how had communist rule affected Czechoslovak society and its ability to adopt democracy?

_____

_____

_____

DOCUMENT 4

"Ultimately, Communism failed because in practice it did not deliver on the material level while its political practices . . . discredited its moral claims. It could not provide a viable socio-economic alternative to the Free Market system . . . Communism . . . by rejecting spiritual values, and by reducing morality to an instrument of politics, made its own success dependent entirely on material performance. And here it could not deliver. . . . As a consequence, Communism's dogmatic self-righteousness reduced idealism to barbaric inhumanity and institutionalized hypocrisy."

—Zbigniew Brzezinski (1993),
Out of Control

According to the reading, what was wrong with the communist system itself that made its failure inevitable?

_____

_____

_____

Essay #2

This task is based on the accompanying documents (Documents 1–4). Some of these documents have been edited for the purposes of this task. The essay is designed to test your ability to work with historical documents. As you analyze the documents, take into account both the source of each document and the author's point of view.

Historical Content: The advance of science and technology since World War II has transformed the world into a global village. The documents below relate how globalization has changed the patterns of human life all over the earth.

Task: Analyze the ideas expressed in the documents in order to understand how globalization has affected all people around the world and presented new challenges for the 21st century.

Part A: These documents relate opinions on the influence of globalization. Examine each document carefully and then answer the question that follows.

Part B: Write a well-organized essay that includes an introduction with a thesis statement, several paragraphs explaining the thesis, and a conclusion. Use evidence from the documents to support your position. Do not simply repeat the contents of the documents. You should also include specific related outside information based on your study of history.

DOCUMENT 1

"For 45 years, from World War II's finish to the end of the Cold War, most agreed that the greatest threat to global security was an all-out war between the two superpowers (US and USSR) that would culminate in the use of nuclear weapons. . . . The post-Cold War era, however, is by no means free of the threat of armed conflict, as demonstrated by continuing warfare. . . . While these conflicts do not have the potential to erupt into nuclear holocaust, they do pose a threat of widespread regional fighting. . . . Moreover, as weapons of mass destruction become more widely diffused, a growing number of these regional wars will entail a risk of chemical and even nuclear attack. Preventing, controlling, and resolving these conflicts . . . will, therefore, constitute the principal world security tasks of the 1990s and beyond."

—Michael T. Klare,
"The New Challenges to Global Security"

According to the text, how has globalization changed the concerns in regard to authority of the international community?

_____

_____

_____

DOCUMENT 2

"While there remains a range of estimates of what the earth's total population will be in the years 2025–2050, the raw figures are daunting, especially when placed in historical perspective. In 1825 . . . about 1 billion human beings occupied the planet, the race having taken thousands of years to reach that total. By then, however, industrialization and modern medicine were permitting population to rise at an increasingly faster rate. In the following hundred years the world's population doubled to 2 billion, and in the following half century (from 1925 to 1976) it doubled again, to 4 billion. By 1990, the figure had advanced to 5.3 billion . . . Behind the raw statistics lies the reality . . . if we do nothing to stabilize the world's population . . . before very long we will have so overpopulated and ransacked the earth that we will pay a heavy price for our collective neglect."

—Paul Kennedy (1993),
Preparing for the 21st Century

According to the reading, how will population impact on globalization and the international community in the future?

_____

_____

_____

DOCUMENT 3

"Civilization has been through periods of simultaneous political and religious upheaval . . . before. Yet modern communications, modern weapons, and modern anxiety make the current one seem even more bewildering. After all, religion is not dead; religious revivalists thrive in many parts of the world where traditional values clash with modern secular and commercial ones. But the struggle is the more turbulent for not having been resolved. Militant Islam is one answer thrown up by a traditional society's bewilderment at the intrusion of modern alien ideas, but, its repressive answers to them—indeed, its seeming embrace of terrorism . . . adds only to the general sense of anomie (absence of social norms)."

—Craig R. Whitney (1993),
"A World Unhinged Gropes for New Rules"

According to the text, how has globalization created a conflict between traditional and modern cultures?

_____

_____

_____

_____

_____

DOCUMENT 4

"To achieve modernization, the Chinese people must first put democracy into practice and modernize China's social system. In addition to being the result of productive forces and productive relations having developed to a certain stage, democracy is also the very condition that allows for the existence of such development to reach beyond this stage. Without democracy, society will become stagnant . . . Judging from history, therefore, a democratic social system is the premise and precondition for . . . modernization."

—Wei Jingsheng (1997),
The Courage to Stand Alone

According to the reading, how has globalization led to the creation of new standards in the development of nations?

_____

_____

_____

_____

_____

_____

ERA IV

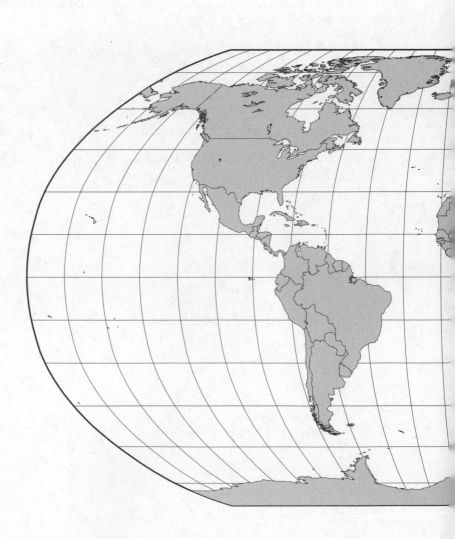

Global Connections and Interactions in the 21st Century

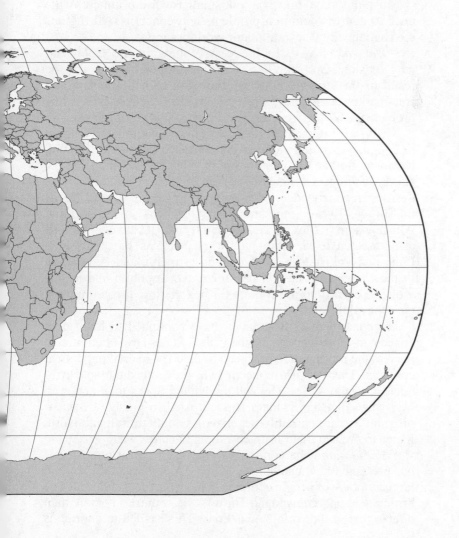

Part A: World Issues

Today's world could be considered a global village, tied together by the ease of rapid travel and nearly instant communication. These ties create interdependence among culture regions and countries. Examples of this interdependence include trade in agricultural and industrial products, the flow of knowledge and ideas from one region to another, and political alliances that provide mutual help and support.

Most important, however, our smaller world is united by the need to address common problems and concerns. All regions are challenged by several major world issues.

• *War and peace.* In the years following the Cold War new tensions and conflicts have developed. Some are the result of the struggle between communist totalitarianism and free-market democracy, while others have their origins in the problems resulting from 19th and 20th century imperialism.

Many are internal conflicts within nations between ethnic or religious groups, such as the former Yugoslavia, Ireland, Rwanda, Somalia, Liberia, Sudan, Darfur, Lebanon, Syria, and East Timor. Others are between ethnic or religious groups desiring independence, such as Palestinians in Israel; Kurds in Turkey, Syria, Iran, and Iraq; Chechens in Russia; and Albanians in Kosovo. Traditional tensions between nations also threaten to develop into wars, such as those between India and Pakistan in Kashmir and Armenia and Azerbaijan in the Caucasus. The UN has attempted to put an end to this violence by promoting forums for negotiating, mediating, and peacekeeping.

Weapons of mass destruction have continued to be a great concern, as both the UN and the United States have attempted to prevent the proliferation or spread of their use in civil or national conflicts. There is also concern with preventing the spread of nuclear weapons. The UN and the United States took action in Iraq when dictator Saddam Hussein tried to pursue a nuclear program and are currently negotiating with both Iran and North Korea to prevent them from developing nuclear weapons.

• *Population.* The continuing growth of world populations has presented new challenges, as the nations least able to feed large numbers of people continue to have the most children. The birth rate in underdeveloped Third World countries is more than double that in industrialized nations. This has led to enormous death and suffering due to famine despite the efforts of the UN and other world health NGOs (nongovernmental organizations) to provide relief. Developed nations, such as India and China, also have problems educating and convincing their people to limit the number of children they have to bring down overpopulation (China has taken drastic measures to limit families to two children). Ignorance and stubborn adherence to traditional practices have hindered efforts of local governments and world health groups to educate people in the Third World to limit their birth rates and bring down overpopulation.

• *Hunger and poverty.* Overpopulation, a lack of modern technology, corrupt governments, and violent conflicts have left much of the world, especially in underdeveloped Third World nations, in hunger and poverty. Populations throughout the world live in primitive conditions with little to eat, no sanitation, a lack of medicines or medical attention, and no means of supporting themselves. Despite the efforts of the UN and world health organizations, hunger and poverty continue to plague people throughout the world.

• *Political and economic refugees.* The global movement of people has increased dramatically throughout the world in recent decades. Often, lack of food, resources, and means of supporting themselves drive populations to move. These are due to natural causes (droughts, floods, disease, natural disasters) or poor government (oppression based on political, racial, ethnic, or religious reasons). Currently there are more than 15 million refugees or people who are forced to move from their homes worldwide. They are often treated harshly in nations that are too poor themselves to support refugees. Wealthier nations, such as the United States, limit immigration of refugees as their own populations are fearful that too many refugees will create strains on their own economies. Many refugees are forced to live in camps under poor conditions and face very uncertain futures.

• *Environmental concerns.* The development of a global economy has led to an increase in the demand for energy. The development of industries and modern technology (electricity, water, sanitation, communication) requires natural resources (coal, oil, gas) to provide the energy needed. This has led to greater development of these resources, which has had a negative effect on the environment. The burning of coal and oil has released much carbon dioxide into the air, which has created health-damaging pollution and acid rain and possibly contributed to global warming. The chemicals created by the use of refrigerators, air conditioners, and manufacturing processes has damaged the ozone layer that protects life on earth from the sun's ultraviolet rays. This has led to cancer in humans and damaged plant life.

Economic development has also done great environmental damage. Farming has led to large-scale erosion of soil worldwide, and the cutting down of forests has both endangered wildlife and remained a major source of carbon dioxide absorption. Environmentalists, scientists, and economists are looking for ways to reduce the damage done and find a means of "sustainable growth" or ways in which world economies can grow without destroying the environment.

• *Economic growth and development.* The expansion of the world's economies has led to an increase in the production of goods and services. Manufacturing moved from "developed" or industrialized nations to "emerging" nations or those becoming industrialized. These emerging nations could also obtain labor at less cost, as the standard of living in those nations was not as high. This created great hardship for those employed in developed nations.

Technological advances in manufacturing in developed nations had already reduced the need for labor. Demands in other areas of development, such as communications (especially computerization), led to the creation of new careers. "Information industries," such as insurance, financial services, market research, and advertising, developed a need for "knowledge workers" or jobs that focus on information.

• *World trade and finance.* The advances in both transportation and communications led to the development of "globalization" (the creation of a global economy) by the late 20th century. This meant that financial interactions quickly became international. Telephone and computer advances made it possible for business to be conducted as easily on the other side of the globe as next door. Many companies relocated to less expensive and less crowded places, no longer needing to be in large cities. Multinational corporations or companies that operate in many different countries quickly developed as well. This allowed businesses to establish manufacturing plants in nations where the resources were located and/or where labor was less expensive, while maintaining offices in the countries that were the greatest consumers. This made access to more products available to more people in more places for less cost.

The movement for "free trade" or the elimination of trade barriers internationally expanded as a result of globalization. The General Agreement on Tariffs and Trade (GATT), which was created after World War II, has been extended throughout the world since the creation of the World Trade Organization (WTO) in 1995. Greater economic integration between nations regionally has resulted in the European Union or EU (1992) and the North American Free Trade Agreement or NAFTA (1994). Similar organizations are in the process of being created in Asia, Africa, and the Middle East.

There has also been much criticism of globalization, in particular from environmental groups. They believe that expanded industry has accelerated pollution and increased environmental damage. Other opponents argue that while there have been some benefits to all nations, the developed countries have been the main beneficiaries. Stronger critics maintain that globalization has been a disaster for underdeveloped nations and that they are worse off now than before. Most of the opposition agrees that investment practices and trade agreements must include aid packages and policies to assist the poorest countries.

• *Energy: resources and allocations.* Part of the criticism of globalization is tied to the use of resources. Developed and emerging nations are increasingly using the vast majority of resources, as their postindustrial and industrial economies are dependent on energy. These countries have a greater number of machines and a higher standard of living that uses the bulk of natural resources available. Despite attempts to develop and exploit more natural resources, underdeveloped nations cannot get enough resources to industrialize. Alternative solutions such as water or solar sources of energy are not sufficient, and there is a fear that nuclear energy will be used to develop weapons of mass destruction. Many of the sources of natural resources are also being exploited at an increasingly faster pace, creating the danger of being exhausted in the near future.

• *Human rights.* The concept of human rights was the result of international legislation in 1948 (Universal Declaration of Human Rights) and 1975 (Helsinki Accords) in response to genocide and political repression in the first half of the 20th century. These are the basic rights of all people to life, liberty, security as a person, and freedom of belief and expression. International organizations, such as the UN and Amnesty International, work to identify, condemn, and create pressure to end human rights abuses by governments and groups throughout the world. Violations of human rights include the suppression of free speech, persecution because of political, religious, or philosophical beliefs, and genocide due to ethnic, racial, religious, or political hatred. Recently, gender equality (equal rights for men and women) and the protection of children have also become human rights issues.

• *Terrorism.* Terrorism is the use of extreme violence to intimidate and create fear in order to force political, social, or religious change. Although the practice is quite old, the creation of more destructive weapons and advanced technology have made it easier for terrorists to kill large groups of people, sometimes from a distance away.

While political or nationalist causes seem to be the reason for terrorism in the 19th and early 20th centuries, most recent motives have been radical religious and/or cultural beliefs. Terrorists do not care who gets killed, and they are so fanatic that the cause is more important than the means. They are willing to use any weapon to kill, even their own bodies, in order to create the fear they believe will force governments and societies to accept their demands. Terrorists target public places where there are many people. This is intended to make people feel unsafe wherever they are. They may also choose to destroy a government or religious site that symbolizes what they hate. An example of this was the attacks on the World Trade Center in New York City and the Pentagon in Washington on September 11, 2001 by Islamic fundamentalists belonging to the Al-Qaeda group. As a result of the attacks, 3,000 people died.

The September 11 attack changed the way Americans looked at terrorism. Up until then most terrorist attacks had occurred in foreign countries, often against diplomatic or military targets. The terrorists were living in the United States and had learned to fly the planes they flew into the World Trade Center and Pentagon there. In response, the federal government created the Department of Homeland Security in 2002 to coordinate national efforts against terrorism. The United States also invaded Afghanistan, which was under the control of the Taliban government. The Taliban was defeated, forcing the terrorists to flee into neighboring countries. By 2010, both Al-Qaeda and the Taliban seemed defeated in Iraq and Afghanistan.

The U.S. withdrawal from Iraq in 2011, however, led to renewed tensions between the nation's Shia, Sunni, and Kurdish populations due to sectarianism and corruption in the Iraqi government. This resulted in the revival of Al-Qaeda, which took advantage of the government's inability to unite the country. Al-Qaeda also began terrorist attacks in other nations in the Middle East as well as in Asia and Africa.

The removal of U.S. forces from Afghanistan in 2014 had similar consequences. The weak and corrupt Afghan government was unable to resolve internal tribal divisions within the country. Both the Taliban and Al-Qaeda reemerged to exploit the unstable situation, which brought the nation close to civil war.

While Al-Qaeda and the Taliban had become rivals, they began to cooperate when faced with the rise of a new and more powerful terrorist group, the Islamic State (IS). Originally a splinter group of Al-Qaeda, the Islamic State of Iraq (ISI) was created in 2006 with the goal of establishing an Islamic state based on Sharia Law in the Sunni Arab areas of Iraq. By 2012, ISI controlled large parts of the country, persecuting and killing the Shia majority, Christians, and all other religious minorities.

In 2011, ISI expanded into Syria, taking advantage of the civil disorder there, to bring down the Assad government and establish a Syrian Islamic state. By 2013 large areas of Syria were controlled by this group. Similar attempts by ISI in Afghanistan and Egypt were less successful.

In 2013, ISI was transformed into the Islamic State of Iraq and the Levant (a term for the countries located in the eastern Mediterranean, including Lebanon, Syria, and Palestine) or ISIL. Its new goal was to recreate the 8th-century Islamic caliphate (religious monarchy), making Baghdad its capital. ISIL slaughtered thousands of civilians of all faiths (including Sunnis who did not support them), committed brutal atrocities, and destroyed holy sites and antiquities (archaeological sites and museums).

By 2017, the combined efforts of the U.S., Russia, Iran, Turkey, and the governments of Syria, Iraq, and Afghanistan had driven ISIL out of much of Syria and Iraq. This group, however, remains a threat in the region. Al-Qaeda and the Taliban also continue terrorist attacks in Iraq and Afghanistan.

These issues, icons of which are shown throughout this book in the margins, show that we live in a world of global interdependence. Today, all regions enjoy the potential for sharing and cooperation and the progress that can result.

Part B: Population Issues and Their Impact

SECTION 1: POPULATION GROWTH IN DEVELOPED AND DEVELOPING NATIONS

Population growth is the easiest issue to recognize but the most difficult with which to deal. In the year 1800 the world population was 1 billion. By 1900 the world population had doubled, reaching 2 billion, and by 1975 it had doubled again and there were 4 billion people. By the year 2000 the world population had reached more than 6 billion. Current UN projections estimate the world population to be 9.8 billion by 2050. Many believe that such a large number of people will strain the earth's "carrying capacity," that is, the ability of its resource base to support people at a reasonably safe and comfortable standard of living.

For government policy makers and many concerned citizens, perceptions of this growth include questions regarding significant risks of food and water shortages, famine, epidemic disease, exhaustion of natural resources, and extinctions among both animal and vital plant species. Adding to the complexity inherent in this issue, researchers and agencies disagree about the most basic question: Will population growth continue at the same accelerating rate throughout the remainder of the 21st century and beyond? Demographers, social scientists who study population issues, have disagreements regarding the various factors that influence growth rates and how they will affect population trends. The changes brought about by the scientific and industrial discoveries have added to the population growth of recent centuries. Increased agricultural productivity has improved nutrition, modern medical knowledge has reduced the number of deaths caused by disease, and improvements in sanitation have bettered health conditions. As a result, more children survive through infancy and more people live longer and healthier lives in both developed and developing nations.

In the developed nations where the production of material goods has increased and protective social and governmental services have been introduced, people have generally decided to have fewer children. Most of these nations have low population growth rates, and some have even reached zero percent population growth. This "demographic transition" seems to occur as increasing prosperity raises living standards and reduces the risks of child mortality. When nations can provide "safety nets" of educational systems, pension plans, health care, and support programs for those who struggle in a variety of ways, people are often less likely to feel that having many children is necessary for their own security.

Consequently, the governments of many developing nations have begun family planning or birth-control programs. They use many techniques, such as advertising and educational campaigns, economic incentives, and restrictive legislation to convince their citizens to have fewer children. China's one-child family law, India's transistor radios for vasectomies campaign, and Singapore's free education only for the first two children policy are examples of the different approaches that have been used. Reducing the birth rate in many developing nations has proved to be difficult, however. Often cultural factors have worked against limiting population growth. In some cultures, economic and social conditions, as well as religious beliefs, lead to the desire, even the necessity, for large numbers of children. Children may be needed to help with the family farm or business, to provide care for elders, or to contribute income from outside jobs. They may also be needed for religious ceremonies (especially funerals), to enhance a family's prestige, or to inherit the family occupation and property and carry the family name into the future.

In some areas, other factors also make limiting population growth difficult. Geographic and historical circumstances have created an uneven distribution of population. Fertile river valleys and coastal plains are capable of producing vast amounts of food grain, and such production requires large labor forces. Consequently, dense populations are both possible and desirable. Eastern China, coastal Japan, and South Asia's Indo-Gangetic Plain are examples of this circumstance.

At the same time, modern agricultural technology has made areas that previously provided only small amounts of food extremely productive with small labor forces. The Great Plains of North America and the North European Plain are two such areas, and they help to provide Americans and Europeans with an abundant food supply and a high standard of living.

GEOGRAPHY

Use of Geography

Population by Region: Estimates, 1950–2015 and Medium-Variant Projection, 2015–2100

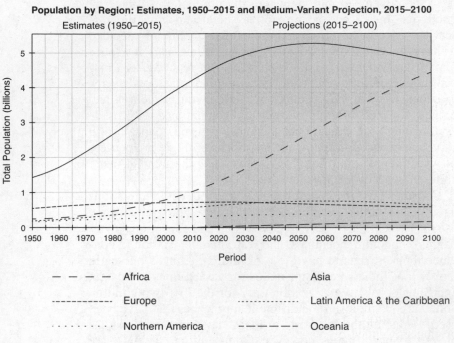

Source: United Nations, Department of Economic and Social Affairs, Population Division (2017).

Urbanization stimulated by the Industrial Revolution has also contributed to uneven population distribution. Today, over 40 percent of the world's population lives in cities. Cities need workers for industries and services. Moreover, urban areas provide many economic and cultural opportunities for their inhabitants. As a result, people migrate from the rural agricultural areas to further crowd and congest urban areas, helping to create squalid, crime-ridden, and unhealthy slums. This trend of rural to urban migration is continuing today.

Population can also be unequally distributed by age. In the developed nations, more people live longer and couples have fewer children. As the population grows older, these societies need to provide services for retired people and care for many elderly. At the same time, there are fewer wage earners to provide tax revenues for such services.

Developing nations, with their growing populations, are faced with large numbers of school-age children. However, they do not have the money to fund education. This deprives young people of the skills and knowledge necessary to compete for jobs in modernized sectors of the economy and results in large numbers of young people being unemployed or underemployed.

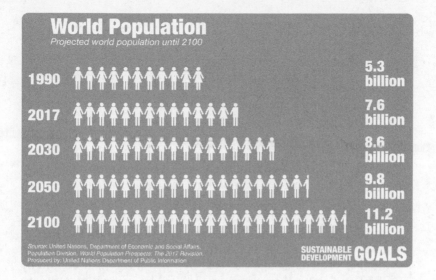

World Population

Projected world population until 2100

1990	👤👤👤👤👤👤👤👤👤👤	5.3 billion
2017	👤👤👤👤👤👤👤👤👤👤👤👤👤	7.6 billion
2030	👤👤👤👤👤👤👤👤👤👤👤👤👤👤	8.6 billion
2050	👤👤👤👤👤👤👤👤👤👤👤👤👤👤👤👤	9.8 billion
2100	👤👤👤👤👤👤👤👤👤👤👤👤👤👤👤👤👤👤	11.2 billion

Source: United Nations, Department of Economic and Social Affairs, Population Division, World Population Prospects: The 2017 Revision. Produced by: United Nations Department of Public Information

SUSTAINABLE DEVELOPMENT **GOALS**

As it relates to the network of world trade, the population issue involves developing relationships that promote fairness in the prices paid for natural resources and agricultural products provided by developing nations. Increased prices for these products would help provide money for these nations to improve education, skill training, industrial capacity, transportation, and communication. These items make up a nation's infrastructure, a necessity for improving living standards and enabling societies to effectively deal with poverty, hunger, and population growth.

Population pressure is not limited to particular culture regions nor is the issue simply that of numbers of humans or even birth or population growth rates. It involves decisions about fairness and equity and how nations will deal with one another in the future. Developing nations react to criticisms of their high birth rates by criticizing how much of the world's natural resources are consumed by the industrialized countries. Indeed, one citizen of a developed nation may consume twenty to thirty times the amount of resources used by an individual in a developing nation.

What might the future hold for population issues? Will a continued high rate of growth add to the ongoing stresses of religious conflicts, political antagonism, environmental degradation, and economic deprivation? Will population pressures endanger lives, create political instability in some nations or regions, or threaten large numbers of people with famines, epidemics, and social upheaval? While the United Nations' estimates depict a slowing of growth rates, they continue to predict that an overall increase is "almost inevitable," particularly in Africa. Other sources cite decreases in replacement fertility rates, that is, the number of children per potential child-bearing woman. This statistic has already declined in economically prosperous areas such as North America, Western Europe, Japan, Australia, and New Zealand. A similar trend seems to be developing among the increasingly larger middle-class segments of high-population nations, particularly China and India. A replacement fertility rate of 2.1 would mean two children per child-producing couple, plus an allowance for infant mortality. One researcher claims that "the evidence shows women are already not having enough children to replace themselves (and their partners)." Another factor that influences the world's population makeup is aging populations (though life expectancy has increased worldwide), and estimates are that the number of persons age 60 or above will more than double by 2050 and more than triple by 2100. Movements of refugees and other migrants are changing the demographic makeup in many regions. For example, Middle Easterners are flooding into Europe, and Central American immigrants are moving into the United States.

SECTION 2: WORLD HUNGER

Among the many negative factors related to population growth, perhaps the most common is hunger. It is estimated that nearly 12 percent of the world's population suffers from a lack of food. Poverty is the single most significant cause of widespread malnutrition. Though 98 percent of malnourished people live in developing nations, the more prosperous regions, too, have significant pockets of those whose diets are severely deficient. Women comprise 60 percent of the world's hungry, a fact that impacts mortality rates among the very youngest children. Poor nutrition is the leading cause of death in children under 5—3.1 million deaths a year according to the United Nations. One in four children in the world suffers slow development and stunted growth, characterized by low height and weight and impaired physical and mental capacity. More than 75 percent of the poorest people grow their own food, making them susceptible to the ravages of climate change and natural disasters, particularly drought.

Although population growth is an underlying cause of hunger and malnutrition in many parts of the world and the increasing numbers of people put a strain on food supplies, the issue is more complex. Many nations do not grow enough food crops. This is often because of policies carried out by former European colonial powers. In these areas, food production was frequently replaced by the production of cash crops for the European market. Also, in some areas, especially in Africa, borders were drawn without regard to natural and traditional agricultural ecosystems (the living community and nonliving environment working together in a cooperative economic system).

Since independence, the governments of some developing nations have ignored the development of agriculture. Instead, leaders have often emphasized industrialization and the growth of cities, hoping to build political support among city workers, the growing middle class, and the educated elite.

Climatic conditions and changes affect the food supply in some areas. Droughts (a long period of dryness, as in Africa's Sahel) often force people to overuse and damage the environment by digging deeper wells, which lower the water table, or by allowing herds to strip sparse vegetation. Floods and storms (as in Bangladesh) can wipe out harvests, ruin arable land, and destroy storage and transport facilities.

Although the developed nations produce a large enough food surplus to ease shortages in crisis areas, a number of obstacles prevent an equal distribution of these surpluses. Simply giving vast amounts of food to needy nations creates dependencies. It also interferes with agricultural prices in other areas. Political differences and policies may hamper the distribution of both food aid and local food supplies. Moreover, corruption, hoarding, and price fixing are often part of the political and economic systems of developing countries.

A rapid rise in food prices in 2010 and 2011 drove millions of people below the UN-designated poverty level. Production had already failed to keep up with the growing population in some less developed areas. In more prosperous economies increased demand for meat from grain-fed livestock and a growing biofuel industry diverted food grains from many needy areas. Unfavorable weather events, national export quotas, use of former farmland for commercial development, water scarcity, and lack of government investment in agriculture and development all contributed to driving the food/hunger equation to the "brink of disaster," as some experts described it.

Finally, many developing nations do not have or cannot afford to develop the necessary factors to produce the technological innovations (new ideas) that could bring about higher crop yields. They also are unable to purchase those items from more developed countries. New, improved seed varieties, chemical fertilizers, pesticides, and farm machinery are all expensive. Also, prices for fuels used in small engines that power farm machinery have increased.

The United Nations website asserts that "a profound change of the global food and agriculture system is needed if we are to nourish today's 795 million hungry and the additional 2 billion people expected by 2050." What can be done, and what is being done to work toward that goal? Family planning provides one fundamental process—fewer mouths to feed. Managing prices for staple food, keeping them relatively stable, eases burdens on the poor, both those selling and those buying. Promoting biodiversity in agriculture can contribute to more nutritious diets, enhanced living conditions for farming communities, and more sustainable farming systems. Providing women with better access to resources could help reduce the malnourished by 150 million. Reducing energy poverty, particularly through access to electricity, would enhance food production for local and global markets. Controlling the conversion of land to nonproductive uses keeps cultivable areas in the agricultural sector. Guaranteeing farmers their land rights and ownership increases their security and their ability to produce needed food. Carefully balancing food production between export markets and local uses provides both nutrition and financial gains in rural communities. Concerted and cooperative efforts by national governments, international organizations, and those who work in the fields are needed to create and implement policies directed toward the goal of eradicating hunger.

SECTION 3: EDUCATION— A GROWING GAP

Development in nations depends on information and technical skills. Education is necessary to make use of resources. However, as communication and information technology leap ahead in the industrialized nations, the developing nations are losing ground in gaining access to these essentials. This is due in part to the shortage of funds available for schools, colleges, and educational media. Also, social or economic limitations often take children out of the educational system. For example, they may be needed to contribute to family care or earnings, or tradition may exclude the participation of females, and children with disabilities may be excluded.

Other factors add barriers to providing education to children in poorer areas. School programs often mimic those of former colonial nations and may be useless for students whose future will differ greatly from that of students in Europe or in North America. Teacher shortages and a lack of teacher-training opportunities often result in inadequate classroom skills and performances. A lack of facilities and teaching materials diminishes the effectiveness of instruction. Scarcity of school sites can create severe overcrowding and may necessitate long distances for students to travel. Most poverty-stricken areas have a high rate of malnutrition among children, hindering their learning abilities.

A lack of security and safety in strife-torn areas of social, political, and military conflict can short-circuit school schedules and hinder attendance. Even where a regular class schedule is available, absenteeism among both teachers and students reduces effectiveness. In spite of an estimated worldwide 80–90 percent increase in primary school attendance since 2000, the above factors and others explain the huge percentage of dropouts around age 12.

Birth rates in most nations can be tied to education; more educated populations tend to have more economic options. These greater opportunities often lessen the need for children as economic assets and lead to a desire for smaller families. In developed nations, too, differences in education levels can create gaps between groups, as between those who have only a secondary education or less and those with college and more advanced degrees; on average, those with more education have higher incomes.

What can the governments of countries with these educational impediments and international organizations concerned with promoting improvements do? The goal should be to get children to school, provide appropriate instruction, and better prepare them to live more productively in and contribute to their societies. The provision of more resources requires planning, organization, and, of course, funds. Some countries have abolished or reduced costs to students' families and added nutritional meals to supplement what families can provide. More extensive training, better salaries, and appropriate classroom resources enhance teachers' abilities. Many educators advocate for "school for life" programs, designed to better fit students' abilities into their communities. They list basic-skills subjects—reading, writing, mathematics, personal health practices, and financial literacy—as well as socially valuable skills—teamwork, problem solving, management techniques, and entrepreneurial practices—as useful and contributive.

Part C: Economic Development and World Trade

Interdependence brought about by scientific, technological, and industrial progress has carried the message of economic development to every nation on earth. Every government strives to improve the standard of living of its citizens in a variety of ways. Improved health, sanitation, and nutrition; broader educational training and employment opportunities; better housing, clothing, and other basic necessities; affordable entertainment; reasonably priced consumer goods; and more leisure time—all of these are elements of economic development.

Accomplishing these things requires the investment of money and human effort, both of which may be strained by the great need. Political leaders must make decisions and set policies, although there may be differing opinions about how their nation can best develop economically.

Within a nation, even close political partners can disagree about how to achieve economic development. In Mahatma Gandhi's vision of independent India, he saw a nation of cottage industries with skilled craftspeople producing goods in their own homes or small shops. However, his follower and India's first prime minister, Jawaharlal Nehru, promoted industrial development and urban growth.

The biggest challenge to political leaders and experts from around the world who wish to promote economic growth is the two-sided nature of the formulation of development plans and policies. The fundamental goal should be to expand the benefits of growth as well as to increase participation in the process by a broad spectrum within relevant populations. At the same time, it is crucial that laws and regulations do not weaken incentives for hard work, wise saving, and careful investing.

SECTION 1: GLOBAL POWER—THE GAP BETWEEN RICH AND POOR

Both developed and developing nations may suffer from an unfavorable balance of trade. Many developing nations earn foreign-exchange capital by selling natural resources at relatively low prices and then must pay high prices for manufactured and consumer goods. In addition, they must borrow capital to finance improvements in their infrastructure, which often leads to massive debts and huge interest costs.

For the world's poorest nations, sometimes referred to as "basket case" economies, the situation can be even more dire. Although the world economy has generally been growing and diversifying, the share of the least developed countries in world trade has steadily declined in recent decades. Like other developing nations, they have difficulty producing competitive goods and services and often lack the ability to export what they do produce. Also, products and services—and the demand for them—are changing rapidly. Struggling economies often lack the capacity to innovate, to access new markets, or to anticipate new opportunities. Social and political instability discourage foreign companies who are reluctant to risk investing in a climate of uncertainty.

These countries may also be more seriously affected by barriers to international commerce—particularly technical regulations and sanitary measures imposed by international agreements and the standards of more developed nations. Information and communication technologies (ICTs) have become increasingly important in all areas of world trade from agriculture to industrial products, consumer goods, and professional services. The rapid growth of this "e-commerce" disadvantages nations with limited access to Internet facilities.

Some economists have speculated that the cancellation of debts ("forgiving loans") owed by developing nations and their businesses to financial institutions such as the World Bank and private banks would be beneficial to the global economy. This would, in theory, promote economic growth by applying assets to development rather than debt service, strengthening national economies and the global economy.

Developed nations consume large quantities of material goods and provide many services for their citizens; also, their workers earn high wages. Consumers in these countries often find it cheaper to buy goods from other nations whose workers are paid less. Buying goods such as automobiles and TVs that are imported from other nations can lead to large trade deficits. Since the citizens of such countries expect high levels of public services, government borrowing and budget deficits may result. Nations with debts and deficits, whether developed or developing, may find the value of their money weak or declining in relation to that of other nations. This further limits their ability to fund economic development.

Often governments use tariffs (import taxes), which raise prices on imported goods, to protect their own industries. Nations with similar interests often form organizations to promote their own interests. The Organization of Petroleum Exporting Countries (OPEC) cooperates on pricing and other issues, and the General Agreement on Trade and Tariffs (GATT) is designed to benefit the industrial nations that have signed the agreement.

Economic growth programs have generally focused on "big development"—heavy industry and manufacturing; infrastructure like dams, roads, and railroads; resource extraction; and large-scale agriculture—and attracting foreign investment for such projects. These ventures create jobs at menial levels, but often the major social and financial benefits of this top-down style go to those at the upper economic levels. The achievement of life-enhancing improvements to create growth that benefits all may require changes in perspective that do not repeat the uneven results of the past. Grassroots programs could empower those at the lower end of the prosperity ladder. Examples of this, which are being tried in a variety of countries, include:

• Financial literacy programs for South African miners teach more efficient planning and reorienting of spending, and these programs engage the miners with financial institutions.

• Enhanced business licensing for would-be small-scale entrepreneurs in India encourages innovations and investments.

• A partnership in East African nations funded a program to process bean crops locally to make them easier to sell to large grocery wholesalers.

• A study involving eight countries across Africa, Asia, and Latin America, assessing affordable access to information and communication technologies, particularly broadband Internet, demonstrated a positive impact on people's opportunity for betterment.

• Neighborhood committees in Mexico City formed health-care clinics and reconstruction groups in response to an earthquake.

Opposition by traditional power elites can provide a major roadblock to promoting such grassroots endeavors. The power elites may consider these endeavors threats to their dominance.

There are many issues regarding trade relations between the more industrialized and prosperous nations of Europe, North America, Japan, and Australia and the more agricultural-reliant nations of Asia, Africa, and Latin America. Trade issues that face the more agricultural-reliant nations include:
- An overdependence on trade with industrialized economies
- Most of their exports go to the industrialized countries
- Most of their exports are raw materials, fuels, and farm products
- There are price fluctuations in their exports
- Manufactured goods tend to be low-tech and labor intensive
- There is a high price for higher-tech manufactured imports

Potential solutions to these issues include:
- Human investments, education, and training
- Material investments, such as transport and communication infrastructure
- Developing intraregional trade networks
- Enforcing world and regional trade agreements that lower barriers

Making the movement of products more "open" and free of the restrictions of tariff policies and import restrictions benefits both sides, but particularly benefits the less-industrialized nations.

SECTION 2: RESOURCE AND ENERGY MANAGEMENT

As science and technology find more ways to use up more of the earth's natural resources, managing scarce or declining resources becomes an ever more critical issue. Developing nations with abundant supplies of nonrenewable mineral resources need to sell them to obtain development capital. Developed nations who use such resources strive to keep the prices for them low and to find ways of recycling and using such resources more efficiently.

In industrial countries, financial resources may be spent on excessive amounts of consumer goods or be lost to corruption or inefficiency (as in some former communist nations). Developing countries are often forced to use much of their capital to pay off their debts and the interest on their loans. In developed capitalist nations, dishonest investing techniques and conspicuous consumption may create waste and inequity.

Human resources are also crucial to development. Many African and Asian societies have suffered a so-called "brain drain," as many of their educated, skilled, or financially prosperous citizens have immigrated to developed nations for better opportunities. The lack of money for investment in education means that developing nations cannot fully develop the potential of the remainder of their population.

Climate change affects all parts of the world, but the poor, poverty-stricken, and powerless in developing nations can be especially vulnerable to its long-term effects, including:

• Rising sea levels could impact large numbers of poor people living in coastal areas.

• Casualties are highest among women and children in natural disasters, including those caused by climate change.

• Grain crops are sensitive to temperature and rainfall variations; declining agricultural production can create food shortages, raise prices, and worsen hunger and malnutrition issues.

• Nations that already have economic issues are less adaptable to changes in climatic circumstances due to shortages of financial resources.

• Sensitivity to temperature and other weather factors can cause physical stresses to both people and livestock, as well as enable the spread of disease.

• The movement by "climate" refugees, dislocated by the social and economic disruptions of environmental change, would create additional political stresses.

Potential actions to mitigate the negative effects of climate change include:

• Policies and plans for development projects should be sensitive to climate change.

• Efforts should be focused on agricultural practices, industrial development, and land use.

• Efforts should be made to reduce large-scale deforestation.

• People need to promote "Green Energy"—solar, wind, and geothermal—and reduce fossil-fuel emissions.

• People need to invest in disaster preparedness to reduce the effects of floods, droughts, earthquakes, and massive storms.

• Research to increase and share knowledge needs to be supported.

SECTION 3: GLOBALIZATION

The McDonald's restaurant in Moscow is the world's busiest. Young children in Philippine villages wear Chicago Bulls' jerseys. German skinheads beat up on Turkish "guest workers." Tourists can buy Kodak film and drink Coca-Cola in Katmandu. Often the most exciting players in Europe's top soccer leagues are Africans or South Americans. In recent decades, some of the most famous Americans in the world have been sports stars— Muhammad Ali, Michael Jordan, and Magic Johnson. Disney theme parks have been built in France and Japan. Apples raised in Chile can be found in American supermarkets. Madonna is criticized by Indians for making a video using Hindu religious images. These are all examples of the so-called globalization of human culture and the world economy.

What are the elements of this process? Modern technology, transportation, and communication have interwoven human activities as never before. Consumer goods, even perishable ones, can be moved great distances in a very short time in order to satisfy the changing tastes of customers. Developed nations in need of workers encourage immigration: companies in richer countries "outsource" jobs to economies where wages are lower; firms in the same countries incorporate in places with much lower tax rates; satellite television broadcasts news, sports, and entertainment around the world; and tourists carry ideas and impressions to their destinations and others back home with them.

International organizations such as the World Bank, the International Monetary Fund, OPEC, the World Trade Organization, and the European Union wield ever-wider influence on the world economy through their policies. The World Trade Organization (WTO) deals with the rules of trade among nations. At its heart are the many agreements negotiated and signed by most of the world's trading nations. The goal is to help producers of goods and services, exporters, and importers conduct their business. The vast majority of WTO members are party to the General Agreement on Tariffs and Trade (GATT), a set of policies that covers international trade in goods. Most also belong to one or more regional trade agreements (RTAs), such as the North American Regional Trade Agreement (NARTA), which further regulate economic relations among its member nations.

Multinational or transnational corporations may exercise the greatest influence in the globalization process and control significant percentages of the world's economic assets. The combined revenues of the world's largest automobile manufacturers, General Motors and Ford, exceed the Gross Domestic Product (GDP) of all of sub-Saharan Africa, and the combined sales of Japan's six largest corporations almost equals the GDP of South America. About half of the 100 largest companies in the world are companies that do business across national boundaries.

Opinions vary as to the consequences of this world-straddling economic pattern. Supporters acclaim its efficiency in promoting economic progress—producing consumer goods, promoting industrialization, creating jobs—but there are also many critics. They claim that it concentrates financial power in the hands of too few nations, most of them in the north and most former colonial powers. Far from creating employment, naysayers decry the loss of jobs to mechanization, especially in developing nations. Population shifts create poverty, prejudice, and conflict and health and equity issues are ignored while pollution increases, biodiversity decreases, and the diversity and integrity of local and national cultures becomes homogenized. These are other criticisms of a process that to some seems beyond the control of any limiting factors.

As the 21st century approaches its third decade, a number of issues regarding globalization continue to create a standard-of-living gap between prosperous and less prosperous countries. Among them:

• Steady economic growth is a key factor in reducing the income divide between rich and impoverished regions; the economies of many nations grow only sporadically.

• The worldwide economic slump that started in 2008 slowed international trade, affecting nations dependent on a limited variety of exports.

• Periodic economic slowdowns tend to affect the well-being of less prosperous nations more severely; they become less likely to attract investment capital for industrial, commercial, and infrastructure development.

• Technological progress has been a driving force for income growth in developing nations; access to technology lags in many poorer regions.

SECTION 4: TRADITION AND MODERNIZATION—FINDING A BALANCE

As developing nations look for ways to improve living standards for their citizens, they often find that modern techniques disrupt or conflict with established cultural patterns. For example, family planning programs may violate religious beliefs (as with the Roman Catholic Church in Latin America); migration from rural areas to urban areas upsets established social structures (for instance, India's caste system); changing roles for women threatens the traditional male-female relationships (as in some Islamic nations); and changing governmental structures may clash with centuries-old economic patterns (China's communes versus family farms).

The Islamic world provides the most obvious example of the conflicting visions of cultural and social change. Fundamentalist Muslims see the influence of modern values and styles (usually labeled "Western" and decadent) as both a threat and an insult to long-established Islamic doctrines and morality. This has, in turn, manifested itself in the violent terrorist actions of a small but extremely militant and active minority.

Part D: Changing Political Power Structures

SECTION 1: RUSSIA TODAY

During much of the period after the end of World War II, world politics was dominated by the so-called superpower struggle, pitting the communist ideology of the former Soviet Union against the capitalist ideas of the United States. This struggle, which involved military, political, and economic competition, has often been called the Cold War, and each nation attempted to build and extend its power and influence. The Cold War was an icy state of tension and hostility between the former Soviet Union and the United States without direct armed conflict.

Although competition between the superpowers was world-wide, it often focused on Europe, where their two opposing alliances faced one another across the Iron Curtain. Here, the Soviet Union and its allies (the satellite states of Eastern Europe) in the Warsaw Pact confronted the United States and its Western European allies in NATO. The Cold War led to an arms race in which both sides built more sophisticated and destructive weapons designed to maintain a balance of terror, or mutually assured destruction (MAD), preventing all-out warfare between the two sides.

During the Cold War, there were periods of stability when both sides sought peaceful coexistence. These periods of détente alternated with times of heightened tensions, such as during the Cuban Missile Crisis of 1961 and the Soviet invasion of Afghanistan in 1979. From time to time, summit meetings were held between leaders of the two nations in order to improve communication and to seek conflict resolution.

Each of the superpowers attempted to extend its influence to other areas of the world. At times, the United States supported military or dictatorial governments opposed to communism, often at the expense of real democracy in those countries. The Soviet Union supported national liberation movements in some nations, often condoning sabotage and terrorism.

The dramatic political changes in Eastern Europe toward the end of the 20th century greatly changed the Cold War pattern of relationships. The ideology of communism and its reliance on totalitarian control were discredited and found ineffective in meeting people's economic and emotional needs. The desires for self-expression and self-determination of the people of Eastern Europe were coupled with a need for higher material standards of living. The result has been the fragmentation of the former Soviet Union into a number of newly independent nations, a closer relationship between several former Soviet satellites and the nations of Western Europe, and a variety of solutions to the problem of transforming economies from centrally planned socialist to some degree of free enterprise.

Russia itself, the dominant force in the former U.S.S.R., experienced some of the most serious transitional pains, as unscrupulous money men and thuggish enforcers turned a free-wheeling market economy into their personal cash cows at the expense of the prosperity and stability of the economy as a whole. Though some Western investors and lenders have seen Russia as a potential growth area, political corruption has made other investors extremely wary. In politics, too, instability as well as personal health problems plagued the government of former Russian president Boris Yeltsin. The resignation of Boris Yeltsin at the end of 1999 led to his replacement by the Russian prime minister, Vladimir Putin, as acting president. Putin won the presidential election held in March 2000. Putin's popularity was due to the Russian people's desire for greater political and economic security, and the Russian army's retaking of Chechnya after a brutal military campaign. President Putin was reelected in 2004. In 2008, Dmitry Medvedev was elected president of the Russian Federation. Vladimir Putin served as his prime minister. Putin was nominated to run for the presidency in 2012. Putin was elected president in May 2012. Dmitry Medvedev was elected prime minister in May 2012.

Under the leadership of Vladimir Putin, Russia has reemerged as a military power. Putin is seeking to promote Russia's national and international interests. His foreign policy and military actions have led to tensions with the European Union and the United States. Russia's attempts to promote its national interest in terms of a land connection to the Crimean Peninsula have led to a stalemated civil war in Ukraine, where the eastern region in part has broken away. International pressure, including economic sanctions affecting Russia, have not led to a resolution of this crisis. Russia is also opposed to the U.S. and EU intentions to place missile systems on its borders, particularly in Poland. In addition, despite a determined effort by Russia and the U.S. to avoid a military confrontation in the Middle East, particularly in the Syrian civil war, the two most powerful military nations have different interests in Syria and the region in general. Despite the fact that both nations are fighting the spread of Islamic terrorism in Syria, they have opposing ideas about the eventual right way to end the conflict and how Syria should be governed after the religiously based civil war finally ends.

SECTION 2: THE DEVELOPING WORLD

Many African, Asian, and Latin American nations have held a different world view, that of a multipolar, or many-sided, pattern of power. The concept of nonalignment for nations that did not wish to be too closely allied with either the West or the Eastern bloc was formulated by Nehru of India. The first meeting of nonaligned nations was held by Sukarno in Indonesia in 1955.

The superpowers often became involved in regional conflicts and disputes. At times, these involvements led to direct superpower confrontations, while at other times, the former Soviet Union and the United States were minimally involved, supplying only weapons or aid. The Korean War pitted communist North Korea and China directly against the United States and its allies. American military involvement in Southeast Asia brought massive Russian support for North Vietnam. The Soviet invasion of Afghanistan brought American weapons and money to aid Afghan *mujaheddin* (freedom fighters) who were resisting Soviet control.

Soviet and American efforts to influence events in the Middle East were frustrated by the ongoing Arab-Israeli conflict. Arab nations used the superpower competition to gain weapons and aid from both sides.

American president Jimmy Carter helped bring about an Egyptian-Israeli peace treaty (Camp David Accords—1979) and President Bill Clinton presided as Palestine Liberation Organization chairman Yasser Arafat and Israeli prime minister Yitzhak Rabin took a major step toward a possible settlement in 1993.

American troops led a UN force in driving Iraq out of Kuwait in 1991 after an invasion by Iraq, but U.S. Marines suffered losses to terrorists in trying to stabilize Lebanon in the midst of a civil conflict.

Elsewhere, many conflicts are regional in nature and do not involve the United States or Russia. India and Pakistan have engaged in hostilities over Kashmir, and China and India have clashed along their disputed borders at several places in the Himalayas. Argentina and Great Britain fought a brief but bloody war over Las Islas Malvinas (the Falkland Islands) in the South Atlantic in 1982, and hostilities broke out between Vietnam and China even though both are communist nations.

In the 21st century, the developing nations of the world are still in need of investment to exploit natural resources and develop their agricultural and industrial potential. The nations of Southeast Asia have fared better in terms of industrial development. Vietnam, Malaysia, Taiwan, and Thailand are examples of developing nations that have made significant progress. African nations, both north and south of the Sahara, still have much to do to develop whatever potential they might have to reduce poverty and improve the standard of living for large segments of their populations. Latin American and Caribbean nations are also seeking ways to develop and expand their economies and improve the lives of most of their citizens.

SECTION 3: ARMS CONTROL

The large sums of money expended in stockpiling nuclear weapons in their arsenals has led the superpowers to search for ways to reduce the massive budgets allocated for their development and deployment. Likewise, the potential for other nations to develop or acquire such weapons has led to efforts to control their spread.

During the 1960s, the Limited Test Ban Treaty (1963), the Nuclear Non-Proliferation Treaty (1968), and similar agreements were the focus of control efforts. Nations without nuclear capability, however, have claimed the right to it for both peaceful means (energy) and to protect themselves against enemies who already possess such weapons. India's 1974 nuclear test possibly spurred Pakistan's quest for an "Islamic bomb."

The United States and the former Soviet Union had many arms-control discussions, some of which have been successful. The 1970s saw limitations placed on certain types of missiles as a result of the first Strategic Arms Limitation Treaty (SALT), while SALT II set limits on the kinds of warheads, missile weights, and types of delivery vehicles. More recently, discussions focused on Strategic Arms Reduction Treaties (START), designed to "build down" (decrease) the numbers and types of weapons each nation possesses. In 1999, the U.S. Senate rejected a treaty to ban nuclear testing.

Arms-control issues have taken on a differing emphasis since the breakup of the Soviet Union. Political and economic instability in Russia and some of the other former Soviet republics have raised concerns about the security of nuclear weapons still in place. Could they be stolen, sold, acquired, and used by rogue nationalists, or even terrorist groups?

For other nations with nuclear capabilities, the key issue has become nonproliferation. In 1998, when India successfully carried out nuclear testing, Pakistan soon developed a nuclear bomb capability. North Korea, too, has attempted to "go nuclear."

The other weapons-control issue involves the development of chemical and biological devices for use in warfare and in some nations, such as Iraq, for control of domestic populations. Former Iraqi president Saddam Hussein played a cat-and-mouse game with arms inspectors from the United Nations throughout the 1990s.

It has become increasingly difficult to control the spread of nuclear weapons and the expanding military role that some nations have undertaken in recent years. For example, North Korea and Iran are both seeking to develop nuclear weapons systems, which will increase the arms race. In addition, the economic growth of China since the 1990s has been accompanied by its expanding military presence in Asia and the surrounding seas. A number of Asian nations claim the South China Sea as part of their offshore territorial boundaries because of the potential energy resources below the surface. China's rise as the leading military and naval power in Asia will be a crucial issue in the 21st century.

In the 21st century, arms control remains more of a hopeful wish than a realizable reality. The spread of weapons in too many countries has accelerated in the last decades and has led to more civil wars, revolutions, terrorism, and crimes. These weapons are mostly sold by the leading industrial nations of the world. The United States, Russia, China, Germany, and France are the leading exporters of weapons. In addition, individual weapons merchants seem to have an endless supply of certain arms, which are available for a price to any individual or organization that can pay for them. Iran and North Korea are examples of nations who either supply weapons or who are developing weapons that have the potential to cause mass destruction and death. Terrorist organizations, such as Al-Qaeda, ISIS, Hezbollah, and Boko Haram, seemingly have no difficulty in obtaining whatever weapons they need. In too many nations, individuals with or without affiliations have been able to obtain illegal weapons. Arms control remains an issue in need of a resolution.

SECTION 4: TERRORISM AS A POLITICAL WEAPON

Today some groups, frustrated by what they feel to be oppression by their own government or the policies of other governments, often turn to terrorism. They use violence or the threat of it to publicize their grievances or to press their demands. Terrorism involves the use of violence against unarmed, innocent civilians. Its special horror lies in the fact that innocent men, women, and children are killed.

Terrorism can involve kidnapping or hijacking, assassination, random murder, or mass killing. It is usually carried out by small groups of highly dedicated, even fanatical individuals who believe they can obtain concessions, frustrate governments, or just gain revenge. Some believe in violence as the only way to fight conditions they view as evil, but most have specific goals.

Among those who turned to terrorism to publicize their demands are the Palestinians, who have carried out global attacks against citizens of both Israel and its supporters, especially the United States. From the 1960s to the turn of the century, branches of the Irish Republican Army that are against Britain's role in Northern Ireland and groups like the Tuparmaros of Uruguay and the Shining Path (Sendoro Luminoso) in Peru used terrorist tactics to defy the governments of those nations. In the United States, a government office building in Oklahoma City, Oklahoma, was blown up by American anti-government radicals, killing 168 people. Terrorist hatred on the part of Islam jihadists led to the World Trade Center and Pentagon murderous atrocities of September 11, 2001.

State-supported terrorism has also become a problem. Countries such as Libya, Iran, and Syria have been accused of providing money and training for Palestinian and Islamic fundamentalist terrorist groups and have supported their activities. But international pressure has created the possibility that some terrorists can be brought to justice. Libya agreed to hand over for trial two suspects in the 1988 bombing of a Pan Am airliner over Scotland, and a Kurdish leader considered by Turkey to be a terrorist was extradited from Kenya. General Augusto Pinochet of Chile, whose government persecuted and killed opponents, was indicted by a Spanish court and arrested in England. In 1999, a British court ruled that Pinochet could be sent to Spain to stand trial. However, Pinochet was never sent to Spain and finally returned to Chile. Nevertheless, his arrest was a warning to other political and military leaders that they could be held responsible for state-sponsored criminal acts against innocent people.

In the 21st century, the use of terrorism as a political weapon has spread to other countries. Somalia and Yemen have become centers of terrorism. Also individual acts of terrorism have taken place in countries such as Great Britain, Spain, and more recently, Norway. Political terrorism knows no boundaries.

On September 11, 2001, the terrorist attack that destroyed the Twin Towers in New York City was a turning point in the use of terrorism as a political weapon. Since this devastating attack, the world has experienced a spike in religiously motivated terrorist incidents. No religion is immune from extremists who commit terrorist actions. However, radical groups have increasingly misinterpreted Islam and used it as the religious source to justify the most destructive and horrible acts. These fundamentalist groups have used terrorism without bounds as a means to obtain their objectives. Al-Qaeda, ISIS, and Boko Haram are just a few of the Islamist terrorist groups that have taken part in or sponsored deadly incidents throughout the world. It has become increasingly obvious that terrorism as a political weapon will remain a problem for many years to come and that solutions must be found that will alleviate the causes and appeal of terrorism to so many young people.

Part E: Environmental Issues

As humans increase their capacity to use the earth's resources through technology, they also become increasingly capable of destroying and polluting the very environment that sustains human and all other life. Human activities now affect the ecology and even the climate of the entire planet. As Margaret Mead, a noted anthropologist, said, "We won't have a society if we destroy the environment. . . ."

Chief among the environmental concerns are possible climate changes caused by the greenhouse effect. Carbon dioxide and other gases produced by modern industries trap more of the sun's heat and energy within the earth's atmosphere, causing global warming. While scientists disagree on the causes of global warming, many feel that even a slight increase in the earth's temperatures worldwide could melt the polar ice caps, raise sea levels, submerge coastal areas, and change growing seasons and agricultural production.

Associated with possible climate change is the issue of the destruction of forests, especially the tropical rain forests. Increasingly, the developing nations are clearing large areas of tropical rain forests. They are exporting timber to obtain foreign capital, converting forests to farmland to grow cash crops such as rubber, and attempting to develop more land for settlement and to raise food crops. It is estimated that three thousand acres of tropical rain forest are destroyed every hour. At this rate, in a hundred years the rain forests could all be gone.

GEOGRAPHY

Environment and Society

GEOGRAPHY

Use of Geography

The destruction of the forests add to the greenhouse effect because it decreases the number of trees and plants on the earth that change carbon dioxide to oxygen. In addition, thousands of plant and animal species may become extinct, reducing the earth's biological diversity and possibly its capacity to sustain other kinds of life. If the rain forests vanish, 40 percent of all living species will be destroyed. This means that millions of species, many of which have not yet even been discovered, will vanish. Finally, changing natural patterns can destroy the usefulness of the soil and the effectiveness of the water supply, thus defeating the original purpose of the attempted change in land use. The soil of the tropical rain forest is extremely poor in many nutrients and can sustain agriculture for only a short time. As a result, farmers move on and cut down more forests. In 1992, the United Nations Conference on Environment and Development was held in Rio de Janeiro. Five major agreements on global environmental issues were signed. In the following years a number of formal treaties designed to protect the environment were negotiated and signed. Among these formal treaties and agreements were the Framework Convention on Climate Change and the Convention on Biological Diversity, which were legally binding on the signing parties. In 1997, the Kyoto Protocol, a treaty that has legally binding targets to limit or reduce greenhouse emissions, became a reality. The majority of industrial nations have already signed, but the United States has refused to accept the provisions of the protocol.

Also at issue is the need to protect endangered species and to conserve the wildlife of the earth. Animals such as leopards and alligators (for their skins), elephants and rhinos (for their tusks and horns), and ostriches (for their feathers) have been hunted almost to extinction to provide luxury consumer goods. The nets used by the tuna-fishing industry have endangered dolphins. Several nations have depleted the whale population for industrial purposes, and the spread of human settlement and recreation areas have reduced the land available for animals and plants.

Increased industrialization means increased pollution and an increased threat to human health. Pollution creates carcinogens that cause cancer. Respiratory diseases result from unhealthful substances in the air we breathe, and chemicals in the water supply and food chain create additional threats. Chlorofluorocarbons used in aerosol sprays and refrigeration units contribute to the depletion of the ozone layer, the part of the earth's atmosphere that filters out some of the most harmful of the sun's rays.

The waste byproducts of energy production are another threat. Acid rain is caused by the burning of fossil fuels and has the capacity to wipe out fish and aquatic plant life when it accumulates in bodies of water. Used-up radioactive fuel from nuclear power plants and other hazardous waste products must be disposed of and their transport across international borders regulated.

Safeguards must be developed to prevent industrial disasters such as those that occurred in Chernobyl in the former Soviet Union and Bhopal in India. Radiation from the accident at the Chernobyl nuclear power plant killed Soviet citizens and spread across northwestern Europe. A poisonous gas leak from an American chemical factory in Bhopal killed and injured thousands. In 2010, in Fukushima, Japan, a nuclear facility was severely damaged because of an earthquake and radiation dangers are still present in areas near to the damaged reactors.

Governments around the world are beginning to cooperate in dealing with these environmental issues, though opinions differ about what to do in specific cases. For example, Brazilians see the clearing of the rain forest as essential to their nation's development. They consider American criticism unfair since the United States has been clearing forest lands for over two centuries. Agreements over the use of the resources of the oceans and areas such as Antarctica may establish patterns for dealing with global environmental issues in the future.

One creative proposal for dealing with environmental issues in developing nations has been related to the debt crises often faced by those countries. Lenders have tied debt cancellation to improved environmental policies on the part of governments, such as slowing the clear-cutting of rain forests.

In the 21st century, many environmental problems remain as concerns that affect the health, well-being, and even the future of life on Earth. Finding clean, fresh water; maintaining natural and organic food production and consumption without the use of pesticides; and combatting air pollution, garbage disposal, atomic waste disposal, and the destruction of the remaining world forests are just some of the environmental problems that humanity faces today.

Perhaps the most pressing and threatening problem that we face, which is related to the environmental problems cited above, is the issue of global warming. The vast majority of climatic scientists agree that Earth is warming at a rate that is too rapid and alarming. Earth did become warmer and then get colder in the past. However, now this natural process is accelerating in our present time. This is due to the gases that result in the pollution that transportation vehicles, industrial production, and the burning of garbage and forests add to the heating of the atmosphere surrounding Earth. The polar caps and certain land areas with ice are undergoing melting at an accelerating pace, particularly at the North Pole and in Greenland. The South Pole also has seen dramatic and worrisome changes. Glaciers are quickly disappearing in many of the world's mountain ranges such as the Himalayas, the Andes, and the Alps. As of 2017, 197 nations agreed to try to limit the causes of global warming by signing the Paris Agreement. Each signatory nation has agreed to do what it can to mitigate the causes and effects of global warming. As of December 2017, President Trump plans to withdraw the United States from this global accord, citing national interests. President Trump's plans will make the United States the only nation that will not be part of the Paris Agreement.

Part F: Human Rights

Along with the industrial and scientific revolutions of the past several centuries has come the democratic revolution. Fundamental to this has been the idea that all human beings possess certain political, social, and economic rights. In 1948 the United Nations adopted the *Universal Declaration of Human Rights*, which states the basic right to dignity for all people, as well as the right to freedom of speech, freedom of assembly, and an adequate standard of living.

In 1975, thirty-three nations of Europe, along with the former Soviet Union and the United States, signed the Helsinki Accords. This agreement included a statement of basic human rights. In spite of these documents, however, human-rights abuses continue around the world. Organizations such as Amnesty International and Human Rights Watch monitor and publicize such abuses. Many nations still have much to do with improving human rights and equality for women. Such improvement received global attention in 2011, with the awarding of the Nobel Peace Prizes. Three women were recipients for promoting humanitarian efforts in their countries: Ellen Johnson Sirleaf and Leymah Gbowee from Liberia, and Tawakul Karman from Yemen.

Another organization concerned with human rights issues is the United Nations Human Rights Council (UNHRC). This agency is responsible for promoting and protecting human rights around the world. It has described cases that would be considered consistent patterns of gross human rights violations. These examples include:

• The alleged deteriorating situation of human rights of people belonging to a minority, including forced evictions, racial segregation, and substandard living conditions.

• The alleged degrading situation of prison conditions for both detainees and prison workers, resulting in violence and the deaths of inmates.

Nevertheless, the UNHRC has been subject to criticism as being politicized toward Israel. Since its creation in 2006, the UNHRC has passed more resolutions, condemning Israel more than the rest of the world combined. By April 2007, the UNHRC had passed 11 resolutions condemning Israel, the only country it had specifically condemned. As of 2015, Israel had been condemned in 62 resolutions by the UNHRC.

Toward Sudan, a country with human rights abuses that were documented by the UNHRC's working groups, the Council has expressed "deep concern." The UNHRC has done almost nothing to call attention to abuses by such nations as China, Iraq, Iran, Syria, Yemen, Egypt, Saudi Arabia, Myanmar, and North Korea.

VIOLATIONS OF HUMAN RIGHTS

Apartheid in South Africa

For over 40 years South Africa's government denied political rights to all citizens not of European background and attempted to establish homelands for blacks. This policy denied the non-white population the use of much of the land and resources of the nation. It severely limited economic opportunities for the majority of the population and preserved the white minority's control of the economy.

The South African system also severely limited the rights of those of Asian or mixed backgrounds and extended full political participation only to those of European ancestry. Efforts by the black majority to gain political rights, including the Freedom Charter of the 1950s as well as demonstrations, often led to violent repression. Several hundred blacks were killed by police at Sharpeville in 1965. Students protesting educational changes were gunned down in 1976, and protests and activism in the 1980s led to continued violence.

Individuals who criticized or campaigned against apartheid suffered banning, that is, restriction in their travel and contacts, or imprisonment. Some, such as Stephen Biko, who died in police custody, were murdered.

When change came, it occurred at a very rapid and surprising pace. Prime Minister F. W. de Klerk, elected in 1990, promised to "dismantle apartheid" and began by releasing revered South African leader Nelson Mandela after 30 years of imprisonment. The formerly outlawed African National Congress was legalized, many rules and laws were changed, and the first free universal elections were held in 1994. Nelson Mandela was inaugurated as the head of the nation.

Though it has struggled with continued racial and ethnic conflict and the resultant poverty and crime, the self-designated "rainbow nation" has made progress both economically and socially. A "Truth and Reconciliation Commission" has been the centerpiece of an ongoing attempt to heal old wounds and set new standards of cooperation.

Totalitarian Governments

Such governments are known for their violations of human rights. The former Soviet Union suppressed and imprisoned dissidents, those who criticized the Communist Party or the government. Forced labor camps and psychiatric wards were used to punish those who spoke out or wrote critical articles or books.

In the spring of 1989, the democracy movement started by Chinese students and activists was violently repressed by the Chinese communist government. It sent tanks and troops to clear the demonstrators out of Beijing's Tiananmen Square.

Military dictatorships in Latin American countries, such as Argentina and Chile in the 1980s, imprisoned, tortured, and murdered those who opposed them. Central American death squads used terrorist tactics to threaten and eliminate those who disagreed with them.

The 1990s saw the replacement of many of the Latin American militarist regimes with democratically elected governments, accompanied by attempts to bring to justice those who perpetrated the human rights violations. There are only vestiges of the totalitarianism of communist Eastern Europe in some of the successor nations, and Western nations continue to criticize the repression of dissidents in China.

Several Arab governments in the Middle East have carried out repressive measures against dissidents and minorities. Egypt, Yemen, Saudi Arabia, Iraq, and Syria received condemnations by human rights organizations.

Genocide

The deliberate extermination of a racial, cultural, or ethnic group is called genocide. The worst-ever example of genocide was the systematic murder of Jewish people in Europe by Nazi Germany during World War II. This policy, which resulted in the death of six million Jews, is known as the Holocaust. There are more recent cases of human rights violations that warrant special consideration. In Cambodia, Rwanda, and Uganda, an untold number were the victims of genocide.

In Uganda, the issue was ethnic. Colonel Idi Amin seized power in 1971 with the support of an army largely made up of soldiers of his own ethnic group. After declaring himself president for life, he led a bloody campaign against members of other ethnic groups, which resulted in over 300,000 deaths, the emigration of most citizens of Asian background, and eventually an armed invasion of neighboring Tanzania in 1979.

The Cambodian tragedy was even more horrible. The fanatical communist Khmer Rouge, led by Pol Pot, gained control in 1977 after the turmoil of the communist takeover in Vietnam. The Khmer Rouge forced the people to leave the cities and killed the educated, the middle class, Buddhist priests, and anyone else of power, authority, or uniqueness in the society. By the time Vietnam helped establish an opposition government in the capital of Phnom Penh in 1985, it is estimated that some four million Cambodians had died.

Africa, too, has seen its version of near-genocide, or what some have called ethnic cleansing. In the small central African nations of Rwanda and Burundi, the rival Tutsi and Hutu ethnic groups battled for political control and in the process massacred thousands of the opposition. In the Darfur region of the Sudan, Black Christians faced extermination by Arabs during 2004–2005.

The focus for the concept of ethnic cleansing has been the Balkans, where the reassertion of nationalist fervor came with the fragmentation of Yugoslavia into its component republics. First in Bosnia-Herzegovina, then in its own region of Kosovo, the government of what is left of the former Yugoslavia (mostly Serbia) has been accused of attempting to drive out, respectively, the Bosnia Muslims, and the ethnic Albanians (Kosovars).

Resurgent Nationalism

Events in the Balkans in particular are evidence of a reassertion of nationalist passions, especially in Europe. Ethnic groups from the Baltic republics to Central Asia gained sovereignty as a result of the breakup of the Soviet Union and there are others such as the Chechens who continue to campaign for independence from Russia. Czechs and Slovaks, Croats, Slovenes, and Macedonians all have established nations based on ethnic and cultural backgrounds, spelling the end of Czechoslovakia and splintering Yugoslavia. Renewed cultural awareness and assertiveness motivates Catalans and Basques in Spain as well as Flemings and Walloons in Belgium. In the United Kingdom, Scots voted to form their own parliament, thereby establishing a greater degree of autonomy.

Part G: Technology

The post–Industrial Revolution refers to changes that have taken place in this century. These changes took place in such fields as the gathering of information technology, communications, and the manufacture of products. These changes have accelerated contact and diffusion among culture regions and promoted global independence. This has, in turn, widened the impact of machines and medical technology on the lifestyles, work patterns, and standard of living of people in all societies.

The Silicon Chip

Computers have been the key to the changes of the post–Industrial Revolution. The tiny low-cost silicon chip has brought the most important change in human communications since the printing press. A silicon chip makes it possible to perform millions of calculations in a second and to store vast amounts of information. Today's largest computers can perform as many as 800 million calculations a second and store 4 million words. These stored data can be retrieved instantly and transmitted to any location on Earth or even into space. Computers today are used in many areas of human activity. These include: international financial and banking transactions and investments; automation of industrial production and product distribution; informational data analysis, sharing, storage, and retrieval; news gathering and spreading via electronic telecommunication; and weapons development, monitoring, and control. Social media, such as instant messaging, Facebook, Facetime, Twitter, etc., have made instant personal communication possible and convenient, and, to a large degree, have replaced "snail mail" and phone calls.

The Green Revolution

The developing nations need to increase their agricultural production to keep up with the population increases in their nations. The efforts of scientists and government leaders to find ways to do this have produced a Green Revolution, that is, an increase in the amount of agricultural production from land already under cultivation and expansion of farming onto previously nonproductive land.

The basis of these improvements has been the development by agronomists (agricultural scientists) of high-yielding plant varieties. These are seeds that can produce greater quantities of crops (especially food grains such as rice and wheat) from an area of land than traditional seeds can produce. However, the new grains are not always as hardy as the older ones, and they need chemical fertilizers, more water, and pesticides to protect them from diseases and insects. Different farming techniques are also necessary to use them effectively.

The Green Revolution needs government support to be carried out. Governments must provide education and information as well as loans to enable farmers to buy the new seeds and the necessary pesticides and fertilizers. They must also build irrigation and transportation systems and provide price supports to guarantee that farmers can sell their products at a profit. In addition, governments must carry out land reform, distributing land in a more equal fashion. Finally, a technology for the Green Revolution (appropriate farm machines and techniques) that is useful in small areas at low cost must be developed and made available.

Although the Green Revolution has led to increased production, in some areas because of the cost of new irrigation systems, hybrid seeds, pesticides, and fertilizers, it has also led to smaller farmers incurring extensive debt and, as a result, losing their land. This has occurred in rural areas all over the globe. The increased use of pesticides and chemical fertilziers may also be the cause of increased cancer rates in many rural areas of the developing world.

Without such government support, the risk is too great for most farmers to try the new methods. One of the criticisms of the revolution in agriculture has been its failure to reach poorer farmers. Only those who already make a profit have the money to invest in new methods and techniques. Another criticism is that some of the changes create threats to the environment— irrigation may disrupt normal water systems; internal combustion engines in machinery, as well as fertilizers and pesticides, pollute the air and water; and overuse of the land can wear it out.

Medical Breakthroughs

The advances in medical technology over the past century have prolonged human life and increased its quality. Vaccinations have helped make humans immune to many deadly diseases, while new treatment techniques have increased survival rates for many others. Likewise, improved treatment of wounds and injuries, as well as organ transplants and artificial body parts, have enabled people to live full lives where in the past they might have been severely disabled.

Attitudes have also changed. People are seen as "physically challenged" rather than handicapped and are encouraged to strive to reach their potential. Accessible public facilities and special activities and support groups have helped to enrich the lives of those with physical disabilities.

Preventing diseases has also become an important medical concern. Scientists have researched the effects of most human activities from smoking to jogging, from eating red meat to living near nuclear power plants. Although there is not always agreement on the implications of such studies, the information does provide people with knowledge and possible choices.

Stem cell research has become an extremely controversial aspect of modern medical technology. Stem cells are the first to develop in embryos and are capable of becoming any of the cell types that make up the human body. Scientists have come to believe that embryonic stem cells, especially, may hold the secrets to the cures for diabetes, Parkinson's, Alzheimer's, and spinal cord injuries, among other conditions. At present these embryonic stem cells come from terminated pregnancies, fertility clinics, cloning, and custom fertilization. There are moral and ethical questions concerning all these sources. In 2004 South Korean scientists announced that they had cloned human embryos and harvested their stem cells. In the United States, the Bush administration has severely restricted funding for stem cell research, whereas abroad many governments are generous in their support.

Biotechnology and genetic engineering hold both a promise and a threat for the future. The development of new organisms (biotechnology) may help control diseases or pollutants, but long-term effects may be hard to predict. And the capacity to alter human genes (genetic engineering) that control a person's individual makeup raises ethical as well as medical issues.

Underlying all this is the issue of cost. Medical treatment grows ever more expensive, even in developed nations. In the developing nations, it is one more factor that must be considered in making decisions regarding use of limited financial resources.

Electric Cars and Self-Driving Cars
Electric cars have been around for some time, but they were not manufactured on a large scale until the 21st century. These cars were not practical until charging stations were established that could make it possible to "refuel" along the route in order to use these cars for long-distance drives. Due to environmental concerns regarding pollution, energy conservation, and

climate change, electric cars will likely be manufactured on an even larger scale in the future.

Driverless cars have video cameras, radar sensors, and laser range finders that allow them to travel without the control of a driver. They are in the testing stage, for the most part. However, most major car producers have plans to create driverless cars. It is expected that they will be available to the public over the next few decades.

Part H: Transportation and Communication

One aspect of our modern world is increased mobility—of resources, manufactured goods, ideas and techniques, and human beings themselves. The horizons of the average North American, Western European, or Japanese have been expanded by the automobile, the jet airplane, the telephone, and satellite television, whereas in Asia and Africa, the bicycle or motor-bike, the train or minibus, and the transistor radio have had a similar impact.

Improved transport systems move oil by supertanker from the Middle East to Japan's industries and move Korean technicians and engineers by jumbo jet to Saudi Arabian oil fields. Paved roads move fertilizer to the rural farms of India's Punjab and rural workers in search of jobs to the cities of Latin America.

China manufactures and uses more bicycles than any other nation. More people ride more trains over more miles in India than anywhere else. Job opportunities for rural Indonesians are increased by their ability to commute to a factory in a nearby town on small Japanese-built motorcycles and bus-vans.

Communication technology also improves people's standards of living. The American investor gathers data using cable TV or satellite and the Internet, and buys and sells using a computer. Cell phones and laptop computers have made it possible for people to work and communicate from the most remote spots on the planet. The Philippine farmer listens to the agricultural and weather reports; the Thai craftsperson watches traditional religious dramas on the government television station.

Mobile phones have become the source of great techno-logical innovation, rapidly replacing traditional land-line tele-phones. Many are now equipped with Internet access as well as the ability to store video games, films, and music, serv-ing as portable PCs (personal computers). iPads and tablets, portable agenda planners with Internet access and communi-cation devices, are another innovation. These are also capable of storing video games, films, and music, as well as the texts of books. With telecommunication companies competing for customers, the prices of both the equipment and monthly costs for services have become affordable to most people and are rapidly replacing other electronic devices. The iPod, a small device with earphones that stores vast amounts of music, video games, and films, has also become very popular, especially with children and teens. The creation of the e-reader (electronic reader), a portable device for reading books, periodicals, and other texts, has challenged the supremacy of printed material. These inventions have made it possible for people to communicate instantaneously anywhere in the world at any time.

Nearly instantaneous news reporting via satellite not only puts citizens in touch with events around the world, but it also puts pressure on politicians, especially those in democratic nations, to consider their actions and policies in terms of "approval ratings." The Internet gives individuals access to a wealth of information, but much of it may be unreliable or even offensive. By the same token, however, a person can become vastly more self-informed and use the information constructively with careful use of the system. An American teacher can, for instance, communicate directly with a Serbian citizen cowering in a basement as NATO bombs rain down on his nation, and get a very different picture from that painted by his own media.

GEOGRAPHY

Environment and Society

However, improved transportation and communications can also have negative effects. The massive oil spill from the ship *Exxon Valdez* in 1989 damaged Alaska's coastline and disrupted its economy. Tokyo commuters wear masks to keep airborne chemicals out of their lungs, and London cab drivers average only 9.2 miles per hour, hoping gridlock will not bring them to a complete standstill.

Terrorists hijack and destroy airliners. Computer hackers develop the potential to disrupt financial, informational, and perhaps even governmental communications systems. Smugglers make millions using boats and airplanes to transport illegal drugs. Each technological innovation also creates the possibility of dishonesty and abuse.

Part I: Space Exploration

The space race began in 1957 when the former Soviet Union launched *Sputnik*, the first satellite. One of the highlights of the space race was the landing of American astronauts on the moon in 1969. Today the space program continues to be the focus of much attention and requires huge amounts of money and resources. Achievements in this area bring great prestige to the nations involved, but some think that the money could be used more effectively elsewhere. In 2003, China launched its space program.

Effects on Global Communication and International Relations

Electronic communication by satellite links has had important effects on both civilian and military aspects of human culture. News and entertainment can be shown live or almost immediately, and nations with "spy-in-the-sky" satellites can monitor the actions and movements of potential enemies.

International crises can develop more quickly but can often be dealt with more easily because of rapid communication. Moreover, when emergencies or disasters occur, aid and relief can be dispatched sooner and with greater effect.

Applications of Space and Space-Based Technology

Both the United States and the former Soviet Union have applied rocket technology from their space programs to the development of intercontinental ballistic missiles (ICBMs) for use as carriers of atomic weapons. The American "star wars," or Strategic Defense Initiative (SDI), was an attempt to apply satellite techniques to the destruction of missiles in flight.

Astronomers have profited from the ability of satellites to look into the depths of space without the interference of the earth's atmosphere. Deep space probes to the farthest reaches of the solar system have extended scientific knowledge in a number of fields. In 2004, the Mars Rovers revealed that Mars was once well watered.

Meteorology and the analysis and prediction of weather patterns have been changed by satellite radar and photography. Such knowledge benefits travelers, businesspeople, farmers, and those threatened by storms or droughts. Other fields, such as medicine, may gain knowledge from the opportunity to conduct experiments in the weightless environment of an orbiting space vehicle. Geographers and geologists have new tools for mapping and analysis of land and water patterns and processes.

Recent Developments

In 2004, the Cassini-Huygens mission was the first to orbit Saturn. This was a United States–European mission that sent back pictures of Saturn's rings and is scheduled to study several of Saturn's moons.

The International Space Station is the largest cooperative scientific project in history. Sixteen nations, including Canada, Belgium, Denmark, France, Germany, Italy, Japan, Netherlands, Norway, Russia, Spain, Sweden, Switzerland, the United Kingdom, the United States, and Japan, are involved in the project. The first assembly of the station took place in 1998. The *Columbia* disaster, which grounded U.S. space shuttles, led to the loss of the main supply ships to the space station; however, repair and maintenance have taken place since. The plans for the space station include studying the effects of long-term exposure to reduced gravity, growing living cells in a gravity-free environment, and studying long-term changes in the earth's environment by observing the earth from outer space.

In 2011, the United States launched the Juno Mission to orbit Jupiter. On December 31, 2011, NASA's GRAIL A (Gravity Recovery and Interior Laboratory) spacecraft entered lunar orbit. In June 2012, China's *Shenzhou 9* spacecraft with three Chinese astronauts on board docked at their Tiangong-1 space station. On December 12, 2012, North Korea succeeded in placing its first satellite in orbit. China launched *Shenzhou 10* to Tiangong-1 in 2013. In December 2013, China's *Chang'e 3* spacecraft made a soft landing on the moon. In September 2014, India's unmanned probe entered orbit around Mars. In 2015, the Japanese *Akatsuki* spacecraft succeeded in entering Venus's orbit. In 2016, North Korea launched a rocket that it claimed carried an observation satellite.

Both Indian and U.S. scientists published articles in the periodical, *Science*, in 2009, indicating that there is more water on the moon than previously thought.

Part J: Mutual Impact and Influence: Europe, America, and Africa-Asia

Much of the history of the past 500 years has focused on the relationships between culture regions that experienced the direct effects of the Industrial Revolution and those that received those effects secondhand. The regions that directly experienced the Industrial Revolution, principally the nations of Europe and North America, are also areas whose cultures are based on the Judeo-Christian and Greco-Roman traditions.

The regions that did not directly experience the Industrial Revolution, such as the Native American cultures of the Americas, the ethnic groups (tribes) of Africa, and the Islamic, Hindu, Buddhist, and Confucian societies of Asia, have been dominated by the West because of its technical and economic power for many of those 500 years. During this period, there has not been much recognition of the contributions of African and Asian cultures to the development of Europe and North America.

Europe's reaction to the availability of trade and resources in Africa, Asia, and the Americas was colonialism and imperialism. The technology of the Industrial Revolution provided the weapons and tools and the development of capitalism provided the financial resources for Europe to colonize these areas of the world and to dominate them. This dominance profoundly affected European attitudes, resulting in feelings of cultural superiority, prejudice, discrimination, ethnocentrism, and racism.

In time, the cultures that came under European control reacted with an awakening of pride in their own cultures. As nationalism developed, Americans, Africans, and Asians often used European ideas of political revolution, democracy, and self-determination against the European colonial powers.

As the 21st century dawned, the influence and impact seemed to be shifting more from the West to the East than had been the case for much of the previous five centuries. Growing capacity in manufacturing and technology coupled with cheaper costs have meant that Asian nations in particular have been net exporters of goods and services. Profits earned in this way have also been invested by Asian companies and governments in European and American concerns, moving relationships in the direction of greater balance.

Remnants of the colonial economic pattern of raw materials moving from Asia and Africa to Europe and America have been supplemented by the development of new service and industrial capacities, especially in Asian nations. Textiles and other lighter manufacturing industries export goods to the EU and North America. Digital communications and the Internet helped create "outsource" informational giants like India and the Philippines.

In the case of fundamentalist Islam, reaction against Western values and cultural styles has led to expanded campaigns of terrorism against European and American institutions, as well as attempts to establish Islamic theocracies such as that of the Taliban in Afghanistan. The destruction of the World Trade Center in New York; bombings in Turkey, Spain, England, and Indonesia; and other violent acts have been carried out by Al-Qaeda and similar or related groups. The expressed goal is a return to basic Muslim beliefs and standards and the destruction of "evil" influences.

Western military "interventions" in Middle Eastern nations earned increased anger and hatred from many Muslims. Among these were American campaigns in Iraq and Afghanistan, the U.S. raid into Pakistan to eliminate Al-Qaeda icon Osama bin Laden, and NATO support of rebels who overthrew long-time dictator Muammar al-Qaddafi in Libya.

The Libyan revolt was one element of 2011's "Arab Spring," a series of popular protest movements in nations across North Africa to Syria and the Arabian Peninsula. Some scholars and politicians saw these uprisings as drawing inspiration from western concepts of democracy. Others cited the "Arab street's" disgust with western governments for their support of despotic and corrupt regimes like that of Hosni Mubarak in Egypt.

The electronic and digital age of the 21st century has changed the nature of the relationship between those areas traditionally referred to as the East and the West. News networks, like CNN and Al Jazeera, have created real-time coverage for worldwide audiences and an instant analysis of events of universal interest and impact. Some analysts see their broad reach and the creation of instant information for millions as influencing governmental policies in a variety of countries. Coupled with the spread of access to the Internet, a greater variety of people have the ability to both access and express information in positive and negative ways. The rise of the Islamic State in the Middle East, in the wake of other fundamentalist Muslim groups, has accelerated the spread of such ideas. Recruitment, both intended and incidental, becomes much more prevalent and often seems to encourage and enable terrorist violence. Conversely, mutual perceptions can be positively enhanced. One recent survey found that Muslims with Internet access tend to have more favorable impressions of Western culture and Christianity than do those without access.

The World Wide Web can also bridge business gaps between firms in widely separated countries, and between companies and customers, revolutionizing day-to-day and long-term practices and policies. Information on buying trends, consumer behavior, and new products is no longer restricted to those with the most money and influence. This makes it easier for investors and entrepreneurs to enter previously restricted markets. At the same time, the speed and spread of the Web can leave behind institutions in nations with inadequate financial and cultural resources for making changes.

Similarly, social and political data and news have become more widely available through more informal means. The news of China's SARS epidemic spread by text message and chat rooms before being released through official channels. Evidence is mixed as to whether this relative openness leads to the weakening or strengthening of autocratic governments.

REVIEW QUESTIONS

Multiple Choice. Select the letter of the answer that correctly completes each statement.

1. People experiencing the revolution of rising expectations today are
   A. eager to accept democracy as the answer to political problems
   B. not interested in receiving assistance from developed nations
   C. dissatisfied with some aspects of their present way of life
   D. determined to follow all their traditional ways of living

2. Rapid population growth in a developing nation is due mainly to
   A. a high standard of living for most families
   B. the availability of medical and health care services
   C. a booming economy and many employment opportunities
   D. the number of marriages among younger teenagers

3. Nations have formed international organizations such as the European Community, the Organization of Petroleum Exporting Countries, and the Organization of African Unity in order to
   A. provide for increased military security and national defense
   B. ensure that they receive a sufficient supply of natural resources
   C. carry out the decisions of the UN Security Council
   D. further their own national interests and improve their situation

4. Political leaders in both the United States and Great Britain have often spoken in favor of peaceful resolution of international conflicts. Yet during the 1980s the armed forces of both nations were involved in military encounters outside their own national boundaries. This observation best supports which of the following conclusions?
   A. Most armed conflicts are deliberately started by one side or the other.
   B. Industrialized nations tend to be more aggressive than developing ones.
   C. A popularly elected government must be warlike to satisfy its citizens.
   D. Nations often place greater value in their self-interest than in peace.

5. "Acid Rain Destroys North American Forests"
   "Chemical Leak in Bhopal, India, Kills Thousands"
   "Nuclear Accident at Soviet Power Plant in Chernobyl"

   These headlines best support which of the following conclusions?
   A. Communist nations produce more pollution than capitalist nations.
   B. Developing nations are responsible for most of the pollution in the world.
   C. Protecting the environment is an issue of worldwide importance.
   D. The United Nations is responsible for solving pollution problems.

6. A modern, well-organized infrastructure is necessary for the economic development of a nation. Which of the following factors would be included in a nation's infrastructure?
   A. network of transportation and communication
   B. written organizational plan for development
   C. technological system for using infrared rays
   D. strong system of family support and unity

7. Nations with a low per capita GNP have
   A. greater life expectancy
   B. greater public expenditure on health per capita
   C. a high infant mortality rate
   D. a high adult literacy rate

Base your answer to question 8 on the chart below.

What Americans Buy from Africans*	
Crude petroleum	$9,900
Coffee beans	$ 599
Platinum	$ 352
Aluminum	$ 292
Diamonds (nonindustrial)	$ 286
Uranium	$ 200
Cocoa beans	$ 137
Iron alloys (for steel)	$ 119

* 1982 U.S./sub-Saharan Africa trade ($ value in millions)

8. Most of the goods exported from Africa to the United States can be described as
   A. high-tech components
   B. consumer goods
   C. raw materials
   D. agricultural products

9. Global issues such as overcrowding and pollution are a direct result of
   A. high unemployment
   B. an agriculture-based economy
   C. population growth
   D. an imbalance in world trade

10. During the 1970s and 1980s, attempts were made by the United States and the former Soviet Union to
    A. share advances in military technology
    B. bring democracy to Eastern Europe
    C. form an alliance against Israel
    D. limit the build-up of nuclear weapons

11. In developing countries, the major reason that people move from rural areas to urban areas is to
    A. gain more political power
    B. escape dangerous chemical fertilizers
    C. find better job opportunities
    D. enjoy more varied entertainment

12. Terrorism in the 1980s and 1990s was used by certain groups primarily to
    A. find a peaceful way of settling international conflicts
    B. draw the attention of the world to their causes
    C. increase humanitarian aid to their people
    D. put pressure on the superpowers to end the arms race

13. Which is most characteristic of a nation whose economy is dependent upon the production of one commodity?
    A. The economy is self-sufficient.
    B. The nation has a subsistence economy.
    C. Economic well-being is closely tied to world market prices.
    D. Industrialization makes it possible to export a variety of goods.

14. A policy of nonalignment may be attractive to a developing nation because it allows that nation to
    A. become a strong military power in its own right
    B. develop an overseas empire
    C. concentrate on domestic problems
    D. gain benefits from both sides in the superpower competition

15. Which has been an important result of improved means of communication and travel?
    A. Changes in one part of the world can greatly affect other areas.
    B. Countries have become more nationalistic.
    C. Barriers to international trade have been abolished.
    D. There is less need for international organizations.

16. The greenhouse effect may cause a dramatic
    A. increase in the world's food production
    B. reduction in the level of the world's oceans
    C. rise in the temperatures of the earth in the 21st century
    D. decline in industrial pollution in the United States and Europe

17. The destruction of tropical rain forests is most alarming on the continents of
    A. South America and Africa
    B. Europe and Australia
    C. North America and Asia
    D. Africa and Antarctica

18. Demographers would most likely study statistics indicating that
    A. China's Gross Domestic Product grew by 7 percent in the 1990s
    B. educational spending in Italy declined between 1995 and 2005
    C. the world's population exceeded 6 billion by the year 2000
    D. ocean temperatures rose by 1.5 degrees in the 20th century

19. Which of the following is a major reason why it is difficult to lower birth rates in developing nations?
    A. Children often contribute to the economic well-being of families.
    B. Traditional religious values may favor small families.
    C. Some governments encourage people to marry at a later age.
    D. Prosperous and educated people usually favor large families.

20. Most developing nations have opted first to
    A. invest in costly industrial projects
    B. expand the health care system for their people
    C. augment their agricultural production to feed their people
    D. expand programs that safeguard their environment

21. Devastating sexually transmitted diseases are hard to control because
    A. there is a need to control population growth in some areas
    B. no medicines are available for their treatment
    C. developed nations refuse to help poorer countries
    D. it is quite easy to change traditional social behaviors

22. Global economic development has led to
    A. decreased foreign investment
    B. multinational interdependence
    C. increased trade barriers
    D. declining world trade

23. The most recent expansion of the European Union has included
    A. all of the countries of Scandinavia
    B. several former members of the Soviet Bloc
    C. the island nations of Ireland and Iceland
    D. newly independent nations from the former U.S.S.R.

24. The primary goal of the European Economic Union is to
    A. achieve economic integration of the member nations
    B. form an economic organization along the lines of NATO
    C. prevent nonmember nations from manufacturing in Europe
    D. create a completely self-sufficient trading network

25. In the 1990s, all the world's leading trading nations
    A. increased the volume of their agricultural exports
    B. tried to avoid a disastrous global economic war
    C. erected trade barriers to protect their national production
    D. gave up the idea of forming economic trading blocs

26. All the following are positive effects of multinational corporations *except*
    A. create jobs where they set up manufacturing plants
    B. bring new manufacturing facilities to developing countries
    C. help national industries by increasing competition
    D. contribute to raising the standard of living of their workers

27. Multinational corporations have a tendency to
    A. serve the interests of the nation where their headquarters are
    B. try to remain within the areas of the United States and Western Europe
    C. be increasingly independent and have an international outlook
    D. invest their profits within the nations where they earn them

28. During the 1990s many developing nations
    A. reduced the amount of foreign debt they owed
    B. happily complied with austerity measures called for by the IMF
    C. avoided borrowing to finance infrastructure projects
    D. became more burdened with debts that were not payable

29. The collapse of communism in the Soviet Union and the nations of Eastern Europe
    A. made more financial aid available for developing nations
    B. led to a growth of employment in these countries
    C. caused greater competition for limited financial aid
    D. resulted in more investment capital for Africa and Asia

30. The decline of the United States currency (the dollar) would result in
    A. U.S. goods becoming more expensive in Europe
    B. foreign automobiles becoming cheaper in the United States
    C. no real change because the dollar is still powerful
    D. American products being cheaper in other world markets

31. The global drug trade is a problem for all of the following reasons *except*
    A. huge sums of drug money are laundered by drug cartels
    B. drug money increases political instability and violence
    C. profits from the drug trade are used mostly for philanthropic purposes
    D. some international banks and businesses cooperate with the drug cartels

32. Cultural diffusion has increased because of
    A. increased automation
    B. technological advances
    C. growing materialism
    D. renewed feminism

33. The growth of materialism in the United States and elsewhere has led to
    A. a questioning of values
    B. gender stereotyping
    C. women's liberation
    D. national self-determination

34. New technological advances have resulted in all of the following *except*
    A. increased automation
    B. reduced working hours
    C. declining consumerism
    D. more leisure time

35. In the 1960s, the rebirth of the women's rights movement in the United States reflected
    A. a demand for equal voting rights
    B. the enactment of a constitutional amendment for women's rights
    C. a desire to end all aspects of sexual discrimination
    D. the overall acceptance by men of the equality of women

36. The disappearance of communism in the Soviet Union and Eastern Europe has led to
    A. greater numbers of people being employed
    B. a decline in ethnic and national consciousness
    C. arrival of religious practice in these areas
    D. more people having a better materialistic life

37. The loss of tropical rain forests leads to
    A. animal and plant life being destroyed
    B. a lessening of the greenhouse effect
    C. less carbon dioxide in the atmosphere
    D. the overall improvement of air quality

38. The Bhopal and Chernobyl incidents are examples of
    A. a nation's ability to control its industrial accidents
    B. policies that governments should follow to control pollution
    C. devastating accidents that can happen if safety is ignored
    D. the need to build more chemical and nuclear plants

39. The nation that consumes the greatest percentage of the world's energy is
    A. Japan
    B. Russia
    C. the United States
    D. China

40. The greatest source of the world's energy used today is
    A. natural gas
    B. oil
    C. coal
    D. electricity

41. The post–Industrial Revolution refers to
    A. a growth in mechanized production
    B. the era of airplane travel
    C. increased use of atomic power
    D. changes in science and technology

42. The computer revolution has led to
    A. the increasing high cost of producing silicon chips
    B. a decline in the use of computer-generated stock trading
    C. enormous changes in the gathering of information
    D. a greater independence for industrialized nations

43. All the following are positive effects of the use of computers *except* the
    A. increased use of computer related instructional programs
    B. improvement in the speed of financial and banking transactions
    C. prediction of election results prior to the polls closing
    D. ability to forecast worldwide weather conditions

44. Space exploration began in earnest in the 1950s after the
    A. United States launched the *Columbia* space shuttle
    B. Soviet Union launched the *Sputnik I* satellite
    C. United States developed the Strategic Defense Initiative
    D. Soviet Union developed the first operational space station

45. All the following are accepted medical advances *except*
    A. laser surgery technology
    B. diagnostic services
    C. genetic engineering
    D. organ transplants

THEMATIC ESSAYS

Essay #1 Theme: Science and Technology
Advances made in science and technology in the 20th century will help humans to resolve health problems and communication issues in the next century.

Task:
1. Explain how scientific and technological advances help resolve human problems.
2. Select two technological advances and explain how they have helped humankind.

Directions: Write a well-organized essay with an introduction to the topic, a body that accomplishes the task, and a summarizing statement.

Hint: You may choose health and communication issues that involve you or people you know.

Essay #2 Theme: Economic Systems
After the end of the Cold War, capitalism emerged triumphant as the world's leading economic system.

Task:
1. Define the economic system of capitalism.
2. Select two capitalist countries and explain how their economic systems are similar and different.

Directions: Write a well-organized essay with an introduction to the topic, a body that accomplishes the task, and a summarizing statement.

Hint: You may use the United States.

DOCUMENT-BASED ESSAY QUESTIONS

Directions: The following two questions are based on the accompanying documents. Some of the documents have been edited for the purpose of this assignment.

Write two well-organized essays with an introduction stating a thesis, a body of several paragraphs that accomplishes the task, and a summarizing conclusion. Use evidence from all of the documents to support the position you take in your thesis. Do not simply repeat the contents of the document; explain things in your own words and relate the information to your thesis. Using your knowledge of social studies, include related information that is not included in the documents.

Essay #1

Historical Context: In Latin America, economic nationalism and foreign investment have been interpreted from different viewpoints and influence how nations make economic and political decisions.

Task: Discuss how different economic ideas about monetary issues such as foreign investment in Latin America can be defended based on the financial and political interests of those who hold that point of view.

Part A: Summarize the main idea expressed in the document.

Part B: Respond in an essay. Your essay should be based on a thesis statement. Your essay should explain how each of the statements in the documents reflect a point of view based on economic or political interests. Use all the documents in your essay.

DOCUMENT 1

"Financial institutions that invest in Latin America have to wrestle with unusual problems to finance their operations. Most of these problems do not plague financial institutions in the developed countries. In Latin America capital is scarce and all business firms suffer from a lack of available cash. Bank rates are high. There is criticism that the automobile business is attracting too much cash to the detriment of other sectors of the economy. National pride is sensitive to the penetration of foreign capital that purchases control of national industries. The price level is under insistent inflationary pressure. Returns to investors have to be correspondingly high."

—M. R. Niefeld (1962), "The American Banker"

DOCUMENT 2

"Let us examine the reasons that the United States government and financial institutions should be interested in investing in Latin America. With a per capita income which averages one eighth of ours they still consume one fifth of our exports. The nations of Latin America possess one of the world's greatest storehouses of natural resources. Roughly one third of our agricultural and raw material imports come from Latin America. Our private investments bring in healthy returns to the investors. There is a great potential for growth of trade."

—Clement G. Motten (1986), "Reasons for Investments in Latin America"

DOCUMENT 3

"It is official US policy to encourage investment abroad. This view arises from a desire to reduce direct government investment and the belief that private investment offers the most effective way to achieve economic growth. However, private investment is highly selective. It tends to favor the areas where the greatest returns can be achieved and avoids problems that are too costly if they interfere with the immediate returns on the capital invested. In addition, private investment in Latin America concentrates on petroleum, mineral, and other natural resources."

Marvin Bernstein (1966), "Foreign Investment in Latin America"

DOCUMENT 4

"The object of foreign investment is to obtain profits for the investors. The first priority of private investment is to select those industries where the returns will be maximized with the least risk and investment in infrastructure. Private investment leads to money being drained from the national economy and sent abroad. Purchase of valuable National industries is a goal of foreign investment. There is no real desire to assist the countries and people in the nation where investments are made by foreign financial interests. The foreign investors often eliminate national competition to gain complete control of a lucrative industry to earn the greatest profits."

—Pablo Casanova (1975), "The Ideology of Foreign Investment in Latin America"

DOCUMENT 5

"The economic growth and the social prosperity of Mexico must depend basically on the Mexican people. Foreign investment is necessary but must be carefully regulated to prevent from creating problems. Mexico has to guard against the outflow of foreign remittances that are the direct result of making too high of a percentage of profits. The types of investments must be analyzed before they are allowed to be made in order that national interests can be protected. The Mexican workers deserve protection from foreign investors who invest because the wages of Mexican workers are lower than in developing countries. Mexico must protect itself from foreign investment that seeks to take over and dominate a selected industry or national market."

—Mario Roman Betata (1965), "Foreign Investment in Mexico"

DOCUMENT 6
A WEALTHY SALVADORAN GIRL

Ana's ancestors have lived at the family hacienda near Ranchador for generations, ever since the first Spanish families settled in the area. Today Ana and her father and mother and brothers and sisters occupy the large, comfortable farm estate that they inherited. They are proud of their Spanish heritage.

Because of the vast inherited land holdings and his good business ability, Ana's father is very wealthy. . . . The family lives on a lavish scale, entertaining many house guests and enjoying a great deal of activity around the swimming pool. . . . There are numerous household servants, and Ana has no idea how many people are employed on her father's fields.

Ana's mother is interested in helping the poorer people of the tiny town of Ranchador, which is the nearest community to the estate, and also the unfortunate people of Santa Ana, just a few miles to the southwest. . . . Ana's mother has worked to help set up free health clinics at Santa Ana. She and her friends hope to open a training school for nurses. . . . They also want to provide housing for the elderly poor of the area.

Ana does not attend a school; she studies under the watchful eye of tutors employed by her parents. In addition to her regular studies, she is given training in art, ballet, and music. . . . She loves to ride her pony about the estate and play games with her brothers. . . .

The principal crop grown by Ana's father is coffee. His trips to the port city of Acajutla are generally to see about the shipment of his crop from the port. However, he also owns an interest in the large modern cement factory in the port city, as well as its oil refinery and its fertilizer and sulphuric acid plants.

Ana's father also has an interest in the largest coffee mill in the world. . . . Ana is not terribly interested in school. She will probably continue her education . . . taking many general college courses and looking forward to marriage.

Adapted from Allan Carpenter and Eloise Baker, *El Salvador* (Chicago Children's Press, 1971), pp. 25, 27. Permission pending.

ANSWER KEY FOR REVIEW QUESTIONS

Pages 66–67

1. B	4. D	7. C	10. C
2. C	5. C	8. B	
3. B	6. C	9. C	

Pages 97–98

1. C	4. C	7. A	10. A
2. D	5. C	8. B	
3. A	6. C	9. B	

Pages 161–163

1. A	5. B	9. B	13. B
2. C	6. C	10. A	14. B
3. C	7. D	11. C	
4. D	8. C	12. C	

Pages 226–228

1. B	5. C	9. B	13. A
2. A	6. B	10. B	14. B
3. B	7. B	11. D	15. A
4. A	8. C	12. A	16. B

Pages 236–237

1. D	4. B	7. B	10. B
2. A	5. B	8. A	11. B
3. B	6. A	9. A	

Page 242

1. C	3. C	5. A
2. A	4. B	

Pages 270–271

1. A	4. A	7. C	10. D
2. C	5. B	8. A	
3. D	6. A	9. C	

Pages 334–341

1. C	13. C	25. B	37. A
2. B	14. D	26. C	38. C
3. D	15. A	27. A	39. C
4. D	16. C	28. D	40. B
5. C	17. A	29. C	41. D
6. A	18. C	30. D	42. C
7. C	19. A	31. C	43. C
8. C	20. A	32. B	44. B
9. C	21. B	33. A	45. C
10. D	22. B	34. C	
11. C	23. B	35. C	
12. B	24. A	36. C	

GLOSSARY

absolutism a system of government where a ruler has complete control over the lives of the people

acid rain the precipitation or rain that falls through polluted air

acupuncture an ancient Chinese practice of sticking needles into certain parts of the body to treat disease and to relieve pain

adaptation adjustment to the conditions of the environment or culture

agriculture using the land to produce crops and raise livestock; farming

agronomist a person who studies soil management and field crop production

ahimsa Indian idea of nonviolent action as suggested by Mohandas K. Gandhi

AIDS the illness known as acquired immunodeficiency syndrome

Ainu among the earliest known people to live in Japan

Allah the one God of Islam

alliance joining together of groups by formal agreement

altitude height of the land above sea level

animism the worship of spirits that are part of the natural environment

annex to join or add to a larger or more important thing

anthropologist social scientist who studies people, their culture, and their different ways of living and behavior

anti-Semitism hostility and prejudice against Jews

apartheid a policy of segregation and political and economic discrimination against non-European groups in South Africa

appeasement satisfying an aggressor's requests in the hope that no more harsh requests will be made

arable fertile; suitable for growing crops

arbitrator a person chosen to settle a dispute between two groups

archaeologist scientist who studies the cultures of prehistoric and historic peoples through their artifacts, such as tools, pottery, building, and writing

archipelago a group of islands

artifacts objects made by either hand or machine representing a particular culture

artisan trained or skilled worker; craftsman

audiencia the highest court of Spanish colonial America

autocrat one person who has supreme, unrestricted power over people

autonomous self-governing; independent

balance of payments a summary of international trade (exports and imports) of a country or region over a period of time

Bantu a large group of Africans who speak a common language

Bedouins nomadic Arabic livestock-raisers and -herders

Bible the holy book of Christians. It contains both the Old Testament and the New Testament. The Old Testament is called the Tanakh by Jews. Jews do not accept the New Testament as a holy book.

bicameral a two-house legislature

bilateral affecting two sides or parties in any negotiation

Boers South Africans of Dutch or Huguenot descent; from the Dutch word for farmers

boycott to refuse to buy and use certain goods

bride price payment made by a man to a woman's father to be allowed to marry her; bride wealth

Bunraku Japanese puppet play

Bushido Japanese Samurai Code of Behavior; similar to the feudal code of behavior of the European knights, called chivalry

cacao the seeds of a tree from which cocoa and chocolate are made

caliph a successor of Muhammad as spiritual and temporal head of Islam

calligraphy artistic writing, especially common in China and Japan

capital the things used to produce goods and services; money used to develop a country's economy

capitalism an economic system based on private rather than government ownership

cartographer someone who makes maps

cash crop the chief agricultural product raised in an economy in order to sell and obtain income

caste social system in which people are grouped according to occupation, wealth, inherited position, or religion

caudillo or **cacique** powerful South American leader or dictator

civilization level of development of a group; includes food-producing ability, government, and methods of communication

clan people within an ethnic group who are descended from a common ancestor

class people grouped according to similar social and economic levels

climate the general existing weather conditions over an area for a long period of time

coalition voluntary union of interest groups, political parties, or nations

collectives a system in which a farming community shares ownership of land and farm machinery

colonialism a situation in which one group, often a nation, has control over and is depended upon by another area or people

colony a body of people living in a separate territory but retaining ties with the parent state

commonwealth a nation or state

commune often rural community characterized by collective ownership and use of property

communication the ability to send or receive information and ideas

communism economic system in which a single party controls the means of production with the aim of establishing a classless society

community a group living together, having the same laws, and sharing common interests

confederation alliance or league

conservation protection of natural resources; conserve, to save for the future

conservatism a desire to maintain traditional customs and practices, and to make any changes very slowly

Containment a policy followed by the United States and the free world during the Cold War, to prevent the spread of communism beyond where it already existed (i.e., China and the Soviet Union)

continent a large landmass; one of the seven great divisions of land on the globe

cooperative a community system operated by and benefiting all members who contribute to it

coup d'etat sudden and violent overthrow of a government by a small group

Creole (criollo) a white person descended from French or Spanish settlers of the U.S. gulf states

crusades military campaigns and pilgrimages by European Christians to win the Holy Land from the Muslims (1096–1204)

cultivated land prepared for the raising of crops

cultural diffusion spread of cultural traits from one group to another

culture the customary beliefs, social forms, and material traits of an ethnic, religious, or social group

cuneiform writing in wedge-shaped characters

customs usual ways of acting in a particular situation

Cyrillic the alphabet used for Russian and other Slavic languages

deficit lacking in amount or quantity

deforestation the action of clearing forests of their trees

deity a god or goddess

delta the land that is formed by mud and sand at the mouth of a river

democracy a political system in which the people participate in the making of their own laws or elect representatives to make the laws

desert a barren, extremely dry area

Détente the friendly relationship between the United States and the Soviet Union during the 1970s

developed nation a nation with a stable economy and a modern standard of living for its people

dharma the law in the Buddhist religion; correct behavior, virtue in Hinduism

dialects a regional or local variety of languages

diaspora the lands where people live outside of their original homeland

dichotomy a division into two individual groups

dictator someone who has taken complete control of a country's government and the lives of the people

dissident one who disagrees with the general opinion or actions of a group

diversity not alike; variety

divine right idea that God has given a ruler the right to rule

doctrine a position or principle taught and believed in by a church or government

drought a long period of dry weather over an area

dynasty a powerful group or family that rules for many years

economic relating to the production, distribution, and consumption of goods and services

ecosystem an ecological unit consisting of a community and its environment

elevation the height of land above sea level; altitude

embargo complete restriction or restraint of trade; refusal to buy a product

encomiendo a grant of land given by the king of Spain for loyal services

environment all of the natural, physical, and cultural conditions that surround and affect people

equator an imaginary line circling the earth and equally distant from the North Pole and the South Pole

ethnic cleansing act of persecuting members of an ethnic group by killing them or by removing them from an area

ethnic group a group of people who have common physical traits, history, and culture

ethnocentrism belief that one's own group or culture is superior to others

euro the European currency introduced in 1999

excommunicate process of expulsion from the Roman Catholic Church, usually because of disobedience and violation of Church rules and laws

exploit to make unfair or selfish use of something or someone

extended family a family that includes other members besides mother, father, sons, and daughters; for example, grandparents

extraterritoriality existing or taking place outside of the territory of a nation

extremists people who go to the greatest extent, including violence, to achieve their goals

faction clique; a party or a group

fallow plowed land that is not planted for one or more seasons

favela a part of a Brazilian town or city where the poor and landless live

federation a union of equal organizations that give power to a central group

fetish any real object worshipped by people for its supposed magical powers

feudalism the political and economic system in which the vassal pledges loyalty and service to a lord in return for land and protection

genocide the destruction of a particular group of people

gentry people belonging to the upper or ruling class of society

Ghats low mountains on the east and west side of the Deccan region in South India

"global village" describes the current state of our world, in which events or actions in one part of the world affect other parts of the world

greenhouse effect harmful warming of the earth's surface and lower layers of the atmosphere, caused by an increase in carbon dioxide in the atmosphere

gross domestic product (GDP) the total value of all goods and services produced in a country during a year

guerilla member of a group that carries on raids and fights an established government

habitat the natural environment in which people, animals, and plants live or grow

hacienda a large land estate or ranch in Spanish America, mainly in Mexico

Haiku a Japanese form of poetry

haj the pilgrimage to Makkah (Mecca) that all Muslims should take as one of their five obligations

Hellenistic Greek culture spread by Alexander the Great on areas he conquered

heritage that which is passed from one generation to the next

hieroglyphics a writing system using mainly pictorial characters

Hindi the major language of India

Hinduism the major religion of India

Hijra the flight by Muhammad from Makkah (Mecca) to Medina in 622. Sometimes spelled as Hegira, its date is the most important date in Islamic history and begins the Muslim calendar.

humanism a belief in the importance of the individual human being, the idea that humans can accomplish great things without regard to supernatural and religious factors. Humanism also emphasized worldly items rather than religious ones. It was a movement that grew during the Renaissance.

hydroelectric relating to the production of electricity through the use of water power

imam leader of the Shi'ite Muslims; prayer leader of a mosque

imperialism a nation's policy of extending its power and dominion over other nations by using force or indirect economic and political control

inflation the great increase in the amount of paper money in relation to the available goods for sale; this situation leads to rising prices

infrastructure the basic transportation and communication system of a nation

interdependence people's dependence on one another

Internet a global computer network that links computers together and enables global communication between users

intervention the policy of interfering in the affairs of another nation

irrigation the watering of crops or other plants by pipes, canals, and ditches

Islam a major world religion that recognizes Allah as the only

God and Muhammad as his Prophet

island a land mass completely surrounded by water

isolation separation from others

isthmus a narrow strip of land connecting two large land masses and separating two large bodies of water

jihad Islamic holy war

joint family a family pattern in which two or more generations live together

Judaism the oldest of the Middle East religions; the main idea of Judaism is the belief in one God (monotheism)

junta a board or ruling body

Kabbah a shrine located in the Great Mosque in Makkah (Mecca) and considered to be the holiest site for Muslims

Kabuki a form of Japanese drama with song and dance

Kami good spirits of nature to the Japanese

karma Hindu idea that every human action brings about certain reactions

kibbutz an Israeli community of farmers who work together and share all the property and income

Koran the holy book of Muslims

laissez faire the theory that government should intervene as little as possible in a nation's economic affairs

landlocked describes an area or region completely surrounded by land without access to a sea or ocean

language a systematic verbal method of communication among a group of people

latifundia large farms, ranches, or plantations in Spanish America

leaching the washing away of nutrients from the soil

leftist a person who favors change or reforms, usually in the name of greater freedom

liberalism a belief favoring change and progress in political and cultural traditions

lines of latitude imaginary parallel lines running east and west around the globe; these lines measure distance north and south of the equator

literate having the ability to read and write a language

llanos plains in Colombia and Venezuela; from the Spanish word for "plains"

mandate an order or command; a commission set up to rule an area

Marxist one who believes in socialism as a method of government

matriarchal a family group led by the mother

medieval the "Middle Ages" or time between the Roman period and the Renaissance in European history; approximately between C.E. 500 and 1500

mercantile system a system in which a colony's only purpose is to provide raw materials for the mother country and act as a market in which products from the mother country can be sold; the colony exists solely for the support of the mother country

mestizo a person of mixed European and Native American ancestry

migration the movement of people from one area or country to another

militarism policy in which the armed forces are made powerful and military interests are most important

militia citizens who can be called to help defend a nation; this generally does not include the regular armed forces

minerals nonliving materials found on or near the earth's surface, such as gold, silver, and lead

missionary person who brings his religion to people who are not members of that religion

mixed economy an economy that has both capitalistic (free market) features and government-directed (command) features

moderate not extreme

moksha the final resting place for all deserving Hindus

monarchy government headed by a king or queen

monopoly economic situation wherein one person or group controls the production, pricing, and distribution of a good

monotheism the belief in one god or supreme being

monsoon a wind in Asia that brings a wet season when it blows from the sea and a dry season when it blows from the land

mosque a building used for public worship by Muslims

most-favored nation a part of most trade agreements that gives each nation the same rights as all other trading partners

mouth the place where a river empties into a sea, lake, or ocean

mulatto a person having one European and one African parent, or a person of mixed European and African ancestry

Muslim someone who practices the religion of Islam

myth a traditional story of supposedly real events that explains a world view of a people or a practice, belief, or natural phenomenon

nationalism loyalty and devotion to one's own country, especially placing it above all others

nationality a group of people who feel they belong together because of common cultural characteristics like language, religion, history, and traditions

nationalization the government take-over of industry and property

natural laws laws and rules about human behavior, occurring naturally, without intervention by people

natural resources industrial materials and capacities provided by nature

navigable deep enough and wide enough for ships to sail on

negotiate to confer or bargain in order to arrive at a settlement or solution to a problem

neutralism a policy of not taking sides in relation to the great world powers

nirvana the stopping of the wheel of rebirth (reincarnation); the goal of all Buddhists

No (Noh) a Japanese form of drama developed in the 14th century

nomad a member of a group that moves from place to place to secure its food supply

nonalignment a policy of not being allied with the great world powers

nuclear proliferation the possession of nuclear weapons by more and more countries

oasis a place in the desert where there is natural spring or surface water

ocean a great body of water that covers three-quarters of the surface of the earth

oligarchy governmental rule by a few or a small group

opium an addictive narcotic drug

oral tradition the practice of passing down stories and information from generation to generation by word of mouth

origin thing from which anything comes; source; starting point

overpopulation a situation in which an area contains more people than available resources can support

Pacific rim refers to the nations of Asia and the Americas that touch both sides of the Pacific Ocean

pact an agreement between two or more nations

paddies rice fields in Asia

pagoda temple or sacred building with many stories (levels) found in India, Southeast Asia, and Japan

pampas the large grassy plains of southern Latin America, especially in Argentina

panchayat a local council in India

parliament a supreme legislative body

Patois a local dialect

patriarch the highest ranking bishop in the Eastern Orthodox Church, usually ministering over a nation

patriarchal a family group led by the father

patriotism love and devotion to one's own country

peasant a small landowner or laborer

peninsula land mass surrounded on three sides by water

peon in Latin America, a field worker who owns no land

per capita GDP the average value per person of the goods and services a country produces in a year

petrodollars money paid to oil-producing countries

petroleum an oily, inflammable liquid used in making gasoline and chemicals

pharaoh a ruler of ancient Egypt

pictograph an ancient or prehistoric drawing or painting on a rock wall

plain an extensive area of flat or rolling treeless country

plateau a broad land area with a usually level surface raised sharply above the land next to it on at least one side

pogrom a violent attack on Jews by non-Jews

population density the average number of persons per unit of area

polytheistic belief in many gods or deities

possession an area under the control of another government

prehistoric refers to a period of time prior to written history

primitive very simple; of early times in a civilization

propaganda the spreading of ideas, information, or rumor for the purpose of furthering one's position or cause to injure another

provincial local; relating to a province or district

quarantine to blockade in order to prevent the transfer of goods

Quechua the language of the Incas, still spoken by the Indians of Peru, Bolivia, Ecuador, Chile, and Argentina

rabbi a Jewish religious leader

race a division of people having certain similar physical characteristics

radical one who favors extreme changes in government or society

rain forest a forest of hardwood evergreen trees that requires very heavy rainfall

rajah Indian ruler

realism a writing style that attempts to portray life as it really happens

rebellion armed resistance or fighting against one's government, political system, or culture

referendum a practice of submitting to popular vote a measure passed or proposed by a legislative body or by popular demands

refugee someone who leaves his or her homeland to seek a safe place to live

region an area of land whose parts have one or more similar characteristics

regionalism loyalty to local economic and social affairs, customs, and traditions

reincarnation the act of returning to some form of life after death

republic a type of government in which leaders are chosen by the citizens

revolution basic change in or complete overthrow of an existing government, political system, or culture

rift valley a split or separation in the earth's crust; the Great Rift Valley extends from southwest Asia (Jordan) to Mozambique in East Africa

rightist one who supports conservativism and resists change

romanticism a writing style that emphasizes human emotions rather than human reasoning

rural having to do with farming and the countryside

Samurai the military class of feudal Japan

Sanskrit an ancient Indian language; the classical language of Hinduism

savanna a grassland in subtropical areas with drought-resistant undergrowth and few trees

schism a division or split among people, usually for political or religious reasons

secede to withdraw from a group or organization

sect a group believing in a particular idea or leader

sectarian a member of a sect; a narrow-minded or bigoted person

secular concerned more with worldly (earthly) matters than with religious matters

self-sufficient able to meet one's own needs without help

Sepoy a native of India employed as a soldier by the English

serf a member of a subservient feudal class bound to the soil and subject to the will of a lord; serfs had few rights or privileges

Shi'ite Muslims who believe Ali and the imams to be the only rightful successors of Muhammad

Shinto the original religion of Japan, having gods (Kami) of nature (sea, river, winds, forests, and sun)

shogun a military leader of Japan before 1867

silt a deposit of sand and mud along a river

slash-and-burn a method of clearing land so that it is temporarily usable for farming; used in tropical areas

social contract the idea that all people have a right to life, liberty, and property, and that, if a government tries to remove these rights, people also have the right to revolt

socialist economy a system in which the government owns the means for production and distribution of goods

source origin; place where something begins

soviet a worker's council set up by the Bolsheviks in 1917; the term was also adopted by them as the name of the communist government of Russia

sphere of influence an area or region within which the influence or the interest of one nation is more important than any other nation

stable steady; firm; not likely to fall

standard of living the level of comfort enjoyed by an individual or a group

steppe flat, treeless plain with short grass found in southeastern Europe or Asia

strait a narrow channel of water connecting two larger bodies of water

subcontinent a landmass of great size but smaller than a continent; for example, India

subsidy a grant or gift of money to assist an enterprise, business, or individual

subsistence farming the production of all or almost all the goods required by a farm family, usually without any significant surplus for sale

suffrage the right to vote

sultan ruler of a Muslim country

Sunni the Muslims of the part of Islam that follow the orthodox tradition

superpower a nation with greater military and/or economic power than other nations

suttee the act or custom of a Hindu widow being cremated on the funeral pyre of her husband

Swahili a Bantu language of East Africa used for trade and government; has many Arabic, Persian, and Indian words

swaraj Indian term for self-rule

taiga a forested area in Russia and other places near the Arctic

Talmud books containing Jewish civil and religious law and tradition

Tanakh refers to the Jewish bible (called the Old Testament by

Christians). Also spelled as Tanach, it consists of holy books in three categories: the Torah, Prophets, and Writings

tariff a tax on goods brought into a country from another country

terraced farmland flat shelves of land, arranged like wide steps on a mountainside

terrorism the idea of using violence and fear of violence to gain an objective

textiles fibers and yarns made into cloth and then into clothing

Third World refers to the developing nations of Asia, Africa, and Latin America

topography the surface features of a place or area

totalitarianism all parts of life—economic, social, political, religious, and educational—are controlled by the state

trade deficit when the imports of a nation exceed its exports

trade surplus exports of a nation are greater than the imports of that nation

tradition the handing down of information, beliefs, and customs from one generation to another

tribalism tribal relationships, feelings, and loyalties

tribe a group of people who share a common language and religion and are united under one leader

tributary the branches of a large river

tropical having to do with the hot areas near the equator

typhoon a tropical storm or cyclone found in the China Sea and Indian Ocean

underdeveloped an area with little industry that is in an early stage of economic development

unique one of a kind

untouchable a person belonging to the lowest caste of the Hindu social order

uprising revolt; rebellion; an act of popular violence in defiance of an established government

urban relating to a city

values attitudes or beliefs considered to be important by a group

vassal a person under the protection of a feudal lord to whom he has vowed his loyalty and service; a subordinate or follower

veld South African steppe or prairie

vernacular the style of language used in a certain area

viceroy the governor of a country or a province who rules as the king's representative

Yoruba an African tribe living in present-day Nigeria

zambo a person of mixed Native American and African parentage in Latin America

Zionism a theory for setting up a Jewish national community in the Middle East and supporting the modern state of Israel

Sample Regents Transition Examination

Global History and Geography

PART I: MULTIPLE CHOICE

Directions (1–30): For each statement or question, write in the space provided the *number* of the word or expression that, of those given, best completes the statement or answers the question.

1 Which of the following was the result of the policies of Peter the Great in Russia?

1 Russia became a constitutional monarchy.
2 Protestantism was adopted as the official religion.
3 The serfs were freed.
4 Western European ideas and technologies were adopted.   1 _____

2 Which of the following was *not* a reason for the decline of the Ottoman Empire?

1 lack of modern military technology
2 loss of territories to other nations
3 movements for independence by ethnic groups in Eastern Europe
4 lack of trade with Western Europe   2 _____

3 Before 1914, nationalism in the Balkans contributed to

  1 the inability of nations to pay reparations
  2 the creation of new independent nations
  3 the acquisition of colonies
  4 the demand for democracy   3 _____

4 Which of the following was *not* a reason for the failure of democracy in Russia?

  1 Most people were not familiar with the concept of democracy.
  2 Tsar Nicholas never allowed a democratic government.
  3 Russia had no history of democratic institutions.
  4 The Provisional Government was experimenting with democracy during a war.   4 _____

5 A large contributing factor for the Bolshevik Revolution of 1917 in Russia was

  1 Vladimir Lenin's New Economic Policy
  2 Rasputin's influence on the government
  3 a shortage of military supplies and food during World War I
  4 Tsar Nicholas's failure to aid the Serbians   5 _____

Base your answer to question 6 on the photos below and on your knowledge of social studies.

6 The first photograph of Joseph Stalin and his fellow Soviet leaders was edited three times between 1926 and 1929 to produce the following three photographs. The gradual removal of the Soviet leaders from the original photograph illustrates the U.S.S.R's development into a(n)

1 democracy
2 aristocracy
3 plutocracy
4 autocracy   6 _____

7 Which of the following events was *not* a direct result of the Cold War?
 1 the building of the Berlin Wall
 2 the policy of détente
 3 the creation of NATO and the Warsaw Pact
 4 the Prague Spring   7 _____

8 The collapse of Communism in the U.S.S.R. and Eastern Europe was due in part to
 1 economic overextension due to the arms race
 2 the lack of jobs for workers
 3 overproduction of consumer goods
 4 overpopulation due to immigration from Eastern Europe   8 _____

9 Which of the following pairs of Eastern European nations was once one country?

 1 Serbia and Bulgaria
 2 Hungary and Poland
 3 Czechia (Czech Republic) and Slovakia
 4 Albania and Croatia   9 _____

10 Violent tensions between Middle East Sunni and Shi'ite Muslims in recent years has been over

 1 interpretations of the Koran
 2 control of waterways
 3 political power
 4 disputes with Israel   10 _____

11 The unification of Germany and the unification of Italy in the 19th century led historians to state that

 1 imperialism could be used to spread European culture
 2 nationalism could be a factor in consolidating political interests
 3 socialism was an effective way of organizing the economy
 4 interdependence was a serious obstacle to waging war   11 _____

12 Former Turkish leader Mustafa Kemal Atatürk was most admired for

1 expanding the construction of mosques
2 increasing the influence of Western ideas and culture
3 issuing decrees and laws in Arabic
4 recognizing the state of Israel   12 _____

Base your answer to question 13 on the photograph below and on your knowledge of social studies.

Tsar Nicholas II

13 The man in this photograph was the leader of a nation that fought another European nation in the 20th century. What European nation did this leader and his nation fight against in the early 20th century?

1 France
2 England
3 Germany
4 the United States of America   13 _____

14 Which of the following choices was one feature of "the final solution"?

    1 an attack on Pearl Harbor
    2 a blitzkrieg over Poland
    3 killings at Auschwitz
    4 bombings of Hiroshima and Nagasaki   14 _____

15 The failure of collective security in the 1930s was seen as a sign of

    1 racist propaganda
    2 appeasement policies
    3 militaristic activities
    4 totalitarian restrictions   15 _____

16 Berlin and Rome became the capital cities of nations formed by the efforts of

    1 Vladimir Lenin and Winston Churchill
    2 Otto von Bismarck and Camillo Benso, Count of Cavour
    3 Adolf Hitler and Neville Chamberlain
    4 Paul von Hindenburg and Giuseppe Garibaldi   16 _____

Base your answer to question 17 on the map below and on your knowledge of social studies.

EUROPE IN 1914

ICELAND

UNITED KINGDOM

NORWAY

SWEDEN

RUSSIAN EMPIRE

DENMARK

NETHERLANDS

GERMANY

BELGIUM

LUXEMBOURG

FRANCE

SWITZERLAND

AUSTRIA-HUNGARY

RUMANIA

SERBIA

BULGARIA

PORTUGAL

SPAIN

ITALY

GREECE

OTTOMAN EMPIRE

ALBANIA

MONTENEGRO

KEY

Allied powers

Central powors

Neutral countries

17 After World War I, which of the following nations lost territory and thereafter no longer existed?

1 France
2 Spain
3 Austria-Hungary
4 Germany

17 _____

18 The phrases "master race," "Aryan," and "genocide" would most often appear in a book on the history of

1 Italy
2 Japan
3 Czechoslovakia
4 Germany   18 _____

Base your answer to question 19 on the map below and on your knowledge of social studies.

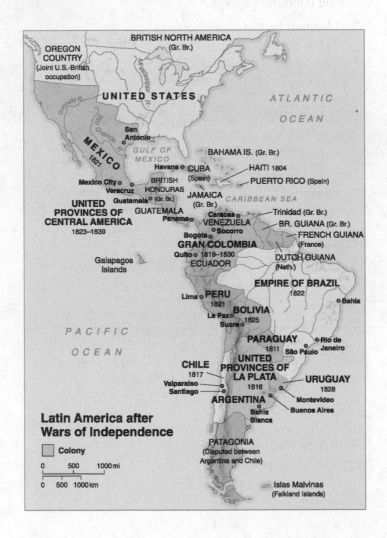

Latin America after Wars of Independence

19 Which three nations were created after the Latin American Wars of independence and were formerly part of the Viceroyalty of Gran Colombia?

1 Peru, Bolivia, and Colombia
2 Colombia, Panama, and Venezuela
3 Venezuela, Colombia, and Ecuador
4 Ecuador, Argentina, and Bolivia   19 _____

20 The French Revolution resulted from all of the following conditions *except*

1 the absolute rule of Louis XVI
2 too much taxation of the Third Estate
3 the persecution of the Huguenots
4 the influence of Enlightenment ideas   20 _____

21 The French Revolution is important for all of the following reasons *except* that

1 it brought about a basic change of relationship between the government and the governed
2 it advanced the idea of representing the democratic rights of the governed
3 it was a direct cause of the Russian Revolution of 1917
4 it removed the remaining feudal features of French society   21 _____

22 All of the following were causes of and preconditions to the beginning of the Industrial Revolution in 18th-century England *except*

1 the availability of investment capital
2 the growth of transportation networks for trucks and railroads
3 the availability of iron ore and coal
4 inventions that led to changes in the ability to produce more products at a lower cost   22 _____

23 The Industrial Revolution in the 19th century was influenced by all of the following *except*

1 the development of banking systems that increased investments
2 inventions that led to the growth of textile production
3 the rise of socialist systems of production and distribution
4 an increased supply of skilled workers in the population

23 _____

24 In the 20th century, Latin American nations experienced a

1 more equal distribution of the income and wealth for most of the population
2 fairer distribution of the available land to all classes in the population
3 rise in the number of governments that came to power via more democratic elections
4 decline in the growth of urban centers due to increased agricultural production

24 _____

25 All of the following are important global issues in the 21st century *except*

1 climatic changes due to global warming
2 the rise of religiously based terrorism
3 employment problems related to technological developments
4 the rise of communist-led governments in Africa and Asia

25 _____

26 All of the following are effects of increased global warming *except*

1 increased melting and the disappearance of glaciers
2 the slow and steady rise of sea levels
3 extreme and severe weather phenomena
4 a greater dependence on fossil-derived fuels   26 _____

27 In the 21st century, the two nations that have seen a significant rise in their GDP are

1 Russia and China
2 China and India
3 France and Germany
4 United States and Japan   27 _____

28 Which of the following was Sun Yat-sen's plan for the development of China?
1 the Cultural Revolution
2 the Five-Year Plans
3 the Four Modernizations
4 the Three Principles of the People   28 _____

Base your answers to questions 29 and 30 on the cartoon below and on your knowledge of social studies.

THE WORLD'S PLUNDERERS
- Thomas Nast, Harper's Weekly, 1885

29 This cartoonist is illustrating which 19th century international process?
1 the spread of industrialization
2 nationalist movements in Africa and Asia
3 expanding European imperialism
4 the unification of colonial areas   29 _____

30 The Grab-Bags carried by each of the figures in this cartoon represent

1 people who were needed to work in the factories of each of these three countries
2 natural resources for enriching the European nations
3 the control of trade routes for shipping raw materials
4 land areas for the settlement of the expanding populations   30 _____

370

In developing your answer to Part II, be sure to keep this general definition in mind:

    (a) <u>discuss</u> means "to make observations about something using facts, reasoning, and argument; to present in some detail"

PART II: THEMATIC ESSAY QUESTION

Directions: Write a well-organized essay that includes an introduction, several paragraphs addressing the task below, and a conclusion.

Theme: Change

> Throughout history, individuals have brought about change in their areas or nations. Their actions have had both positive and negative effects on the people of their areas or nations.

Task:

> Choose *three* individuals from your study of global history and geography from 1750 to the present and for *each*
>
> - Discuss two changes that each of these individuals brought about in his/her region
> - Assess whether the changes brought about by each of the three individuals had either a positive impact or a negative impact in the area or nation that he/she was involved in

You may use any individual from your study of global history and geography from 1750 to the present.

**Do *not* use an individual from the
United States in your response.**

Guidelines:

In your essay, be sure to:
- Develop all aspects of the task
- Support the theme with relevant facts, examples, and details
- Use a logical and clear plan of organization, including an introduction and a conclusion that are beyond a restatement of the theme

In developing your answers to Part III, be sure to keep these general definitions in mind:

(a) <u>describe</u> means "to illustrate something in words or tell about it"

(b) <u>discuss</u> means "to make observations about something using facts, reasoning, and argument; to present in some detail"

PART III: DOCUMENT-BASED QUESTION

This question is based on the accompanying documents. The question is designed to test your ability to work with historical documents. Some of these documents have been edited for the purposes of this question. As you analyze the documents, take into account the source of each document and any point of view that may be presented in the document. Keep in mind that the language used in a document may reflect the historical context of the time in which it was written.

Historical Context:

> Throughout history, protest movements have formed in response to government policies and actions. Some examples of protest movements are ***the women's rights movement in Great Britain***, ***the pro-democracy movement in China***, and ***the anti-apartheid movement in South Africa***. These protest movements have resulted in different government responses.

Task:

> Using the information from the documents and your knowledge of global history and geography, answer the questions that follow each document in Part A. Your answers to the questions will help you write the Part B essay in which you will be asked to
>
> Choose *two* protest movements mentioned in the historical context and for *each*
>
> - Describe the historical circumstances surrounding this protest movement
> - Discuss an action taken by the protesters
> - Discuss a government response to this protest movement

Part A: Short-Answer Questions

Directions: Analyze the documents and answer the short-answer questions that follow each document in the space provided.

Document 1

SOME REASONS FOR SUPPORTING WOMEN'S SUFFRAGE

- Because it is the foundation of all political liberty that those who obey the Law should be able to have a voice in choosing those who make the Law. . . .
- Because Parliament cannot fully reflect the wishes of the people, when the wishes of women are without any direct representation. . . .
- Because the Laws which affect women especially are now passed without consulting those persons whom they are intended to benefit. . . .
- Because to deprive women of the vote is to lower their position in common estimation. . . .

Source: "Fourteen Reasons for Supporting Women's Suffrage,"
National Union of Women's Suffrage Societies,
British Library online (adapted)

1 According to the National Union of Women's Suffrage Societies, what is *one* issue faced by women as a result of being denied the right to vote? [1]

_____

_____

Document 2

Source: "*The Suffragette*," April 25, 1913 online at
History Cooperative (adapted)

2 Based on this document, state *one* action taken by women in
Great Britain to obtain rights. [1]

_____

_____

Document 3

This is an excerpt from a speech given by British suffragist Emmeline Pankhurst in 1913.

> . . . "Put them [women] in prison," they [men] said; "that will stop it." But it didn't stop it. They put women in prison for long terms of imprisonment, for making a nuisance of themselves—that was the expression when they took petitions in their hands to the door of the House of Commons; and they thought that by sending them to prison, giving them a day's imprisonment, would cause them to all settle down again and there would be no further trouble. But it didn't happen so at all: instead of the women giving it up, more women did it, and more and more and more women did it until there were three hundred women at a time, who had not broken a single law, only "made a nuisance of themselves" as the politicians say. . . .

Source: Candace Gregory, ed., *Documents of Western Civilization, Volume II: Since 1500*, Thomson Wadsworth

3*a* According to Emmeline Pankhurst, what was **one** action British women used to draw attention to their issues? [1]

_____

_____

3*b* According to Emmeline Pankhurst, what was **one** way the British government responded to these actions? [1]

_____

_____

Document 4

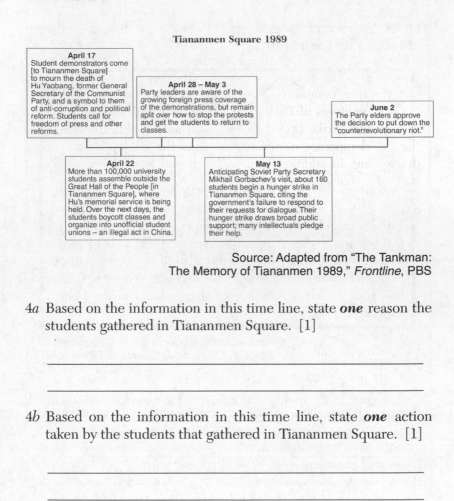

Tiananmen Square 1989

April 17
Student demonstrators come [to Tiananmen Square] to mourn the death of Hu Yaobang, former General Secretary of the Communist Party, and a symbol to them of anti-corruption and political reform. Students call for freedom of press and other reforms.

April 28 – May 3
Party leaders are aware of the growing foreign press coverage of the demonstrations, but remain split over how to stop the protests and get the students to return to classes.

June 2
The Party elders approve the decision to put down the "counterrevolutionary riot."

April 22
More than 100,000 university students assemble outside the Great Hall of the People [in Tiananmen Square], where Hu's memorial service is being held. Over the next days, the students boycott classes and organize into unofficial student unions – an illegal act in China.

May 13
Anticipating Soviet Party Secretary Mikhail Gorbachev's visit, about 160 students begin a hunger strike in Tiananmen Square, citing the government's failure to respond to their requests for dialogue. Their hunger strike draws broad public support; many intellectuals pledge their help.

Source: Adapted from "The Tankman: The Memory of Tiananmen 1989," *Frontline*, PBS

4a Based on the information in this time line, state **one** reason the students gathered in Tiananmen Square. [1]

_____

_____

4b Based on the information in this time line, state **one** action taken by the students that gathered in Tiananmen Square. [1]

_____

_____

Document 5

... The manifesto that follows was typical of the many melodramatic last wills and testaments produced by the [student] hunger strikers. Circulated prior to the hunger strike, it was apparently a committee document prepared by the "Hunger Strike Volunteers of Peking's Institutions of Higher Education." The hunger strike upped the political ante [political stakes] in the pro-democracy movement for now the students were also demanding, in addition to democracy and freedom of speech, concrete changes including the resignations of Li Peng and Deng Xiaoping. Both leaders were seen by the demonstrators as the spiritual (if not actual) authors of the *People's Daily* editorial of April 26 and the most important opponents of democratic change. . . .

"Open Declaration of a Hunger Strike"

In this May of glowing sunshine, we are starting our hunger strike. In this moment of beautiful youth, we must resolutely put behind us the beauty of life. But how unwilling we are, how unreconciled!

But our nation has come to a critical juncture: inflation is sky-rocketing, government corruption is rampant, power is in the hands of few high-ranking officials, bureaucrats are corrupt, a large number of patriots have fled into exile, and social order grows daily more chaotic. Fellow-countrymen, all fellow-countrymen of conscience, at this crucial moment for the survival of the nation, please hear our voice:

The country is our country!
The people are our people!
The government is our government!

If we do not dare to cry out, who will?

If we do not dare to act, who will? . . .

Source: Pei-Kai Cheng et al., eds., *The Search for Modern China*,
W.W. Norton & Company (adapted)

5*a* According to this document, what is **one** reform the Chinese students were trying to achieve? [1]

_____

_____

5*b* According to this document, what is **one** problem facing China? [1]

_____

_____

Document 6

Several hundred civilians have been shot dead by the Chinese army during a bloody military operation to crush a democratic protest in Peking's (Beijing) Tiananmen Square.

Tanks rumbled through the capital's streets late on 3 June as the army moved into the square from several directions, randomly firing on unarmed protesters.

The injured were rushed to hospital on bicycle rickshaws by frantic residents shocked by the army's sudden and extreme response to the peaceful mass protest. . . .

Source: "1989: Massacre in Tiananmen Square," *BBC*, June 4, 1989

6 Based on this news report from the BBC, state an action taken by the Chinese government in response to the protest movement in Tiananmen Square. [1]

_____

_____

Document 7

This is an excerpt from a pamphlet on the racial situation in the Union of South Africa. It sets out the general principles of apartheid established by the National Party in 1948.

> ... The party [National Party] therefore undertakes to protect the White race properly and effectively against any policy, doctrine or attack which might undermine or threaten its continued existence. At the same time the party rejects any policy of oppression and exploitation of the non-Europeans by the Europeans as being in conflict with the Christian basis of our national life and irreconcilable with our policy.
>
> The party believes that a definite policy of separation (*apartheid*) between the White races and the non-White racial groups, and the application of the policy of separation also in the case of the non-White racial groups, is the only basis on which the character and future of each race can be protected and safeguarded and on which each race can be guided so as to develop his own national character, aptitude and calling. ....

Source: National Party, "The National Party's Colour Policy,"
March 29, 1948

7 According to this excerpt from this National Party pamphlet, what was *one* way the National Party justified its racial policy? [1]

_____

_____

Document 8

1952 Campaign for the Defiance of Unjust Laws

... When the ANC [African National Congress] launched its Campaign for the Defiance of Unjust Laws in 1952, Mandela was elected National Volunteer-in-Chief. The Defiance Campaign was conceived as a mass civil disobedience campaign that would snowball from a core of selected volunteers to involve more and more ordinary people, culminating in mass defiance. Fulfilling his responsibility as Volunteer-in-Chief, Mandela travelled the country organising resistance to discriminatory legislation. Charged and brought to trial for his role in the campaign, the court found that Mandela and his co-accused had consistently advised their followers to adopt a peaceful course of action and to avoid all violence.

For his part in the [1952] Defiance Campaign, Mandela was convicted of contravening [disobeying] the Suppression of Communism Act and given a suspended prison sentence. Shortly after the campaign ended, he was also prohibited from attending gatherings and confined to Johannesburg for six months. . . .

Source: Nelson Mandela, Biographical Details,
African National Congress online

8a What is *one* action the African National Congress and Nelson Mandela suggested black South Africans take against the white nationalist government? [1]

_____

_____

8b According to this biography on the African National Congress website, what is *one* consequence Nelson Mandela faced as a result of his actions? [1]

_____

_____

Document 9

This excerpt is taken from a 2006 National Public Radio program in which Nthato Motlana and Bongi Mkhabela were interviewed. Nthato Motlana played a critical role in the aftermath of the Soweto uprisings and Bongi Mkhabela was responsible for planning the student march in Soweto.

Thirty years ago, the uprising of a group of schoolchildren changed South Africa forever. . . .

But on June 16, 1976, students in Soweto township outside Johannesburg decided to hold a protest against a government policy mandating that all classes be taught in Afrikaans, the language of South African whites.

What started as a student demonstration exploded across South Africa, helping to change the course of the nation's history by galvanizing the struggle to dismantle apartheid. . . .

Newscast: At 8:15 in the morning, and precisely according to plan, students simultaneously marched out of five schools in Soweto, intending to protest the Afrikaans issue in a mass meeting at the Orlando Football Stadium. . . .

Nthato Motlana: Then it became really a torrent, a sea of young, black faces. Masses of students, I mean, we'd never seen such a demonstration in many, many years. And at that point, the police tried to stop the march from going on to Orlando Stadium.

Bongi Mkhabela: I've never seen that many police. And you didn't only have police at that time, you had the Defense Force. So you actually had the Army.

Nthato Motlana: They intervened by, first of all, setting dogs. And I saw these police dogs set onto these kids, man, and I saw moments of real courage, especially from the girls.

Bongi Mkhabela: I mean, this is a group of kids, kids with shining black shoes and little white socks and teeny little tunics. And they are singing freedom songs, holding one another. We actually looked cute. It's unbelievable to think that anyone could have stood firm on their feet and actually shot into that crowd. . . .

Source: "Soweto 1976: An Audio History," *NPR*

9 According to this National Public Radio program, what was *one* action taken by the South African government to end the student protests in Soweto? [1]

_____

_____

Part B: Essay

Directions: Write a well-organized essay that includes an introduction, several paragraphs, and a conclusion. Use evidence from *at least four* documents in your essay. Support your response with relevant facts, examples, and details. Include additional outside information.

Historical Context:

> Throughout history, protest movements have formed in response to government policies and actions. Some examples of protest movements are ***the women's rights movement in Great Britain***, ***the pro-democracy movement in China***, and ***the anti-apartheid movement in South Africa***. These protest movements have resulted in different government responses.

Task:

> Using the information from the documents and your knowledge of global history and geography, write an essay in which you
>
> Choose *two* protest movements mentioned in the historical context and for *each*
>
> - Describe the historical circumstances surrounding this protest movement
> - Discuss an action taken by the protesters
> - Discuss a government response to this protest movement

Guidelines:

In your essay, be sure to:
- Develop all aspects of the task
- Incorporate information from *at least four* documents
- Incorporate relevant outside information
- Support the theme with relevant facts, examples, and details
- Use a logical and clear plan of organization, including an introduction and a conclusion that are beyond a restatement of the theme

Answers
Sample Regents
Transition Examination
Global History and Geography

Answer Key

PART I (1–30)

1. 4	9. 3	17. 3	25. 4
2. 4	10. 3	18. 4	26. 4
3. 2	11. 2	19. 3	27. 2
4. 2	12. 2	20. 3	28. 4
5. 3	13. 3	21. 3	29. 3
6. 4	14. 3	22. 2	30. 2
7. 4	15. 2	23. 3	
8. 1	16. 2	24. 3	

PART II: Thematic Essay   See Answers Explained section.

PART III: Document-Based Essay   See Answers Explained section.

Answers Explained

PART I

1. **4** When Tsar Peter the Great came to power, Russia was considered backward and inferior compared to the western European powers of the 17th and 18th centuries. Russia had spent its early history under indirect Mongol control that left it relatively isolated from Western Europe, which had experienced a renaissance in technology and learning. Russia had no warm-water port and no navy, and thus Peter the Great was determined to "westernize," or modernize, Russia and make it a competing European power. He invited Western military leaders to Russia to learn from them, and he even traveled to Western Europe to learn shipbuilding firsthand. His military efforts awarded him a port on the Baltic Sea and the establishment of Russia's first navy.

WRONG CHOICES EXPLAINED:

(1) Russia remained an absolute monarchy until the Revolution of 1905, 180 years after Peter the Great, when Tsar Nicholas II was faced with either establishing a form of military dictatorship or providing a constitution.

(2) Russia was never a Protestant country; it has been Russian Orthodox from the 10th century until the present day.

(3) Russia did not free the serfs until 1861, more than 130 years after Peter the Great.

2. **4** The Ottoman Empire had a rich history of trade with Western Europe beginning in 1453 when it seized control of the eastern Mediterranean region, conquering the city of Constantinople (which was renamed Istanbul in 1923). Along with the Venetians in Italy, the Ottomans traded extensively, controlled trade throughout the Mediterranean Sea, and continued to expand trading contacts with Western Europe from the 16th century to the 20th century. In the 16th and 17th centuries, the French, Dutch, and British made a variety of trade agreements with the Ottomans, and European powers viewed Ottoman ports as a market for European finished goods. Although trade with Western Europe had declined by the time the Ottoman Empire fell after World War I, that was not a leading cause of the empire's collapse.

WRONG CHOICES EXPLAINED:

(1), (2), and (3) All of these choices were strong reasons for the Ottoman Empire's collapse. The empire allied with Britain and France against Russia in the Crimean War in the mid-19th century. Despite defeating the Russians, the Ottoman Empire was revealed as being militarily weak as it continued to lose lands after a rebellion in the Balkans. The Slavic people in Bosnia, Herzegovina, Montenegro, and Bulgaria were aided by the Russians in their rebellion against the Ottomans, who were too weak militarily to maintain control of the lands they had previously held. Additionally, other lands were annexed by Austria-Hungary and Russia, and the empire lost territories in Africa as well.

3. **2** Prior to 1914, nationalism in the Balkan region led to the formation of newly independent states that had previously been under the control of the Ottoman Empire. Some of the many ethnic groups under the empire's control began to form nationalist movements. Albanians, Serbs, Bulgarians, and other ethnic groups won their independence, which led to the creation of Montenegro, Albania, Serbia, Bulgaria, Greece, and Macedonia.

WRONG CHOICES EXPLAINED:

(1) Nationalism in the Balkans did not lead to the inability of nations to pay reparations. Nationalism is defined as loyalty and devotion to a nation. This loyalty and devotion did not lead to the lack of ability to pay reparations, which involve making amends for a wrong that has been done by paying money.

(3) Nationalism in the Balkans led to the loss, not acquisition, of territories as new nations were created from areas that were previously held by the Ottoman Empire.

(4) Nationalism in the Balkans did not immediately lead to a demand for democracy as nations in the Balkans first and foremost desired independence from the Ottoman Empire that previously controlled them.

4. **2** Although he was reluctant about it, Tsar Nicholas II promised more freedoms after "Bloody Sunday" during the Revolution of 1905. In 1906, to appease the people, he approved the creation of Russia's first Parliamentary body, called the Duma, although it was dissolved after just a few months due to his fear of a constitutional monarchy and his hesitance to share power.

WRONG CHOICES EXPLAINED:

(1) and (3) Most people in Russia were not familiar with the concept of democracy and had no experience governing democratically, which contributed to the failure of democracy in Russia. By the early 20th century, when democratic reforms were made, Russia had been under the control of the Romanov dynasty and an absolute monarchy for centuries, so there was little understanding of what a democracy is.

(4) The Provisional Government was attempting to govern and was experimenting with democracy while Russia was involved in World War I, which also contributed to the failure of democracy in Russia. During periods of crisis like war, when decisions need to be made quickly, democratic institutions often slow down the decision-making process. Therefore, the chaos of war inhibited Russia's ability to carry out democratic institutions.

5. **3** Tsar Nicholas II made a poor decision to entangle Russia in World War I when the country was unprepared to handle the economic and military costs of the war. Generals were poorly trained as were their troops, and Russia proved itself to be no match against Germany, which inflicted devastating casualties on advancing Russian soldiers. Many soldiers began to defect or ignore orders, and at home, food and fuel were in short supply, leading many to desire change and an end to the war. The monarchy, which was already losing influence in the eyes of the people, was viewed as no longer having control over the nation. This directly led to the March Revolution of 1917 as well as support for the return of Vladimir Lenin to Russia and the communist Bolshevik Party.

WRONG CHOICES EXPLAINED:

(1) Vladimir Lenin's New Economic Policy was a result of the Bolshevik Revolution; it was not a cause for this revolution. In 1921, Lenin's new policy promoted small-scale capitalism to help peasants sell their surplus and to allow small factories and businesses to operate under private ownership.

(2) While Tsarina Alexandra's relationship with Grigori Rasputin and his increasing influence on the government led many to distrust the royal family, his influence alone does not explain the outbreak of the Bolshevik Revolution.

(4) Tsar Nicholas II aided the Slavs in Serbia during World War I.

6. **4** The progression of these photographs from Joseph Stalin and his fellow Soviet leaders to eventually just Stalin standing alone illustrates the U.S.S.R's development into an autocracy. An autocracy is the rule of one individual. These photos illustrate that Stalin was in power all on his own by 1929.

WRONG CHOICES EXPLAINED:

(1) A democracy is a government in which the people have the power to vote. This is not the form of government through which Stalin came to power.

(2) An aristocracy is a government ruled by the nobility. None of the communist leaders were of noble birth.

(3) A plutocracy is a government ruled by the wealthy. The Soviet leadership was not based on wealth.

7. **4** The Prague Spring was not a direct result of the Cold War, but rather it was a long-term and indirect result of Soviet policies of censorship. In 1968, Prague, the capital of Czechoslovakia, became a center of reform and new ideas that were viewed by Community Party official Leonid Brezhnev as a rejection of communist ideals. Therefore, the Prague Spring was quickly put to an end.

WRONG CHOICES EXPLAINED:

(1), (2), and (3) These choices were all direct results of the Cold War. In the immediate aftermath of World War II, Europe was divided between democratic Western Europe and communist Eastern Europe. By 1949, as a result of fears of Soviet aggression, many Western European nations joined the United States and Canada to form a defensive military alliance called NATO, or the North Atlantic Treaty Organization. Viewing NATO as a threat, the Soviet Union formed its own alliance, the Warsaw Pact, which included East Germany, Czechoslovakia, Romania, Albania, Bulgaria, Poland, and Hungary. In 1961, East Germans built a barrier, called the Berlin Wall, to separate East and West Berlin, which further enhanced the Cold War divisions. By the early 1970s, however, with the realization that the United States and the U.S.S.R. could both gain from increased trade and a decrease in the threat of nuclear war, a policy of détente, or a release from tension, was adopted.

8. **1** The fall of Communism in the U.S.S.R. and Eastern Europe in the late 20th century was caused by many factors, including economic overextension due to the arms race. As the Cold War continued into the 1980s, U.S. President Ronald Reagan began an extensive military buildup, and the Soviet

Premier Mikhail Gorbachëv could not afford to keep up with the costly arms race.

WRONG CHOICES EXPLAINED:

(2) With Gorbachëv's introduction of *perestroika*, the Soviet economy was somewhat revived, allowing for more private ownership and making the economic system more productive, not less productive.

(3) Consumer products were not overproduced during this time period because, despite the reforms of *perestroika*, Communism was not completely dispelled. Underproduction and a lack of ability to keep up with demand were hallmarks of capitalism, and therefore overproduction was not a leading cause of Communism's collapse.

(4) Overpopulation due to immigration from Eastern Europe was not a major issue during the late 20th century in this region of the world.

9. **3** Czechoslovakia (Czechia and Slovakia) was one of many nations formed out of the former Austro-Hungarian Empire and was recognized as an independent state at the end of World War I. The joined state fell apart in 1992 due to many factors, including ethnic differences between the Czechs and the Slovaks and Czech domination of local government in the region, which left the Slovaks feeling marginalized.

WRONG CHOICES EXPLAINED:

(1) Serbia and Bulgaria were often enemies throughout history, engaging in many conflicts. They were never one nation.

(2) Despite the fact that Hungary and Poland have had a long history of camaraderie due to a shared cultural history, they were never one nation.

(4) While both Albania and Croatia are members of NATO, they were never one nation.

10. **3** The issue of political power has led to violent tensions between Middle East Sunni and Shi'ite Muslims in recent years. For example, in Iraq, after the fall of Saddam Hussein and the dominance of the Sunni sect in government, with support from the United States, political control fell into the hands of the Shi'ite sect, leaving the Sunnis feeling sidelined. In an attempt to reassert their influence, the Sunnis fought back, which has led to sectarian violence.

WRONG CHOICES EXPLAINED:

(1) The main cause of the Sunni–Shi'ite split in the 7th century was the question of leadership and who would become Muhammad's successor, or caliph. The divide had little to do with religious interpretations of the Koran and was much more of a political dispute, even at the time of the Islamic schism.

(2) In the regions where the vast majority of sectarian violence occurs, mainly Iraq, Syria, and Pakistan, there is no dispute over the control of major waterways.

(4) While there have been conflicts between Muslims throughout the Middle East and Jews in Israel, these disputes have not contributed to Muslim sects fighting each other.

11. **2** Feelings of nationalism caused empires like the Austrian Empire to fall, but it also led to the unification of states such as Italy and Germany. Both Italy and Germany were decentralized states in the mid-19th century, but feelings of shared cultural identity led to the desire to unify under one government. Camillo di Cavour and Giuseppe Garibaldi united Italy, while Otto von Bismarck united Germany. In addition to a shared cultural identity, the presence of a common enemy helped create nationalist sentiments. For example, in Germany, the 1871 defeat of France, a common enemy of all German states, helped Bismarck bring the southern states into Germany.

WRONG CHOICES EXPLAINED:

(1) While imperialism was thought to be a method by which European culture could be spread to other regions, it was not a factor in the unification of Italy and Germany.

(3) Neither Italy nor Germany were socialist nations. Therefore, socialism was not a contributing factor to either country's unification in the 19th century.

(4) Germany's desire for independence from the domination of the Austrian Empire led to the wars that allowed for the unification of the nation.

12. **2** Mustafa Kemal Atatürk became president of the newly formed Republic of Turkey in 1923. At the end of World War I, the Ottoman Empire was forced to give up most of its territories beyond the lands controlled by modern-day Turkey. After fighting off Greek advances, Atatürk overthrew the last Ottoman sultan and sought to create a "Western," or modern, republic. He made various reforms, including separating religious law and secular law and creating a legal system based on European law rather than on Islamic law. Due to his goals of modernization and Westernization, Atatürk is often compared to Peter the Great of Russia.

WRONG CHOICES EXPLAINED:

(1) Atatürk was known for his secular (non-religious) reforms, which made Turkey more like the European republics of the early 20th century. He was not known for a devotion to Islam or for the construction of mosques.

(3) Atatürk used Europe as a model for legal code reform. Arabic is the language of the Koran and is widely spoken in areas of the Middle East.

(4) Atatürk died in 1938. Israel was not recognized as a state until 1948.

13. **3** Tsar Nicholas II, who was the leader of Russia from 1894 to 1917, led his nation in the battles against Germany during World War I.

WRONG CHOICES EXPLAINED:

(1) and (2) France and England were both allies of Russia during World War I. Russia did not fight against France or England during the early 20th century.

(4) The United States of America joined in the fight against Germany during World War I. Russia did not fight against the United States in the early 20th century.

14. **3** "The final solution" was Adolf Hitler's attempt at creating racial purity by purging Germany and Europe of Jews and other groups deemed

inferior during World War II. Concentration camps, such as Auschwitz, were constructed to carry out the plan to exterminate Jews and several other groups, and many died in gas chambers after being exposed to cyanide.

WRONG CHOICES EXPLAINED:

(1) The attack on Pearl Harbor was perpetrated by Japan. It led to the United States' involvement in World War II.

(2) Blitzkrieg, or "lightning war," was a German military strategy used to create psychological shock during World War II.

(4) The atomic bombings of Hiroshima and Nagasaki were perpetrated by the United States in an effort to end the war against Japan.

15. **2** The League of Nations, formed in the aftermath of World War I, was meant to provide a sense of collective security. However, the League was challenged in the 1930s by Adolf Hitler in Germany who defied the Versailles Treaty (which limited the size of Germany's army) by ignoring the treaty's restrictions. To avoid another global conflict, Britain and France supported appeasement, or giving into German aggression, and it was these appeasement policies that reflected the League's failure to provide collective security and its eventual failure to prevent global conflict.

WRONG CHOICES EXPLAINED:

(1) The purpose of a body like the League of Nations was to promote collective security and prevent another global conflict like World War I. Therefore, racist propaganda was not a sign of its failure; allowing Germany to become an aggressor was a sign of its failure.

(3) The purpose of collective security was to prevent militarism.

(4) Totalitarianism rose in the 1930s with the rise of Benito Mussolini and Adolf Hitler.

16. **2** Both Otto von Bismarck and Camillo Benso, Count of Cavour were nationalist leaders who led their nations, Germany and Italy, with capitals at Berlin and Rome, respectively, to unification. In the 19th century, nationalism, or the belief that a single "nationality" or ancestry should be united under one government independent of outside influence, was one of the most powerful ideas. Nationalism tore apart empires like the Austrian Empire, the Russian Empire, and the Ottoman Empire, while leading to the development of new nations, such as Germany and Italy.

WRONG CHOICES EXPLAINED:

(1) Vladimir Lenin was the leader of the Bolshevik Revolution against the Romanov dynasty in Russia, whereas Winston Churchill was the prime minister of the United Kingdom during World War II.

(3) Adolf Hitler was the Chancellor of Germany in the 1930s through World War II, and Neville Chamberlain was the prime minister of the United Kingdom until 1940.

(4) Paul von Hindenburg was a German World War I general and president until his death in 1934, long after the unification of Germany. Giuseppe Garibaldi did in fact aid in the unification of Italy.

17. **3** Following World War I, Austria-Hungary was broken up into different nations, including Yugoslavia, Czechoslovakia, and Hungary.

WRONG CHOICES EXPLAINED:

(1) and (2) France and Spain did not lose land as a result of World War I.

(4) Germany did lose land as a result of World War I, but it still continued to exist as a nation following the end of this war.

18. **4** The phrases "master race," "Aryan," and "genocide" are most often associated with Nazi Germany, Chancellor Adolf Hitler, and the Holocaust. Hitler believed that in order to lead Germany to victory, he needed to "cleanse" German society of those he deemed "subhuman." He believed the Aryan race was the master race, and he led a genocide aimed at many subgroups but particularly targeted at the Jewish people. Capitalizing on a long history of anti-Semitism in Europe, Hitler was able to carry out his genocide, leading to the deaths of 6 million Jews in Europe.

WRONG CHOICES EXPLAINED:

(1), (2), and (3) Neither Italy nor Japan nor Czechoslovakia believed in the idea of a supreme Aryan master race, although Japan did commit acts of genocide in China, for example, during the Nanking Massacre in 1937.

19. **3** Venezuela, Colombia, and Ecuador were created after Simón Bolívar's dream of uniting all of the lands of the former Viceroyalty of New Granada into the Republic of Gran Colombia proved to be an unrealistic goal. This goal was not feasible due to the opposition of the Creole class in the three subregions of the former viceroyalty.

WRONG CHOICES EXPLAINED:

(1) Peru was part of the Viceroyalty of Peru, which was established in 1543 and dissolved in 1824. Bolivia was originally part of the Viceroyalty of Peru, but it became part of the Viceroyalty of Rio de la Plata in 1776.

(2) Panama was originally a province of Colombia and only became a nation in the early 20th century when it broke away from Colombia during the time that the Panama Canal was being built.

(4) Argentina was originally part of the Viceroyalty of Peru, but it became the main part of the Viceroyalty of Rio de la Plata in 1776.

20. **3** The persecution of the Huguenots, or French Protestants, was more closely associated with the reign of Louis XIV, the "Sun King," as opposed to Louis XVI, who was king at the time of the French Revolution. In 1685, Louis XIV revoked the Edict of Nantes, which was a promise of religious tolerance, leading to the persecution of the Huguenots. Hundreds of thousands of Huguenots fled France as a result, which led to economic decline as the Protestants were some of the most productive workers. This all occurred a century prior to the French Revolution.

WRONG CHOICES EXPLAINED:

(1) Louis XVI's absolute and weak leadership helped create the conditions in France that led to the outbreak of revolution. During his reign, France faced major economic problems, including a bankrupted treasury and a sharp

increase in the price of bread. His lack of leadership failed to address these economic problems, which led to resentment of his absolute rule.

(2) The Third Estate, which made up 97% of France's population and included the middle and peasant classes, paid almost all of the taxes in France prior to the French Revolution. The First and Second Estates, which made up 3% of France's population and included the Roman Catholic Church's clergy and the rich nobility, paid almost nothing in taxes. This unfair distribution of the tax burden led to resentment and eventually the revolution.

(4) By the mid-18th century, Paris had become the center of Enlightenment ideas. The Enlightenment was a philosophical movement that encouraged new ideas about where the government gets its power and authority. Such ideas led the people in France to demand liberty and equality, and some called for an end to absolute monarchy.

21. **3** The Russian Revolution of 1917 occurred well over a century after the French Revolution and was influenced by the principles of communist ideology as opposed to Enlightenment philosophy. Therefore, the French Revolution was not a direct influence on the outbreak of revolution in Russia in the early 20th century.

WRONG CHOICES EXPLAINED:

(1) The French Revolution ended absolute hereditary monarchy in France, and, at least in the short term, put into power a government that was created by the people with a written declaration of rights.

(2) The revolution, in the short term, led to the creation of a National Assembly that drafted the Declaration of the Rights of Man, which outlined civil rights to protect individual freedoms. Essentially, the government was viewed as a body to protect the natural rights of the governed.

(4) The division of France into the Three Estates was a remnant of feudalism in France. The revolutionary leaders were all members of the Third Estate and thus abolished this archaic social system.

22. **2** Although the expansion of railroads was a cause of and a precondition to industrialization, trucks and automobiles in general were not in wide use until the first half of the 20th century. Since the Industrial Revolution took place in England in the 18th century, the growth of transportation networks for trucks could not have been a precondition that led to the Industrial Revolution.

WRONG CHOICES EXPLAINED:

(1) One of the reasons why the Industrial Revolution began in England was because it had an economy and a banking system to support investments. Business people invested their money to manufacture new machinery to help production grow.

(3) England was rich in natural resources, such as iron ore and coal, which were used to fuel machinery and construct the machines, buildings, and tools necessary for industry.

(4) England was a center of innovation in the 18th century, which led to the development of textile manufacturing and factories that could produce more products with fewer materials that therefore could be sold at a lower cost.

23. **3** The rise of socialist systems of production and distribution was an *effect* of the Industrial Revolution rather than being a *cause* or *influencing factor* that led to it. As theorized by writers like Karl Marx, industrialism created a society in which the rich were getting wealthier at the expense of the workers. This type of thinking ultimately lead to communist revolutions throughout the world.

WRONG CHOICES EXPLAINED:

(1) The expansion of the banking system allowed for both businesses and individuals to borrow money to invest in the expansion of their businesses and to invest in new machinery.

(2) Many inventions led to the growth of the textile industry, such as the flying shuttle, which doubled the work a weaver could do in a single day. Later, the spinning jenny increased the number of threads a spinner could work with at one time. These were later combined to produce the spinning mule, which made threads finer and stronger.

(4) Although an increase in the supply of skilled workers was not completely necessary to create the conditions that led to industrialization, the revolution was influenced by skilled workers in the areas of banking, investment, and innovation.

24. **3** In the early 19th century, many Latin American countries won their independence from colonial powers like Spain and Portugal, which left them with governments that included a variety of forms of authoritarian rule well into the 20th century. Despite the irregular occurrence of democracy by the mid-20th century, some governments were chosen through more democratic means. Women in many parts of Latin America gained suffrage by the mid-20th century, and women even held high office in Argentina, Chile, and Bolivia.

WRONG CHOICES EXPLAINED:

(1) Unfortunately, as in many parts of the world, Latin America saw more income inequality and increasing gaps between the rich and the poor into the 20th century. One clear example of this is in Chile under the regime of Augusto Pinochet in the 1970s. The economy experienced rapid growth, but the cost of living increased with it, leading to a widening gap between the rich and the poor.

(2) Again, gaps between the rich and the poor grew in the 20th century, and a small percentage of the population—the wealthy elite—controlled the majority of the land.

(4) Urban centers grew during the 20th century as many economies strengthened in Latin America.

25. **4** The rise of communist-led governments in Africa and Asia were issues of the early to mid-20th century, not the 21st century. The U.S.S.R.'s influence over Africa at the time led to the rise of Communism in countries like Somalia and Ethiopia. In the mid-20th century, the world witnessed the rise of Communism in Asian countries like China, North Korea, and Vietnam. By the 21st century, however, Communism had fallen or weakened considerably on both continents in the wake of the fall of the Soviet Union.

WRONG CHOICES EXPLAINED:

(1) Climate change due to rising temperatures has remained an issue into the 21st century. Despite controversies over its causes, the vast majority of climate scientists agree that Earth's temperatures are rising, which has led to fears of droughts and famine in various parts of the world.

(2) Terrorism, fueled by extremist religious ideology, has led to the rise of highly organized terrorist groups like Al-Qaeda, which perpetrated the attacks of September 11, 2001, as well as the rise of ISIS, which has claimed responsibility for a variety of terrorist attacks throughout Europe since 2013.

(3) Technology has increasingly been cited as a cause for rising unemployment rates across the globe. As technology has progressed, and as humans have been increasingly replaced by machines and other technologies, economists fear a growth in the rate of unemployment in the future.

26. **4** Global warming has had many consequences in the 21st century, but a greater dependence on fossil-derived fuels is not a direct effect of rising global temperatures. Instead, some view the increased dependence on fossil fuels as a direct *cause* of global warming rather than an *effect* of it (although this remains a controversial political issue). Fossil fuels release gases like carbon dioxide into the atmosphere and are thought by some to trap heat from escaping, leading to what is known as the "greenhouse effect."

WRONG CHOICES EXPLAINED:

(1) Increased melting and the disappearance of glaciers is argued to be a direct effect of global warming. As Earth's temperatures begin to rise, even just by a few degrees, the polar ice caps and glaciers in regions around northern Norway are beginning to melt.

(2) As Earth's temperatures rise, causing glaciers and ice caps to melt, sea levels rise as a result. This is thought to have a devastating effect on coastlines, which are experiencing destructive erosion.

(3) In addition to melting glaciers and rising sea levels, global warming has been argued to have a direct influence on extreme and severe weather phenomena. Hurricanes, for example, rely on warm water for fuel to intensify and, as water temperatures rise, so does the occurrence of higher intensity extreme weather.

27. **2** Both China and India have experienced the fastest economic growth in the 21st century. Both countries have benefited from increased exports. Unlike China, which has largely benefited from manufacturing exports, India's exports are mainly in services (especially information technology). Additionally, state investments, as opposed to private investments, have led to economic growth and the rise of the GDP in both countries.

WRONG CHOICES EXPLAINED:

(1) While China is experiencing rapid economic growth, Russia's economy has declined rather than expanded. Multiple factors have led to this decline, but some include too much protection of state-owned companies at the expense of private enterprise and the declining price of oil, a major Russian export.

(3) While France and Germany have maintained stable economies, they have not experienced the type of rapid economic growth that China and India have. Germany continues to be an economic leader in the European Union, while France has continued to suffer from slow growth and problems with unemployment.

(4) While the United States and Japan experienced major economic growth in the latter part of the 20th century, both countries have experienced a slow rise in the overall GDP in the 21st century.

28. **4** The Three Principles of the People was Sun Yat-sen's plan for the development of China when he became president of the new Republic of China in 1912, after millennia of imperial rule. The goal of the Three Principles was to create a more modern government based on nationalist principles. The first principle was that of nationalism and the goal to end foreign control after centuries of outsiders controlling China politically and economically. The second principle was based on democracy and bringing about rights for the people. The third principle was to achieve economic security to protect the livelihood of the Chinese people. Despite these desired reforms, Sun Yat-sen's death in 1916 and China's involvement in World War I led to chaos and to the rise of the Chinese Communist Party.

WRONG CHOICES EXPLAINED:

(1) The Cultural Revolution was implemented by Mao Zedong, after the failure of the Great Leap Forward, to reinforce communist ideals of social equality and to revive the revolution's spirit. During the period from 1966 to 1968, the Red Guards, or students who had pledged their devotion to Mao, attempted to destroy the old non-Maoist ways of life.

(2) The Five-Year Plans were outlined under Stalin in the U.S.S.R., beginning in 1928, for the purpose of developing the national centralized economy.

(3) The Four Modernizations were goals established by Zhou Enlai and later implemented by Deng Xiaoping in the 1970s and 1980s, embracing some capitalist ideals that allowed for some private business and profit. The goals focused on progress in agriculture, industry, technology, and defense and led to economic growth in the latter part of the 20th century and in the early 21st century.

29. **3** Germany, Russia, and Britain were all involved in acquiring colonial areas on other continents and consolidating them into profitable empires.

WRONG CHOICES EXPLAINED:

(1) None of the three nations represented in this cartoon was interested in developing heavy industry in the colonial areas.

(2) While European imperialistic activities helped stimulate African and Asian nationalism, there is no representation of those movements in this cartoon.

(4) Britain and Germany both acquired colonies in widely spread areas of the world.

30. **2** The imperialist nations were seeking natural resources, such as land and raw materials, for the agricultural and industrial sectors of their economies.

WRONG CHOICES EXPLAINED:

(1) Though Britain and Germany had thriving industrial sectors in 1885, their workers were native to those countries. Russia had a less industrialized, more agricultural economy.

(3) While trade routes were important for moving raw materials, the control of the national resources of these colonial areas had to come first.

(4) While many Britons and some Germans were sent to the colonial areas, they were generally only there temporarily for control and exploitation, not for permanent settlement.

THEMATIC ESSAY: GENERIC SCORING RUBRIC

Score of 5:
- Shows a thorough understanding of the theme or problem
- Addresses all aspects of the task
- Shows an ability to analyze, evaluate, compare and/or contrast issues and events
- Richly supports the theme or problem with relevant facts, examples, and details
- Is a well-developed essay, consistently demonstrating a logical and clear plan of organization
- Introduces the theme or problem by establishing a framework that is beyond a simple restatement of the task and concludes with a summation of the theme or problem

Score of 4:
- Shows a good understanding of the theme or problem
- Addresses all aspects of the task
- Shows an ability to analyze, evaluate, compare and/or contrast issues and events
- Includes relevant facts, examples, and details, but may not support all aspects of the theme or problem evenly
- Is a well-developed essay, demonstrating a logical and clear plan of organization
- Introduces the theme or problem by establishing a framework that is beyond a simple restatement of the task and concludes with a summation of the theme or problem

Score of 3:
- Shows a satisfactory understanding of the theme or problem
- Addresses most aspects of the task or addresses all aspects in a limited way
- Shows an ability to analyze or evaluate issues and events, but not in any depth
- Includes some facts, examples, and details
- Is a satisfactorily developed essay, demonstrating a general plan of organization
- Introduces the theme or problem by repeating the task and concludes by repeating the theme or problem

Score of 2:
- Shows limited understanding of the theme or problem
- Attempts to address the task
- Develops a faulty analysis or evaluation of issues and events
- Includes few facts, examples, and details, and may include information that contains inaccuracies
- Is a poorly organized essay, lacking focus
- Fails to introduce or summarize the theme or problem

Score of 1:
- Shows very limited understanding of the theme or problem
- Lacks an analysis or evaluation of the issues and events
- Includes little or no accurate or relevant facts, examples, or details
- Attempts to complete the task, but demonstrates a major weakness in organization
- Fails to introduce or summarize the theme or problem

Score of 0: Fails to address the task, is illegible, or is a blank paper

PART II: THEMATIC ESSAY QUESTION

Many individuals throughout the course of history have played a vital role in bringing about change within societies around the world. While some individuals have brought negative changes, many have brought progress to their nations. Although there were some negative consequences of the reigns of Catherine the Great of Russia, Napoleon Bonaparte of France, and Mustafa Kemal Atatürk of Turkey, all three individuals challenged the traditions in their respective societies in order to bring about social progress.

Catherine the Great lived during the Age of Enlightenment and was inspired by the philosophical movement to bring social progress to Russia. Her reforms, however, led to limited advancement, particularly for the peasants and the serfs. By the time she ascended to the throne in 1762, she was well-versed in Enlightenment ideals of freedom, equality, and natural rights and desired to put these concepts into practice. Inspired by the ideas of Voltaire and Montesquieu, she sought to change the relationship between the ruler and the state to one in which the monarch exists to serve the state and its citizens. She therefore recommended abolishing capital punishment and allowing for freedom of religion. Although she did not accomplish either of these goals, she was able to pass other limited reforms, such as relaxing censorship laws and encouraging education for the nobility and for the middle class. Despite her desire to reign according to the ideals of the Enlightenment, an uprising by the serfs led her to change her mind about ending serfdom and, instead, the revolt made her realize that without the support of the nobility, her power could be challenged. As a result, she gave the nobility complete power over the serfs, and they were not freed until almost a century later.

Similarly to Catherine the Great, Napoleon Bonaparte sought to achieve some of the Enlightenment goals of the French Revolution for France but not without limitations to women and slaves. After a decade of instability resulting from the Reign of Terror and later from the control of the government by the Directory, Bonaparte brought peace and stability to the nation. While strengthening the central government, he created a government that sought to serve the state and its citizens as opposed to a government that was served by the state and its citizens. He helped to create a meritocracy by establishing government-run "lycees," or public schools open to males of all stations and whose graduates were appointed to public office based on achievement rather than privilege. Additionally, his legal system, the Napoleonic Code, was comprehensive and eliminated certain legal injustices that had previously existed within criminal law. Bonaparte also created coherent civil laws relating to property and family. Despite the progress that a complete legal system brought to France, the Napoleonic Code discriminated against women in that it ensured the supremacy of men over women as women were deprived of individual rights. Additionally, the population in general was deprived of certain liberties established during the Revolution, such as freedom of speech and the press. Lastly, slavery was reinstated in France's Caribbean colonies.

A third individual who brought progress to his nation was Mustafa Kemal Atatürk, who successfully "Westernized," or modernized, the new nation of Turkey after the Ottoman Empire's defeat in World War I. After overthrowing the last Ottoman sultan, Atatürk became the first president of the new Republic of Turkey. He wanted to make it a modern nation built on Western ideals. Using the nations of Europe, as well as the United States, as examples, Atatürk passed sweeping reforms, including separating Islamic law from national law while abolishing religious courts and passing new secular laws. Additionally, he brought about social progress by granting women the right to vote and giving them the ability to hold public office. Lastly, he improved the economy by creating government-funded programs to industrialize the nation and spur economic growth. By the time of his death in the late 1930s, Turkey had a new national identity based on Western standards and ideals. His reforms were so influential that he received the nickname "Atatürk," or "father of the Turks," by the Turkish people.

Individuals have historically been responsible for bringing about change within nations and societies. While progress has not been the only consequence of reformers' actions, individuals such as Catherine the Great of Russia, Napoleon Bonaparte of France, and Mustafa Kemal Atatürk of Turkey managed to bring a great deal of progress to their respective nations. Both Catherine the Great and Napoleon Bonaparte brought reforms influenced by Enlightenment philosophy, while Mustafa Kemal Atatürk successfully Westernized Turkey to make it a more modern nation. These nations would not be the same today if not for the actions of these individuals.

PART III: DOCUMENT-BASED QUESTIONS

Part A: Short Answers

Document 1

1) According to the document, one issue faced by women as a result of being denied the right to vote was that laws were being passed that affected women, but those laws were being passed without women's consent and without women being consulted.

Note: This response receives full credit because it correctly identifies an issue faced by women as a result of their lack of suffrage. Being subjected to laws that they had no power to participate in deciding on or voting on was an issue that women faced prior to achieving suffrage in the early 20th century.

Document 2

2) Based on this image, one action taken by women in Great Britain to obtain rights was organizing a march or a parade to bring attention and awareness to the suffragette movement.

Note: This response receives full credit because it correctly identifies an action that women took to obtain the right to vote. The newspaper, entitled *The Suffragette*, shows women marching and exclaims "March On! March On!" at the bottom of the publication.

Document 3

3a) According to Emmeline Pankhurst, one action British women used to draw attention to their issues was bringing petitions to the House of Commons.

3b) According to Emmeline Pankhurst, one way the British government responded to these actions was by imprisoning women.

Note: These responses receive full credit because they correctly identify one action British women used to draw attention to their issues and one way the British government responded to the women's actions. The document clearly states that women bringing petitions to the House of Commons was viewed as a "nuisance" and, therefore, the women were imprisoned despite not having broken any laws.

Document 4

4a) Based on this time line, one reason why the students gathered in Tiananmen Square was to mourn the death of Hu Yaobang, who was viewed as a symbol of anti-corruption and political reform.

4b) Based on this time line, one action taken by the students that gathered in Tiananmen Square was boycotting classes and organizing into unofficial student unions.

Note: These responses receive full credit because they correctly identify one reason why students gathered in Tiananmen Square and one action taken by the students that gathered in Tiananmen Square.

Document 5

5a) According to this document, one reform the Chinese students were trying to achieve was democracy and freedom of speech by calling for the resignation of leaders viewed as those who oppose democratic reforms.

5b) According to this document, one problem facing China was that power was in the hands of a few high-ranking officials who were viewed as corrupt.

Note: These responses receive full credit because they correctly identify one reform the Chinese students were trying to achieve and one problem that faced China during this time period.

Document 6

6) Based on this news report from the BBC, one action taken by the Chinese government in response to the protest movement in Tiananmen Square was using military force against the protesters, resulting in several hundred civilians being shot dead.

Note: This response receives full credit because it states one action taken by the Chinese government in response to the protest movement in Tiananmen Square. The government fired on unarmed protesters, killing hundreds and injuring many others.

Document 7

7) According to this excerpt from this National Party pamphlet, one way the National Party justified its racial policy was to say that it served to protect both races to ensure that each race could develop its own national character.

Note: This response receives full credit because it states one way the National Party justified its racial policy. According to the National Party, they implemented apartheid laws of segregation so as to protect and safeguard "the character and future of each race."

Document 8

8a) One action the African National Congress and Nelson Mandela suggested black South Africans take against the white nationalist government was civil disobedience without violence.

8b) According to this biography on the African National Congress website, one consequence Nelson Mandela faced as a result of his actions was being given a suspended prison sentence.

Note: These responses receive full credit because they state one action the African National Congress and Nelson Mandela suggested that black South Africans take against the white nationalist government and one consequence Nelson Mandela faced as a result of his actions.

Document 9

9) According to this National Public Radio program, one action taken by the South African government to end the student protests in Soweto was to set police dogs on the crowd of protesters.

Note: This response receives full credit because it correctly states one action taken by the South African government to end student protests in Soweto.

DOCUMENT-BASED QUESTION: GENERIC SCORING RUBRIC

Score of 5:
- Thoroughly addresses all aspects of the task by accurately analyzing and interpreting at least **four** documents
- Incorporates information from the documents in the body of the essay
- Incorporates relevant outside information
- Richly supports the theme or problem with relevant facts, examples, and details
- Is a well-developed essay, consistently demonstrating a logical and clear plan of organization
- Introduces the theme or problem by establishing a framework that is beyond a simple restatement of the task or historical context and concludes with a summation of the theme or problem

Score of 4:
- Addresses all aspects of the task by accurately analyzing and interpreting at least **four** documents
- Incorporates information from the documents in the body of the essay
- Incorporates relevant outside information
- Includes relevant facts, examples, and details, but discussion may be more descriptive than analytical
- Is a well-developed essay, demonstrating a logical and clear plan of organization
- Introduces the theme or problem by establishing a framework that is beyond a simple restatement of the task or historical context and concludes with a summation of the theme or problem

Score of 3:
- Addresses most aspects of the task or addresses all aspects of the task in a limited way, using some of the documents
- Incorporates some information from the documents in the body of the essay
- Incorporates limited or no relevant outside information
- Includes some facts, examples, and details, but discussion is more descriptive than analytical
- Is a satisfactorily developed essay, demonstrating a general plan of organization
- Introduces the theme or problem by repeating the task or historical context and concludes by simply repeating the theme or problem

Score of 2:
- Attempts to address some aspects of the task, making limited use of the documents
- Presents no relevant outside information
- Includes few facts, examples, and details; discussion restates contents of the documents
- Is a poorly organized essay, lacking focus
- Fails to introduce or summarize the theme or problem

Score of 1:
- Shows limited understanding of the task with vague, unclear references to the documents
- Presents no relevant outside information
- Includes little or no accurate or relevant facts, details, or examples
- Attempts to complete the task, but demonstrates a major weakness in organization
- Fails to introduce or summarize the theme or problem

Score of 0: Fails to address the task, is illegible, or is a blank paper

Part B: Essay

Throughout history, there have been many examples of governments around the world that have attempted to disenfranchise groups of their citizens, both politically and socially. In many instances, citizens have formed protest movements to dissent against such policies in an attempt to attain more equity. The pro-democracy movement in China and the anti-apartheid movement in South Africa are two examples of such protests. While both the pro-democracy movement in China and the anti-apartheid movement in South Africa were peaceful movements to achieve the goals of political reform and equality, the governments in both countries resorted to using violence to maintain their policies of restriction.

The dominance of one-party rule by the Chinese Communist Party led to dissent and protests that were met with violence ordered by the government in China. When the Communist Party came to power in 1949, a one-party system was created under the leadership of Mao Zedong, who did not tolerate criticism of the government. By the 1970s, in the wake of the Cultural Revolution, the government had loosened restrictions and allowed for more freedom to criticize government actions. This brief period of liberalization became known as "The Beijing Spring," and many of the pro-democracy ideals put forth during this period continued to be influential into the 1980s. By the latter part of the 20th century, however, China's government was viewed as corrupt and ineffective, leading many to call for democracy. Following the death of the former General Secretary of the Communist Party, Hu Yaobang, who was viewed as a symbol of anti-corruption and political reform, students began to gather in Tiananmen Square to mourn. Over the next few days, over 100,000 university students had gathered and began organizing into unofficial student unions, an illegal act in China, and some even began a hunger strike. According to the students, the reason for the hunger strike was the government's failure to respond to their requests for dialogue (Doc. 4). As the days and weeks of protests went on, the government began to respond with violence. In June of 1989, the government violence peaked as several hundred civilians were shot dead by the Chinese army, which used tanks to randomly shoot unarmed protesters (Doc. 6). One of the most famous images of the events of the pro-democracy movement is that of an unidentified man standing in front of a column of tanks, attempting to stop the advancement of the government's military suppression. The fate of "Tank Man" is unknown, but he has become a symbol of peaceful protest in the wake of a violent reaction from the government.

Similarly to China, policies of social and racial inequity in South Africa led to peaceful protests and actions such as civil disobedience, which were ultimately met with violence by the government. South Africa's history of social and racial inequality can be traced back centuries to Dutch and British colonization of the region in the 17th and 18th centuries, and racial segregation had become the predominant social structure by the early 20th century. After South Africa gained its independence from Britain in 1910, the Land Act was passed, marking the beginning of segregation by forcing black Africans to live on reserves and restricting them from working as sharecroppers. The African National Congress (ANC) was created during this period to oppose racial discrimination and segregation, but the situation became worse when the National Party, a white Afrikaner party, won the election of 1948 using the slogan "apartheid," which literally means "apartness." The Afrikaner Nationalist Party justified their policy of apartheid by claiming it allowed for the protection and cultural growth of both the "White races" and "non-White racial groups" (Doc. 7). Apartheid policies, however, created racial segregation and social inequalities, similar to the Jim Crow laws in the southern U.S. states, which eventually led to the civil rights movement in America. Like African Americans, black South Africans were restricted from using the same public facilities as whites, and the laws went as far as denying non-white participation in national government. Black South Africans organized peaceful protests and acts of civil disobedience. For example, in 1952, led by Nelson Mandela, the ANC organized a mass civil disobedience campaign that grew in numbers to create an act of mass defiance, which led to Mandela being given a suspended prison sentence (Doc. 8). In the 1970s, when the government passed legislation forcing all schools to use Afrikaans and English in their instruction, black school children in the segregated township of Soweto organized a peaceful demonstration to protest the use of the language of the "oppressor." In response to the protests, the government responded with violence as the government had in the pro-democracy movements in China. In an effort to stop students from joining the protests in Orlando Stadium, where the protests were to be held, the government set dogs on school children and eventually fired into the crowd, killing and injuring many (Doc. 9). Peaceful protests and acts of civil disobedience eventually brought apartheid to an end by 1991.

The attempt to attain more political and social equality through peaceful means has been demonstrated in many ways throughout history. The government's first response to these movements in both China and South Africa was to react with violence. In China, during the pro-democracy movement, many innocent university students were killed at the hands of their own government. Likewise, anti-apartheid leaders like Nelson Mandela were jailed, and children were killed protesting segregation laws and policies. Although both protest movements resulted in violence, these protesters' courageous actions certainly made an everlasting impact on the history of their country.

INDEX

NOTES

NOTES

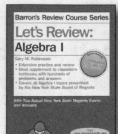

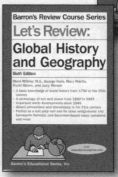

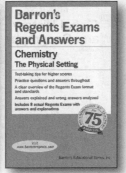

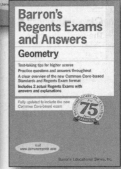